THE INSIDERS' GUIDE TO
Greater Denver

THE INSIDERS' GUIDE TO

Greater Denver

by
Laura Caruso
and
Robert Ebisch

The Insiders' Guides® Inc.

Co-published and marketed by:
Boulder Publishing Co. Inc.
1048 Pearl St.
Boulder, CO 80302
(303) 442-1202

Co-published and distributed by:
The Insiders' Guides® Inc.
The Waterfront • Suites 12 &13
P.O. Box 2057
Manteo, NC 27954
(919) 473-6100

•

SECOND EDITION
1st printing

•

Copyright ©1995
by Boulder Publishing Co. Inc.

•

Printed in the
United States of America

•

ISBN 0-912367-88-1

Preface

Welcome to Greater Denver and *The Insiders' Guide®to Greater Denver*. Whether you're relocating, or just visiting for business or pleasure, we're sure you'll enjoy our sunny, friendly area and find this guide quite helpful. Actually, even long-time residents might learn a thing or three. We've been living in the area for a combined total of 30 years, and still discovered new places to go and things to do while researching this guide.

This is a guide, and not a directory. While we've made sure to include all the leading tourist attractions, restaurants, hotels and just about every other leading thing in the Greater Denver universe, our choices are to a great extent personal choices. But that's one of the things that makes this guide so valuable. We give honest, knowledgeable information on Denver and the surrounding counties of Adams, Arapahoe, Douglas and Jefferson. Although Boulder is sometimes considered part of the Denver metro area, it's very different in mood and is separated by a greenbelt and a psychological barrier from metro Denver. Some Boulderites don't visit Denver for years at a time, except for trips to the airport. So we treat Boulder only peripherally here. There is, however, an Insiders' Guide®devoted entirely to Boulder and Rocky Mountain National Park.

Denver, and Colorado's entire Front Range for that matter, are experiencing explosive growth. This has positive results, such as the blossoming of cultural attractions and job markets. And it has negative results, such as the impact of growing population on urban sprawl, increased traffic congestion and descreased wildlife habitat. But much of what makes people want to move here is still intact. The climate is moderate, recreational activities abound, and some of the most beautiful scenery in the country is within a few hours' drive.

This isn't a directory, but neither is it a novel. You don't have to pick it up and read it straight through. In fact, we can't imagine anybody doing that. Check the table of contents, and read selectively on a need-to-know or want-to-know basis. Each chapter has its own introduction, so it's clear what's included and how it's organized. However, if you are new to the area, begin by reading through the Area Overviews and Getting Around chapters.

And when you're done, let us know what you think. Did we leave out your favorite restaurant? Did we neglect to mention some really nifty place to visit, thing to do or fact worth knowing? Send suggestions for future editions to the publisher, and we'll do our best to check them out. Seriously. We're not kidding.

About the Authors

Laura Caruso has lived and worked in the Denver-Boulder area since 1980, with the exception of the time she spent as art critic for the *Kansas City Star* in 1990 and 1991. She earned her undergraduate degree at Middlebury College and holds a master's degree in journalism from the University of Colorado, where she has taught beginning reporting and public affairs reporting. Nationally, she has published feature stories and art reviews in *Family Circle*, *Backpacker*, *Ms.* and *American Craft*, among other magazines. She has also written for many Colorado publications, including the *Boulder Daily Camera*, the *Rocky Mountain News* and *The Bloomsbury Review*.

Robert W. Ebisch first came to Colorado at the age of 1 month, promptly left and came back nearly every following year of his youth. That's because his father, a University of Wisconsin geography professor, spent virtually all of every summer from 1950 to the mid-1960s car camping with his family around the western United States. A good deal of that time was spent in Colorado, where Bob developed passions for trout fishing, flipping pancakes over an open fire and climbing up mountains and running down their scree slopes and boulder fields.

Love for the use of language and the telling of a good story, instilled by Bob's mom and dad, led to an early interest in writing. After earning a physics degree at the University of Wisconsin, Bob completed a master's degree in journalism and worked for newspapers and magazines.

Not until 1982 did he move to Colorado for good, when his wife Jane came to attend law school at the University of Colorado. In the years since, they have enjoyed the countless attractions and byways of the state and thanked the happy twist of fate that brought them to Colorado. They count themselves as quasi-natives by virtue of the fact that their two children, 6-year-old Nick and 2-year-old Beth, were born here.

Now living in the Greater Denver community of Wheat Ridge, Bob has been freelancing full time since he left the staff of the Boulder *Daily Camera*, the daily newspaper of Boulder, Colorado, in 1989.

Acknowledgments

Thanks to Rich Grant and Jean Anderson at the Denver Convention and Visitors Bureau; to Lisa Gesner and Alice Logsdon at the Boulder Bookstore; to Ronda Haskins and Charlotte Smokler at the *Daily Camera*; to my knowledgeable co-author, Bob Ebisch; to Reed Glenn and Shelley Schlender, co-authors of *The Insiders' Guide to Boulder and Rocky Mountain National Park*; to longtime Denverites Gerry Brimmer, Patty Conroy, Susie Cotton, Judy Goater, Ken Morr and Carolyn McDonald for sharing some of their favorite things about the city they call home; to M.S. Mason and Justin Mitchell, for the expert advice on the Arts and Nightlife chapters, respectively; to Steve Klodt at DIA and Bonnie McCune at the Denver Public Library; and special thanks to Joe Burleson.

— Laura

We don't write in a vacuum; there's no way we could have produced this book without the help, wisdom and forbearance of countless good people. First and foremost, of course, I wish to thank my wife, Jane Ebisch, who put up with yet another year of authorial distraction as well as contributing greatly to Insiders' Tips and general editorial content. Topping the list after Jane is real-estate guru Karen Cutrell, a Re/Max West Realtor without whose help the Neighborhoods and Real Estate chapter would have been totally lame. Dude. Great debt is also due to a host of others including baseball guru Larry Theis; golf guru Tom McMahon; cycling gurus Mike Schiebout and Doug and Jo Stiverson at Westside Cycling and Fitness; Becky Parrington, of the Wheat Ridge post office, and her son Nick; the reference librarians at the Lakewood Public Library; Judy Waller and the reference gang at the Boulder Public Library, and the *Denver Business Journal*.

— Robert

Table of Contents

Directory of Maps

Denver's Surrounding Counties

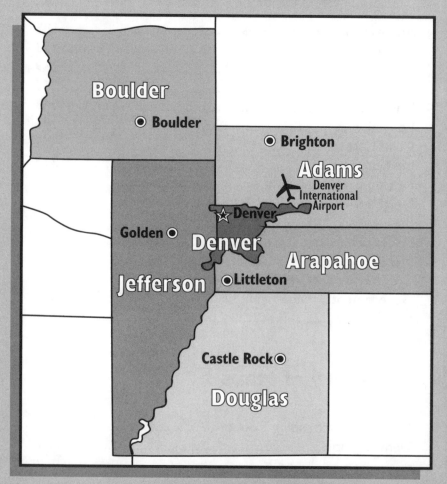

Boulder

Boulder ◉ Boulder

◉ Brighton

Adams
Denver International Airport

☆ Denver

Golden ◉

Denver

Jefferson

Arapahoe

◉ Littleton

Castle Rock ◉

Douglas

Denver

Colorado

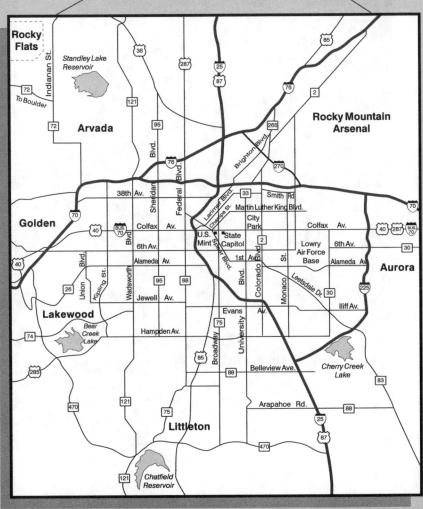

Buffalo Bill (William F. Cody) was one of early Denver's most famous citizens.

Inside
Area Overviews

The temperature is 77 degrees, according to the disc jockey on a popular Denver radio station. But at the Continental Divide, just an hour's drive away, the ski conditions are righteous. It's November 13, and already the Loveland, Keystone and Vail ski areas are open. "Nearly 80 degrees and they're skiing in the mountains," he crows, as though the delightful insanity of it all is more than he can bear. "Oh man, only in Denver."

"The great braggart city," English traveler Isabella Bird called Denver during an 1872 visit. Denver can't be blamed for a little conceit. It is today, as it was 100 years ago, the largest metropolis between California and Missouri, between Dallas and Seattle. An expansive self-regard still comes easily to the present inhabitants of Greater Denver, the metropolitan area roughly defined by the City and County of Denver and its four suburban counties, Adams, Arapahoe, Douglas and Jefferson.

Only about 40 percent of Greater Denver's present citizens were born here. An obvious testimony to their pride — and maybe a little resentment of all the newcomers — is the "Native" bumper sticker so visible on the highways. The other 60 percent of Greater Denver's residents came here by choice. Some of these may mock the native's hubris with bumper stickers that are identical except for the disappearance of the "t," but they are no less bullish on the area's attractions and achievements.

Natives and newcomers alike are uneasy about the threat that growth poses to quality of life through new real-estate developments springing up willy-nilly amid prairie and mountain scenery. But, boosterism runs rampant on such projects as the new Denver International Airport, which finally opened in 1995. It was a year and a half past the opening deadline, mainly due to horrendous bungling that resulted in a "state-of-the-art" baggage handling system that didn't work, and the decision to build a backup system. The money this cost by the time the airport opened, ran one local joke, could have been better used hiring thousands of people to form a human bucket brigade that would pass suitcases hand-to-hand from the aircraft to the luggage carousels.

Denver's airport, its publicists like to point out, is now the nation's largest. Its 53 square miles cover an area twice the size of Manhattan. Construction began by moving half as much dirt as it took to build the Panama Canal. It could contain both Chicago's O'Hare International Airport and the Dallas-Fort Worth Airport with 5 square miles left over.

Even before the airport opened, Colorado began a serious binge of buyer's remorse over far more than the baggage bungling system. The cost estimated in 1988 at $1.4 billion had reached nearly $5 billion. It was employing about half the number of people originally projected, and carrying far fewer passengers. Instead of 120 gates as projected, it had 87. High passenger fees tacked onto ticket prices, to pay for the airport, along with other airport hassles have fed Colorado Springs a growing business of Denver residents willing to drive an extra 70 miles to catch a flight.

Still, many people point to similar headaches at the beginnings of other great airports, headaches forgotten in future years when those airports fulfilled their promise. And the boosters take an enormous sense of pride in the grandeur of the enterprise and what they expect it to do for the city. Lying near the geographic center of the nation, Denver is already a major hub of the nation's railroad, airline and highway systems. Now the airport is supposed to transform Denver's position midway between Munich and Tokyo, Canada and Mexico, into a focus of worldwide trade and transportation.

Geography has a lot to do with Denver's historical image of itself as lying at the hinge of the North American continent. No matter where you are in Denver, you have only to look west to see the Rocky Mountains running north and south like a wall dividing west from east. The first slopes of the Foothills begin at the edge of Greater Denver. Behind the Foothills and front ranges you can see the gray back ranges rising to the jagged spine of the North American continent, the Continental Divide.

Self-styled since the 1800s as the "Queen City of the Plains," Denver might lay equal claim to being the Monarch Metropolis of the Mountains. Its urban fabric extends into the mountains on the west and overlays the first swells of the Great Plains to the east. The mountains are what drew Paleolithic hunters to the sheltering slopes and fertile hunting grounds of the Foothills. Between the housing developments of Jefferson County on Denver's southwest fringe, archaeologists have found 10,000-year-old sites where mammoths and camels appear to have been killed by human hunters. Later, modern Indians, principally the Ute, Comanche, Apache, Arapaho, Cheyenne and Kiowa, gravitated to the area for hunting, trade and war.

From Cottonwood Groves to Convention Centers

Settling the Land

Non-native Americans came first from the south, beginning with Spanish expeditions in the 1600s. During the next two centuries a slow movement of mostly agrarian colonists from Mexico and New Mexico gave a distinctly Hispanic culture to the southern part of the state. The City of Pueblo, less than a two-hour drive south of Denver, was Mexican territory until the United States grabbed the Southwest in the war with Mexico in 1848. As Colorado grew, the ancestors of today's Hispanic citizens generated much of the sweat that built the state's mining, railroads and agriculture.

Invaders from the east came faster and hit harder. In 1858, little more than 50 years after the first mountain men began trapping furs in the Rockies, a party of prospectors panned gold from the Platte River in what is now the City of Englewood on Denver's southern edge. It wasn't enough to pay each man more than about $10 a day, but it was enough to start the rush.

The history of modern Denver began at the confluence of the South Platte River with tiny Cherry Creek, where cottonwood groves sheltered the camps of Indians and early explorers such as John C. Fremont. By the beginning of 1859, the City of Denver was established at the confluence by friends of James W. Denver, then governor

No matter where you travel in Colorado this year...

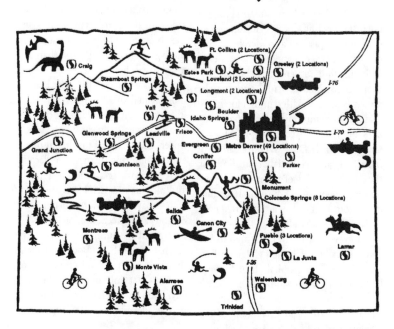

You are always close to a friend!

of Kansas Territory. By the middle of 1859, the cottonwood groves had been axed into oblivion and replaced by some 400 cabins and a lot of bare dirt and mud.

Striking Gold

Gold strikes in the mountains brought not just a growing swarm of fortune-seekers from the east but also merchants, industry and other elements of a real city, including the bad elements in boom town proportions. Denver had "more brawls, more pistol shots with criminal intent . . . than in any community with equal numbers on Earth," according to Horace Greeley. "Uncle Dick" Wootton, an early merchant, later recalled that "stealing was the only occupation of a considerable portion of the population, who would take anything from a pet calf, or a counterfeit gold dollar, up to a sawmill."

However, as Denver matured to become the capital of the new Colorado Territory in 1867 and capital of the State of Colorado in 1876, it acquired a certain air of refinement. "A shooting affray in the street is as rare as in Liverpool," noted Isabella Bird in 1872, "and one no longer sees men dangling to the lamp posts when one looks out in the morning." Still, she noted, Denver was not a very pretty sight, a city that "lay spread out, brown and treeless, upon the brown and treeless plain, which seemed to nourish nothing but wormwood and the Spanish bayonet."

The kind of money needed to polish the city's rough edges was not long in coming from Colorado's growing cattle, mining, railroad, steel, banking and other industries. Gambling houses and painted ladies still characterized the city in journalistic accounts of the time. Yet a new class of aristocrats began decorating Denver's Capi-

tol Hill neighborhood with mansions that have now become tourist destinations. Silver strikes in the mountains in the late 1870s caused another mining boom that poured money into the city until the silver market collapsed in 1893 and threw Denver into a depression. But more gold strikes in the mountains, along with the growth of Colorado agriculture and manufacturing industries, brought Denver into the 20th century more given to creating parks than cavorting in bawdy houses.

Still the Queen City of the Plains was more plain than queenly, as one visitor put it. Major credit for making the queen look like a lady generally goes to Mayor Robert Speer, who pursued his dream of a City Beautiful during the first two decades of this century with expanding neighborhood and mountain parks. He is also credited with the laying of hundreds of miles of sewers and paved streets, turning Cherry Creek from a garbage dump into the centerpiece of what is today Speer Boulevard, planting thousands of trees and promoting other projects that culminated in the Denver Civic Center, which was completed nearly two decades after his 1918 death.

War Spurs Growth

Despite the Great Depression, Denver's population grew by more than 50 percent between 1910 and 1940. But, it was World War II that initiated the area's greatest surge of growth when fear of attack on the nation's coasts transformed the area into a center of military and other government functions. Within a year after Pearl Harbor, major employment bases appeared in facilities such as the Denver Federal Center, the Rocky Mountain Arsenal and Fitzsimmons Army Medical Center. Those who came for war-related opportunities stayed on when the war was done, and Greater Denver now contains some 50 percent of Colorado's population.

Optimism and Diversification

Since World War II, the local economy has had its ups and downs, but Greater Denver has never lost that growth momentum. The last slump came during the 1980s, while the rest of the nation was booming and Greater Denver was reeling from an oil bust. Now the region has come back with a new and more diversified economy. Optimism is visible in the unprecedented spending on transportation infrastructure, including the new Denver International Airport, the city's new light-rail transportation system and the rebuilding of the intersection of Denver's two major interstates, I-70 and I-25, which had been nicknamed the "mousetrap" for its ability to foul the traffic of this growing city.

Denver is to a large extent reinventing itself in this decade. The new $126-million Colorado Convention Center opened in 1990. That same year saw the opening of the new Cherry Creek Shopping Center, Greater Denver's prestige retail mall that boasts the state's first outlets of stores such as Lord & Taylor, Saks Fifth Avenue and Nieman Marcus.

Nowhere is revivification more evident than in the area known as the Central Platte Valley, where the city began around the confluence of the South Platte River and Cherry Creek. As the railroads arrived in the 1870s and Denver grew up and grew outward, the Central Platte Valley became the rail and warehousing district. By the 1980s, the Central Platte Valley had become an urban wasteland, with a smattering of businesses in old buildings and a lot of trash-strewn vacant fields crisscrossed by railroad tracks. Now the area is rebounding as the focal point of the new Denver. City planners envision a planned community of green spaces and residential, retail, office and entertainment developments. Much of the vision is still blue sky, but some of its anchor developments are already in place. In 1995, the 50,000-seat stadium known as Coors Field opened on the edge of the Central Platte Valley as home for Denver's major-league baseball team, the Colorado Rockies. Just a half-mile southwest down the valley, Elitch Gardens, Denver's premier amusement park, opened its 60 acres of fun in 1995 after a move from the city's far west side, where it had been located since 1890. Another announcement in 1995 was the selection of a site just across the South Platte River from Elitch Gardens for the $67-million Ocean Journey

While Denver's weather is envied across the country, contrary to popular belief, the city doesn't have 300 days of sunshine per year. Not long ago, the state climatologist's office tried to calculate how Greater Denver could live up to the claim and found that 300 days is an accurate figure if you count as a "day of sunshine" those days in which the sun shines for more than 45 minutes. Denver does get more sunshine than Miami. It gets less than San Diego, but hey, who doesn't?

Insiders' Tips

aquarium, slated for a 1998 opening. Planned for a space between Elitch Gardens and Auraria Parkway in the Platte Valley is a new $132-million arena for the Denver Nuggets and the Colorado Avalanche, Colorado's new professional hockey team. This entertainment complex is also supposed to include a $20-million film-production studio, Colorado Studios.

Rebounding ahead of the Central Platte Valley has been Lower Downtown, the turn-of-the-century, red-brick business and warehousing district along the valley's edge. In the last decade, it has become a renovated historic district of restaurants and brewpubs, prestigious offices, condominiums and apartments around Denver's historic railroad terminal, Union Station. Lower Downtown is particularly hot now that the Colorado Rockies baseball team's new Coors Field opened there in 1995. On the north side of Lower Downtown, the area becoming known as the ballpark neighborhood, has seen the opening of hundreds of new housing units and 20-30 restaurants and bars since 1994.

Big City Pains

Of course, not everything is perfect about Greater Denver.

Tourists strolling amid the stately buildings and luxuriant flower gardens of Denver's Civic Center could attract glares and catcalls from groups of transients lounging in the shade. Park your car in the wrong place, and you may well return to find the driver's window smashed out and the stereo missing. Today's "gang problem" that exists in every sizeable city exists in Denver as well, and so do the other, less-organized sources of flying bullets. Part of Denver's identity crisis comes from the city's celebrating its Western history of blazing guns on the raw frontier of yesteryear, while simultaneously wringing its hands over the popping pistols on the urban frontier of this year. Yet, crime in Denver does not distinguish it from other metropolitan areas. In terms of its crime rate, Denver lies between Lubbock, Texas, and Springfield, Massachusetts. Denver is more dangerous than Des Moines, safer than Seattle.

One of Denver's most notorious negatives is what locals call "the brown cloud," the yellow-brown layer of air pollution often visible in the air above the city. Denver may be 1 mile above sea level, but it actually lies in a geographic depression. The High Plains rise for 50 miles or so as one travels to the east, and of course the mountains rise like crazy to the west.

Summer visitors may wonder, "What brown cloud?" During warm weather, convection carries the pollution up where the winds can carry it away. High-pollution days are most frequently announced during the winter, when temperature inversions trap and concentrate air pollution in the depression. Unfortunately, this means that those who buy a house with a wood-burning fireplace may be buying a house with wasted wall space; those nights on which a merry crackling fire would be most comforting often seem to be the same nights when it's against the law to build a fire.

Insiders' Tips

You can use all kinds of reference sources in seeking information about Greater Denver, but your best bet generally is that incomparable resource known as the reference librarian.

Greater Denver Vital Statistics

- Denver was named for James W. Denver, governor of Kansas Territory when the city was founded.

- Denver became the capital of the new Colorado Territory in 1867 and capital of the State of Colorado in 1876.

- Population: 1,762,000. This is as of the most recent estimate by the Denver Regional Council of Governments on January 1, 1994. It includes the City and County of Denver (483,250), Adams County (285,275), Arapahoe County (427,875), Douglas County (88,925) and Jefferson County (476,675).

- Location: At the base of the Rocky Mountains about a third of the way across Colorado from Wyoming to New Mexico.

- Terrain: Rocky Mountain Foothills on the west, rolling plains on the east.

- Altitude: Gee, how high is "The Mile High City?" A bronze disk imbedded in the western steps of the State Capitol building proclaims "ELEVATION 5,280.000 FEET." The words, "ONE MILE ABOVE SEA LEVEL" are chiseled just below.

- Climate: Mild. Dry heat in summer makes days bearable, nights pleasantly cool. Snow seldom stays long on the ground during winter.
  Average maximum temperature in the summer is 85 degrees; minimum is 56. Average maximum winter temperature is 45 degrees; minimum is 18.
  Average annual rainfall is 11 inches. Average annual snowfall is 60 inches. Average number of days with snow, ice pellets or hail of 1 inch or more in depth: 18.
  Clear days: 115. Partly cloudy days: 130. Cloudy days: 120.

- Denver government consists of a mayor and a city council. The current mayor is Wellington Webb, re-elected to a second term in 1995.

More irritating is feeling it in the lungs and eyes. Some of us don't even notice it. But those with allergies or respiratory conditions can find it distressing. It's ironic, considering that many of Greater Denver's early inhabitants — including Mayor Robert Speer — came here because the clean, dry air was celebrated as a cure for tuberculosis.

Still, those who compare Denver's air pollution to that of Los Angeles are being ridiculous. During 1993, Los Angeles had more than 100 days during which it exceeded federal air pollution standards. Denver crossed the line on just two days. And 1994 was Denver's first year without a single violation. Even without air pollution, breathing is a bit more difficult at 1 mile of altitude. This is typically a mild and temporary problem. Only during the first week or so in Denver do some visitors feel headachy and strangely out of sorts. Since Denver is a gateway to the mountains, however, visitors need to take seriously the dangers of acute altitude sickness, a collapse of the body's ability to take in and metabolize oxygen.

Striking without warning, altitude sickness can be frightening, devastating, and even deadly. Those who exert themselves in the mountains need to take a few days to get used to the altitude and drink an abnormally large amount of water; otherwise they could find themselves beset by abdominal cramps and hyperventilation. A couple of years ago, a healthy male 26-year-old skier from Texas suddenly dropped dead on one of the mountain ski slopes to the west. What at first appeared to be an inexplicable heart attack turned out to be the result of acute altitude sickness.

As the population grows, rush-hour traffic jams are worse than natives have ever known. If you're from Chicago or Los Angeles, you may find Denver's traffic jams unimpressive. Former Los Angelenos newly transplanted to Denver can be heard claiming to commute to downtown from homes in the mountains in the time it would take them to drive 1 mile at rush hour in L.A. Most people, however, find Denver traffic tremendously unpleasant.

One of the nation's grossest misconceptions about Denver concerns the weather. Seen from far away, Denver is hard to distinguish from the mountains that are so important to its national image. More than 80 percent of Colorado's population lives in the "Front Range," the increasingly interconnected metropolitan areas ranging from Greeley on the north to Pueblo on the south along the base of the mountains. Front Range weather is surprisingly mild.

Someone in Chicago or Cleveland may hear of new snow falling on 6-foot snowpacks in the Rockies, then call a friend in Denver and find out the temperature here is 70 degrees.

Long cold spells do set in periodically from November to February. And Denver does get some whopping snowstorms, more in March than in any other month. Every year sees at least one storm that leaves highways littered with abandoned vehicles. But a few days later, don't be surprised to see people out working in their yards. On April 10, 1995, for example, a snowstorm dumped up to 15 inches on the Denver area. On the morning of April 11, people woke up to 20 degrees and kneedeep snow. Two days later it was 80 degrees, and birds were hopping on dry green lawns. Snow melts particularly fast during the late winter and early spring when Chinook winds come roaring down from the mountains at speeds that have been clocked as high as 143 miles per hour. These warm, dry "snow-eaters" literally suck the moisture out of the snow before it can reach the soil, and they have been known to raise Front Range temperatures by as much as 36 degrees within two hours. They've also been known to tear the roofs off houses, topple trees and blow semitrucks right off the interstate.

Mild on average, Greater Denver is the land of weather extremes, one of the reasons why the National Center for Atmospheric Research is just up the road in the City of Boulder. Meteorologists joke that the area is ideal, because they can go golfing in the morning and chase thunderstorms in the afternoon. Hail is a big part of the area's weather experience. After a particularly violent hailstorm in July 1990, cars all over the area looked like someone had gone at them with ball-peen hammers, and insurance companies were handing out new roofs like candy.

Denver Suburbs

Much of what we've already said about Greater Denver has focused on the City of Denver, but the suburban counties have their own lives and characters. Pretty impressive ones, too. While the City and County of Denver's population declined by 32,000 during Colorado's recession in the 1980s, the population of Greater Denver's suburban counties — Arapahoe, Jefferson, Douglas and Adams — grew by 212,000. Now that Colorado's economy has begun attracting people and companies again, the suburban counties are reaping the lion's share of the growth.

Jefferson County, West of Denver

Among Greater Denver counties, Jefferson County is second only to the City and County of Denver itself in population and is on the verge of becoming second to none. Jefferson County's estimated 476,675 population at the beginning of 1994 was just 6,575 less than Denver, which was 483,250. Since we don't have more recent estimates for all of the counties, it's hard to say, but it's a good guess that Jefferson County has since then passed Denver in population. Jefferson County Planning and Zoning in 1995 estimated 484,854 people in the county.

The county wraps around the western end of the metropolitan area and extends from Denver's western edge up to include such mountain communities as Evergreen and Conifer and reaches into the Pike Na-

tional Forest. Only Douglas County rivals Jefferson as far as scenic beauty is concerned. However, Jefferson County is eclipsed only by Douglas County concerning median income of its inhabitants. Generally reputed as a conservative area, Jefferson County in 1992 elected a Democratic majority of county commissioners for the first time since the 1940s. Being on the mountain side of Greater Denver, Jefferson tends to attract the residents who are most motivated by quality of life. Colorado's image is one of mountains, and when people immigrate here, those who can afford to locate in or near the mountains generally go that route. Jefferson County has a highly educated population and a high percentage of dual-income families.

Greater Denver's gateway to the mountains, Jefferson County is traversed by streams of skiers and other motorists on I-70 west or on U.S. Highway 6 through scenic Clear Creek Canyon, the historic main thoroughfare to the gold and silver meccas of the 1800s. Many of these passersby notice little more of Jefferson County than the City of Golden below to the north or the upscale homes of mountain communities that dot the hills along the route farther into the Foothills.

But "Jeffco," in the local slang, is also an urban county in which cities such as Arvada, Westminster, Wheat Ridge and Lakewood represent a continuum of the urban fabric reaching out from Denver.

Jefferson County has been hit hard in recent years by drastic workforce reductions at Martin Marietta, but the company ac-

---

If you're a low-altitude person like many first arriving in Denver, you may wonder why you have a nagging, slight headache. Don't worry; it's just the altitude. Drink lots of water and your physiology should be Denverized within a week.

quired General Dynamics in 1994 and merged with Lockheed Corporation in 1995 to become Lockheed Martin Corporation, and its employment in 1995 is actually expected to increase over 1994. The end of operations at Rocky Flats, the federal defense plant in the county's northwest quadrant, also has been a drag on the local economy. Yet the county is still highly industrialized, with an emphasis on high technology. Golden, the county seat, claims Greater Denver's highest population percentage of technology Ph.Ds. Up to a third of the students at Golden's Colorado School of Mines stay on in Jefferson County after they graduate. Jefferson County is the regional geotechnology, materials, mining and energy business cluster.

The U.S. government is the county's largest employer with the mammoth Denver Federal Center in Lakewood, Jefferson County's largest city, and the National Renewable Energy Laboratory in Golden. The Denver Federal Center has been laying off right and left, though, and the National Renewable Energy Laboratory in 1995 was in the shadow of the federal budgetary axe.

Arapahoe County, East and South of Denver

Back when it was Arapahoe County of the Kansas Territory, it once covered nearly half of the present state of Colorado. Now Arapahoe County covers about 800 square miles reaching halfway from Denver to the Kansas border. Arapahoe holds the biggest part of Denver's eastern suburbs and folds under the south side of Denver to encompass such south Denver suburbs as Englewood, Cherry Hills Village and Littleton, the county seat. Arapahoe County today is the powerhouse of Greater Denver's eastern side, having jumped 33 percent in population between 1980 and 1990 and reached an estimated 427,875 by the start of 1994.

Arapahoe contains most of the City of Aurora, and Aurora contains nearly 50 percent of the county's population as well. Aurora is the state's biggest city in area and its third-largest in population. Since World War II, Aurora has been heavily influenced by the military. It contains Fitzsimmons Army Medical Center (the city's second-largest employer), bordering Lowry Air Force Base on the west and embracing Buckley Air National Guard Base (the city's largest employer) on the east. The closing of Lowry Air Force Base in 1994 has slapped the city's economy in the face, and so did the federal decision in 1995 to close Fitzsimmons, but Lowry is already attracting plenty of development interest. So is the old Stapleton International Airport on Aurora's boundary.

The county's second- and third-largest cities, Englewood and Littleton south of Denver, also suffered from workforce reductions during the early 1990s at Martin Marietta, now Lockheed Martin, in nearby Jefferson County. At the decade's dawn, Martin Marietta was Littleton's largest employer. Littleton's employment base has become increasingly diversified. Littleton

Downtown Denver from new Elitch's Tower.

still has something of a small-town feel, but its school system has produced Scholastic Aptitude Test scores that rank in the top echelons of Greater Denver.

Englewood was a prairie when Colorado's first gold discovery occurred there in 1858. By the late 1800s, however, the fruit orchards of Englewood had given that city its modern name from the Old English words for "wooded place." Denver's ladies and gentlemen preferred it for Sunday carriage drives and picnics. Since that time, Englewood has developed a strong business community. Today Englewood has Colorado's largest concentration of biomedical/biotechnology companies and, for its size, Greater Denver's strongest concentration of Japanese companies.

Adams County, Northeast of Denver

Adams County ceded 53 of its square miles to the City of Denver so that Denver could build its new airport. But Adams County is still Greater Denver's largest county. Lying north of Arapahoe County, the approximately 1,200 square miles of Adams County extend as far to the east as Arapahoe County but much wider north to south.

Adams County is perhaps Greater Denver's most economically diverse county, hosting agriculture, heavy industry, transportation and high-tech companies. It does have an image as Greater Denver's big-shouldered, blue-collar county, thanks to the spread of warehouses, smokestack industries and oil refineries that can be seen steaming like volcanoes on winter mornings as you drive along interstates 70 and 270. At the same time, it has its share of communications, biopharmaceuticals and computer software and hardware companies. That's in Adams County's eastern, urbanized zone. The county's square mileage is predominantly a rural area of farming and ranching. Even in Brighton, the county seat, one of the most celebrated citizens is the nation's most well-known "cowboy poet," Baxter Black.

Jumping out at anyone who looks at a map of Greater Denver is a large blank space east of Commerce City with a scattering of lakes and the lettering, Rocky Mountain Arsenal (Restricted Area). Once the site of Cold War chemical weapons manufacturing, the arsenal is a 27-square-mile area often said to contain the most polluted square mile on earth. As a Superfund site, it's in the process of a federal cleanup effort exceeding $1 billion. Meanwhile, off-limits to hunters and other human intrusion, it has become the most impressive wildlife refuge in Greater Denver. A continuous traffic of weekend visitors and weekday school groups take the guided tours on double-decker buses to view eagles, elk and other wildlife that call the arsenal home.

While dealing gracefully with its past, Adams County is well-positioned for its future. Surrounding the new airport, Adams County will be a primary beneficiary of economic spin-offs as well as a primary recipi-

ent of new airport noise. Not everyone wanted the Denver International Airport there, and not everyone is satisfied with the way it has been developed. In return for 53 square miles of its land, Adams County was supposed to get economic growth related to development around the airport. The cargo complex was originally proposed for the north side of the new airport, where residents expected more jobs and development. When the City of Denver moved the complex to the south side of the airport, some saw it as a betrayal.

In the long term, however, Adams County expects substantial benefits. Despite strong growth in Greater Denver, the county still has a good availability of land and buildings at affordable prices. Despite having Greater Denver's second-lowest population —January 1, 1994 estimate: 285,275 — after Douglas County, the county's percentage population growth between 1990 and 2010 has been projected as Greater Denver's second-fastest after Douglas County. Adams County's own airport, Front Range Airport, is just 3 miles from the Denver International Airport and rather new itself, having begun operations in 1983. The abundance of air transportation has enhanced basic industries such as metalworking, food-processing and wood products in Adams County's southwestern corner, as well as the 120th Avenue corridor of high-technology companies in the county's northwestern corner.

Insiders' Tips

Last year, Colorado got its third area code, 970, covering the northern and western portions of the state formerly covered by the 303 area code. South Colorado and southeast of Greater Denver still have a 719 area code. Now, 303 covers Greater Denver and Boulder and the gambling towns of Central City and Black Hawk, and unless otherwise noted in this book, all telephone numbers can be assumed to have a 303 area code.

Douglas County, South of Denver

Flowing through the Pike National Forest southwest of Denver, the South Platte River has some of the most celebrated trout fishing — it was once called "the St. Peter's Basilica of trout fishing" by *Time* magazine — on Colorado's Front Range. This is Douglas County.

Highlands Ranch is one of Greater Denver's most popular planned communities, with average recent home-sale prices topping $200,000 in a gracious and open, almost country environment. With a population of 31,220 as of July 31, 1995, an increase of 16 percent from the 27,000 population a year earlier, Highlands Ranch is not far from eclipsing the nearby cities of Littleton and Englewood in size, and it's expected to reach a population of 100,000 by the year 2015. This too is Douglas County.

Including the three municipalities of Castle Rock, Larkspur and Parker, as well as a piece of Littleton, Douglas County is the only metro county that does not share a boundary with the City and County of Denver. It's separated from Denver by a slice of Arapahoe County that wraps under the city's south side. Douglas County is Greater Denver's sparsely populated southern frontier. It has some impressive planned communities such as Highlands Ranch and Castle Pines, but it's mostly open country. The county's three incorporated municipalities of Castle Rock, Larkspur and Parker are small. Douglas is the only Greater Denver county in which the vast majority of its population lives in unincorporated communities. On average, Douglas County is Greater Denver's prestige living zone, with the region's highest median income and home prices. Douglas County is also the region's major bedroom community, with by far the highest ratio of people commuting outside the county to reach their jobs.

As the focus of what local planners call the Denver/Colorado Springs Development Corridor, Douglas is also Colorado's fastest-growing county with a population that ballooned 230 percent between 1980 and 1990. With 29 planned communities and 319 subdivisions covering nearly 18 percent of the county, Douglas anticipates a half-million new residents by the year 2030. Pretty big vision for a county that had an estimated total of 88,925 as of January 1, 1994, but it's a growing area. The Hahn Company in 1995, for example, announced a $164-million Park Meadows Town Center mall at the intersection of I-25 and C-470, and other projects have been popping up all around it.

Meanwhile, the county plans to keep as much as 70 percent of its 841 square miles as open space in the form of ranches, greenbelts and public parks. Taking the county as a whole, it sometimes seems almost as much a part of Colorado Springs as it is of Denver. The county seat of Castle Rock, so named for the monolith-capped hill that towers above it, is just short of halfway to Colorado Springs, and most of its workers commute to one metropolis or the other.

Photo: Daily Camera/Lourie Zipf

Denver's light-rail system began downtown service in fall 1994.

Inside
Getting Around

Denver's first streets were laid out parallel to Cherry Creek. Later, streets were laid out north-south and east-west, so that now the old part of town — downtown — is at an angle to the rest of the metropolis, a fact made immediately clear by looking at a map. This may sound confusing, and it can be at times. Still, getting around really isn't that difficult. For one thing, the mountains are always to the west. Even natives occasionally use this trick to orient themselves.

You'll need to look at a map to see what we mean, but generally, from downtown Denver, Aurora is to the east; the Denver Tech Center, Englewood and Greenwood Village are to the south; Littleton is southwest; Lakewood, Wheat Ridge and Golden are to the west; Arvada, Broomfield and Westminster are to the northwest; and Commerce City, Northglenn and Thornton are to the north.

"Downtown" refers to the area that is roughly bounded by 13th Avenue on the south, Speer Boulevard (which follows Cherry Creek) on the west, the South Platte River on the north and Grant Street

on the east. Most streets downtown run one-way. 17th Street, where most of the banks and big office buildings are located, is in many ways the heart of downtown. The 16th Street Mall is also an important thoroughfare, as free shuttle buses run up and down its 1-mile length, connecting the two RTD (Regional Transportation District) bus terminals at Civic Center and Market Street. The shuttle buses operate between about 5:30 AM and 1 AM on weekdays, from about 6 AM to 1 AM on Saturdays and from 7 AM to 1 AM on Sundays. Frequency depends on the time of day and ranges from one every 10 minutes to almost one a minute during the morning and afternoon rush hours. The 16th Street Mall is closed to auto traffic between Market Street and Broadway.

Somewhere around Larimer Street — or is it Market? — downtown becomes Lower Downtown, or "LoDo" (say "low-dough"). The boundaries are extremely vague. Dana Crawford, who spearheaded the Larimer Street rejuvenation, defines the area narrowly as Larimer and Market streets west to Union Station, from 20th Street to Cherry Creek. A broader defini-

Lost? Look for the mountains: They'll always show you which direction is west.

Photo: Daily Camera/Nico Toutenhoofd

Denver International Airport opened February 28, 1995.

tion extends farther west to the Platte River. Well, at least you'll have an idea of what people are talking about when you hear them say LoDo. Coors Field is in LoDo — or at least on the perimeter.

Capitol Hill is the name given to the area just east of downtown.

Our Area Overviews chapter, which talks about the different counties that make up Greater Denver, should also help you orient yourself. For descriptions of neighborhoods, see our Neighborhoods and Real Estate chapter.

Logistics: Finding an Address

In central Denver, east-west streets are numbered, with bigger numbers to the north and smaller numbers to the south (for example, 17th Street is south of 23rd Street).

Broadway is the dividing line between east and west in addresses. Ellsworth Avenue is the dividing line between north and south.

Maps Unlimited, 899 Broadway, 623-4299, has every kind of map you'll ever need to find your way around — topographic,

recreational and illustrated. They also stock guidebooks.

Main Arteries and Thoroughfares

Interstate-25 runs north-south through Denver in a line from Colorado Springs to Cheyenne (and farther, of course, in each direction). Just north of downtown, it intersects Interstate 70, which runs east-west through the city and is the major route to the mountains. The always-busy intersection of these two highways is known as the Mousetrap, a testament to its congestion. In bad weather or at rush hour, avoid it if you can.

Interstate 225 makes a loop southeast of the city, passing through Aurora and hooking up again with Interstate 25 near the Denver Tech Center area.

Other major thoroughfares are Sixth Avenue (U.S. Highway 6), which joins up with I-70 at Golden; Santa Fe Drive (U.S. Highway 85), a north-south route that can be a good alternative to I-25; and Broadway. Colfax Avenue (Colo. Highway 40) is a major east-west route, but, like Broadway, it has a lot of traffic and traffic lights

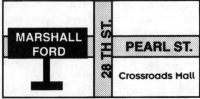 

Art at the Airport

As one of the largest public construction projects in recent years, with an original budget of more than $3.2 billion, Denver International Airport had a correspondingly large amount of money to spend on art. That's because Denver, like so many other cities, has a percent-for-art ordinance that specifies that an amount equal to 1 percent of the total costs of new city construction be set aside for art at the site. This added up to about $7.5 million worth of art commissions divided among 25 projects.

That sounds like a lot of money and a lot of art — and it is — but DIA is so big that the art still can seem tucked away. It's an airport, not a museum, and nobody would ever mistake the two. Still, a traveler is unlikely to pass through DIA without at least noticing some of the art. The main areas to look for art are in the center and wings of each concourse, along the underground train passages and throughout the main terminal.

Here are a few of our favorites:

A 30-foot-high fiberglass blue mustang is the first piece of art people will see as they come into the airport via Peña Boulevard. Made by well-known New Mexico artist Luis Jiminez, the rearing horse has eyes that shoot out laser-like beams of red light. Like DIA, the sculpture has experienced its share of delays and probably won't be installed until 1996 at the earliest.

Near the carousels in the baggage claim area, check out the two whimsical suitcase gargoyles by Terry Allen. They go by the name "Notre Denver."

Also in the baggage claim area are two colorful murals painted by Denver artist Leo Tanguma, a Chicano activist-artist whose general procedure is to involve the community in creating his murals.

Across the main terminal from Tanguma's murals is Gary Sweeney's "America, Why I Love Her," two big photomural maps of the United States with the artist's small framed snapshots of odd bits of Americana — ever seen the Frog Fantasies Museum in Eureka Springs, Arkansas? — tacked onto the appropriate locations. Sweeney used to work as a baggage handler for Continental Airlines. On Denver's spot on the map, he included a little sign that says: "You are here . . . but your luggage is in Spokane." Needless to say, not everybody was amused, especially when glitches in the automated baggage system caused multiple delays in the airport opening date.

On the balustrade at the top of the escalators that connect level five and level six in the main terminal are 28 glossy, vibrant ceramic vases by internationally known ceramist Betty Woodman. Although Woodman has exhibited widely in the United States and Europe, this was her first public commission.

One of our favorite pieces is the interior garden created by Michael Singer in Concourse C. These mossy ruins are visible from below as you exit the train and from above in the concourse.

The Denver International Airport is home to $75 million worth of commissioned artwork, including "America ... Why I Love Her" by Gary Sweeney.

Artists have worked on the floors of DIA in several places, including the main terminal and Concourse B, so if you watch where you're walking, you'll see pictographs, fossils and more inlaid in the terrazzo floor. In the food court areas in Concourse A you'll notice colorful tile patterns that appear to be abstract — but go up the escalator, take a look from above and you'll see that they form foreshortened figures of people. Barb McKee and Darrell Anderson collaborated on this project.

Finally, on the way out of the airport you may notice a line of rusted farm implements. It's not that there wasn't time to clean up — this is part of an art project created by Sherry Wiggins and Buster Simpson to acknowledge that agriculture was historically one of the primary uses of the land on which DIA was built.

Curious passersby can get a brochure that identifies and locates the art at DIA in the information booths in the main terminal and in concourses A and C.

— so it's hardly a quick way to get from one side of town to another. Speer Boulevard connects downtown with Cherry Creek.

Rush hour comes early in Denver: Assuming all goes well, the highways have cleared by 9 AM, and the evening rush hour starts at about 4:30 PM. As mentioned, the Mousetrap is perhaps the most congested intersection, but traffic also runs heavy southbound on I-25 in the evening from downtown to the Tech Center.

There are HOV (high-occupancy vehicle) lanes set up to encourage carpooling on several of Denver's major commuter routes including S. Santa Fe Drive, eastbound U.S. Highway 36 and I-25 north of downtown.

Denver's notorious "brown cloud" has prompted much hand-wringing about auto exhaust pollution. The pollution is worse in winter when temperature inversions clamp down on the city. Under a program called Clean Air Colorado, air quality is monitored between November and April of each year and voluntary "no drive" days are declared when things look particularly bad. (On these high pollution days, woodburning is banned.) News programs regularly broadcast the status, or you can call the Air-Quality Advisory Line, 758-4848.

Parking is tight but not impossible downtown. Options for drivers are on-street meters and lots. Bring coins and small bills.

Public Transportation

RTD

The Regional Transportation District, RTD, runs buses throughout the city and suburbs and in October 1994 began the first phase of light-rail service.

LIGHT RAIL

Light rail runs along a central corridor (the Metro Area Connection, or MAC) from 30th Avenue and Downing Street through Five Points neighborhood, downtown Denver, the Auraria campus and then along railroad right-of-way to the Gates Rubber Plant at I-25 and Broadway. The 5.3-mile route includes 14 stations and connects with bus routes to the south at the I-25/Broadway station. Fares are the same as for local buses: $1 during peak times and 50¢ at off-peak times.

RTD would like to expand the light rail system, but whether or not it can do so depends largely on the availability of federal funding as well as public response to the first phase. The next likely expansion of the system would be along Santa Fe Drive to Mineral Avenue in Littleton.

BUSES

RTD runs local, express and regional bus service. Local buses operate on many routes downtown and cost $1 during peak times, 50¢ at off-peak times. Express routes travel longer distances without as many stops; the basic fare is $1.50. Regional routes run to Boulder and other outlying areas; fare is $2.50. The regional buses are comfortably upholstered, with reclining seats and air-conditioning. In all cases, exact change is required. Tokens, ticket books and monthly passes are available at supermarkets, and many discounts apply (for senior citizens, students and the disabled). RTD recently added a $3 day pass, good for unlimited travel on all local bus routes and light rail. It can be purchased at the Market Street and Civic Street stations and

Insiders' Tips

Parking is tight downtown, but that's not the only reason to use public transportation. There's also Denver's air pollution problem, which worsens in the winter. While they may not be convenient for all metro travelers, RTD buses and light rail to and from downtown are as fast as and no more expensive than driving, especially if you plan to leave your car parked in one spot all day long.

Photo: Daily Camera/Louie Zipf

Denver's infamous Mousetrap: I-70 and I-25 north of downtown.

on the Cultural Connection Trolley. For schedule and route information, call 299-6000, or stop in at the Market Street Station at 16th and Market streets.

RTD's Downtown Express service began in September 1994; it benefits commuters who live north of downtown. Two-way bus lanes run along the middle of I-25 from 58th Avenue to the downtown Market Street Station on a newly completed extension of the 16th Street Mall that runs past Union Station. In September 1995 the lanes were extended as far north as 70th Street, and carpools of two or more persons (in addition to buses) are now allowed to use the lanes.

For information about public transportation to and from the airport, see the airport sections later in this chapter. RTD also provides transportation to professional football and baseball games; check

our Spectator Sports chapter, or call 299-6000 for details.

Taxis

Generally, you don't just wave down a cruising taxi on a Greater Denver street, although it's possible downtown; you usually call ahead. Taxi services operating in Greater Denver include Yellow Cab, 777-7777; Zone Cab, 444-8888; and Metro Taxi, 333-3333.

Leaving Town: Buses and Trains

Trains

Like many cities in the West and Midwest, Denver has a Union Station that dates back to the 19th century and used to be

East Colfax Avenue is the original Colo. Highway 40 into the Rocky Mountain area and, until I-70 was built, Aurora was the first city that travelers encountered coming into the Denver area. Hence, Aurora's claim as the gateway.

Insiders' Tips

much busier than it is now. There are plenty of proposed scenarios for renovating Union Station, but it's not obsolete as a railroad station yet. Among the east-west trains that still run through Denver is the famous *California Zephyr*, which travels an amazingly scenic route across the Continental Divide and through Glenwood Canyon on its way to Salt Lake City and, eventually, Oakland, California. In the winter, a ski train makes the round trip to Winter Park; see our Ski Country chapter for details. Union Station is in Lower Downtown at Wynkoop and 18th streets. For Amtrak information, call (800) USA-RAIL. For recorded information about Amtrak departures and arrivals in Denver, call the Denver Amtrak ticket office, 534-2812.

Buses

The Denver terminus for Greyhound and other private bus lines is at 20th and Curtis streets (1055 19th Street), only a few blocks away from RTD's Market Street Station. Generally, RTD provides bus service to points less than an hour away, such as Boulder and Longmont. See the section on public transportation in this chapter. Longer trips, including trips to Fort Collins and the mountains, originate at the 20th and Curtis station. Because both stations are downtown, make sure you know whether someone is talking about the RTD Market Street Station or the Greyhound Station. For Greyhound fare and schedule information, call (800) 231-2222 or 293-

6555. As seems to always be the case with big-city bus terminals, this one is not located in the nicest part of town. There's no reason to avoid it; just be alert.

Airport

Is there anybody out there who hasn't heard about Denver International Airport and can't recite at least one joke about the baggage system or what DIA stands for? Its postponed opening dates (four, before it opened on February 28, 1995), distance from downtown (24 miles) and escalating price tag ($4.9 billion is a modest estimate) generated "no respect" from the rest of the nation. Denverites are, however, learning to live with it, and some claim to love it. DIA is larger than Dallas-Fort Worth Airport and Chicago's O'Hare Airport combined, extending over an area of 53 square miles. It is the first major U.S. airport to be built from the ground up in nearly 20 years. DIA's five runways can land three aircraft at once using state-of-the-art radar, an improvement over Stapleton International Airport, which closed for business when DIA opened.

RTD still uses Stapleton as a transfer center for skyRide, its service to DIA, and skyRide passengers can park at Stapleton for free. The remainder of Stapleton's 4,700 acres will likely be developed as some kind of commercial mix, with an urban park component, but all that's still up in the air.

DIA is situated to the north and east of Denver and is accessed via Peña Boulevard. Peña Boulevard can be reached via

Insiders' Tips

Park at Stapleton for free and take skyRide to the Denver International Airport — it's the cheapest and easiest way to go. Our only complaint: the small bus shelter where you wait at Stapleton isn't much protection in really foul weather.

Exit 284 off I-70. Travelers from the north can get to the new airport by taking 104th Avenue or 120th Avenue to Tower Road and then driving south to Peña Boulevard. There are numerous stoplights on this route, however.

If you're dropping someone off or picking someone up, there is no charge for the first 70 minutes you spend after passing the DIA toll booth. After that, charges for short-term parking run from $2 to $4 an hour, up to a maximum of $10. Long-term parking costs $5 a day in the uncovered lot or $10 a day in the covered lot.

You could let RTD do the driving. skyRide operates five major routes, from Boulder along U.S. Highway 36 to Stapleton and DIA (Route AB); from Cold Spring Park-n-Ride in Lakewood through downtown to Stapleton and DIA (Route AF); from Stapleton and Montbello to DIA (Route AS); between Highlands Ranch and the Denver Tech Center to DIA (Route AT); and from Northwest Jefferson and Adams counties (Route AA). One-way fare for the suburban routes is $8; from downtown, $6; and from Stapleton, $4. skyRide passengers can park their cars at Stapleton for free. For skyRide information, call RTD at 299-6000.

DIA is a handsome airport, with a dramatic tented roof of Teflon-coated fiberglass fashioned into 34 peaks symbolizing the Rocky Mountains. From a distance, the roof also looks like an encampment of teepees, a nod to the site's historical usage as American Indians' migratory land. Inside, many surfaces are brushed steel, and $7.5 million worth of commissioned art adorns the floors, walls and ceilings (see our sidebar in this chapter for a fuller description of the art).

DIA has three concourses and a main terminal, all of which are connected by underground trains. There is also a pedestrian bridge between Concourse A and the main terminal that provides a good view of the airfield.

Travelers should appreciate DIA's retail shops and restaurants, which, by the terms of their concession contracts, are prevented from charging more than 10 percent above what comparable prices are elsewhere in Denver. Also, there are more brand-name stores and food outlets than in Stapleton. Benjamin Books, with branches in all concourses, has a fine selection of hardcover and paperback books that's far superior to the usual newsstand fare. The main information and paging number at DIA is 342-2000.

Airlines

The following major airlines serve Denver:

America West	(800) 235-9292
American	(800) 433-7300
Continental Airlines	398-3000
Delta	(800) 221-1212
Frontier	(800) 432-1359
MartinAir Holland	(800) 366-4655
Mesa Airlines	(800) 637-2247
Mexicana	(800) 531-7921
Northwest	(800) 225-2525
TWA	(800) 221-2000
United Airlines/United Express	(800) 241-6522
USAir	(800) 428-4322
Vanguard	(800) 826-4827

Photo: Daily Camera/Lourie Zipf

Valet service is a hallmark of the famed Brown Palace Hotel.

Inside
Accommodations

Greater Denver is a community of travelers, those who traveled here to live, those who travel here for vacations and, increasingly, those who travel here on business. It's a popular spot for conventions, and it's one of those places where the residents seldom have any trouble convincing people from other states to come and visit.

The appetites of travelers for good accommodations are well matched by the approximately 15,000 hotel and motel rooms in the Denver area. Whether your tastes tend toward the magnificent or the humble, you'll find plenty of choices.

One good general source of hotel information is the Colorado Hotel and Lodging Association Inc. They have a *Colorado Accommodations Guide* that you can get by writing them at 999 18th Street, Denver 80202, or by calling their Colorado reservations service line, (800) 777-6880. By calling that number, you can also get information on availability and make reservations at hotels anywhere in the state.

Lodging prices in the mountain resorts show amazing bargains in the off seasons of spring and fall, but Denver hotels, tending to be less vacation- and more commerce-oriented, don't show that much variation year round. As commercial hotels, however, they do tend to give much better rates on weekends than during the week, which is, of course, a boon for the working person who wants a weekend getaway.

Our listing rates hotels according to a three-symbol price key, representing average room cost per night during the week for a double occupancy.

Less than $80	**$**
$81 to $120	**$$**
More than $120	**$$$**

The average room rate is not what you'll pay all the time, of course. Most hotels have a wide range of rates on any specific day, and, in addition to good weekend rates, most offer special package deals. Romantic weekend packages are popular with hotels, often lumping together such things as tickets and a limousine ride to a show, carriage rides or dinner at a local fine restaurant into a single price.

At the more moderately priced downtown hotels, you might want to check and see what kind of conventions they have going. We once stayed at a downtown Denver hotel with a convention of some teenage group, and there was running up and down the halls until close to midnight. Later, at 3 AM, the fire trucks came with sirens blaring because a youthful prankster had pulled a fire alarm.

The two biggest sources of hotel bookings are business, including conventions, and tourism. Business travelers stay in the greatest numbers at hotels in downtown Denver, the Denver Tech Center to the southeast and points in between. Tourists will generally stay anywhere they can get a good price, but near downtown is the preferred location for seeing "the sights" of Denver.

If you're interested in seeing Rocky Mountain National Park and want Denver to be part of your trip, choose from the many lodgings on Denver's northwest quadrant. The near-east side of Denver is the most convenient place to stay if you're visiting the Denver Museum of Natural History, Colorado's second-most popular attraction. Lodgings on the west side of Denver provide the best access to Golden, the home of the Coors Brewery. The west side also allows for fast access to downtown and makes for a speedy mountain getaway via I-70. Sporting events are another big attraction, and the downtown or the near-west side are prime lodging locations for ready access to the Colorado Rockies at the new Coors Field, the Denver Broncos at Mile High Stadium or the Denver Nuggets at McNichols Sports Arena.

Big news for Denver is that hotels are finally going up around Denver International Airport. The first of them should be open by January of 1996, a Fairfield Inn by Marriott, part of a $1-billion Denver International Business Center planned along Tower Road between 64th and 72nd avenues, just a few miles from the terminal. A $70-million Westin Hotel has been announced, expected to open in 1997, right at the airport itself. Supposedly you'll be able to take an escalator from the terminal right into the hotel. Also slated for a 1997 opening is a 200-room Courtyard by Marriott, just north of the Fairfield Inn by Marriott.

The U.S. Travel Data Center in Washington, D.C., tells us that we get about 13 million "pleasure trips" from out of state each year, but the Denver firm of Browne Bortz and Coddington estimates about 7 million actual tourists per year, the largest segment of that being people coming to visit

friends and relatives. If they're not crashing on the living room floor, a large percentage of them are staying in Greater Denver hotels and seeing the local sights. Not everybody is in love with the great outdoors.

Tourists spend more than $6 billion here each year, and about half of that amount is associated with the ski industry. We get more tourists in the summer, but skiers are bigger spenders. On the other hand, skiers do most of their skiing in the mountains, tending to hop the first rental car or resort shuttle they can catch out of town. So for the skiers, for attendees at the many conferences held at mountain resort areas, and for all those who want a place to stay in the mountains in the summer, we need to point out that you don't have to do much touch-tone punching to find lodgings.

Besides calling the toll-free reservations number listed above for the Colorado Hotel and Lodging Association, you can call a central reservations number at every major resort for help with prices and availability. See the Ski Country chapter in this book. Also consult the gray pages of the Denver phone book.

Hotels in the southeastern part of Greater Denver, especially around the Denver Tech Center area, seem far from the new Denver International Airport northeast of the city. But they're actually closer in terms of time and traffic than many more central areas, thanks to I-225 that runs up the east side of the metro area to connect with I-70. Hotels in that area are also closer than it would seem to the mountains via I-70, thanks to C-470, the completed southwest quadrant of Denver's future beltway. C-470 offers a low-traffic highway across the south side of Greater Denver, curving up along the edge of the Foothills to meet I-70 west near Golden. It's a faster and less nerve-wracking route than you would otherwise take from the southern half of Greater Denver, which requires you to travel I-25 through the most congested parts of the city before you reach I-70.

A lot of hotels have free continental breakfast, free transportation, free newspapers delivered to your door, free attached parking, free or discounted access to a nearby athletic club, free free free. In most of our listings, we haven't detailed all the frees, but do make a point of asking when you check in. Sometimes they may forget to tell you that you don't need to buy breakfast in the morning.

All hotels, bed and breakfasts, and hostels in this listing accept credit cards.

One fact that you may not notice in looking for a hotel, but of which you should be aware to save yourself confusion and possible grief, is that many Englewood addresses are not in Englewood. For some perverse reason, the post office lists many addresses around the Denver Tech Center as being Englewood addresses, even though Englewood is a good 5 miles to the northwest. We've noted this up-front in each such listing.

Hotels

Denver

ADAM'S MARK DENVER HOTEL

1550 Court Pl.   *893-3333*
$$$

The Adams Mark has undergone a $20-million renovation, mostly during 1995, converting it from a 740-room hotel to a 620-room hotel. That has allowed them to enlarge many of the smaller rooms, as well as renovate room interiors. Completed in 1995 was the Concorde Club on the concierge level, with concierge service daily. The concierge level is the top two floors of the hotel, with panoramic views, and the Concorde Club, exclusively used by guests on those floors, is a central area with seating for up to 75 where there's daily continental breakfast, afternoon tea, hors d'oeuvres and a nightly dessert service. Every room in the hotel is now equipped with work space and the phones have speed dial and speaker action, and dataports. The hotel has more than 70,000 square feet of meeting space, two restaurants and a martini bar with live entertainment nightly, a

---

File this one under ancient secrets of the Brown Palace Hotel. The Navarre Building, 1727 Tremont Place, across the street from the Brown Palace, was built in 1890 as the Brinker Collegiate Institution, the first coeducational college west of the Missouri River. Nine years later, it was converted into the Hotel Richelieu, the city's most elegant gambling house and brothel. In its basement, you can still see rails disappearing into the wall where rail carts once traveled a tunnel beneath Tremont Place delivering fine foods from the Brown Palace kitchens. Legend has it that these carts also delivered Brown Palace patrons too discreet to be seen above ground entering and leaving the Hotel Richelieu.

Insiders' Tips

florist, a print shop, currency exchange, a gift shop, a business center, an airline ticketing office, a beauty salon and barber shop, and a fitness center with sauna, steam room, exercise equipment, an outdoor heated pool and a sundeck. It's on the 16th Street Mall a block away from the Denver Civic Center and four blocks from the Colorado Convention Center.

BEST WESTERN EXECUTIVE HOTEL
4411 Peoria St.   373-5730
$

When they were calling this the Best Western Airport Inn, there were a lot of other airport hotels that were closer to Stapleton International Airport. Good fortune, however, has now made it much closer than those other airport hotels to the new Denver International Airport. So the Best Western Executive Hotel, as it's now called, has capitalized on good fortune by putting about $4 million into sprucing up for its newly prominent airport role. It now has 199 rooms, each featuring work areas and small sitting areas. In 1995 they opened a new restaurant, the Cockpit Grill. The hotel has an outdoor courtyard pool and a fitness center as well.

BEST WESTERN LANDMARK HOTEL
455 S. Colorado Blvd.   388-5561
$

This is Best Western's most central hotel, within walking distance of the Cherry Creek Shopping Center. It has 279 rooms, a restaurant, meeting space for 600, an attractive indoor pool and hot tub with skylights and a poolside lounge.

BROWN PALACE HOTEL
321 17th St.   297-3111
$$$

This is, flat out, Denver's most famous hotel, and deservedly so. If you want a central downtown location, prestige accommo-

dations and a historic experience all in one, you can't do better than the Brown Palace. The list of celebs and potentates who have stayed here since Henry C. Brown opened the doors in 1892 includes every U.S. president since Teddy Roosevelt, except for Jimmy Carter and Bill Clinton; the Beatles and Elvis Presley; English queens, kings, princes, princesses and emperors from England, Sweden, Romania, Japan and others; and entertainment industry names ranging from Lionel Barrrymore to Bruce Willis. Flo Ziegfield wanted to stay there but they wouldn't let him bring his dog in, so he stormed off in a huff.

When the Brown Palace opened, it represented the state of the Victorian art in Italian Renaissance hotel design, with a sunlit, eight-story atrium lobby and tiers of balconies above white onyx walls. It has 230 rooms and 25 suites, more than 13,000 square feet of meeting space; an elegant dining room; an award-winning restaurant, The Palace Arms (described in our Restaurants chapter); a tavern; a lounge and, once again, a central location at the head of 17th Street.

THE BURNSLEY
1000 Grant St.   830-1000
$$

Equipped for and specializing in the extended stay, the Burnsley also compares with the finest Denver hotels in its offering for even the one-night visitor. It's all apartment-style suites, and each tastefully furnished unit has a fully equipped kitchen, separate living room, dining area and bedroom with king-size bed. The Burnsley also has an on-site, self-serve business center and outdoor pool, as well as complimentary passes to a nearby fitness center. In case you don't want to cook in your kitchen, there's also a restaurant. There's a complimentary buffet breakfast, happy hour and parking. We've put the $$

symbol on this entry, because it's been costing $95-$119 for stays of one to seven days, but as an extended stay hotel it costs more like $70 per night when you're there for 30 days or more.

THE CAMBRIDGE
1560 Sherman St.   *831-1252*
$$

On the upslope of Capitol Hill just two blocks from the head of 17th Street, "the Wall Street of the Rockies," the restaurant, lounge and 27 individually decorated suites of this hotel have an atmosphere of senior executive elegance. They bill themselves as "Denver's Personal Hotel." It's an exclusive, fine European sort of place, with complimentary continental breakfast and newspaper.

CHERRY CREEK INN
600 S. Colorado Blvd.   *757-3341*
$$

This inn has one of Denver's nicer locations. It's right on the Cherry Creek greenbelt and near the Cherry Creek shopping/arts/dining area. It's something of a business-traveler hotel, emphasizing desks in the rooms and a business center that can help with things such as notebook computers, faxes and aid in preparing presentations for the 10,000 square feet of meeting/social space. It has a heated outdoor pool, restaurant, gift and sundry store and beauty shop, as well as complimentary passes to a nearby health club.

COMFORT INN DOWNTOWN DENVER
401 17th St.   *296-0400*
$

You can see the big yellow letters, "Comfort Inn," high on the side of this 229-room downtown hotel. Although it's an economy hotel, it's connected by a skywalk across Tremont Place to the Brown Palace Hotel, one of Denver's luxury inns. That

means the Comfort Inn can offer as amenities the restaurants, lounges, meeting spaces and elegant lobby of the Brown Palace. The Comfort Inn is near the head of 17th Street, where the State Capitol and Civic Center and Denver Art Museum are a short walk away, and where you can hop one of the free shuttles on the 16th Street Mall to Larimer Square and Lower Downtown.

COURTYARD BY MARRIOTT
7415 41st Ave. E.   *333-3303*
$$

Aside from the trademark gazebo by the indoor pool in the courtyard, the Courtyards by Marriott are the basic upscale hotels for the discerning business traveler. This one is also distinctive as the Courtyard nearest the airport, positioned off I-70 on Denver's northeast side, 1 mile from the old Stapleton International Airport and 17 miles from the new Denver International Airport.

DAYS HOTEL
4950 Quebec St.   *320-0260*
$

Just north of old Stapleton International Airport, this hotel is also a good bet for travelers coming into the new Denver International Airport because I-70 whizzes right past the hotel. DIA is 18 miles away. It has 195 rooms, an outdoor pool, dining and conference center space for 200.

DENVER MARRIOTT CITY CENTER
1701 California St.   *297-1300*
$$

Marriott's flagship hotel in the city, the Denver Marriott City Center lies in the thick of downtown activities. Within a block of 17th Street, less than two blocks from the 16th Street Mall and less than four blocks from the Colorado Convention Center, it has prestige accommodations in 613 rooms. The fitness center has an indoor pool, exercise room, whirlpool and sauna. The hotel is a big meeting center, with more than 25,000 square feet of space, including the city's largest ballroom.

DENVER MARRIOTT SOUTHEAST

I-25 at Hampden Ave.   758-7000

$$

The Denver Marriott Southeast is about halfway between downtown Denver and the Denver Tech Center. It's a big place, with 595 guest rooms and nearly 16,000 square feet of meeting space. Inside the hotel, there are two restaurants and a sports bar, indoor and outdoor pools, a hydrotherapy pool and an exercise room. You've got the Wellshire Municipal Golf Course a little more than a mile west and a lot of theaters and restaurants within a couple of miles.

DENVER MARRIOTT TECH CENTER

4900 S. Syracuse St.   779-1100

$$

On the edge of the City of Denver's farthest southeast corner, and right off I-25, this hotel is well-named for its access to the Denver Tech Center area. There are good views of the mountains here. Recreational facilities include not just a workout room, indoor and outdoor pools, a sauna, a steam room and a whirlpool, but also racquetball and handball courts, massage and tanning beds. The hotel has 623 rooms, more than 35,000 square feet of meeting space, two restaurants and a deli.

EMBASSY SUITES

7525 E. Hampden Ave.   696-6644

$$

Of four Embassy Suites hotels in Greater Denver, this one is the closest to the Denver Tech Center. Near the intersection of Hampden Avenue and I-25, it's just 2 miles from DTC with fast access to downtown as well. Each suite has a living

room as well as a bedroom, and guests can enjoy exercise facilities, an indoor pool, banquet facilities and free cooked-to-order breakfast in the atrium.

EMBASSY SUITES HOTEL AND ATHLETIC CLUB AT DENVER PLACE

1881 Curtis St.   297-8888

$$$

This fine big beauty of a hotel is Embassy Suites' downtown flagship. It's a little more than two blocks from the 16th Street Mall and all its attractions. It's also close to the pubs and shops and galleries of Lower Downtown. The hotel has 337 suites with one or two bedrooms and a living room and also has 193 furnished apartments "for relocating executives and consultants." The hotel has an outdoor swimming pool. A highlight of the hotel is its Athletic Club at Denver Place. It costs $10 extra for hotel guests, but it's a 65,000-square-foot, three-tier facility with an indoor swimming pool; racquetball, squash and basketball courts; what the hotel claims is the longest indoor running track in Denver; cardiovascular equipment and circuit training area; aerobic and conditioning classes; and a masseuse. There's also a deli, cafe and restaurant at the hotel.

EMBASSY SUITES- DENVER AIRPORT HOTEL

4444 N. Havana St.   375-0400

$$

Amid construction of a new generation of airport hotels at the new Denver International Airport, this is one of the closer ones offering fine accommodations. Fifteen miles west of the new airport, it's also just off I-70 for connections west and close to I-70's intersection with I-225 for connections south. It has 212 suites, a restaurant and lounge, indoor pool, steam room, sauna, whirlpool, exercise equipment, outdoor sundeck, grand ballroom, 12 execu-

The Tabor Center is also home to the Westin Hotel.

tive meeting suites, complimentary cooked-to-order breakfast in the atrium and complimentary cocktails and nonalcoholic beverages for two hours every evening.

EXECUTIVE TOWER INN

1405 Curtis St.   571-0300
$$

Near the Denver Performing Arts Complex and two blocks from the 16th Street Mall and the Colorado Convention Center, the Executive Tower Inn is convenient. Its 337 guest rooms are luxurious. It has two restaurants, a lounge and 22,000 square feet of meeting space. Its Tower Athletic Club is an outstanding exercise and relaxation center. They've got an Olympic-size indoor swimming pool, steam rooms, saunas, indoor and outdoor jogging tracks, exercise rooms, aerobic classes, a whirlpool and courts for tennis, racquetball, squash and volleyball.

FAIRFIELD INN BY MARRIOTT

1680 S. Colorado Blvd.   691-2223
$

Just a block north of I-25 on Colorado Boulevard, the Fairfield Inn by Marriott is midway between downtown Denver and the Denver Tech Center. Three miles to the north and west is Cherry Creek. The hotel packs 166 rooms into 10 stories, with three levels of covered parking, an indoor pool, exercise facility and continental breakfast served in the lobby.

FAIRFIELD INN BY MARRIOTT-DIA

6851 Tower Rd   576-9640
$

Oh joyous day for the business traveler! Slated for a December 1995 opening, a date that shouldn't slide any later than January 1996, this is the first DIA airport hotel to open. It will be the only one open until 1997. It's a modest beginning to future accommodations development around DIA, with 107 rooms and a free continental breakfast but no restaurant. Midday and evening food are available in the form of microwavable vending-machine fare. Still, it's got a meeting room and van transportation to and from the airport, and it's real close. While many fine hotels are still available around the old Stapleton International Airport and northeast Greater Denver, they tend to be 14-18 miles away. This one is just 4 miles away from DIA. The City of

Denver is still fiddling with Peña Boulevard intersections though, and it can get confusing out there on the plains. So directions are necessary: Coming south from the airport on Peña Boulevard, you can exit on Tower Road and go south to the hotel. Coming north from the city toward the airport on Peña Boulevard, exit at 56th Street, go east 1 mile to Tower Road, and then north on Tower Road about 1.5 miles, where you'll see the hotel on the left.

HAMPTON INN
DENVER-AIRPORT/I-70
4685 Quebec St.　　　　　388-8100
$

This Hampton Inn offers 138 rooms near what used to be Stapleton International Airport. At about 18 miles from Denver International Airport, that can still be considered convenient until a good hotel community grows up around DIA. It offers a complimentary continental buffet breakfast.

HOLIDAY INN DENVER DOWNTOWN
1450 Glenarm Pl.　　　　　573-1450
$$

This downtown Denver hotel is centrally situated 1½ blocks from the 16th Street Mall and an equal distance from the U.S. Mint. Holiday Inn's city center prestige hotel, it's a 21-story highrise with 394 rooms, a restaurant, lounge, banquet capabilities, conference rooms for up to 350 and an outdoor, rooftop pool open in season.

HOLIDAY INN
DENVER INTERNATIONAL AIRPORT
15500 E. 40th Ave.　　　　371-9494
$$

This was the nearest hotel to DIA, pending the opening of the Fairfield Inn by Marriott right on the airport's western edge in January 1996. It has 256 guest rooms

and 66,000 square feet of meeting space and public areas. Located north of the Chambers Avenue Exit from I-70, almost in the City of Aurora, it also has a restaurant and lounge, indoor pool, whirlpool, sauna and fitness room.

HOLIDAY INN
DENVER-NORTH/COLISEUM
4849 Bannock St.　　　　　292-9500
$

You'll see it on the west side of I-25 as you whiz by just north of I-25's intersection with I-70. That intersection is not the most scenic place in the area, but you can't find a better location for immediate access to all four points of the city compass. In addition to 218 rooms and eight two-bedroom suites, they've got an outdoor heated pool with a wading pool for the kiddies, a full-service dining room, a deli and a tavern, Teddy's, that got Channel 7's nod as one of the top-seven clubs in Colorado.

HOLIDAY INN-
DENVER QUEBEC STREET
4040 Quebec St.　　　　　321-6666
$$

Holiday Inn's second-closest hotel to the old Stapleton International Airport, this hotel continues to serve the new airport and the west side of Denver. It's just off I-70, so there's also fast access to downtown Denver and points west. It has a restaurant, outdoor pool and 4,000 square feet of meeting space.

HOLTZE EXECUTIVE PLACE
818 17th St.　　　　　　607-9000
$$$

Downtown Denver's newest hotel, opened in 1995, is a 250-room extended-stay hotel resulting from a $20 million renovation of one of 17th Street's oldest buildings, the American National Bank Building at 17th and Stout Streets. While the one- and two-bedroom suites, with full kitchen and dining room, go for $129 and $169, the basic rooms go as low as $99. Many of the rooms have big windows overlooking 17th Street, while others look into an interior atrium with a rock garden and waterfall beneath skylights. The hotel does not serve meals, but nearby restaurants will deliver meals to guest suites. The Holtze also includes street-level retail including the La Salsa restaurant and Starbucks Coffee.

HOWARD JOHNSON DENVER WEST
4765 Federal Blvd.   433-8441
$

Off I-70 at Federal, Howard Johnson Denver West is next to Rocky Mountain Park and Lake, an easy walk from Regis College, and 1½ miles from Lakeside Amusement Park. Close to the business areas around I-25 and on the near-west side convenient to downtown, this Howard Johnson has 92 guest rooms, an outdoor pool, a restaurant and cocktail lounge, and meeting facilities for up to 130.

HYATT REGENCY DENVER DOWNTOWN
1750 Welton St.   295-1234
$$$

Looking down from highrises on the northeastern end of Capitol Hill, the eye is immediately attracted to a large outdoor jogging track and tennis court next to a pool on one of the rooftops in downtown Denver. That's a part of the Hyatt Regency Denver Downtown, which completed a $2.3 million renovation in the fall of 1994 on a Colorado theme that includes a huge Colorado sandstone fireplace in its lobby, a restaurant (two former restaurants combined to form one grand restaurant called 1876) and 25 deluxe suites. In all, the Hyatt has 511 rooms, with 40,000 square feet of meeting space, the previously mentioned rooftop recreational facilities and special rates

at one of Denver's best health clubs a block away.

HYATT REGENCY TECH CENTER
7800 E. Tufts Ave.   779-1234
$$$

The Tech Center Hyatt is an outstanding visual landmark in this part of the Tech Center because it's surrounded by a lot of open ground and because, of course, it's a Hyatt. The landscape is so open around it, you have great views of the Rockies even if you're standing in the parking lot. A majestic 469-room facility, it's designed to give you the sense of being inside a large old Colorado train station. But it doesn't look old at all, and its grand ballroom, four banquet rooms and four meeting rooms make it a favorite meeting place for the business/convention crowd. A rooftop restaurant and lounge makes for scenic dining, and relaxation opportunities include an indoor pool, sauna, hot tub, exercise room and lighted tennis court.

LA QUINTA INN-AIRPORT
3975 Peoria Way   371-5640
$

This is one of those airport hotels that was not as close to Stapleton International Airport as were the airport hotels on Quebec Street to the west. Now, however, it's closer to the new Denver International Airport to the northeast.

Located on I-70 west of the intersection with I-225, it's also convenient to the Denver Coliseum and to the city of Aurora. It's your classic moderate-price business-traveler hotel. The 112 rooms are attractive but basic affairs with small work tables. You can go for a little extra with "King Plus" rooms with king-size beds, recliners and two telephones. One of those phones is a dataport phone, accessible to computer. Complimentary airport shuttle is available. The hotel underwent an exterior renovation in 1994 and completed an interior renovation in 1995. It has a heated outdoor pool, free continental breakfast and a guest laundry facility.

LA QUINTA INN-CENTRAL

3500 Park Ave. W.   458-1222
$

Just north of downtown Denver, La Quinta Inn-Central is a three-story hotel of 105 rooms with an outdoor swimming pool and a newly renovated lobby. A continental breakfast is offered. It's right next to Coors Field, close to Elitch Gardens amusement park, and convenient to downtown, the west side and the sports complexes of Mile High Stadium and McNichols Arena.

LA QUINTA INN-SOUTH

1975 S. Colorado Blvd.   758-8886
$

It's nice to find an inexpensive but pleasant place to stay in the central business location of I-25 at Colorado Boulevard, midway between downtown Denver and the Denver Tech Center. La Quinta Inn-South is such a place, with the dependable La Quinta features of quiet, comfortable rooms with the "King Plus" features mentioned in the entry above, an outdoor heated pool, a continental breakfast and a guest laundry facility. This particular area of Colorado Boulevard also has a lot of mid-range and chain restaurants to choose from.

LOEWS GIORGIO HOTEL

4150 E. Mississippi Ave.   782-9300
$$

There's enough elegant Italian styling to make your head swim at this 12-story hotel near the intersection of I-70 and I-225 in northeast Denver. Inside the lobby, library, 7,000 square feet of meeting rooms and 200 guest rooms, all you see is custom furnishing, marble, murals, frescoes and continental antiques. The Tuscany Restau-

rant has exclusively Italian wines. Guests interested in exercise can take advantage of the aerobic center, which has equipment such as exercise bikes and rowing machines.

OXFORD HOTEL

1600 17th St.   628-5400
$$$

The 81-room Oxford Hotel is in the heart of Lower Downtown's recently renovated red brick district, one block from Union Station, a block from the fabulous Wynkoop Brewing Company's restaurant, bar, cabaret and billiard parlor; across the street from an antique shop and adjacent to an art gallery. The Oxford was built a year before the Brown Palace Hotel, by the same architect, and was once the pre-eminent lodging for travelers arriving in Denver by rail. It's not generally considered to be as beautiful as the Brown Palace Hotel, but the surroundings are more historic. The Cruise Room bar is a popular nightspot, since the Oxford is easy walking distance from the other nightspots of Lower Downtown and Larimer Square. And, it's just three blocks away from the new Coors Field, home to the Colorado Rockies. McCormick's Fish House and Bar is one of Denver's best places to eat. Next door on the other side of the art gallery is the Oxford Club, a very nice health club with barbering and styling available upstairs at the Oxford Aveda Salon.

QUALITY INN DENVER SOUTH

6300 E. Hampden Ave.   758-2211
$$

At the intersection of Hampden Avenue and I-25 north of the Denver Tech Center, and less than 2 miles from I-25's intersection with I-225 north toward the airport, the Quality Inn South is well-positioned for travel. Besides its 185 guest rooms, restaurant, lounge and banquet facilities, this newly refurbished hotel has an outdoor pool, sauna and hot tub.

RAMADA INN DOWNTOWN

1150 E. Colfax Ave.   *831-7700*
$

East Colfax is not the most scenic street in Denver, but you're in the Capitol Hill area here, and you're about halfway between the city center and the Colfax/University Avenue area. There are some fine restaurants within a few blocks, not to mention the attractions of the Denver Botanic Gardens and City Park, with the Denver Zoo and Denver Museum of Natural History. The Ramada has 146 rooms at very reasonable prices and a heated outdoor pool with a hot tub.

RAMADA INN AIRPORT

3737 Quebec St.   *388-6161*
$

An airport-accessible location is the main feature of this Ramada, along with a restaurant, lounge, meeting rooms and 148 guest rooms, including 90 king rooms. There is also a heated outdoor pool and complimentary transportation to Denver International Airport, 17 miles away.

RAMADA MILE HIGH STADIUM

1975 Bryant St.   *433-8331*
$$

One of the most convenient hotels to Denver sporting events, this 13-story, circular tower of 167 rooms is separated from McNichols Sports Arena only by Mile High Stadium. And those sports venues are right across I-25 from downtown Denver. The restaurant and lounge is on the 14th floor, with great views of the area, including downtown Denver. The hotel also has an outdoor pool, exercise facilities and more than 2,100 square feet of meeting space. It was called the Holiday Inn Denver Sports Center until the beginning of 1994.

RED LION HOTEL

3203 Quebec St.   *321-3333*
$$$

One of the finer "airport hotels," the Red Lion is just off I-70 at Stapleton International Airport and offers ready access to the new Denver International Airport as well. It was known as the Registry Hotel until 1990. It has an outdoor hot tub, an indoor pool and exercise equipment for the guests in its 576 rooms. As with other large hotels, it's a major meeting venue with 26,000 square feet of space, as well as two restaurants, a cafe, a lounge and a sports bar.

REGENCY HOTEL

3900 Elati St.   *458-0808*
$

On the heights across the South Platte River and I-25 from downtown Denver, the Regency is one of the near-west side's visual landmarks, thanks to the spherical spaceframe dome of its Picadilly Rotunda.

A few years ago, urban archaeologists went probing to find an underground tunnel that supposedly used to exist between Union Station and the Oxford Hotel. They didn't find the tunnel, but according to local legend, Teddy Roosevelt's aides once used it to whisk him from Union Station to the hotel when they decided he'd had too many spirits to be seen by the public.

Insiders' Tips

It's a convention hotel, with 400 rooms and 63,000 square feet of conference space, but the regular Joe and Jane can enjoy its amenities, including restaurant, piano lounge, indoor and outdoor pools, exercise areas and saunas.

RESIDENCE INN BY MARRIOTT-DENVER DOWNTOWN

2777 Zuni St.   458-5318
$$

Residence Inns are equipped as extended-stay accommodations, with per-night prices dropping substantially if you're there more than a week. Each unit has a fully equipped kitchen and living room area; either one-bed studio suites, or two-bed, loft-style penthouse suites. This one lies just off Speer Boulevard across the Central Platte Valley and I-25 from downtown Denver. It has a heated outdoor swimming pool, two hot tubs and an exercise room. As well as a central dining room with complimentary breakfast and dinner, they'll do your grocery shopping for you for free (you just pay for the groceries).

SHERATON INN DENVER AIRPORT

3535 Quebec St.   333-7711
$

Sheraton's bow to the importance of northwest Denver's air travel corridor, this 195-room hotel off I-70 is a fast, clean high-way-ride away from takeoffs and touch-downs at Denver International Airport. The 2-year-old lobby has a nice, understated, burgundy/mahogany elegance, and the indoor swimming pool, hot tub and exercise area are in a pleasant two-story space with two walls of windows to the outside. Just outside the glass doors from the pool is an 18,000-square-foot courtyard with gazebo and picnic tables, often used for barbecues and company picnics. The Sheraton also has a restaurant and 7,500 square feet of meeting space. And there's complimentary airport shuttle service.

SIGNATURE SUITES

1833 Williams St.   399-2222
$

Good for the extended stay or the short visit, Signature Suites offers 38 one-bed-room suites with fully equipped kitchens and separate sleeping and living areas. You'll find a TV in each suite. Signature Suites is just south of the medical complex including Children's Hospital, St. Joseph Hospital and Presbyterian/ St. Luke's Medical Center, a short walk from downtown and the Denver Zoo and Denver Museum of Natural History in City Park.

STAPLETON PLAZA HOTEL AND FITNESS CENTER

3333 Quebec St.   321-3500
$$

The full title of this hotel says a good deal about the health club amenities and canny marketing. The health club has fitness consultants, aerobics classes, racquet-ball courts, a heated outdoor pool, a whirl-pool, a steam room sauna and very nice exercise equipment. The hotel's 303 guest rooms are arrayed around a striking, 11-story atrium lobby. Boardrooms are available on each floor, and the hotel has an 18,000-square-foot conference center, a business-services center, a restaurant and a lounge.

STOUFFER RENAISSANCE DENVER HOTEL

3801 Quebec St.   399-7500
$$$

Formerly the Stouffer Concourse Hotel, and changing its name again in 1996 to the Renaissance Denver Hotel, this is another hotel that has in the past focused on business from Stapleton International Airport. Now it continues to offer high-end accommodations to air travelers from the new airport as well as people doing business in the north and east sides of Greater Denver. Just south of I-70, it has great connections to downtown Denver and the west. It has 400 guest rooms, three Club Floors with enhanced facilities and service, a restaurant, a health club with spas and indoor and outdoor pools and more than 25,500 square feet of meeting space. They provide complimentary transportation to and from DIA.

WARWICK HOTEL

1776 Grant St.   *861-2000*
$$

The accommodations shine in this tony hotel on Capitol Hill. All of the 194 rooms have Thomasville furniture. The hotel features a number of romantic and night-on-the-town weekend packages and free towncar service to downtown and fashionable Cherry Creek. The open-air, rooftop pool is a nice touch in agreeable weather, and there are complimentary health club privileges.

WESTIN HOTEL TABOR CENTER

1672 Lawrence St.   *572-9100*
$$$

Although the alphabet places this downtown hotel at the bottom of our list, it really deserves to be near the top, if not the first on the list. All downtown hotels can claim a central location, but the Westin is truly central to the best shopping, entertainment and nightlife of downtown Denver. It's on the 16th Street Mall, at the Tabor Center complex shopping mall, and it's a short walk away from the historic buildings, wonderful shops and fine dining of Larimer Square and Lower Downtown Denver. The hotel itself is palatial, with 420 rooms, including guest suites of up to 2,400 square feet, a great restaurant and lounge, and enough ballroom and meeting space

(19,400 square feet, including a 200-seat auditorium) to make it one of the city's preferred gathering spots. Its Augusta restaurant is one of the city's best. The lobby lounge is a great place for people-watching. There's a health club, racquetball courts, an indoor/outdoor pool with a channel that allows you to swim between them, a sauna and a nice hot tub on the western sundeck by the outdoor pool.

WYNDHAM GARDEN HOTEL-DENVER SOUTHEAST

1475 S. Colorado Blvd.
$$ *757-8797*

Just north of I-25 on Colorado Boulevard, this hotel offers fast access to downtown and the Denver Tech Center, and it's also in a commercial area with a lot of restaurants and movie theaters an easy walk away. Besides 250 rooms, it has a cafe, lounge and ballroom on the lobby level. It was the Ramada Denver Midtown until the beginning of 1996.

Adams County

INN AT THE MART

401 E. 58th Ave.
Denver   *297-1717*
$

Though Denver is the mailing address, the Inn at the Mart is actually in a patch of unincorporated Adams County. That's a relatively unimportant distinction, though, because it's on I-25 north of I-70; it's well connected to Denver and its environs. It's also adjacent to the Merchandise Mart, a prime business venue from which the hotel takes its name. It has 156 rooms, a restaurant, a lounge, balconies on every room above the second floor, an outdoor heated pool, a beauty/barber shop and a post office.

La Quinta Inn-North

345 120th Ave. W.
Westminster   252-9800
$

When you stay this far north on I-25, you're putting yourself in a position convenient not just to Greater Denver but to the northern attractions as well: Weld County, Fort Collins, Cheyenne, Rocky Mountain National Park via U.S. Highway 36, Big Thompson Canyon via U.S. Highway 34 out of Loveland, etc. Still, the Westminster La Quinta has commercial areas and companies, such as the headquarters of Gerry Baby Products, nearby.

Rooms are basic but tidy and attractive, and you can opt for a "King Plus" room with a king-size bed, recliner chair and two telephones. One of those phones is a dataport phone, accessible to computer. This is the only La Quinta in Greater Denver with privileges at a nearby health club, and it also has a heated outdoor pool, free continental breakfast and guest laundry facility. Nearby restaurants include Applebee's, Village Inn, Perkins and Gussie Steak House.

Radisson North
Denver Graystone Castle

83 E. 120th Ave.
Thornton   451-1002
$

You can't miss this place, because it is in fact a gray stone castle. The medieval theme is carried out in some of the interior decoration, but it's a modern hotel with close to 9,000 square feet of meeting space and 137 rooms. Enjoy controlled access to the "Camelot Level" on the fifth floor, a restaurant, a pub lounge, an indoor heated swimming pool, a hot tub, sauna and an exercise room.

Ramada Limited Denver North

110 W. 104th Ave.
Northglenn   451-1234
$

If you want a Greater Denver address but also ready access to Fort Collins and points north, or to Rocky Mountain National Park, this is a dandy location. And it's still just 10 miles north of downtown Denver.

Its 140 rooms have recently been renovated with in-room refrigerators. It has a self-service laundry facility on site as well as an on-site Applebee's restaurant and a free breakfast bar in the lobby. There's a weight room facility and an outdoor swimming pool in an interior courtyard in addition to a special small pool for kids. The hotel has meeting and banquet rooms for up to 175 people. Within walking distance are a shopping mall, night clubs, other restaurants, movie theaters and bowling.

Arapahoe County

Courtyard by Marriott

6565 S. Boston St.
Englewood   721-0300
$$

As we warned at the beginning of this chapter, many Englewood mailing addresses are not in Englewood. This is one of them. The Courtyard by Marriott is in Greenwood Village's southeastern tip, near the intersection of I-25 and Arapahoe Road. This Courtyard bills itself as "the hotel designed by business travelers," and that's appropriate for its setting in the Denver Tech Center area. The hotel has large rooms, most with king-size and double rooms, and suites with closed-out bedroom and living room area. The hotel offers a minigym, indoor pool and Jacuzzi, and of course the courtyard with gazebo and barbecue grills. The Courtyard Cafe serves breakfast buf-

The Brown Palace Hotel is an elegant turn-of-the-century landmark.

fets, and the hotel also has a lounge bar open Monday through Saturday.

DENVER HILTON SOUTH

7801 E. Orchard Rd.
Englewood 779-6161
$$

It's not in Englewood, but in Greenwood Village, right on the southern border of the Denver Technological Center. It has 305 rooms, a restaurant, a lounge, an exercise room, a pool and sauna, a boardroom and meeting suites and a Grand Ballroom. This is a very attractive suburban hotel — a feeling of elegance greets you when you enter its polished lobby and see the multistory, sunlit open spaces of its central lounge.

DOUBLETREE
HOTEL DENVER SOUTHEAST

13696 E. Iliff Pl.
Aurora 337-2800
$$

On I-225 in Aurora, the Doubletree-Southeast has the best of that side of town as well as fast connections south toward the Denver Tech Center and north to the airport. The Doubletree-Southeast offers

248 rooms, a restaurant with a very impressive upscale atmosphere, as well as cafe, bar, executive conference suites, health club and indoor pool. All the rooms have two double beds or king-size beds.

DRURY INN DENVER AIRPORT

4400 Peoria St.
Denver 373-1983
$

A well-situated inn for the price-conscious traveler, the Drury Inn is off I-70 between the old Stapleton International Airport and the new Denver International Airport. A free breakfast bar and evening cocktails and snacks are available in the lobby. This hotel has a heated outdoor pool and meeting rooms.

EMBASSY SUITES,
I-25/ARAPAHOE ROAD

10250 E. Costilla Ave.
Englewood 792-0433
$$

Embassy Suites is not in Englewood, but on the southern boundary between Greenwood Village and unincorporated Arapahoe County. Close to the Denver Tech Center, Inverness Business Park and

I-25 and a half-block from Southshore Water Amusement Park, this hotel has 236 two-room suites that each include a separate living room with a sofa bed and a dining/work table. The restaurant has Southwestern and traditional cuisine, and you can work your meal off at the fitness center, indoor pool and whirlpool, or at a nearby full-service health club.

HAMPTON INN DENVER/AURORA
1500 S. Abilene St.
Aurora   369-8400
$

Serving a central location in the City of Aurora, this hotel is also located along I-225 for fast access north to the Denver International Airport and south to the Denver Tech Center and Colorado Springs. The hotel has 132 rooms with coffee makers and ironing boards and irons. The hotel also provides a free continental breakfast buffet, outdoor swimming pool and conference space.

HAMPTON INN DENVER-SOUTHEAST
9231 E. Arapahoe Rd.
Englewood   792-9999
$

The Hampton Inn Denver-Southeast is not in Englewood, despite the mailing address. It's in the hotel cluster on the southeastern tip of Greenwood Village, adjacent to the intersection of Arapahoe Road and I-25, south of the Denver Tech Center. The hotel has 152 rooms, an outdoor swimming pool, workout facilities, in-room coffee service, ironing boards and irons in all rooms, and free continental buffet breakfast.

HOLIDAY INN DENVER
SOUTH-CENTENNIAL AIRPORT
7770 S. Peoria St.
Englewood   790-7770
$$

Not in Englewood but in unincorporated Arapahoe County, this Holiday Inn

is conveniently situated at the Centennial Airport, near the Denver Tech Center, on the way to Colorado Springs, close to C-470 around the southwest side of Greater Denver, and with good connections to the Denver International Airport via I-25, I-225 and I-70. Known as the Clarion Hotel Denver Southeast until it became a Holiday Inn in 1994, the hotel has 120 guest rooms, 50 of which are suites with separate bedrooms and living rooms. It has a cafe and lounge, an outdoor pool, a health club with sauna, a ballroom and six flexible meeting/banquet rooms.

HOLIDAY INN DENVER SOUTHEAST
3200 S. Parker Rd.
Aurora   695-1700
$

The Holiday Inn's Parker Road address is right on I-225, connecting north to I-70 and south to I-25. It's also right on the edge of Cherry Creek Reservoir State Recreation Area, in case you can work in some time for swimming, boating or riding. There is also a rifle range. The hotel has 475 rooms, a restaurant and special rates at an adjacent fitness center with racquetball courts, exercise equipment, indoor running track, swimming pool and saunas.

LA QUINTA INN-AURORA
1101 S. Abilene St.
Aurora   337-0206
$

Aurora Regional Medical Center is right across I-225 from this centrally located Aurora hotel, and I-225 provides quick access north to the airport and south to the Denver Tech Center, Douglas County and points south. It has a heated outdoor pool and laundry facilities, and includes a free continental breakfast and free cable TV. Nearby restaurants include Coco's, Bennigan's, Black-eyed Pea and The Italian Fisherman. Rooms are basic but tidy and attractive, and you can opt for a "King Plus" room with a king-size bed, recliner chair and two telephones. One of those phones is a dataport phone, accessible to computer.

RADISSON HOTEL DENVER SOUTH
7007 S. Clinton St.
Englewood 799-6200
$$

No, it's not in Englewood. Despite the mailing address, it's just off I-25 at the far southeastern tip of Greenwood Village between the Denver Tech Center and Centennial Airport. It's a good place to stay if your Denver stay includes business or pleasure in Colorado Springs. Like other big hotels in this open part of town, it has great views of the mountains, especially from the Plaza Club levels on the ninth and 10th floors, where you have concierge service, complimentary complete breakfast in the morning and cocktails and hors d'oeuvres in the evening. The rooms total 263; the conference center meeting space totals 8,100 square feet. The hotel has a restaurant, lounge, exercise facility, outdoor heated pool and whirlpool.

RESIDENCE INN BY MARRIOTT-DENVER SOUTH
6565 S. Yosemite
Englewood 740-7177
$$

No, it's not in Englewood. It's actually on the border of unincorporated Arapahoe County and Greenwood Village in the Denver Tech Center area. That needs to be said for the benefit of those who want to find this tasteful, extended-stay hotel in the Denver Tech Center area. Even the "studio suites" include a fully equipped kitchen. Set in a neighborhood environment, the hotel has an outdoor swimming pool, heated spa and complimentary passes to a nearby fitness club.

THE INVERNESS HOTEL AND GOLF CLUB
200 Inverness Dr. W.
Englewood 799-5800
$$$

It's not in Englewood but in unincorporated Arapahoe County just west of Centennial Airport. At the intersection of I-25 and County Line Road, one of I-25's last major intersections before it heads south through Douglas County to Colorado Springs, it's centrally located in the "Piedmont Megalopolis," as some are beginning to call the increasingly interconnected Front Range urban landscape. Absolutely stunning from the outside, the Inverness Hotel's high-tech/high-style exterior fits the state-of-the-art conference facilities in the interior, with 33 meeting rooms including auditoriums, conference rooms, boardrooms and breakout rooms with sophisticated audiovisual accommodations built in and aided by audiovisual specialists in a central control room. The hotel was named as "Best Conference Facility" in *Colorado Business Magazine*'s February 1995 "Best of Colorado Business" feature and also was voted Denver's best overall hotel by the 1995 Zagat survey. But you don't have to attend a conference to enjoy the adjoining

Inverness Golf Course, home of the Colorado Open. The hotel has its own pro shop, as well as a billiards room, three lighted tennis courts, indoor and outdoor pools, saunas, indoor and outdoor whirlpool baths, health club with aerobics studio, exercise circuit and exercise equipment. Guests in the 302 rooms can also enjoy three fine restaurants, including the award-winning, four-diamond Swan Restaurant.

Jefferson County

BROOMFIELD GUEST HOUSE
9009 W. Jeffco Airport Ave.
Broomfield   469-3900
$$

The Broomfield Guest House could almost be listed in our Bed and Breakfast section, with its quiet country-inn ambiance, its complimentary breakfast, its "great room" with fireplace and collection of books. Then again, it has amenities similar to those found in a hotel such as a laundry room, conference and meeting rooms, an on-site catering and special events coordinator and a corporate atmosphere. One might describe it as a "corporate B&B," although it's not just for the business crowd. The great room and patio are good places for wedding-related events as well as corporate cocktail parties. Each separate suite has its own private entrance and fireplace, kitchenette, private bath and king bed. Some have whirlpool baths and separate sitting rooms.

BROOMFIELD MANOR HOTEL
570 Hwy. 287 & Midway Blvd.
Broomfield   466-7311
$

This is our only hotel listing in Boulder County, but Broomfield is also a part of Jefferson County, and the Broomfield Manor Hotel has long been the city's workhorse economy hotel. It has 60 rooms, along with a restaurant, lounge and banquet room. In the same building is a beauty shop, barber shop, nail shop and insurance agency.

COMFORT INN SOUTHWEST DENVER
3440 S. Vance St.
Lakewood   989-5500
$

On the south end of Lakewood, less than a mile from the Foothills Golf Course and just south of U.S. 285 west to C-470 and the mountains, the Comfort Inn is one of the cost-conscious alternatives for lodging in the southwest metro area. Each room has contemporary furnishings and a king-size bed or two queens. Eight of the rooms are two-room suites. The hotel has a small fitness center with a rowing machine, exercise bike, stair climber and sit-up bar; an outdoor heated pool with a hot tub; free continental breakfast; and guest laundry and valet service. In 1995, they got the Gold Award for the second year in a row, from Choice Hotels International.

DAYS INN-DENVER WEST/GOLDEN
15059 W. Colfax Ave.
Golden   277-0200
$

Another cost-conscious alternative on the west side, this Days Inn sits at a major node of the west side's transportation web. You can go straight west to Golden, hop on I-70 west or east, or jog south to catch U.S. Highway 6 for a fast, no-stoplight run to downtown Denver. This Days Inn has 155 rooms, a restaurant, heated outdoor swimming pool, hot tub and sauna and exercise area and meeting/banquet facilities.

DENVER MARRIOTT WEST
1717 Denver West-Marriott Blvd.
Golden   279-9100
$$

One of the first places people mention when asked about fine accommodations on the far-west side, Denver Marriott West is set in the Denver West Office Park just off I-70 in Golden. Guests in its 307 rooms are 20 minutes from downtown Denver. After 10 minutes on I-70 west you'll be in the mountains. It has an indoor and outdoor pool, exercise equipment, saunas, a hydrotherapy pool, restaurant, cafe, lounge and 8,300 square feet of meeting/banquet space.

DOUBLETREE CLUB HOTEL
137 Union Blvd.
Lakewood   969-9900
$$

On the far western side of Lakewood, between the Denver Federal Center and Red Rocks Community College, the Doubletree Club is a great staging point for business and tourism excursions around the west side of Greater Denver. A straight shot west for a couple of miles on U.S. Highway 6 connects you to I-70. This hotel has 170 rooms, complimentary transportation within a 5-mile radius, a dining room, exercise room, outdoor pool, sauna and whirlpool.

ECONO LODGE
715 Kipling St.
Lakewood   232-5000
$

This economy hotel is just north of U.S. Highway 6. It's convenient for trips to Golden and the mountains and a fast, straight shot from downtown Denver. It has 65 suites with full kitchens, an outdoor heated swimming pool and a fenced play area. Two fine restaurants and lounges are within easy walking distance.

FOOTHILLS EXECUTIVE LODGING
6565 W. Jewell Ave.
Lakewood   936-3070
$

You can't take advantage of the extended-stay accommodations at Foothills

unless you commit to at least three days, but you get a full apartment for what a room of equivalent quality would cost you at most hotels. The address listed is only the mailing address for the management of Foothills Executive Lodging, and 6565 W. Jewell is actually in Lakewood. More important is that this family-owned company has 11 different lodging sites around the Denver area. One is in Littleton near the Denver Tech Center, and the others are clustered in Lakewood on the west side. There are close to 70 units in all, some apartments and some condos; some of which Foothills Executive Lodging owns, some they rent and some they manage. You can choose between one-, two- and three-bedroom units. All complexes have outdoor pools. Most have workout rooms, but if they don't, Foothills Executive Lodging can arrange for local health club memberships.

HAMPTON INN DENVER-SOUTHWEST
3605 S. Wadsworth Blvd.
Lakewood   989-6900
$

Just south of U.S. Highway 285, on the southern tip of Lakewood where it borders unincorporated Jefferson County, the Hampton Inn Denver-Southwest is convenient to the mountains and to the big employers of southwest and western Jefferson County such as the Denver Federal Center, Martin Marietta, US West, Coors and Manville. It has 148 rooms, an outdoor swimming pool, free continental buffet breakfast, meeting rooms, neighborhood surroundings and the Foothills Golf Course nearby.

LA QUINTA INN-GOLDEN
3301 Youngfield Service Rd.
Golden   279-5565
$

This is a great location for fast access to the mountains on I-70 west, or to the business and tourist attractions of Jefferson County. Practically out its front door, 32nd Avenue winds west past the Adolph Coors Co. brewery to the City of Golden. On the other side of I-70, an extensive shopping center has nearly everything you might need, including a Starbucks Coffee shop that opened in 1993. The hotel has 129 rooms on three floors and a heated outdoor pool.

LA QUINTA INN-WESTMINSTER MALL
8701 Turnpike Dr.
Westminster   425-9099
$

Just south of U.S. Highway 36, east of Sheridan Avenue, this hotel puts you in an intermediate location between Denver and Boulder. And Sheridan, of all the north/south thoroughfares on the west side, is one of the fastest moving, so that means a decent connection with I-70 to the south. You're also right next to some of the west side's biggest shopping and entertainment areas along north Sheridan and Wadsworth, including the Westminster Mall Shopping Center on the other side of Sheridan. The hotel has 130 rooms, a heated outdoor pool, continental breakfast and guest laundry facilities. Rooms are basic but tidy and attractive, and you can opt for a "King Plus" room with a king-size bed, recliner chair and two telephones. One of those phones is a dataport phone, accessible to computer.

RAMADA HOTEL DENVER/BOULDER
8773 Yates Dr.
Westminster   427-4000 or (800) 868-4001
$$

Perched on a nice Rocky Mountain vantage point just north of U.S. Highway 36, this is a good hotel for those seeking ready access both to Greater Denver and Boulder County to the northwest. It's a classy place with com-plimentary continental breakfast, cocktails and hors d'oeuvres served Monday through Friday in the private Summit Club on the Concierge floor. In addition to its 180 rooms, including "Jacuzzi Suites," it has more than 8,000 square feet of meeting space, a restaurant, a lounge and a very nice whirlpool, sauna and indoor swimming pool.

RODEWAY INN-DENVER WEST
7150 W. Colfax Ave.
Lakewood   238-1251
$

Until May 1994, this hotel was known as Denver Lakewood Inn. It's a nice, inexpensive hotel for business and vacation travelers. Just off of two major east-west thoroughfares, W. Colfax Avenue and U.S. Highway 6, and less than 5 miles east of I-70, it's a good location for access to both downtown Denver and the mountains. There's an onsite restaurant, Sammy's, a heated outdoor pool and free coffee 24 hours a day in the lobby. That's about it for amenities, but the 122 rooms are recently refurbished in what manager Sammy Toole calls "Rodeway requisition" style, with light-colored walls, nice clean carpets and king-size and double beds.

SHERATON DENVER WEST
HOTEL & CONFERENCE CENTER
360 Union Blvd.
Lakewood   987-2000
$$

Aimed at the business traveler, with a full-service business center and 18,000 square feet of meeting space in 16 meeting rooms, this 242-room hotel is also one of the nicest places to stay on your vacation. Right off U.S. Highway 6, it's a great staging point for trips to the mountains; it's also in a thriving business and commercial area of western Greater Denver. The Sheraton has its own restaurant and an in-house health club, weight room, indoor pool and sauna. If you want to go whole hog, the oversized rooms on the Concierge Floor have whirlpool tubs and other amenities.

TABLE MOUNTAIN INN

1310 Washington Ave.
Golden   277-9898
$$

The Table Mountain Inn shares an important characteristic with the Westin Hotel Tabor Center in our Denver listings: the alphabet places it at the bottom, but it should be at or near the top for the county. First of all, it's charming as all-get-out with its Santa Fe-style architecture and interiors. Second, its Southwestern-cuisine restaurant, The Mesa Bar & Grill, is not just a hotel restaurant but a westside treasure that people drive from other nearby cities just to enjoy. Third, it's right on the main street of downtown Golden in the midst of the neighborly, small-town atmosphere. It's within walking distance of the Coors Brewery and the Colorado School of Mines to

boot. It has 32 rooms and a bar adjoining the restaurant.

Bed and Breakfast Inns

There are some who don't care for the bed and breakfast experience; they want a modern room, a pool, a restaurant, a gift shop and a lobby. But others enjoy the charm, personal touch, intimacy and the often historic surroundings of a bed and breakfast inn. Greater Denver has such inns that compare with the best anywhere.

If you want a more complete exposition on bed and breakfasts up and down the Front Range and throughout the rest of Colorado, the Bed & Breakfast Innkeepers of Colorado has more than 100 inspected and approved establishments in its listings for the state. You can call them at (800) 83-BOOKS and order their directory over the phone by credit card.

In the use of our price-key symbols ($, $$ or $$$), representing double occupancy during the week, we've tried to represent an average price of accommodations for each bed and breakfast inn, but remember

The Embassy Suites Hotel is in downtown Denver.

that the inns often have a limited number of rooms at widely varying price ranges. All of the bed and breakfasts in our listing accept credit cards, and none of them accept pets. None of them will turn away people with children, but in some cases as indicated, children may be difficult to accommodate due to limits on the number of people allowed in rooms or the inability to add an extra bed to rooms.

ANTIQUE ROSE

1422 Washington Ave.
Golden   277-1893
$$

The Antique Rose Bed & Breakfast Inn has just four rooms in an 1880s Queen Anne Victorian home, with gables, dormers and fishscale and diamond-shaped shingles. Originally the home of Senator and Mrs. Richard Broad Jr., it later became a boarding house for Colorado School of Mines students. It has historic designation and was opened as a bed and breakfast in 1993 by host Sharon Bennetts. In the southern end of Golden's historic business district, it is an easy walking distance from Golden's many historic and tourist attractions. Office services are also available. Children are difficult to accommodate, because no room has more than one bed, and there are no cots or rollaways.

CAPITOL HILL MANSION

1207 Pennsylvania St.
Denver   839-5221
$$$

All the fineries you expect from a bed and breakfast inn can be found in this mansion of ruby sandstone along with all the sense of place and history you expect in the historic inn experience. One of the owners co-wrote Denver's official walking tour. The mansion is on the National Historic Register, having been built in 1891 as one of the last great mansions raised before the silver crash put a temporary damper on lo-

cal development. It's in an area near the State Capitol, surrounded by ornate historic structures built when Capitol Hill was snob knob. The exterior is a turreted, balconied affair with a grand curved porch. The interiors live up to even the most aristocratic expectations, with crafted, patterned plaster and golden oak paneling opening to a dramatic sweeping staircase with stained and beveled glass windows. The public parlors are inviting, and each room is individually decorated with such touches as brass beds, claw-foot tubs, private balconies, curved-glass windows, high ceilings, fireplaces, oak floors, a solarium and a hand-painted mural. Soothing music, soft lighting and jetted tubs are among the other attractions. There are eight guest rooms in all, each with a private bath, some with whirlpools. Those with kids should know that Capitol Hill Mansion has only one room in which it allows children younger than 15 years of age.

CASTLE MARNE

1572 Race St.
Denver   331-0621
$$$

Victorian architecture with an eccentric flair is the charm of this bed and breakfast on Denver's near-east side, 20 blocks from downtown and an easier and more scenic walk from the Denver Zoo, the Denver Museum of Natural History and the Denver Botanic Gardens. Built in 1889, Castle Marne really looks like a small castle. Its designer was eclectic architect William Lang, who also designed Denver's famous "Unsinkable" Molly Brown House, now a major landmark and tourist attraction. Castle Marne is striking on the outside, stunning on the inside. Some of the guest rooms have their own Jacuzzi tubs for two. Three of the rooms have private balconies with hot tubs for two. All have furnishings chosen to bring together authentic period antiques, family heirlooms and exacting reproductions to create a mood of tranquil and elegant charm. You can find that same mood in the parlor, a serene retreat of high ceilings and glowing, dark woods and the cherry-paneled dining room. The Castle's big visual treasure is what they call their Peacock Window, a circular, stained-glass beauty partway up the grand staircase. The Castle also has a gift shop, game room, Victorian garden, an airy veranda and a guest office for the business traveler, including computer. Restrictions on children are: only well-behaved children older than 10. Although that is the only restriction on children at Castle Marne, this bed and breakfast does have a maximum allowable occupancy of two persons per room.

THE CLIFF HOUSE LODGE & COTTAGES

121 Stone St.
Morrison   697-9732
$$$

In the charming town of Morrison amid the red-rock splendor of the Morrison Geological Formation, this bed and breakfast is housed in a sandstone Victorian built in 1873 by Morrison's founder, George Morrison. George built an addition for his quarry miners back around the turn of the century, and his house became a hotel. Now it's a bed and breakfast, although it's really more properly described as a country inn. Only two suites are actually in George's house. The rest are private, separate cottages, where candlelight breakfasts are brought to the cottage door. Special offerings are the honeymoon suites, which include private hot tubs, entertainment centers and woodburning fireplaces. Accommodating children may be difficult here, since the Cliff House does not have futons, cots or rollaway beds.

FRANKLIN HOUSE

1620 Franklin St.
Denver   331-9106
$

You may find fancier bed and breakfasts in Denver, but you won't find one at such inexpensive prices in such a great location. Franklin House's hosts George and Sharon Bauer describe it as Denver's only European-style inn. By that they mean that it's nothing fancy, just comfortable rooms with a nice breakfast and homey charm rather than Victorian charm, even though the building itself is an 1890s home. They have eight rooms, a sitting room with a TV, books, music and a backyard patio. The Bauers speak German, Spanish and a little French, although they don't get enough French visitors to keep real sharp on the latter. If you drew a triangle with points at downtown Denver, the Denver Botanic Gardens and City Park, with its Denver Zoo and Denver Museum of Natural History, Franklin House would be just about in the middle of the triangle.

HAUS BERLIN

1651 Emerson St.
Denver   837-9527 or (800) 659-0253
$$

Haus Berlin is an 1892 Victorian townhouse, which has always been known as the Haskell House because it was built for Thomas Haskell, founder of Colorado College in Colorado Springs. It's on the National Historic Register and sits on a tree-lined street surrounded by similar structures. That's about as Victorian as Haus Berlin gets, however, because the interior is mostly northern European furnishings with just a few antiques. Christiana Brown, co-owner and host with her American husband Dennis Brown, is a native of Berlin. The original paintings and other works of art that decorate Haus Berlin are a mixture picked up by the couple in their

European and Latin American travels and during the 12 years they lived in the Virgin Islands. All linens used in the hotel are cotton, and there's a pretty backyard with flower gardens where guests can opt to enjoy their breakfast in the warmer months. Haus Berlin is between downtown and City Park, an easy walk from the Denver Zoo and the Denver Museum of Natural History. It's just a couple of blocks from the medical cluster of Saint Joseph Hospital, Children's Hospital and the Presbyterian/St. Luke's Medical Center. There are also some nice restaurants along the nearby stretch of 17th Street. It's hard to accommodate children here as there are no futons, cots or rollaway beds.

HOLIDAY CHALET

1820 E. Colfax Ave.
Denver 321-9975
$

We listed the Holiday Chalet in our hotel section last year, because it's advertised as a hotel and doesn't have the typical bed and breakfast arrangement. Each suite has its own kitchen, and it's a self-serve breakfast. Holiday Chalet provides a variety of cereals, fruit juice, Pop Tarts, breakfast bars, cocoa, coffee and tea, and guests provide whatever they want in terms of fresh fruit, canned goods, meat and milk. This Victorian-charm hotel is a restored, three-story brownstone mansion built in 1896 for a prominent Denver jeweler. The present owners represent the third generation of the same family that has served guests here. It's situated for easy walking to the Denver Zoo, the Denver Museum of Natural History and the Denver Botanic Gardens. It's about 10 blocks from downtown.

JAMESON INN

1704 Illinois St.
Golden 278-0351
$$

On a shady street on the campus of the Colorado School of Mines, a five-minute walk from downtown Golden, the Jameson Inn is a 1914-vintage building in English Norman Cottage style and officially designated as one of Golden's historic landmarks. Alexander Jameson, a pioneer and judge during the gold-rush days, performed the wedding of Adolph and Louisa Coors in 1879. The Jameson Inn includes a parlor with a fireplace, a shady courtyard with fountain, games, books, movies and cable TV. For business travelers, there's a desk and phone in every room and access to a fax machine.

LUMBER BARON INN

2555 W. 37th Ave.
Denver 477-8205
$$$

Denver's newest bed and breakfast, the Lumber Baron was refurbished and open for business in the summer of 1994. But it goes way back before that, being an 1890s brick mansion built by John Mouat, a Scottish immigrant who ran a major millwork and construction supply company. He put six different kinds of wood into his house's fancy woodwork. The first two floors have 12-foot ceilings, there's a 2,000-square-foot ballroom on the third floor, and there is space for banquets and event rental. The Lumber Baron has five suites, three of them with Jacuzzis for two.

MERRITT HOUSE

941 E. 17th Ave.
Denver 861-5230
$$

Four blocks east and three blocks north of the State Capitol, the Merritt House is about as historic as a bed and breakfast can get. It was designed by Frank Edbrooke, the same architect who designed the Brown Palace Hotel, the Oxford Hotel, the Tabor Grande Opera House and a lot of other historic treasures. It's also in the Swallow Hill District, which is on the National Register of Historic Places and is named for its original real-estate developer, not because it was buzzing with swallows. The 1889 Merritt House has 10 guest rooms, and guest rooms and common areas reflect the elegance of 1880s era. All the rooms, however, have a telephone and cable TV, and some of the private bathrooms include whirlpool Jacuzzis. Otherwise, they have antiquarian furnishings such as queen-size, four-poster beds or brass beds, brass chandeliers, wing-back chairs and oriental carpets.

ON GOLDEN POND
7831 Eldridge St.
Arvada 424-2296
$

"For European hospitality and a relaxing blend of country comfort," states this bed and breakfast's brochure. You drive semi-rural roads to a long gravel drive leading up past a horse pasture on the left and goats on the right, through a lane overhung by bushes, trees and flowers, to the entrance. Neighbors are far away, and the 10 acres truly offer a quiet, country atmosphere. There are five rooms, four of which look south on manicured grounds with a duck pond and gazebo. Your host, Kathy Kula, is a native of Germany, and this is the only German-speaking accommodation on the west side of Greater Denver. But it's great for every nationality, and for some reason they get a lot of British visitors who are in Colorado for the bird-watching. Among the amenities of this location are a hot tub and pool, and you can bicycle and walk the country roads and ride horseback in the

foothills. Breakfast is served on the deck or indoors, and there is a traditional late-afternoon kaffeeklatsch with coffee and pastries. Although the room average is under $80, there is also the lovely Peacock Room for $100 per night and the Blackbird Room at $90.

QUEEN ANNE INN BED & BREAKFAST
2147 Tremont Pl.
Denver 296-6666
$$

The Queen Anne Bed & Breakfast Inn is in a restored area on the edge of downtown: the Clements Historic District, Denver's oldest continuously occupied residential neighborhood. The Queen Anne itself consists of two adjacent Victorian buildings in the Queen-Anne style of architecture, of 1879 and 1886 vintage, both of which are on the National Historic Register. They give you a list of guidebook editors to write to, and that's because they know they're a good bet for favorable review with their elegantly restored interiors, period furnishings, eager service and 14 quaintly homey rooms featuring individual baths, writing desks, piped-in chamber music at your control and fresh flowers. Rooms range from $75 to $155. This inn has been rated one of the best of Denver by *Westword* and among the seven most romantic destinations in Colorado by a local television station. The new Coors Field is also about a 15-minute walk away, which hasn't hurt the bed and breakfast's business.

VICTORIA OAKS INN
1575 Race St.
Denver 355-1818
$

Guests rate this as a pearl, largely due to its welcoming and gracious owners and homey ambiance. It's a restored 1896 mansion with just nine rooms and a lot of atmospherics such as antiques, leaded-glass windows, original oak woodwork and tile fireplaces. It's nicely located, too, for easy access to some of the finest amenities of Denver's near-east side. Little more than a mile west is the State Capitol, and beyond it, downtown Denver. Less than a mile of pleasant walking can take you to Cheesman Park, City Park and three of Denver's finest attractions: the Denver Botanic Gardens, the Denver Zoo and the Denver Museum of Natural History. Due to some bad experiences with children, the owners prefer not to have them as guests.

Hostels

Hostels are for the truly cost-conscious traveler who is not looking for frills or even a bathroom in the room. If you're traveling on a budget and love an offbeat atmosphere and what might seem like bohemian accommodations to the folks at the Westin and the Hyatt, there's nothing like that special camaraderie that prevails in the hostel environment.

They used to call these things "youth hostels," because older folks tended to think they were OK for kids but declassé for adults, or that they were just plain dives for hippies and the down-and-out. Now, in a more enlightened era, we know that all ages can enjoy the hostel experience. OK, hostels sometimes look from the outside like flop houses, and they're sometimes in seedier parts of town. Then again, some of them are unexpectedly attractive. One thing for sure is they tend to be close to the center of town, with prices that allow you to stay for a week on what would be one night's price at a reasonably fancy hotel. Our price key, explained in the beginning of the chapter, doesn't really tell you how cheap they are, because prices for the following hostels range as low as $8.50 per night. Denver has several choice venues for the hosteler.

You can get the full scoop on hostels in the Denver area and the rest of Colorado by calling American Youth Hostels-Hostelling International at (202) 783-6161, for anywhere in the United States. There's also a Boulder number, (303) 442-1166, that's good for Colorado hostels. We've listed below the downtown Denver possibilities.

Hostels listed below all accept major credit cards but no personal checks. There are no age restrictions on occupants, except that people younger than 18 cannot check in without a parent or guardian.

DENVER CENTRAL YMCA
25 E. 16th Ave.
Denver   861-8300
$

The Y is just off the Civic Station bus terminal for the 16th Street Mall, a prime location. The Y has 189 rooms, with no phone and no TV, ranging from a single without a bathroom to a double with a bathroom. One thing about the YMCA is that few hotels can claim a health club that is nearly as extensive as the Y's. Exercise facilities cost $3.50 a day for residents and include an indoor pool, two gyms, two indoor running tracks, a Nautilus center, other exercise equipment and handball and racquetball courts. No alcohol is allowed, and pets aren't welcome either. The rooms are clean, secure and comfortable.

DENVER INTERNATIONAL YOUTH HOSTEL
630 E. 16th Ave.
Denver   832-9996
$

The Denver International Hostel is just six blocks east of Broadway and the edge of the downtown. It's all dormitories, meaning you share bedrooms with other people, but the dormitories are separated into men's and women's sections. How many people share a room? It depends on the night. Bathrooms are down the hall. They have showers, a kitchen you can use and a common room with a TV, library and stereo, balconies, storage and sports equipment. You have to check in between 8 and 10 AM or between 5 and 10:30 PM, when the office is open. There's no curfew; you get keys to come and go when you please.

MELBOURNE HOTEL & HOSTEL
607 22nd St.
Denver   *292-6386*
$

An old hotel, the Melbourne is a member of the American Youth Hostel Association. Rooms have sinks and beds. Bathrooms are off the hall. Ten of the 16 rooms in this hotel are not a part of the hostel but simply hotel rooms. The six hostel rooms are dormitories, meaning you share a room with three to five people. Wine and 3.2 beer are allowed, but no hard liquor.

The Melbourne is Denver's most child-accommodating hostel. It has four family rooms, each of which has a double bed plus a set of bunk beds.

An employee gets ready for the mealtime rush at Rock Bottom Brewery
in downtown Denver.

Inside
Restaurants

Dining out, like shopping, is an area where Greater Denver has shown dramatic improvement in recent years. Lots of hot young chefs are busy in the kitchens here, enough so that their food has collectively earned the name "Rocky Mountain cuisine."

What this means is an emphasis on game and other local products, like trout and lamb (Colorado has the country's fourth-largest population of lamb and is the country's largest processor of lamb). Southwestern touches abound; many of the new chefs are liberal in their use of chiles, cilantro, tomatillos and black beans.

Of course there's plenty of old-fashioned Rocky Mountain cuisine to be had, too: a number of restaurants pride themselves on what they're able to do with buffalo meat. Buffalo, along with other game such as elk and pheasant, has long been on the menu at Denver's oldest restaurant, The Buckhorn Exchange. Leaner than beef, buffalo is enjoying a resurgence of popularity nationwide, and Colorado restaurateurs like Sam Arnold of The Fort and Will McFarlane of the Denver Buffalo Company are leading the way. McFarlane raises

his own herd on a spread in the eastern part of the state near Kiowa. The strong-stomached Denver diner may want to sample Rocky Mountain oysters, which are — how shall we put it? — the private parts of the male buffalo or male cattle, sautéed or breaded and deep-fried.

Getting fresh seafood used to be a problem in Denver, but no more. Pacific Coast fish such as salmon and river fish such as trout are widely available and consistently good. Maine lobster isn't hard to find either, but fans of clams and oysters on the half shell will have a more difficult (though not impossible) time fulfilling their desire; those are about the only things that Denver restaurants are lacking.

As for ethnicity, Greater Denver counts among its blessings several Ethiopian eateries and top-notch Vietnamese, Japanese, Korean, Mexican, Peruvian and Brazilian restaurants. There are also plenty of California-influenced bistros, especially in the Cherry Creek area. Most serve pastas, burgers and pizzas made in on-site woodburning ovens.

In this section we've left out chain restaurants like Chili's and Pizza Hut, not

> If you're on the lookout for a low-fat, low-sodium meal, check your menu for HealthMark selections. HealthMark is a Denver organization that analyzes recipes and gives its stamp of approval to those that meet its criteria.

Insiders' Tips

because we have anything against them, but on the assumption that readers already know what to expect at these places without our going into detail. Locally owned chains that operate within the Greater Denver area only are included, as visitors couldn't be expected to know their fare. A national chain may have slipped into the listings here and there, either inadvertently because we didn't know it was one of many, or because to omit it would leave a particular geographic area under-represented. In the case of exceptional merit, we've bent our rules on chains.

As can be imagined, no one book could ever describe all of Greater Denver's restaurants. We've picked out the best and the brightest, as is our mandate throughout this guide. Some are special-occasion places, others are neighborhood joints. Some are widely known local institutions, others much less so. We also tried to be clear about whether it's the food, the ambiance, the crowd, the service or all of the above that makes a place worth a visit. Obviously we don't expect everyone to agree with all our choices, and restaurants are notoriously mutable creatures, apt to get better or worse or go out of business without warning. Hours and days of operation change, too, so we suggest you call before you go. Also, while some restaurants serve continuously, others close between lunch and dinner, so if it's a mid-afternoon bite that you're after, definitely call first.

For dining out with children, take a look at our Kidstuff chapter where we have described restaurants that cater to kids or places where the entertainment is at least as much of a draw as the food. If you're looking to combine eating with music, or if you're more in the mood for a bar than a restaurant, check our Nightlife chapter.

We've listed restaurants alphabetically by category, based on our experience that

Denverites, like most Westerners, are more inclined to drive to a destination than to pick a restaurant on the basis of what's within walking distance. At the end of each listing, however, we've given an indication of location. Downtown restaurants are all within walking (or free shuttle bus) distance of downtown hotels. Restaurants we've described as being central are usually more than a half-mile walk from downtown. Each restaurant is in Denver unless otherwise noted.

Listing by category has its own set of problems, of course. In Denver, it seems that every third restaurant has at least a few Mexican-inspired items on the menu, and steakhouses and seafood restaurants usually cross over into each other's territory. We placed restaurants by their specialty, but if you read the descriptions themselves you'll get a better sense of what else each offers.

Denver is a very casual city and the suburbs even more so. It's possible to eat a $100 dinner in shorts and sandals and not feel like the waiter is looking down at you. But, Denverites generally do dress up for a nice meal. In general, price is a good guide as to how formal a restaurant is: the more expensive, the more dressed-up the clientele. Consider location, too: at virtually all the restaurants we've listed in West Denver, a person who shows up dressed to the nines is going to feel very much out of place. Another rule of thumb is that restaurants that don't take any credit cards tend to be the most casual and located in neighborhoods that aren't the most fashionable. (This isn't necessarily true of coffeehouses and bakeries, however.)

Most of the restaurants listed in this chapter accept major credit cards; we have specified those that do not.

Unless we've noted otherwise, all restaurants are open for lunch and dinner.

Many downtown restaurants serve lunch on weekdays only.

Most Greater Denver restaurants accept local (but not out-of-state) checks. Occasionally a check guarantee card is required, and, of course, there are some restaurants that don't take checks at all. Policies change, so call first if this is important to you.

Also, the nonsmoking movement is strong along Colorado's Front Range (especially in Boulder) and a growing number of restaurants are totally nonsmoking. Once again, if this is an issue for you, it's best to call ahead. Or, you can get a copy of the *Colorado Guide to Smoke-Free Dining* by calling the Group to Alleviate Smoking Pollution (GASP) at 444-9799.

To give an idea of price, we've used the following symbols:

Average dinner entree less than $7	$
Average dinner entree $8 to $11	$$
Average dinner entree $12 to $16	$$$
Average dinner entree $17 and higher	$$$$

Remember that lunch at an expensive place is likely to be quite a bit less costly than dinner, although the price difference varies from restaurant to restaurant.

Happy dining!

African

THE ETHIOPIAN RESTAURANT
2816 E. Colfax Ave.   322-5939
$-$$

How's this for choice: we give you three Ethiopian restaurants to choose from, all located on Colfax Avenue from nearly downtown to nearly Aurora. The small, homey Ethiopian Restaurant has a warm pink dining room and reasonable prices. No smoking; beer and wine only (including Ethiopian honey wine). Checks are accepted, but credit cards are not. (Central/East)

MESKEREM ETHIOPIAN RESTAURANT
1501 E. Colfax Ave.   860-0591
$$

An Ethiopian meal is a wonderful, sensual experience. Various spiced vegetable and meat dishes are served family style with a crepe-like bread called injera. You roll the food up with the bread with your fingers — no silverware! The restaurant is nicely decorated and has an extraordinarily gracious staff. Reservations are recommended on the weekends. (Central)

QUEEN OF SHEBA
ETHIOPIAN RESTAURANT
7225 E. Colfax Ave. at Quebec St.   399-9442
$

The most casual and smallest of Denver's trio of Ethiopian restaurants, Queen of Sheba nonetheless has the same smiling service. Prices here are rock-bottom inexpensive. No smoking; beer and wine only; no credit cards. Checks are accepted. It's closed on Mondays. (Central/East)

MATAAM FEZ MOROCCAN RESTAURANT
4609 E. Colfax Ave.   399-9282
$$$$

It's often said that a meal at Mataam Fez is more than a meal; it's an experience. A five-course Moroccan feast (priced at $23.50 per person) is served in sumptuous, tented surroundings with entertainment on the weekends. This nonsmoking restaurant is open for dinner only. There is also a location in Boulder. (Central)

American

ACAPPELLA'S
1336 E. 17th Ave.   832-1479
$-$$

Outdoors on a summer night, you'll feel as though you've stepped into a Bruce Springsteen song at this fun, casual restaurant that serves up possibly the best Philly cheesesteaks in the city. There are Caribbean entrees, in addition to burgers and such, and a cappella music on the weekends. It's closed on Sundays. (Central)

AUBERGINE CAFE
225 E. Seventh Ave.   832-4778
$$

Sean Kelly, formerly of Barolo Grill, is the mastermind behind this nifty little spot. "Aubergine" is French for eggplant, and while grilled, roasted and pureed eggplant are on the menu — and sometimes eggplant risotto — the restaurant also serves meat and fish. Still, it's vegetarian heaven. There's an outdoor patio and the restaurant serves beer and wine only. It's closed Mondays. (Central)

AUGUSTA
1672 Lawrence St.
At the Westin Tabor Center   572-7222
$$$$

Named for the first wife of 19th-century silver tycoon Horace Tabor, Augusta has a Manhattan-style dining room with a wall of curved windows overlooking the downtown skyscrapers. The interior is sleek and dark, hung with Erte prints, and draws almost as much praise as executive chef Roland Ulber's inspired updating of traditional hotel dining-room fare. The lobster tacos are a specialty of the house, as are the lamb and the beef tenderloin with wild mushrooms and cognac. Service is top-

Inventive chef Radek Cerny started European Cafes in Denver and Boulder.

notch. The Augusta is a five-star, AAA Four-Diamond restaurant and one of Denver's very best. Reservations are recommended. (Downtown)

AVENUE GRILL

630 E. 17th Ave.   *861-2820*
$$-$$$

Denver's young movers-and-shakers gather at the long bar here and do business at the banquettes with their cellular phones. This is not a place to hide out in a dark corner, as there are none. So what's to eat? Salads, sandwiches, burgers, a few Southwestern dishes, a tasty cioppino and some killer desserts. Oh, and this is a great people-watching spot. (Central)

BAYOU BOB'S

1635 Glenarm St.   *573-6828*
$

Itching for some jambalaya, red beans and rice, a po'boy sandwich, shrimp gumbo or fried catfish? Bayou Bob's is one of the few places in town that serves authentic Louisiana Cajun food. The downtown restaurant moved from its 17th Street location around the corner to the Paramount Building in fall 1995. There's a second location

geared more toward family dining at 5650 Greenwood Plaza Boulevard in the Denver Tech Center area, 740-7772. Bayou Bob's doesn't serve lunch on Sunday. (Downtown, Southeast)

BRECKENRIDGE BREWERY

2220 Blake St.   *297-3644*
$

The emphasis here is on the microbrewed beers and ales, but no one need go hungry with a menu that includes hearty pub fare for lunch and dinner. Close to Coors Field, it's a great place for an after-game brew. (Downtown)

BRICK OVEN BEANERY

1007 E. Colfax Ave.   *860-0077*
$

When you've had enough of yuppified restaurants with nouvelle this and that, this Denver cafeteria will satisfy your desire for plain homestyle food at low prices. Their motto is "Honest Fast Food," and to that end they offer rotisserie chicken, lamb chops, mashed potatoes and hot open-face sandwiches. You can choose from great soup and chicken and black-bean chili, and you can even get a cocktail. (Central)

THE BROKER

821 17th St.   292-6065
$$$-$$$$

The Broker is situated in what was once a bank — some tables are in the old vault. It serves classic and contemporary American entrees and is known for its steaks and its ice-cold peeled shrimp. It's a popular place for a business lunch downtown and they have a good wine list and excellent desserts. There are additional locations at E. 39th Avenue and Peoria Street, 371-6420, and in Greenwood Village at 5111 DTC Parkway, 770-5111. Unlike the Boulder branch of this restaurant, which is noted for its Sunday brunch, the Denver outposts serve lunch and dinner only. (Downtown, East and Southeast)

CAFE PARADISO

2355 E. Third Ave.   321-2066
$$$

This small, popular Cherry Creek eatery distinguishes itself from the crowd by its no-butter, no-cream preparation of eclectic salads, pasta dishes and entrees. However, anything goes when it comes to the luscious desserts. Reservations are recommended at this nonsmoking restaurant. Cafe Paradiso is closed on Sunday. (Cherry Creek)

CHAMPION BREWING COMPANY

1442 Larimer St.   534-5444
$

Part of the same family of restaurants as the Mexicali Cafe, the Cadillac Ranch and Josephina's, Champion has prime sidewalk seating in Larimer Square. Count on this young, fun place for terrific munchies, beer brewed on the premises and a menu that runs the gamut from Jamaican jerk chicken to fajita salad. (Downtown)

THE CHERRY CRICKET

2641 E. Second Ave.   322-7666
$

The Cherry Cricket is known for its famously juicy burgers and its extensive roster of microbrews. It's a loud neighborhood joint in a neighborhood that otherwise tends to be subdued. (Cherry Creek)

CLIFF YOUNG'S RESTAURANT

700 E. 17th Ave.   831-8900
$$$$

Cliff Young's is one of Denver's best and most innovative restaurants, though with the departure of the restaurant's namesake owner, Denverites are watching carefully to see if the high standards hold. The food has always been astonishingly creative, but the prices are high, making this a special occasion choice for Denverites and out-of-town visitors. There's live music every night in the gracious dining room. Cliff Young's is a AAA Four Diamond Award winner. No lunch is served on weekends. Reservations are recommended. (Central)

EL RANCHO
RESTAURANT & MOUNTAIN LODGE

El Rancho Exit 252 off I-70   526-0661
$$$

A restaurant and lodge about 18 miles west of Denver near Genesee, El Rancho has a rustic atmosphere and seven fireplaces. The main dining room has a view of the Rocky Mountains and serves such regional specialties as prime rib and trout. The cinnamon rolls are locally famous. Open since 1948, El Rancho serves lunch, dinner and Sunday brunch, with live entertainment Thursday through Saturday evenings. The eight lodges are fun for a weekend getaway or for out-of-town visitors. (West suburbs)

THE FIREHOUSE BAR & GRILL
1525 Blake St.   820-3308
$-$$

Some like it hot, so they hustle on over to the Firehouse Bar & Grill, where the chilie pepper reigns. The origin of the spicy stuff on the plate may be Italy, Asia or Mexico at this easygoing downtown spot that features hot-and-spicy food from all over the world. None of our categories really covered this one, so we put it here under American — as in melting pot. No checks. (Lower Downtown)

FLICKER'S FILLY
1585 S. Pearl St.   744-2520
$$

Formerly the Philadelphia Filly, this charming little restaurant done up in cozy teal and red acquired a new name and new owners in mid-1995. Some favorites from the former menu remain: the "Filly" mignon and the "Filly" cheesesteak (the latter at lunch only). New offerings emphasize seafood and pasta. This nonsmoking restaurant is closed Monday but open Sunday for brunch. (South central)

GOODFRIENDS
3100 E. Colfax Ave.   399-1751
$

The name says it all: Here's an easygoing place to get together with friends and enjoy sandwiches, burgers or Southwestern food, with virtually everything on the menu prepared in low-fat fashion upon request. (Central/East)

GREENS
1469 S. Pearl St.   744-1940
$$

Formerly a humble natural-foods joint on East Colfax, Greens edged upscale in decor and cuisine when it recently moved to South Pearl Street. The urbane interior features saffron-hued walls in the dining room and a rubbed-denim color in the bar. Although there are still plenty of vegetarian dishes, the menu includes contemporary American presentations of steaks and lamb chops, too, often with a Southwestern twist. The menu changes seasonally. On Sundays, it's dinner only. (South central)

GUNTHER TOODY'S
4500 E. Alameda Ave.
Glendale   399-1959
$

You'll feel like you're in a scene of the movie *Grease* at this '50s-concept diner, with gum-chewing waiters and waitresses. The food is classic American fare, and the milkshakes will bring out the kid in you. We highly recommend it for children. Breakfast is served here. There are two other locations, one in Englewood at 9220 E. Arapahoe Road, 799-1958; the other in Arvada at 7355 Ralston Road, 422-1954. (East, Southeast and West suburbs)

MARIA'S BAKERY & DELI
3705 Shoshone St.   477-3372
$

A delightful, out-of-the-way spot, Maria's serves sandwiches so thick you have

A good way to sample Greater Denver's better — but more expensive — restaurants is to go for lunch instead of dinner. You'll enjoy the same great quality at lower prices.

Insiders' Tips

• 59

to eat them with a fork and knife. The self-service bakery and deli doubles as the owners' home. You order in the garage, eat in the beautiful large garden or, during cooler weather, inside the house. It serves lunch only, Tuesday through Friday. Enter through the wrought-iron gate on 37th Avenue. They don't accept credit cards, but do take checks. (West Denver)

MARLOWE'S

511 16th St.   595-3700
$$$

The epitome of Denver's singles scene in the '80s, Marlowe's remains a popular gathering spot for lunch, dinner or after work. The restaurant serves steaks, seafood, salads, pasta and a fresh Maine lobster special on Saturday nights. Saturday is dinner only; closed Sunday. (Downtown)

MERCURY CAFE

2199 California St.   294-9258
$-$$

In addition to hosting one of the best and most eclectic performing-arts series in town, the funky, friendly Mercury Cafe serves late breakfast, lunch, dinner and weekend brunch, with an emphasis on natural foods. The food is as varied as the entertainment lineup; a meal here might include tofu enchiladas, steaks, salmon or sandwiches. They don't accept credit cards, but checks are OK. Closed Mondays. (Downtown/Central)

MUSTARD'S LAST STAND

2081 S. University Blvd.   722-7936
$

You can't get more American than hot dogs, french fries and root beer floats, all of which this plain little joint does to perfection. Its location near the University of Denver guarantees a steady clientele, but older folks sneak over for the Polish sausage, too. No credit cards are accepted, but checks

are OK. The original Mustard's Last Stand is at 1719 Broadway (at Arapahoe Avenue) in Boulder; 444-5841. (South central)

MY BROTHER'S BAR

2376 15th St.   455-9991
$

The unmarked entrance to this corner tavern looks foreboding, but really, everyone is welcome. A mixed crowd gathers here for burgers (vegetarian version available) and beers, and there's a pleasant shaded patio out back. It's a good place to keep in mind when you're hungry late at night as they serve past midnight. They're closed Sundays. (Downtown/Platte River area)

PALACE ARMS

321 17th Ave.
At the Brown Palace Hotel   297-3111
$$$$

The poshest of the Brown Palace's three restaurants, the Palace Arms is one of the very few places in Denver where gentlemen are required to wear jackets and ties. The setting and service are superb, holdovers from a more formal era. The room is decorated with antiques dating from the 17th century, including a pair of dueling pistols said to have belonged to Napoleon. The fare is contemporary regional cuisine, and the award-winning wine list features close to 1,000 titles. Reservations are strongly recommended. (Downtown)

PARAMOUNT CAFE

511 16th St.   893-2000
$

A favorite for people-watching, the Paramount's outdoor seating area extends into the 16th Street Mall. This casual lunch or dinner spot serves burgers, sandwiches and Tex-Mex food at low prices in a setting reminiscent of the '50s. It's closed Sundays, except for once in a while, when they feel like staying open. (Downtown)

PEARL STREET GRILL

1477 S. Pearl St.   778-6475
$

A big, friendly bar and restaurant with a particularly nice outdoor patio, the Pearl Street Grill serves soups, salads, sandwiches, burgers etc., along with a large selection of beers on tap. It offers brunch on the weekends. No reservations taken. (South central)

RACINE'S

850 Bannock St.   595-0418
$

Housed in a former auto-dealer showroom, Racine's is a big, laid-back place that's fun for breakfast, weekend brunch, lunch, dinner or anything in between. The menu has something for everyone, from sandwiches to pastas to a selection of Mexican entrees. An in-house bakery makes carrot cake, muffins and Racine's locally famous brownies — in addition to the usual chocolate with or without nuts, flavors include white chocolate, peanut butter and German chocolate — all ready to be packaged up and taken home. (Central)

REIVER'S

1085 S. Gaylord St.   733-8856
$$

A popular watering hole in the Washington Park neighborhood, Reiver's is best known for its burgers. Clarissa Pinkola Estes, author of the bestselling *Women Who Run With the Wolves*, is one of the restaurant's many regulars. Reservations are accepted, except on Fridays. It's a great place for a casual Saturday or Sunday brunch. (South central)

ROCK BOTTOM BREWERY
1001 16th St.   534-7616
$$

A huge brewpub, with outdoor seating on the 16th Street Mall, the Rock Bottom Brewery is related to the Walnut Brewery in Boulder. It's popular from lunch well into the evening and the extensive menu includes salads, pastas, barbecued meats and sandwiches. (Downtown)

ROCKY MOUNTAIN DINER
800 18th St.   293-8383
$-$$

A retro-Western diner with handsome green leather booths, the Rocky Mountain Diner serves big portions of meatloaf, chicken-fried steak and pot roast with mashed potatoes and vegetables. Save room for the white chocolate banana cream pie and the many old-fashioned soda-fountain drinks available, too. Smoking at the bar only. (Downtown)

THE ROSE TEA ROOM
7425 Grandview Ave.
Arvada   420-3333
$

A prettily decorated tea room housed in a 100-year-old former print shop in historic Olde Town Arvada, the Rose Tea Room is a wonderful spot for a ladies' lunch or afternoon tea. They even do a proper English high tea, with a pot of tea, sandwiches, pastries, scones and fruit, but you must reserve your place in advance. They also serve breakfast every morning, and dinner Friday and Saturday night (average entree, $12-$16). (West suburbs)

SHIP TAVERN
321 17th St.
At the Brown Palace Hotel   297-3111
$$$

Located in the Brown Palace Hotel (but accessible through its own entrance off Tremont Place), the Ship Tavern is mod-

eled after a classic English pub and is crammed with replicas of actual ships from America's Clipper period. The food is classic, too: prime rib, fish, chicken, lamb chops and sandwiches. (Downtown)

STRINGS
1700 Humboldt St.   831-7310
$$$

Diners rated this classy spot as Denver's best in the first Zagat consumer survey of Rocky Mountain restaurants. Denverites like its distinctively eclectic California-Italian menu of pasta, seafood, warm salads and grilled dishes; they appreciate the artistic presentation; they enjoy its extensive wine list; and they like its friendly owner, Noel Cunningham. The place is a perfect example of the vibrant spirit that typifies Denver, where more casually dressed diners mingle with the "Dynasty" set. Reservations are recommended. (Central)

TODAY'S GOURMET: HIGHLAND'S GARDEN CAFE
3927 W. 32nd Ave.   458-5920
$$$

Today's Gourmet serves creative food in a pleasantly renovated Victorian house on Denver's up-and-coming west side. The menu changes daily but the emphasis on fresh, healthful ingredients remains the same. (West Denver)

TRINITY GRILLE
1801 Broadway   293-2288
$$$

A popular spot for lunching lawyers, the Trinity Grille is brisk and shiny with polished wood, brass railings and a black-and-white tile floor. Steaks, soups, sandwiches, fish and homemade pasta dishes are the mainstay of the menu. The Cobb salad, in particular, is highly recommended. Closed Sundays; lunch on weekdays only. (Downtown)

WAZEE LOUNGE & SUPPER CLUB
1600 15th St.   623-9518
$

It's back to the '40s, or some other unspecified prior decade, at this laid-back pizza-and-burgers joint. A Lower Downtown favorite for years, it's hard to say just what makes this place so neat. The diverse crowd? The bohemian ambiance? The pizza? Regardless, it remains popular year after year. It's closed Sundays. (Downtown)

WYNKOOP BREWING COMPANY
1634 18th St. at Wynkoop   297-2700
$

Housed in the historic J.S. Brown Mercantile Building, the Wynkoop led the way in the resurgence of Lower Downtown. Denver's first brewpub, it was founded in 1988 and serves a variety of handcrafted ales and pub fare for lunch and dinner, such as potpies with quinoa crust, at reasonable prices. The main dining area is noisy, crowded and often smoky — not necessarily a reason to stay away, we're just warning you. Upstairs there's a classic pool hall. Reservations are accepted for large groups only. Sunday brunch is served. (Downtown)

YORK STREET CAFE & BAR
2239 E. Colfax   331-0533
$$$

Housed in an historic former bank, the York Street Cafe is a cosmopolitan restaurant that features live jazz on Thursday, Friday and Saturday nights. The food is easygoing but not plain, with a grilled-fish special daily and a lobster special on Thursday nights. (Central)

ZENITH AMERICAN GRILL
1735 Arapahoe St.   820-2800
$$$

With its sleek, modern interior and creative American cuisine, Zenith has soared into the ranks of Denver's best restaurants since opening in 1991. Executive Chef Kevin Taylor's menu changes seasonally and is based on pastas and grilled meats and fish with innovative sauces. This is a good place for vegetarians who want to eat gourmet food. Reservations are suggested for dinner. No lunch on weekends. (Downtown)

American/Southwestern

CAFE IGUANA
300 Fillmore St.   377-8300
$-$$

Cafe Iguana is chef Kevin Taylor's (of Zenith fame) venture into Southwestern cuisine, in the chic Cherry Creek neighborhood. Taylor started out serving Yucatan and Oaxacan specialties but has segued into more familiar Southwestern cuisine. Cafe Iguana mixes a mean margarita. (Cherry Creek)

CITY SPIRIT CAFE
1434 Blake St.   575-0022
$

Sharpen your wits with a Smart Drink — made with soda water, juice and assorted herbal extracts — in this bright and spirited restaurant that turns into an avant-garde music center at night. The tables, floors and walls are all done up in colorful mosaic tiles, and the crowd is an interesting mix of artists and office workers. Most of the food is vegetarian, and sometimes the kitchen's inventions are a little far out, but you won't have any trouble if you stick with such proven favorites as the vegetarian green chili, the City Smart Burrita (sic) or the City Quesadilla. You'll enjoy espresso drinks and nice desserts, too. (Downtown)

The New Denver Central Library

Of all the major construction projects underway in Greater Denver over the past few years, the new Denver Central Library is hardest to miss because it's right in the middle of town. The library gets a lot of use: It receives more visits from the public than the Museum of Natural History, the Denver Broncos, the Denver Zoo or the Denver Performing Arts Complex. By all measurements (circulation, registered card holders, per capita book holdings and so forth), the Denver Public Library ranks first or second out of all urban libraries in the nation.

Library users aren't the only ones interested in the new building; architecture aficionados are checking it out, too. The new library — called the Central Library to distinguish it from the many Denver Public Library branch libraries — was designed by the internationally acclaimed firm of Michael Graves Architect in association with the Denver-based firm Klipp Colussy Jenks DuBois Architects.

What most stood out when the design for the new library was revealed in 1991 was that it had color; admirers of Michael Graves will instantly recognize the distinctive palette as one of his signature architectural devices. The new building has a facade of sandstone reds, limestone greens, yellows and buffs that pay tribute to the library's Western setting. A series of different rooflines repeat the shapes of Denver's skyline. It has seven stories above ground and three below. It was built with almost $72 million of public money, complemented by a $6-million private philanthropy campaign.

The main portion opened to the public in spring 1995; later that summer artist Edward Ruscha installed a 70-panel work of art in the four-story Schlessman Hall, which connects the east and west tower entries. The Children's Library and Pavilion was slated for completion in late 1995 or early 1996.

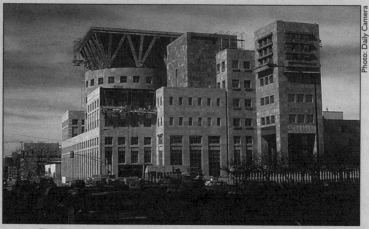

Photo: Daily Camera

The Denver Public Library remodeling/addition construction is transforming its corner of downtown Denver.

On its west side, the new building is connected by an outdoor plaza and a new underground concourse with the Denver Art Museum, which is in the midst of some serious renovations of its own.

Inside, the library will now have room to display its own impressive art collection. The paintings, rare books, maps, photographs, manuscripts and ephemera, owned and managed by the Western History and Genealogy Department, form one of the largest such collections in the world, and the only one open to the public. Other improvements inside include a high-tech computer network.

If you are especially interested in architecture, you may want to get in touch with the Denver Art Museum's Department of Architecture, Design & Graphics which, although its focus is not strictly local, has an active design council and sponsors lectures and other special events. Contact them at 640-7571.

You may write or call the Central Library, 10 W. 14th Avenue Parkway, 640-6200.

CROCODILE CAFE

1630 Market St.   *436-1144*
$$

A high-energy restaurant with brick walls, a big bar and a 20-foot-long fake crocodile suspended from the ceiling, "Croc's" serves mainly Mexican food at reasonable prices. There are also burgers, seafood and a wall-to-wall happy hour. (Downtown)

GOVNR'S PARK

672 Logan St.   *831-8605*
$

Once a dry cleaners, Govnr's Park is now a big, boisterous neighborhood restaurant and tavern with sandwiches, burgers and Southwestern dishes on the menu. The front patio, shaded by a large awning, is especially nice for an informal Sunday brunch. (Central)

SILVERHEELS SOUTHWEST GRILL

1122 Washington St.
Golden   *279-6390*
$$-$$$

A newly opened branch of a popular Summit County restaurant, Silverheels specializes in meat and fish grilled on a stone slab, with a Southwestern flair. There's live music most nights (always on Friday and Saturday). Reservations are recommended on the weekends. (West suburbs)

American/Steaks

AURORA SUMMIT

2700 S. Havana St.
Aurora   *751-2112*
$$$$

A classic steakhouse, with a dark, woodsy masculine ambiance, the Aurora Summit serves only the finest grade of U.S.D.A. prime, aged, corn-fed beef. In the tradition of steakhouses, there are also seafood entrees. In the large front lounge, there's a piano bar Monday through Saturday nights. Reservations are preferred. (Southeast)

BEACON GRILL

303 16th St. (second level)   *592-4745*
$$$

This isn't strictly a steakhouse, but what

is, anymore? And they do make a big deal out of their Double-J Limousin beef, a breed of cattle raised on Colorado's Western Slope that's naturally lower in fat. Chef David Minty's smoked salmon cheesecake appetizer is also drawing raves. There's a great big patio that overlooks the 16th Street Mall, and there's live jazz Wednesday nights. Dinner is almost twice the price of lunch, something to keep in mind if you're on a budget. Beacon Grill is closed Sunday; reservations are recommended, even for lunch. (Downtown)

THE BUCKHORN EXCHANGE
1000 Osage St.   534-9505
$$$$

The Buckhorn Exchange is Denver's oldest restaurant. It was founded in 1893 by "Shorty Scout" Zeitz, who, along with his family, amassed an astounding collection of animal trophies, including moose, elk, buffalo and bear. More than 500 stuffed animals and birds are displayed — it's sort of like dining in a natural history museum. The menu, accordingly, runs to traditional Western fare: beef, barbecued pork ribs and game meats. For something more unusual, try the rattlesnake or alligator tail appetizers. Vegetarian alert: You may feel a little squeamish here, but if you can put up with the dead heads on the wall, call ahead and the restaurant will put together a vegetarian plate just for you. Dinner entrees are expensive ($20 and up), but lunch is quite reasonable, with almost everything priced at $10 and less. Thursday through Saturday nights feature folk and cowboy music in the saloon upstairs. It's probably more popular with tourists than locals, but there's no other place like it. Reservations are recommended for dinner. (Central)

CADILLAC RANCH
1400 Larimer St.   820-2288
$$-$$$

The Cadillac Ranch prides itself on its Texas-size certified Angus steaks and its howdy-pardner friendliness. The fun, colorful decor consists of cowboy boots, saddles, horseshoes and car parts. There's a second-floor patio with a clear view of the Rocky Mountains. In addition to steaks, there's Route 66 Rotisserie Chicken and a whole mess of sandwiches and salads. Reservations are suggested. (Downtown)

DENVER BUFFALO COMPANY
1109 Lincoln St.   832-0880
$$$

More than just a restaurant, the Denver Buffalo Company complex includes a trading post, art gallery, deli and food mart in addition to the Western-style main dining room. A nicely appointed private dining room that seats up to 30 can be reserved in advance for special occasions. Buffalo is, as you might have guessed, the No. 1 choice here, all of it raised on the company ranch near Kiowa in eastern Colorado. There are chicken, seafood and pasta entrees as well. (Central)

THE DENVER CHOPHOUSE & BREWERY
1735 19th St.   293-3628
$$$

For years there were few places to eat in Lower Downtown. Then, as Coors Field was built, sports bars, brewpubs and steakhouses sprang up on every corner. The Denver ChopHouse is one of the most successful of the newcomers; reservations are definitely suggested for weekends. The outdoor barbecue area, with its patio and rolling roof, is a big draw. The ChopHouse is affiliated with Boulder's Walnut Brewery. (Lower Downtown)

THE FORT

19192 Rt. 8
Morrison   697-4771
$$$$

The Fort combines Wild-West flair with classy fare: Where else do waiters open bottles of champagne with a tomahawk? Located in the Foothills, the restaurant is a full-sized adobe replica of Bent's Fort, Colorado's first fur-trading post. Owners Sam and Carrie Arnold were among the first restaurateurs to feature buffalo meat on the menu; other unusual entrees include elk, quail, rattlesnake and Rocky Mountain oysters. More traditional preparations of trout and steak are available, and for those who wish to sample a little bit of everything, there's a game plate. As we said about the Buckhorn Exchange, there's no place else like it. Reservations are recommended. (West suburbs)

MORTON'S OF CHICAGO

1710 Wynkoop   825-3353
$$$$

One of the last holdouts in Denver's Tivoli Center, a brewery turned shopping mall turned community-college student union, Morton's has finally moved to Lower Downtown. A classic, classy steakhouse, Morton's is always mentioned when people talk about where to get the best steaks in town. It serves dinner only; reservations are recommended. (Downtown)

Asian

AKEBONO

1255 19th St.   295-1849
$$-$$$

Located in colorful Sakura Square, Akebono is a handsome, coolly lit Japanese restaurant with a sushi/sashimi bar and a full menu including gyoza, fried oysters, teriyaki and tempura dishes. It's closed Mondays. (Downtown)

L'AUBERGE ZEN

9955 E. Hampden Ave.   751-3571
$$$-$$$$

We feel pretty confident stating that L'Auberge Zen is Greater Denver's only French and Japanese restaurant, with a sushi bar located next to a rather continental-looking dining room. Go ahead and order French if that's what you're in the mood for, but the critics have generally lavished their praise on the Japanese entrees. It's closed Monday and doesn't serve lunch on weekends. (Southeast)

CHAO-PRAYA THAI

5411 Quebec
Commerce City   287-2210
$$

Some of the best Thai food in the area can be found at this surprisingly gracious truck-stop location. The family-owned restaurant traces its history back to Laiad Chittivej, a remarkable immigrant who opened the first Thai restaurant in Denver. Hot means hot, so don't be shy about

New York Bagel Boys, on the corner of Hampden Avenue and Monaco Street Parkway, is widely perceived as making the best bagels in Greater Denver. But with new bagel shops springing up all over town, they've got some strong competition!

Insiders' Tips

asking for the level you feel comfortable with. Virtually everything on the menu can be made vegetarian. (Northeast)

CHEZ THUY HOA
1500 California St.   623-4809
$$

Chef Hoa developed her reputation and her loyal clientele at the T-Wa Inn (T-Wa is the approximate English phonetic spelling for "Thuy Hoa") before moving to this modest downtown eatery. Jammed at lunch, the restaurant has a large menu with a number of particularly tasty grilled meat dishes. Portion sizes are generous. The soft-shell crab is the house specialty. Only dinner on Sundays. (Downtown)

IMPERIAL CHINESE
RESTAURANT & LOUNGE
431 S. Broadway   698-2800
$$

Imperial does indeed live up to its name, with staggeringly opulent decor that looks like the set for *The Last Emperor*. The restaurant specializes in seafood, but don't pass up the sesame chicken, or, if you're in the mood for the royal treatment, the fabulous Peking duck. Reservations are accepted for parties of four or more only. (Central)

J'S NOODLES
945-E S. Federal Blvd.   922-5495
$

Many of Greater Denver's best and most authentic Asian restaurants are located along South Federal Boulevard. For many aficionados of Thai food, this plain storefront restaurant tops the list for its combination of outstanding Thai food and low prices. They do not accept credit cards, but checks are OK. (Southwest)

LONG BINH
940 S. Federal Blvd.   935-4141
$

Long Binh is a modest Federal Boulevard eatery that is often mentioned when you ask Denverites about their favorite place for Vietnamese food. The noodle bowls and the crispy egg rolls are special favorites, and the staff receives compliments for their friendly manner. (Southwest)

MORI SUSHI BAR & TOKYO CUISINE
2019 Market St.   298-1864
$$-$$$

Just a baseball's throw from Coors Field on the corner of Market Street and 20th Avenue, Mori Sushi offers a great selection of sushi, noodle dishes (the seafood udon noodles are a personal favorite) and other Japanese specialties in a pleasant setting that includes a small aquarium. The restaurant is popular with downtown workers at lunch. At dinner the menu expands into what seems like a book, but rest assured, you're unlikely to make a bad choice. (Downtown)

NEW ORIENT
10203 E. Iliff Ave.
Aurora   751-1288
$$

A small, simply decorated restaurant, New Orient serves Vietnamese, Chinese and "Amerasian" cuisine, updating traditional recipes with creative touches. What this means is that you can have roast-duck soup and pineapple-paprika shrimp for lunch, with cappuccino mud torte for dessert. Seafood is a specialty at this nonsmoking restaurant. Reservations are recommended on the weekend. (Southeast)

Photo: Daily Camera

A heady experience for carnivores, the Buckhorn Exchange will make vegetarian plates on request.

NEW SAIGON

630 S. Federal Blvd.   936-4954
$$

Yet another Federal Boulevard restaurant, New Saigon is a perennial winner in local weekly *Westword*'s "Best Vietnamese Restaurant" category. One of Denver's first Vietnamese restaurants, it's been in business more than 10 years. Despite tons of competition, its loyal fans can't be lured away from the spicy beef and the acclaimed fish dishes. (Southwest)

SEOUL FOOD

701 E. Sixth Ave.   837-1460
$

A friend who has lived in Korea swears that the most authentic Korean food in town is cooked and served at this casual eatery. The bee bim bob (a mixed vegetable dish) and the bulgogi (Korean beef) are favorites, as well as the barley tea. It's closed Sundays. (Central)

SONODA'S

3108 S. Parker Rd.
Aurora   337-3800
$$$

Proprietor Kenny Sonoda calls his casual restaurant a "Japanese seafood house and sushi bar," and indeed the menu features changing seafood specials depending on what's fresh and available. Local restaurant critics are fond of the sushi. Sonoda is planning to open a second location in Lower Downtown on Market Street just across from the bus station. (Southeast)

SUSHI DEN

1487 S. Pearl St.   777-0826
$$$

A chic, modern restaurant that just happens to be a sushi bar, Sushi Den does a superb job with cooked fish, too. The standout is the steamed fresh fish in a bamboo basket. Lunch isn't served on weekends. (South Central)

SUSHI HEIGHTS

2301 E. Colfax Ave.   355-2777
$$

A tidy Japanese restaurant with classical music playing in the background, Sushi Heights gets raves for its sushi and its reasonably priced lunch specials. It's closed Sunday and doesn't serve lunch on Saturday. (Central)

T-WA INN

555 S. Federal Blvd.   922-4584
$$

The T-Wa Inn has a huge menu that emphasizes seafood. The point is driven home by the foyer's aquarium filled with giant silver arrow wanna fish (for decoration only). The Asian decor is exotic without being overwhelming. Should you desire Vietnamese coffee, it will be French-pressed for you right at the table. (Southwest)

T-WA TERRACE

6882 S. Yosemite St.   741-4051
$$$

Located in the Southgate shopping center just south of Arapahoe Road, the T-Wa Terrace was started by one of the founders of the T-Wa Inn. Recommended dishes include the Vietnamese egg rolls and the soft-shell crab. Lunch isn't served on Sunday. (South/Greenwood Village)

VIETNAMNA

1600 California St.   534-6909
$

Fresh spring rolls, bowls of grilled meat over noodles, curry dishes and sweet Vietnamese iced coffee are the highlights at this casual cafeteria-style restaurant. This non-smoking restaurant is open for lunch only from 11 AM to 4 PM weekdays. (Downtown)

YOISHO RESTAURANT

7236 E. Colfax Ave.   322-6265
$

A tiny, tiny Japanese restaurant with a devoted following, Yoisho has a simple menu with mostly fried Japanese dishes (no sushi here) and notable gyoza dumplings. There's no smoking, no alcohol, no credit cards and it's closed Sundays. Checks are accepted. (East)

Barbecue

SAM TAYLOR'S BAR-B-Q

The Links at City Park Golf Course
2500 York St.   297-2268
$

Is Sam Taylor's smoky-sweet and spicy barbecue the best in town? Lots of folks say it is. The setting is fine, too, on the golf course at City Park. In summer you can sit outside and stare at the greenest lawn in Denver. (Central/East)

WOLFE'S BARBEQUE

333 E. Colfax Ave.   831-1500
$

Here's hope for committed vegetarians: in addition to Wolfe's scrumptious traditional barbecued meats, you can get smoked, grilled tofu and vegetarian baked beans at this eatery near the State Capitol. This favorite is open Monday through Friday only. (Central)

Bistros

BISTRO ADDE BREWSTER

250 Steele St.   388-1900
$$

Bistro Adde Brewster serves unpretentious lunches and dinners in a very French-looking subterranean setting. Entrees include grilled duck, bistro burgers and baked eggplant. Low-fat HealthMark selections are available. It's closed Sunday. (Cherry Creek)

Bistro Loco and Cocoloco

1525 15th St.   446-8768
$$-$$$

Bistro Loco serves a set meal at lunch and dinner: several choices in each of three price ranges that include bread and salad. The menu runs to game, and also includes grilled fish, pasta and their pizza rustica. One glance at the rich, dark, chocolate truffles in the adjacent sweet shop, Cocoloco, and you just know the desserts are up to par. (Downtown)

Chives American Bistro

1120 E. Sixth Ave.   722-3800
$$

Yet another bistro par excellence, Chives is known for its martinis and is Denver's only champagne bar, with a selection of champagnes by the glass. Sophistication extends to its frequently changing menu, which is based on interesting ethnic combinations. For dessert, there's truly exceptional chocolate lasagne. Chives is open for dinner only and serves until midnight every night and 1 am on Fridays and Saturdays. (Central)

La Bonne Soupe

1512 Larimer St.   595-9169
$$

The prix fixe lunches are the big attraction at this simple French bistro: soup, salad, bread, a glass of wine or coffee and dessert for around $6. Country French entrees including poulet chasseur and

bouillabaise are on the menu at dinner, and prices shoot up accordingly. The outdoor patio in Writer Square is most agreeable. If the name and concept sound familiar, perhaps you've been to La Bonne Soupe in New York City — it's not a chain, but the owners are friends. (Downtown)

Napa Cafe

2033 E. Colfax Ave.   377-6869
$$$

One of the hottest new restaurants of 1995, Napa Cafe is the latest from Cliff Young, whose moniker still graces an elegant restaurant on 17th Street. It serves Americanized bistro food and gets good reviews for its extensive and well-priced wine list. Reservations recommended. (Central)

Pour la France

730 S. University Blvd.   744-1888
$

A likable French cafe and bakery with branches in Aspen and Boulder, Pour la France offers light lunches and dinners — perhaps a pissaladiere (a French pizza) or a Mediterranean salad — and excellent pastries and desserts. The dense, dark melt-in-your-mouth chocolate truffle cake is a chocoholic's fantasy come true. This is also a good spot for breakfast, a mid-morning coffee break or a late-night glass of champagne. (South central)

Rattlesnake Grill

3000 E. First Ave.   377-8000
$$$

The Rattlesnake Grill was the most-talked-about restaurant of 1994-95: Its prin-

Insiders' Tips

cipals include Jimmy Schmidt, chef and part-owner of the first Rattlesnake Club in Denver in the 1980s. It serves stylish food, from hamburgers to grilled fish, in a tony setting filled with a stylish crowd. What seemed so innovative in the '80s is, however, not nearly so cutting-edge in the '90s, especially in chic Cherry Creek where unusual ingredients, artistic presentation and swanky decor are more the rule than the exception. Reservations recommended. (Cherry Creek)

SFUZZI
3000 E. First Ave.   321-4700
$$

Sfuzzi bills itself as an Italian bistro, although more than one local restaurant critic has noted the California influence on the decor and the menu. Located in the posh Cherry Creek Shopping Center, Sfuzzi features a central woodburning pizza oven and an open kitchen. Specialties include grilled and smoked meats and, of course, pizzas. The young and the beautiful eat here, and the restaurant is noted as much for its people-watching as its food. Reservations are accepted. (Cherry Creek)

Continental

THE SWAN
200 Inverness Dr. W.   799-5800
$$$$

Inside the sprawling Inverness Hotel south of the Denver Tech Center, The Swan is sophisticated but light and open in its decor. The cuisine is traditional continental, with knockout presentations of lamb, lobster and steaks. The restaurant has received the AAA Four Diamond Award every year since 1991. It's open for dinner only, Tuesday through Saturday. (Southeast)

BRIARWOOD INN
1630 18th St.
Golden   279-3121
$$$$

The Briarwood Inn isn't that far from downtown, and not far at all for those who live in Denver's western suburbs, but it's a world away from the hustle-bustle. A romantic getaway, the formal, old-fashioned Briarwood Inn is Victorian in its decor and continental in its cuisine. Complete meals are served, including appetizers, dessert and entrees such as prime rib and fresh seafood, at prices ranging from $22 to $39 a person. It's especially nice when it's decorated for the winter holidays, or for a sumptuous Sunday brunch. Lunch isn't served on weekends. (West suburbs)

THE BURNSLEY HOTEL
1000 Grant St.   830-1000
$$$-$$$$

The intimate dining room at this small Capitol Hill hotel is extravagantly wallpapered and almost fussily furnished. This is the place to go when you don't want to run into everyone you know and would rather sink into a banquette and sip a martini than schmooze. The food is Americanized continental cuisine of lamb, chicken and seafood with frequently changing specials. We've been hearing good things about the $7.25 breakfast buffet, too. (Central)

CHINOOK TAVERN
265 Detroit St.   394-0044
$$$

There's always a hot new place in Cherry Creek, and in the spring and summer of 1995 it was the Chinook Tavern, which opened in the space formerly occupied by the bistro Cache Cache. The menu is German-influenced but the translation is a very contemporary one, and the warm decor avoids any Bavarian cliches. (Cherry Creek)

ELLYNGTON'S

321 17th St.
At the Brown Palace Hotel   297-3111
$$$$

Best known for its lavish champagne brunch (with Dom Perignon, if you've got the bucks for it), the classy and urbane Ellyngton's also serves a tasteful breakfast and lunch. (Downtown)

EUROPEAN CAFE

1515 Market St.   825-6555
$$$

Simply put, this is one of Denver's best restaurants and a personal favorite of ours. Its French/continental cuisine is exquisitely conceived and executed; the presentation is artful but not forced; the service is impeccable; and the surroundings are elegant. the original European Cafe, at 2460 Arapahoe Avenue in Boulder, 938-8240, is still going strong, and there's now a third location at 5150 S. Quebec (I-25 and Belleview) in the Denver Tech Center, 770-6500. Reservations are recommended. (Downtown, Southeast)

LITTLE RUSSIAN CAFE

1424 Larimer St.   595-8600
$$-$$$

The Little Russian Cafe serves hearty peasant fare such as stuffed cabbage, dumplings and borscht, in a smashing red dining room. Stop in after lunch for apple strudel and tea served Old-World style in silver-handled glasses, or later in the evening for a shot of ice-cold homemade flavored vodka. There is also a Little Russian Cafe in Boulder. Reservations are recommended on the weekend. Lunch isn't served Saturday and Sunday. (Downtown)

THE MANOR HOUSE

No. 1 Manor House Rd.
Littleton   973-8064
$$$

In a beautiful setting perched atop Ken Caryl Ranch, the Manor House serves Colorado continental cuisine, including roasted duck, lamb chops, steaks and prime rib on weekends. Salmon is a specialty. The 1914 Southern-style mansion was the original manor home for Ken Caryl Ranch. Dinner only is served, Tuesday through Sunday. Reservations are requested. (Southwest)

SOREN'S RESTAURANT

315 Detroit St.   322-8155
$$$

Sunny and airy, with a lovely patio, Soren's dates from pre-Cherry Creek Shopping Center days and has always struck us as somehow Scandinavian in its decor. The restaurant is noted for its Sunday brunch. Lunch and dinner selections include meat, fish and substantial salads. A classical guitarist plays on Friday and Saturday evenings and during Sunday brunch. Reservations are accepted. (Cherry Creek)

WELLSHIRE INN

3333 S. Colorado Blvd.   759-3333
$$$-$$$$

Housed in an English Tudor mansion on the grounds of the Wellshire Municipal Golf Course, the Wellshire Inn is richly decorated with 100-year-old tapestries, stained glass and handsome wood paneling. Owner Leo Goto serves sophisticated continental fare, including rack of lamb and salmon. There are nightly specials. Lunch, breakfast and Sunday brunch are served. (Southeast)

Delicatessens

THE BAGEL DELI
6439 E. Hampden Ave. at Monaco 756-6667
$-$$

A big, family-style kosher restaurant and deli that serves breakfast, lunch and dinner until 7:30 PM, The Bagel Deli has been in business in Denver since 1967. Never mind nouvelle; come here when you want chopped liver, Dr. Brown's sodas, gefilte fish, knishes, blintzes and oversized deli sandwiches including, of course, corned beef on rye. A second, more centrally located branch is at 6217 E. 14th Avenue, at Krameria Street, 322-0350. It stays open until 5 PM. (Southeast)

NEW YORK DELI NEWS
7105 E. Hampden Ave.   759-4741
$

Similar in offerings, prices and easygoing style to The Bagel Deli, The New York Deli News also serves breakfast, lunch and dinner. You'll enjoy great pumpernickel bread, pastrami, bagels, corned beef and — loosen your belt — genuine New York-style cheesecake. (Southeast)

ZAIDY'S DELI
121 Adams St.   333-5336
$-$$

Zaidy's may very well be the closest thing to an authentic New York Jewish deli as can be found in Greater Denver. This is a prime source for potato latkes, smoked fish and matzoh ball soup just like your grandmother used to make. Come for breakfast or lunch Monday through Wednesday; breakfast, lunch and dinner Thursday through Sunday. (Cherry Creek)

French

LA COUPOLE
2191 Arapahoe St.   297-2288
$$$

Situated in the old brick Hotel Paris building, La Coupole boasts one of the most beautiful dining rooms in Denver, with its old wood floors and stained-glass ceiling. At the entrance is a lovely enclosed courtyard with several tables shaded by umbrellas. The fare is classically French, with a country touch. This is a terrifically romantic restaurant, but not too fussy for business lunches either. On Friday and Saturday evenings starting at 8 PM there's live jazz; reservations are essential at these times. (Central/Downtown)

LE CENTRAL
112 E. Eighth Ave.   863-8094
$$

Le Central styles itself as "the affordable French restaurant" and does a good job of living up to that claim without skimping on quality. The restaurant is a charming series of low-ceilinged rooms; the food is country French. Sunday brunch is a treat. (Central)

THE NORMANDY FRENCH
RESTAURANT AND CHEZ MICHELLE
1515 Madison St.   321-3311
$$-$$$$

The Normandy is the epitome of a fine French restaurant, where guests enjoy updated French cuisine in a setting that's like an elegant home. Aware, however, that the cream-and-butter excesses of traditional French fare are not as welcome in the '90s as they once were, the Normandy has switched to a style of cooking that emphasizes reduced sauces over heavy sauces. There's lots of seafood, chicken and salmon on the menu in addition to more traditional favorites. They've also added a restaurant-within-a-restaurant, called Chez Michelle, which serves casual bistro food in a garden-like setting at prices considerably lower than in the main restaurant. Lunch isn't served on weekends; it's closed on Mondays. (Central)

PHILIPPE'S

120 Madison St.   322-1483
$$$

Lightened-up French cuisine is served in this longtime Cherry Creek favorite that occupies a former home. The backyard patio is especially fine. Enjoy a salad at lunch — *Westword* calls the Caesar salad the best in town — or steak tartare. Philippe's is closed Sundays. (Cherry Creek)

TANTE LOUISE

4900 E. Colfax Ave.   355-4488
$$$$

Often called the most romantic restaurant in Denver, Tante Louise is known as much for its extensive, award-winning wine

list with more than 300 selections and its attentive service as for its contemporary French-American cuisine. Located in a lovely old home, the restaurant has lots of little private nooks that are renowned for encouraging marriage proposals. Tante Louise has been in business since the early 1970s and has received the AAA Four Diamond Award. Dinner only is served every night except Sunday. Reservations are recommended. (Central)

Greek

CENTRAL 1

300 S. Pearl St.   778-6675
$$

A nothing-fancy Greek restaurant not far from the Mayan Theatre, Central 1 has been pleasing customers with its souvlaki and gyros since the early '80s. Closed Sunday. (Central)

YANNI'S

2223 S. Monaco Pkwy.   692-0404
$$

This is a classic Greek family-run taverna, with a blue-and-white interior and outdoor tables with umbrellas. The menu

Cadillac Ranch, in downtown Denver's Larimer Square, prides itself on its Texas-size certified Angus steaks.

leans heavily on traditional, hearty dishes like moussaka and pastitsio. On Friday, Saturday and Sunday nights, they spit-roast a lamb. Knock back a shot of ouzo and let the dancing begin! (Southeast)

Health Food/Natural Foods

THE HARVEST RESTAURANT & BAKERY
430 S. Colorado Blvd.   399-6652
$-$$

The Harvest had its start as a natural foods restaurant in Boulder and has since branched out into Denver. There are many vegetarian items on the menu, as well as chicken and meat salads and sandwiches, plus lots of homemade baked goods and a potent, aromatic spice tea. The low-key Harvest is particularly good for breakfast and for solo diners, who can choose to sit at a shared community table. It's near Cherry Creek and there is an additional location at 7730 E. Belleview, 779-4111, in Greenwood Village in Southeast Denver. Both locations are non-smoking. (Cherry Creek, Southeast)

HEALTHY HABITS
865 S. Colorado Blvd.   733-2105
$-$$

The casual Healthy Habits, just east of the Cherry Creek neighborhood, offers an all-you-can-eat salad buffet, plus soup and pastas. The muffins are a standout. And despite the name, desserts are not banished from the premises. This nonsmoking restaurant has a location in Golden at 14195 W. Colfax, 277-9293, and also one in Boulder. (Cherry Creek, West suburbs)

Indian

DELHI DARBAR
1514 Blake St.   595-0680
$$$

Downtown's only Indian restaurant is refined in its decor and in its wide range of tandoori dishes, which include two kinds of Cornish game hen and quail in addition to the more usual chicken. We're particularly fond of the murgh tikka saag, a chicken in a spinach sauce. The $5.95 lunch buffet is an especially good value, and vegetarians will appreciate the many meatless entrees. There is also a Delhi Darbar in Boulder.(Downtown)

INDIA'S
3333 S. Tamarac Dr.   755-4284
$$-$$$

India's is a feast for the senses, with its tantalizing aromas, colorful cloth hangings and hypnotic Indian music. Located in a strip shopping mall just behind Tamarac Square, India's is Denver's oldest Indian restaurant and one of the finest you are ever likely to encounter. The curries are hot and spicy, and the tandoori dishes are very popular. Reservations are recommended. (Southeast)

International/Eclectic

SAFFRON RESTAURANT
6600 S. Quebec St.   290-9705
$$$

A quiet, elegant little restaurant, Saffron uses a Mediterranean style of seasoning in all its dishes, which range from pastas to beef, lamb and chicken preparations. Saffron, mint, curry and lemon are common flavorings. Prime rib is served on Saturday nights; on Sundays the restaurant is closed. Reservations are requested on the weekend. (Southeast)

TRANSALPIN
416 E. Seventh Ave.   830-8282
$$

A sophisticated dining experience, with a seasonally changing menu that draws on cuisines from around the world, Transalpin serves interesting food at great prices. (Central)

Italian

AL FRESCO

1523 Market St.   534-0404
$$$

In the same renovated brick building in Lower Downtown that houses the European Cafe, the sophisticated Al Fresco specializes in Northern Italian food and was Denver's first restaurant to feature a woodburning pizza oven. The $5.50 express lunch is a great way to sample this fine food at a bargain-basement price. Al Fresco has a Capitol Hill branch in Denver at Ninth Avenue and Lincoln Street, 894-0600, in the location formerly occupied by Bistro 100, and also a location in Boulder. The heated, enclosed patio is nice on those days when you'd like to eat outside but it's not quite warm enough. The Capitol Hill branch is closed Sundays. Reservations are accepted at both locations. (Downtown/Central)

AMADEO'S

5025 W. 44th Ave.   455-5078
$

A homey Italian restaurant with a big glass case of bakery items, Amadeo's is open for lunch only, 11 AM to 2 PM Monday through Friday. Look for the cheery red, white and green awning about two blocks south of Sheridan Boulevard. Cash only. (West Denver)

BAROLO GRILL

3030 E. Sixth Ave.   393-1040
$$$

Since its opening in 1992, Barolo has skyrocketed into the ranks of the hottest of the city's hot spots. The food in this pretty

restaurant could be called "Cal-Ital," combining as it does Northern Italian recipes with California ingredients. Wines are an especially good value. It serves dinner only, Tuesday through Saturday; reservations are strongly recommended. (Central)

BASIL'S CAFE

30 S. Broadway   698-1413
$$

Basil's is a small, noisy, urban place along a stretch of South Broadway where adult movie theaters mingle with antique shops. The hand-rolled ravioli and fresh pastas are made on the premises, as are the breads and desserts. Basil's does pizza one better with its panini, bread dough wrapped around vegetables and cheeses and topped with marinara sauce. Basil's has lots of vegetarian selections. It's closed Sundays; beer and wine only. (Central)

CIAO! BABY

7400 E. Hampden Ave.   740-0990
$$-$$$

Ciao! Baby, owned by Noel Cunningham of Strings fame, is one of the city's most fashionable see-and-be-seen spots. Done up in bright and shiny black, red and white, the restaurant is in the Tiffany Plaza shopping center. The upscale fare includes salads, pizzas, pastas and Italian-influenced meat and fish preparations. Don't pass up the thin, crispy breadsticks. Italian-language instruction tapes play in the restrooms. Reservations are strongly recommended. (Southeast)

DARIO'S

2011 E. 17th Ave.   333-5243
$$

An old-fashioned, cozy little Swiss-Italian neighborhood restaurant with traditional red-and-white checked tablecloths,

Dario's serves veal, seafood, poultry and, of course, pasta dishes. No lunch on weekends. (Central)

JOSEPHINA'S
1433 Larimer St.   623-0166
$$

A longtime Larimer Square favorite, Josephina's is known for its pizza and live jazz. In warm weather patrons try for a table on the sidewalk that provides a better spot from which to watch the comings and goings on this pedestrian-friendly block. A second location in Tamarac Square, 7777 E. Hampden Avenue, 750-4422, in southeast Denver has the same pizza-pasta-plus menu but a more refined and airy ambience. (Downtown, Southeast)

LITTLE PEPINA'S
3400 Osage St.   477-3335
$$-$$$

A veritable institution in West Denver, Little Pepina's has been around since 1938, and it looks it; the lavish maroon and pink decor is the height of mid-century style. But we mean this in the most complimentary way and hope they never change a thing. The generously proportioned fare includes pastas, fish, chicken, veal and an assortment of classic desserts highlighted by cheesecake, cannoli and the layered Sicilian cake called zuccata. Closed Mondays. (West Denver)

MIKE BERARDI'S
2115 E. 17th Ave.   399-8800
$$

The Berardi family has, in one form or another, been operating restaurants in the Boulder/Denver area for decades. Their newest venture is a sophisticated, Manhattan-syle trattoria, with an uncomplicated menu of pastas and meat and fish dishes. A strolling opera singer performs nightly. (Central)

PAGLIACCI'S
1440 W. 33rd Ave.   458-0530
$$

Family-run for 50 years, Pagliacci's is another West Denver institution. The neon clown on the roof is famously visible from I-25 but not from the restaurant itself, which has a handsome, grotto-like interior. If you can't stay for a meal, you can get the minestrone to go. It serves dinner only. (West Denver)

PASTA'S
9126 W. Bowles
Littleton   933-2829
$$$

Pasta's is a big, friendly, family-run southern Italian restaurant that specializes in big portions and solicitous service. The staff will treat you like a relative as you enjoy their pastas, chicken, veal and seafood entrees. It's open every day for lunch and dinner except Sunday when they serve dinner only. (Southwest)

RANELLE'S
1313 E. Sixth Ave.   831-1992
$$$

A tiny and dearly loved northern Italian restaurant, Ranelle's is known for its sophisticated pasta dishes, but also for its excellent soups and good wine list. Reservations are strongly recommended. Closed Sunday and Monday. (Central)

Mexican

THE BLUE BONNET LOUNGE
457 S. Broadway   778-0147
$

This hole-in-the-wall Mexican joint was "discovered" by Denver yuppies in the '80s and remains popular — prepare to wait a while for a table. There's nothing fancy here, but there's lots of it with great big margaritas to wash it all down. (Central)

CASA BONITA
6715 W. Colfax Ave.
Lakewood   232-5115
$

Unaccompanied adults take note: the food is decent at this place, but the real attraction is the Disneyland-like entertainment, which is geared toward children. For details, see our Kidstuff chapter. (Southwest)

EL NOA NOA
722 Santa Fe Dr.   623-9968
$

Located in an authentic Mexican-American neighborhood, which is the site each year of a Cinco de Mayo parade and street festival, El Noa Noa dishes out tasty enchiladas, burritos, tacos and rellenos. Breakfast is served all day. In good weather, enjoy the large patio with wrought iron chairs and a fountain. It has other locations at 1920 Federal Boulevard, 455-6071, in West Denver and downtown at 1543 Champa Street, 623-5321. (Central, Downtown, North)

EL TACO DE MEXICO
714 Santa Fe Dr.   623-3926
$

This simple joint holds its own, despite stiff competition from larger and better-known El Noa Noa next door. It's open for breakfast. No credit cards are accepted, but checks are OK. There's a second location at 2463 Sheridan Boulevard in Edgewater, 237-7174, in Northwest Denver. (Central, North)

JUANITA'S UPTOWN
1700 Vine St.   333-9595
$$

A yuppified restaurant that's very popular, Juanita's earns compliments for its reasonably priced food and fun atmosphere. The fajitas are the house specialty. A similar spirit prevails at the Juanita's in Boulder at 1043 Pearl Street, 449-5273. (Central)

LA ESTRELLITA
7617 W. 88th Ave.
Westminster   422-3700
$

This is the third Mexican restaurant owned and operated by the Montoya family in the Denver metro area; the others are in Brighton and Boulder. The award-winning green chile is available hot, medium, mild or vegetarian, and by the quart for take-out. You'll enjoy the casual atmosphere. (North)

LA LOMA RESTAURANT
2527 W. 26th Ave.   433-8300
$-$$

In the Diamond Hill neighborhood just west of I-25 at Speer Boulevard, La Loma is rather incongruously housed in an 1887 Victorian home that's renovated into a sprawling restaurant with a series of dining rooms. The restaurant is known for its big margaritas and its authentic food. (West Denver)

LAS DELICIAS
439 E. 19th Ave.   839-5675
$

This family-run restaurant has expanded to three locations, and loyal customers still can't get enough of their Michoacan-style carnitas and fajitas, carne adobada, taquitos, carne asada and steak ranchero. It offers great breakfasts in addition to lunch and dinner. You'll find other locations at 50 E. Del Norte, 430-0422, in north Denver and 1530 Blake Street, 629-5051. (Central, North, Downtown)

MEXICALI CAFE
1453 Larimer St.   892-1444
$-$$

This is a big, fun, colorful place with a nice location in Larimer Square. They describe themselves as a "Bordertown Diner," and make an especially big deal about their fajitas. There's a good selection of barbecue items, more than at most Tex-Mex places. The outdoor tables are prized for people-watching. (Downtown)

MEXICO CITY LOUNGE & CAFE
2115 Larimer St.   296-0563
$

Denverites make a big fuss about authenticity when discussing the comparative merits of restaurants. No argument here: this is the real thing. The green chile and burritos are favorites, and breakfast is a real eye-opener. If you're a fan of menudo, this is the place to go. Checks with guaranteed check card only are accepted. No credit cards. (Downtown)

MORRISON INN
301 Bear Creek Ave.
Morrison   697-6650
$-$$

A fun, Americanized restaurant in an 1885 building in the heart of the Foothills town of Morrison, the Morrison Inn is known for its custom-made (not pre-mixed) margaritas. (West suburbs)

ROSALINDA'S MEXICAN CAFE
2005 W. 33rd Ave.   455-0608
$

Run by the Aquirre family since 1985, RosaLinda's is a small, plain place with great burritos, enchiladas and soft chile rellenos. You say you want a neighborhood restaurant? Check out this one. There are a few tables on the sidewalk. (West Denver)

TAQUERIA PATZCUARO
2616 W. 32nd Ave.   455-4389
$

An ultra-casual restaurant in an authentic Spanish-speaking neighborhood, Taqueria Patzcuaro draws fans of its green chile and soft tacos from all over the city. Checks with check guarantee card only. No credit cards. (West Denver)

Middle Eastern

CEDARS
1550 S. Federal Blvd. at Florida Ave. 936-2980
$$-$$$

A Lebanese family owns and operates this attractive 100-seat restaurant, which serves terrific falafel, tabbouleh and more sophisticated Middle Eastern fare. Save room for the baklava. (Southwest)

FETTOUSH
1448 Market St.   820-2554
$$

Downtown's new Middle Eastern restaurant has cooling mint-green accented decor and reasonable prices for its kabobs, gyros, falafel, curries and lamb dishes. A sidewalk patio keeps diners in touch with the LoDo scene. (Downtown)

JERUSALEM RESTAURANT
1890 E. Evans Ave.   777-8838
$

A tiny, eight-table restaurant that does a bustling take-out business, Jerusalem is popular with students from the University of Denver campus nearby. Everything is good here, including the kebabs, hummus, baba ghanouj and phyllo pastries. Students cramming for an exam no doubt also appreciate the fact that Jerusalem is virtually always open, from about 9 AM to at least 3 AM. The space crunch is eased somewhat by the outdoor patio. (South central)

Pizza

ARMANDO'S OF CHERRY CREEK
201 Milwaukee St.   320-6300
$

This casual New York-style pizzeria in the heart of Cherry Creek North has many fans, and the double-crusted spinach pizza with black olives is especially well-thought-of. Take-out is available. There are other

The Augusta in the Westin Hotel in theTabor Center is one of Greater Denver's finest restaurants.

locations at 837 16th Street downtown, 825-6668, and in Aurora at 16611 E. Smoky Hill Road, 690-6660. There is a $10 minimum for credit card purchases. (Cherry Creek, Downtown and East)

BEAU JO'S PIZZA
2700 S. Colorado Blvd.   758-1519
$-$$

The original Beau Jo's is still in Idaho Springs, and is a beloved stopping point on the way home from skiing for Denverites who crave thick-crusted pizza loaded with toppings. Finally, Beau Jo's opened up branches in southeast Denver, Arvada and Boulder. The Arvada location is at 7805 Wadsworth Boulevard, 420-8376. (South central, West suburbs)

BONNIE BRAE TAVERN
740 S. University Blvd.   777-2262
$-$$

The crowds! The noise! The pizza! This astoundingly popular, 60-year-old neighborhood pizza joint is locally famous and always busy, busy, busy. It's a fun place, but don't come here if you're in a hurry. Take-out is available. (South central)

PASQUINI'S PIZZERIA
1310 S. Broadway   744-0917
$

A nifty little pizzeria with an artsy interior and mosaic-topped tables, Pasquini's serves New York-style thin crust, sauceless and thick-crust Sicilian-style pizzas and individual pizzettas with interesting toppings. Also on the menu are calzones and subs. Pasquini's is nestled amidst the antique stores on South Broadway, at Louisiana Avenue. The Blu Luna Room upstairs features live music nightly, everything from jazz to blues to acoustic. Take-out and delivery are available. (South central)

PIZZA COLORE CAFE
1512 Larimer St.   534-6844
$-$$

The Rocky Mountain offshoot of a small New Jersey chain, Pizza Colore has a menu that's built around a clever gimmick: pizzas come with sauces of red, green or white, the three colors of the Italian flag. Other Italian entrees, plus calzones, are available. No smoking, except on the patio, which is where you'll want to be anyway in good weather. Pizza Colore has an upscale cousin in Cherry Creek, Cucina Colore, at 3041 E. Third Avenue, 393-6917. (Downtown)

Seafood

FRESH FISH COMPANY
7600 E. Hampden Ave.   740-9556
$$$

The aquatic theme extends to the decor at this big restaurant, which consists of walls of beautiful tropical aquariums. Mesquite grilling is a specialty here, and the $14.95 Sunday brunch, with all-you-can-eat crab legs and shrimp, is very popular. On Sunday nights there's a lobster bake. (Southeast)

MCCORMICK'S FISH HOUSE & BAR
1659 Wazee St.   825-1107
$$$

In McCormick's elegant dining room can be found some of the freshest fish in Denver. If oysters are in season, this is one of the few places in town to get them. The menu changes daily to take advantage of what's fresh. McCormick's "The Time Is the Price" menu, available from 5 to 6 PM, is one of the best bargains going. If you order one of the evening's special selections at 5:45 PM, you pay $5.45. This is a great deal and a good choice for pre-theater meals (the Denver Performing Arts Complex is just a few blocks away). Private dining rooms are available; call for information. Breakfast is served, too, beginning at 6:30 AM weekdays. New to the lineup is weekend brunch. (Downtown)

PALMETTO GRILLE
8090 E. Quincy Ave.   689-9569
$$$

Done in cool Miami Beach hues of aquas and pinks, the laid-back Palmetto Grille serves more than just seafood, but counts fresh fish as one of its specialties. Pork chops and grilled meats are also popular choices. Desserts receive high marks, especially those that contain chocolate. The outdoor patio doesn't have an ocean view, but that's about all we can find to complain about at this friendly spot. (Southeast)

240 UNION
240 Union Blvd. at Sixth Ave.
Lakewood   989-3562
$$-$$$

The menu changes seasonally at this creative restaurant, which specializes in seafood. Pastas and pizzas round out the offerings. It has a fine pedigree: two of its three owners are Noel Cunningham, of Strings restaurant fame, and executive chef Matthew Franklin, who did a stint at the original Rattlesnake Club, Denver's most innovative restaurant of the 1980s. The restaurant has recently undergone extensive remodeling, and now sports a modern, open look with lots of cherry, marble and glass. There's a nice enclosed patio and a wall-to-wall open grill. No lunch is served on weekends. (West suburbs)

South American

CAFE BRAZIL
3611 Navajo St.   480-1877
$$$

Cafe Brazil is a tiny, intimate restaurant in what used to be an Old World Italian neighborhood that has become more ethnically mixed. The neighborhood has a strong artistic inclination with an alternative gallery and theater space in the same block. It may not look like much from the outside, but trust us, the food is terrific. Try the feijoada completa, Brazil's national dish. It combines black beans, meat, fruit and rice in a most delicious way. Cafe Brazil is open for dinner only and is closed Sunday and Monday. Reservations are highly recommended on the weekends. No credit cards are accepted, but checks are. (West Denver)

LOS CABOS
2727 Sixth Ave. W.
455-5258
$

The specialty here is Peruvian seafood, and there is a selection of Mexican entrees, too, including a superb Snapper Veracruzana. This self-proclaimed "first Latin American nightclub, restaurant and sports bar in Denver" has the added attraction of salsa music on Friday and Saturday nights. No credit cards are accepted, but checks are OK. To get there, take the Bryant Street exit from Sixth Avenue. (West Denver)

SABOR LATINO
3463 W. 32nd Ave.   *455-8664*
$-$$

A small, charming place in an interesting neighborhood, Sabor Latino serves South American and Mexican cuisine. Specialties of the house include Colombian tamales and South American empanadas, baked or fried. A nice selection of Chilean wines is available. No reservations are taken and it's closed Sundays. (West Denver)

Less Than a Meal: Coffeehouses, Ice Cream Parlors, etc.

ALL FOR THE BETTER
3501 S. Clarkson St.
Englewood   *781-0230*
$

A sweet, old-fashioned ice-cream parlor that also serves soup and sandwiches, All for the Better is across the street from Swedish Medical Center. Checks are accepted. No credit cards. (Southeast)

BLUEPOINT BAKERY
1307 E. Sixth Ave.   *839-1820*
$

Bluepoint devotees are fierce in their praise of this bakery's bread, which ranges from densely brown and chewy to light as a feather. The sourdough is great, and there are more unusual breads, too, such as tomato-basil or olive. Rather than the giant cookies you'll find elsewhere, Bluepoint's are petite treats. Checks are accepted, but not credit cards. It's closed Sundays. (Central)

CAMPAGNA BAKING
1710 S. Broadway   *698-9393*
$

Campagna's rustic breads are manna for those who appreciate a real, hard crust. They also make muffins and pastries, and sell Italian meats and cheeses. Coffee is available, too. The bakery's open every day except Monday, and their products are

In 1944, Louis Ballast grilled a slice of cheese onto a hamburger at his Denver drive-in restaurant, and patented the invention as "The Cheeseburger." Other claimants can take up their case with the Denver Metro Convention & Visitors Bureau, which stands by this bit of trivia.

Insiders' Tips

widely carried in local supermarkets. (South)

COMMON GROUNDS

3484 W. 32nd Ave.   458-5248
$

A coffeehouse in the European tradition, Common Grounds doubles as a community center for the Highlands neighborhood. Lots of free reading material, boardgames and a piano for would-be Liberaces make this a place to stop and sit a spell. Pastries, cakes, muffins and bagels are available. In the evenings, there might be a poetry reading or jazz concert. Sign of the times: This coffeehouse prohibits smoking. No credit cards. Checks are accepted. (West Denver)

ECONOMY GREEK MARKET

1035 Lincoln St.   861-3001
$

A Denver institution since 1901, the Economy Market stocks hard-to-find varieties of imported feta cheese and olives, as well as other Greek and Mediterranean specialties. It's open every day except Sunday for breakfast and lunch, featuring gyros and other deli items. (Central)

JOSH & JOHN'S NATURALLY HOMEMADE ICE CREAM

1444 Market St.   628-0310
$

Started by two boyhood friends in their 20s, Josh & John's now has stores in Boulder, Colorado Springs and Denver. About 13 flavors are available at any given time. Try the coffee crunch, citrus bliss or the Rocky Roy, named after the state's governor. It's open from 11 AM to midnight. Checks are accepted, but not credit cards. (Downtown)

LE DELICE

250 Steele St.   331-0972
$-$$

Actually, you can get lunch here, a slice of quiche or a salad to fortify you in the midst of a Cherry Creek shopping excursion. You can even get a light dinner most evenings until 7 PM. But our primary reason for including this very French bakery is the extravagant array of mouthwatering tortes, cookies and pastries. Closed Sundays. There's a second location downtown at 1512 Larimer Street in Writer Square, 446-0694. (Cherry Creek, Downtown)

LIKS

2039 E. 13th Ave.   321-1492
$

Formerly known as Lickety Split, this old-fashioned ice cream parlor is the place to go for a New York egg cream or a fabulously indulgent sundae. The homemade ice creams come in such tempting flavors as Almond Roca and Cheesman Park, a strawberry-cheesecake concoction named for the park a few blocks away. Don't fret if they're out of your favorite flavor; they'll put it on the request list and call you when it's available. Checks with check guarantee card only. No credit cards. (Central)

THE MARKET

1445 Larimer St.   534-5140
$

You can make a meal out of the gourmet offerings at The Market, which include made-to-order deli sandwiches and a changing variety of soups and salads. But it's not really a restaurant, so we've included it in this category. The baked goods, top-of-the-line chocolates and shelves of imported food items make this as much a shopping destination as a dining spot, and the espresso bar is always busy. Bring a cup of cappuccino and a plate of biscotti out to a table on the sidewalk and watch the world go by. (Downtown)

NEWSSTAND CAFE
630 E. Sixth Ave. at Washington St. 777-6060
$

A wonderful sip-and-read coffeehouse a few blocks from the famed Esquire Theatre, the Newsstand attracts an interesting, literary crowd. Cafe food and pastries are available in addition to espresso drinks, and with more than 1,000 magazines, newspapers and books (including audio, travel and Internet books) for sale, no one need suffer for lack of reading material. (Central)

OMONIA BAKERY
2813 E. Colfax Ave. 394-9333
$

This authentic Greek bakery will satisfy a craving for baklava, koularakia, kataifi or galataboureko. A napoleon is available, too, and of course there's strong coffee to go with whatever sweet your heart desires. No credit cards. Checks are accepted. (Central)

PARIS ON THE PLATTE
1553 Platte St. 455-2451
$

Popular with neighborhood artists, some of whom exhibit their paintings here, Paris on the Platte is connected to a used bookstore. If coffee isn't enough, sandwiches, salads and soups are available. (Downtown/Platte River)

RHEINLANDER BAKERY
5721 Olde Wadsworth Blvd.
Arvada 467-1810
$

Authentic German rye bread tops the list at this charming family-run Old World bakery in Arvada's historic Olde Town district. Coffeecakes, Danish pastries, Euro-

pean-style tortes and cookies can be had here, too. Checks are accepted. There's a second location at 10354 N. Federal in Federal Heights, 469-8572, and a third at 8025 N. Sheridan unit U, 427-5664. The Sheridan location specializes in wedding cakes. All locations are closed Sunday. No credit cards. (Western suburbs)

ROSALES MEXICAN BAKERY
2636 W. 32nd Ave. 458-8420
$

This family-operated bakery features authentic Mexican pastries and bread baked fresh daily, as well as a selection of imported Mexican items. Open daily 7 AM to 10 PM. No credit cards. (West Denver)

ST. MARK'S COFFEEHOUSE
1416 Market St. 446-2925
$

The bohemian alternative to the much more crowded Market on Larimer Street, St. Mark's serves coffee, cappuccino and baked goods from 7 AM to midnight and until 1 AM on weekends. Cash only. (Downtown)

STELLA'S COFFEEHOUSE
1476 S. Pearl St. 777-1031
$

Stella's is almost certainly the only Denver coffeehouse with a branch in Amsterdam — the owner's family runs a cafe by the same name in that European city. Stella's has lots of outdoor seating and scrumptious baked goods and desserts. They also serve a light lunch menu. The adjoining Amsterdam Room has live entertainment on weekends and can be booked for private meetings and parties. No smoking is allowed, a custom we suspect doesn't hold true for the trans-Atlantic Stella's. It's open until 1 AM on weekends. (South Central)

Two-steppers step out to country music at the Grizzly Rose.

Inside
Nightlife

Despite its fabled reputation as a cowtown, where folks turn in early and rise with the sun, Denver does have a nightlife. It boasts one of the best country-and-western dance clubs anywhere, fine jazz and more yuppified pool halls than you can shake a billiard stick at. Denverites are avid moviegoers who flock to the historic Mayan Theater for its eclectic offering of art and foreign films. We also attend the annual Denver Film Festival in droves each October.

In this chapter we survey Denver's nightlife, stopping in at a few of our favorite bars, brewpubs, live music venues, comedy clubs and movie houses. This isn't meant to be a comprehensive listing; for that kind of inclusiveness, the best place to turn is *Westword*, Denver's free weekly paper. The Friday editions of *The Denver Post* and *Rocky Mountain News* also carry weekend entertainment listings. The newspaper *Out Front* is a good source of information about gay and lesbian nightlife. The

paper is free and widely distributed, but if you can't find a copy, call 778-7900.

Because people interpret "nightlife" so broadly — it includes everything from a coffeehouse with live poetry readings to an outdoor rock concert at a stadium to a blues club — there is some inevitable overlap with other chapters. A brewpub such as the Wynkoop that serves dinner also draws a late-night billiards crowd. City Spirit Cafe attracts downtown workers for lunch but fills up with a more bohemian crowd for its live music at night. If a listing in this chapter has an asterisk (*) after its name, that means it's described in further detail in the Restaurants chapter.

Theater and dance performances and concerts, such as those at the Denver Performing Arts Complex, are covered in the Arts chapter. We direct your attention to such popular in-town music venues as the Paramount Theatre, the Ogden Theatre and the Swallow Hill Music Hall. As opposed to concert halls, where advance tick-

---

Under 21? A number of clubs cater to the too-young-to-drink set. One way to find them is to contact city parks and recreation departments, which often sponsor alcohol-free events. Telephone numbers for recreation departments are listed in our Recreation chapter. Or laugh yourself silly at the Chicken Lips Comedy Theater, 534-4440, which is open to all ages. Swallow Hill Music Hall, 777-1003, is another youth-friendly venue.

Insiders' Tips

eting is recommended, most of the live music venues described in this chapter serve food and drink and can be visited on a drop-in basis, although this too is no hard-and-fast rule. Finally, you'll find family attractions that don't shut down at dusk, such as Elitch Gardens, described in the Tours and Attractions chapter.

Keep in mind, too, that today's hot spot could be tomorrow's Siberia. No guidebook could ever hope to keep up with the strange twists of taste that make one place worth lining up for and another worth taking pains to avoid. It seems every bar in town added a pool table in 1993; whether this is a trend with staying power or whether we'll see them replaced with aquariums or climbing walls is anybody's guess. And, of course, music and dance clubs change their format and hours frequently. If you're looking for a specific kind of music, it's always best to call ahead.

After years of a system that permitted individuals 18 and older to buy 3.2 percent beer but nothing stronger, the Colorado legislature simplified matters by raising the drinking age for any kind of alcoholic beverage to 21. Closing time at bars and nightclubs is generally 2 AM, but most restaurants stop serving at 11 PM or even earlier.

Colorado is not a state that takes drunk driving lightly. Penalties for driving under the influence or driving while impaired are severe. If you've had too much to drink, any restaurant or bar will call a taxi for you. If you're headed up to Central City and Black Hawk for an evening of gambling (we write about this at the end of this chapter), we strongly recommend that you avail yourself of one of the shuttle services rather than driving your own car.

Bars and Other Gathering Spots

Duffy's Shamrock Restaurant & Bar, 1635 Court Place, 534-4935, really comes into its own on St. Paddy's Day, but it's a classic Irish drinking establishment the rest of the year, too. Nothing fancy, mind you, but a right neighborly place.

The restored **Oxford Hotel**, 1600 17th Street, 628-5400, one block away from Union Station, boasts a restaurant and bar complex that's among the city's best. The intimately sized **Cruise Room** was modeled after a lounge on the Queen Mary and has a wonderful art-deco interior that dates back to the lifting of Prohibition in 1933. A favorite with visiting authors, the Cruise Room is a great place for a late-night drink, especially if your taste runs to martinis. The bar doesn't have live music, but the jukebox is well-stocked with jazz and Big Band music.

For more-public occasions, the roomy corner bar at **McCormick's Fish House and Bar***, 1659 Wazee Street, 825-1107, attracts a big crowd after 5 PM for Guinness Stout on tap and other libations. If you decide to stay for dinner, some of the freshest fish in town can be had in McCormick's main dining room just across the hallway.

The grande dame of Denver hotels, **The Brown Palace**, has three dining rooms, including **Ellyngton's***, and the formal **Palace Arms***, where gentlemen diners are requested to wear jackets and ties. **The Ship Tavern*** is the most casual (though not necessarily the least expensive) of the trio and a good place to stop in for a drink or a bite to eat. It's more restaurant than bar, but with its dark wood and nautical decor, it has the feel of an English pub.

The lobby of the Brown Palace Hotel is a charming and elegant place to go for tea or cocktails.

Photo: Daily Camera/Lourie Zipf

The walls and ceiling are hung with models of actual ships from America's clipper period. The Ship Tavern can be entered through the Brown Palace Hotel lobby, at 321 17th Street, or from the street at Tremont Place. The general number for all Brown Palace services is 297-3111.

The upstairs bar at **The Buckhorn Exchange***, 1000 Osage Street, 534-9505, has been a Denver institution for more than 100 years — Colorado's first liquor license is posted on the wall. The hand-carved, white-oak bar dates from 1857 and was brought over from Germany. Weekends, there's live music in the adjacent Victorian parlor.

A few restaurants that are equally good spots for a pre-dinner or late-night drink and a nosh are: **Marlowe's***, 595-3700, at 16th Street and Glenarm Place; **The Paramount Cafe***, 893-2000, next door to Marlowe's at 511 16th Street; the glitzy Texas-style **Cadillac Ranch***, 820-2288, 1400 Larimer; and the **Avenue Grill***, 861-2820, 630 E. 17th Avenue, the choice of Denver's young movers and shakers. In Cherry Creek, try the **Rattlesnake Grill***, 377-8000, in the Cherry Creek Shopping Center. See the Restaurants chapter for more information.

Live Music

Once on the edge of gentrified Denver, **El Chapultepec**, 1962 Market Street, 295-9126, used to be a slightly dangerous place to drink beer, eat a burrito and listen to jazz. It now finds itself in the rising shadow of Coors Field and encroached upon by brewpubs, art galleries and designer tile shops. So far, the essential attraction — sizzling jazz — has remained the same. El Chapultepec is open every night; there's no cover charge.

Brendan's Market Street Pub, 1624 Market Street, 595-0609, serves up live blues every night at a subterranean lair in lower downtown (LoDo to Insiders). Monday nights are set aside for an all-comers-welcome blues jam. Casual dinner is served. Brendan's happy hour lasts a long, long time — from 7 PM Sunday to 7 PM Thursday, with drink specials, free pool and free pizza and wings Monday through Friday from 5-7 PM.

A swanky spot that's one of Denver's few true nightclubs (as opposed to a restaurant with music), **Butterfield Eight**, 175 Fillmore Street, 388-8808, has hip-hop dance music Tuesday and Saturday evenings and Top 40 on Friday nights.

Nearby in the former site of the Bay Wolf, at 231 Milwaukee Street, 399-1111, is **Vartan Jazz Club**, which since its opening in 1994 has quickly established itself as one of the city's best venues for Big Band, Latin and Brazilian jazz — and lots more. And here's a '90s twist: no smoking. Some performances require tickets and reservations, other nights there's no cover charge at all.

Jimmy's Grille, 320 S. Birch Street, Glendale, 322-5334, packs 'em in for reggae and Tex-Mex food and burgers. Some of reggae's biggest stars have played here on Thursday through Saturday nights; there's also jazz on Tuesday nights.

There's no cover and no minimum drinks charge at **Josephina's***, 1433 Larimer Street, 623-0166, where there's live entertainment every night of the week. Bands and musicians — mostly of the classic rock variety — have the stage all week. Josephina's serves casual Italian food (pizza and pastas). No reservations are accepted for Friday and Saturday nights, but reservations are suggested for the rest of the week.

A funky, mostly vegetarian restaurant (they describe their menu as "ethno-healthy cuisine"), **City Spirit***, 1434 Blake Street, 575-0022, sponsors jazz, acid jazz and blues on the weekends and sometimes other nights as well. Be warned: This is generally not the kind of background music that enhances a meal or encourages conversation.

Acappella's* is a popular, casual restaurant that, true to its name, features a cappella music on the weekends. It's lo-cated on restaurant row at 1336 E. 17th Avenue, 832-1479.

The **York Street Cafe & Bar***, 2239 E. Colfax Avenue, 331-0533, is a big, bustling restaurant with some of the best jazz in town on Thursday, Friday and Saturday evenings in a sophisticated setting. Menu offerings include lobster, pastas, salads and fresh fish. There's a $6-per-person minimum while the music is playing.

Although the skyscrapers of downtown Denver are visible from the windows of **La Coupole***, 2191 Arapahoe Street, 297-2288, the lace curtains, wood floors, snippets of overheard French and gracious outdoor courtyard make patrons feel like they're dining in Paris. This elegant French restaurant is one of the most beautiful rooms in Denver in which to enjoy a meal and, on Friday and Saturday nights from 8 to 11 PM, live jazz. Reservations are recommended.

A downtown restaurant and bar frequented by the after-work crowd, **The Mall Exchange**, 1580 Lawrence Street, 573-1400, is crowded, smoky and jumping with blues and jazz every Friday and Saturday night. Located across from the Tabor Center on the 16th Street Mall, the Mall Exchange has a full menu and outdoor tables for people-watching.

During most of the week, **Soapy Smith's Eagle Bar**, 1317 14th Street, 534-1111, is popular with students from the nearby Auraria Campus, who come to drink a beer and enjoy live music. Wednesday nights are for jazz; Thursday through Saturday for ska, funk and rock; and on Sunday, rockabilly rules.

A relatively new restaurant with an ambitious schedule of live jazz is the **Beacon Grill***, 303 16th Street, 592-4745. One of the owners of this hip downtown spot is Rich Salturelli, a familiar name in the Denver jazz scene as former proprietor of the

Movies Filmed in Denver

Even if you've never been to Denver, you may have seen it in the movies. The hit movie *Die Hard*, starring Bruce Willis, had major scenes filmed at the old Stapleton Airport. Portions of Woody Allen's 1973 film *Sleeper* were shot in Denver and vicinity, including the exterior of the National Center for Atmospheric Research in Boulder and a modernist home visible from I-70 near Genesee that's known locally as the *Sleeper* house.

Between July 1994 and June 1995, some 12 feature films, 43 documentaries and television docudramas, three music videos and 72 commercials — plus other film and video projects — were filming in Denver, according to the Mayor's Office of Art, Culture & Film, which keeps tabs on such things. The office provides technical assistance and coordinates public safety for film and video producers.

Among the films being shot in Denver in 1994-95 were Warner Brothers *Under Seige II: "In Dark Territory,"* with Steven Seagal; and Boat Drink Productions' *Things to Do in Denver When You're Dead*, starring Andy Garcia. *In Dark Territory* has scenes in Lower Downtown (LoDo), including around Union Station and Coors Field. *Things to Do* was shot largely in the Five Points neighborhood at 26th and Welton, including the historic old Rossonian Hotel. For some key scenes, the Rossonian's bar was transformed into a malt shop. *Elephant Man* (also known as *Nickel and Dime*), with Bill Murray, was also filmed in Denver and Colorado during this period.

The closing of the 100-year-old Elitch Gardens amusement park in Lakeside (Elitch's moved to a new site in the Platte Valley along I-25) has

The bar at the old Rossonian Hotel in Five Points was transformed into a malt shop for the film Things To Do In Denver When You're Dead.

opened up new possibilities for filmmakers who might need to demolish an amusement park. Elitch's has put the word out, through the Mayor's Office of Art, Culture & Film, that the old site, Twister roller coaster and all, is available as a location and that for the right price, some lucky producer can blow it all up.

now-defunct jazz club the Bay Wolf in Cherry Creek. Opened in December 1993, the Beacon Grill has live jazz in the lounge Thursday, Friday and Saturday nights. In the summer there's also jazz Wednesday nights on the spacious second-level patio that overlooks the 16th Street Mall.

Dancing

I-Beam, 1427 Larimer Street, 534-2326, presents live entertainment, Top-40 and disco music, dancing and billiards for the twentysomething set.

Modeans, 1410 Market Street, 623-3532, draws a young crowd on Wednesday through Sunday nights for alternative music and dancing; they also have '80s New Wave nights. There is a small cover charge.

The DJs at the **Aqua Lounge**, 17th and Clarkson, 832-FISH, entertain the young and energetic with New Wave to Top-40 to retro '80s music, depending on the evening. There's a small cover charge most nights. It's closed Sundays and Mondays.

Another popular R&B joint is **Ziggies Saloon**, 4923 W. 38th Avenue, 455-9930, which is regarded by many as Denver's No. 1 blues bar. There's live music Wednesday through Sunday nights. On Sunday afternoons there's a no-cover-charge acoustic jam.

For live alternative rock, try **Seven South**, 7 S. Broadway, 744-0513, on Friday and Saturday nights. Regulars say the jukebox, with the kind of selection you won't find in Howard Johnson's, is a fine substitute the rest of the time.

Under the same roof (but acoustically

separate) are **Packard's** and **Panama Red's**, at 2797 S. Parker Road in Aurora, 695-1751 or 695-1752. Panama Red's plays Top-40 music and attracts a young crowd; at Packard's, the thirtysomething set listens to '50s and '60s music. But once you've paid the modest cover charge, you can divide your time between the two bars. It's open Tuesday through Sunday nights; some food is served.

Roadhouses

Herman's Hideaway, 1578 S. Broadway, 777-5840, is a live music showcase with a large dance floor. The entertainment can vary from rock to zydeco. Advance ticketing is advisable for special bookings of nationally known acts; call Herman's or TicketMaster, 830-TIXS.

Buffalo Rose Saloon, 1119 Washington Street, Golden, 279-5190, was established in 1851. The saloon presents a variety of musical acts, from well-known rock groups to folk singers, Wednesday through Saturday nights. Tickets are available at the Saloon or from TicketMaster, 830-TIXS. A full menu is served until 10 PM.

Even folks from the plains brave the narrow mountain roads to make the scene at the **Little Bear**, 28075 Colo. Highway 74, Main Street, Evergreen, 674-9991. Neither the route nor the rollicking roadhouse atmosphere are for the timid, but it's a fine place to listen to national and local rock, folk and blues musicians. Advance tickets for special bookings are available at TicketMaster, 830-TIXS. Pizza and burgers are served from 11 AM; open every day.

Country-and-Western Nightclubs

Grizzly Rose Saloon & Dance Emporium, 5450 N. Valley Highway, 295-2353 (concert line, 295-1330), was voted the nation's No. 1 country music dance hall by the Country Music Association, and it's where the big names come to play when they're in town. With a 5,000-square-foot dance floor and headliners such as Willie Nelson, Waylon Jennings and Toby Keith, it's not hard to see why the Grizzly Rose is the undisputed favorite in the live-music C&W category. Advance ticketing is recommended for national acts; call the Grizzly Rose or TicketMaster, 830-TIXS.

Stampede Mesquite Grill & Dance Emporium, 2430 S. Havana at Parker Road, Aurora, 337-6909, is a new club with a giant racetrack dance floor, line dancing and lessons, a yuppie clientele and an antique bar. For reservations at the restaurant, which is on a second-floor balcony overlooking the nightclub, call 696-7686.

Locals swear that **Ollie's Roundup**, 5195 Morrison Road at Sheridan Boulevard, 935-8377, is where the very best dancers can be found. If you're looking to see if you measure up, or just want to watch competition-level two-stepping, this is the place to go. The DJs start spinning the songs at 9 PM, seven nights a week, and lessons are available every night, too.

Teddy's Restaurant and Lounge, in the Denver North Holiday Inn, 4849 Bannock Street, 292-9500, near the intersection of I-70 and I-25, has a different musical format every night. Tuesday night is reserved for country music with local KYGO disc jockeys. Happy hour with free hors d' oeuvres runs from 5 to 7 PM. Teddy's is a full-service restaurant serving breakfast, lunch and dinner.

Mixed Bag

The reincarnation of a legendary Denver nightclub of the '70s and early '80s, the **Mercury Cafe***, 2199 California Street, 294-9281, offers everything from swing dancing and Big Band music to performance art, comedy, theater and lectures. Mercury Cafe serves lunch, dinner and weekend brunch, with an emphasis on natural foods; it doesn't accept credit cards.

Similar in inclusiveness to the Mercury Cafe (and located just a block away), is **Muddy's Java Cafe**, 2200 Champa Street, 298-1631. Muddy's offers comedy on some nights and poetry readings on others. Over the course of a week, expect to find theater, jazz, folk and blues.

Brewpubs, Sports Bars and Pool Halls

After 5 PM is a busy time for the **Wynkoop Brewing Company***, 18th and Wynkoop Streets, 297-2700, Denver's first brewpub. Opened in 1988, the Wynkoop offers comedy downstairs, dining on the first floor and pool upstairs, all in the historic J. S. Brown Mercantile Building, c. 1899.

Denver's greatest concentration of nightspots are in Lower Downtown (LoDo) and Cherry Creek. Head on over and follow the crowds.

Insiders' Tips

Regulars like the Railyard Ale. Wynkoop also brews its own root beer. The billiards room has 22 pool tables, dart lanes and shuffleboard, as well as a full-service bar. Cue rentals and lessons are available; call for more information. Validated parking is available across the street. Also, **Comedy Sports**, billed as Denver's longest-running comedy show, occupies the lower level of the building with performances Thursdays, Fridays and Saturdays. Reservations are recommended; call 297-2111.

A microbrewery/sports bar/restaurant in a great location in Larimer Square, **Champion Brewing Company***, 1442 Larimer Street, 534-5444, has the requisite pool tables and big-screen TVs. But there's also plenty of outdoor seating for prime people-watching. You might opt for a mug of the Home Run Ale, a gold-medal winner in the 1993 American Beer Contest.

Yet another brewpub and pool hall, the huge, sunny **Rock Bottom Brewery***, 1001 16th Street, 534-7616, is popular with the young lawyers and bankers who work on 17th Street. There's live jazz music Friday and Saturday nights and in the summer, on Thursday nights too.

The **Breckenridge Brewery***, 2220 Blake Street, 297-3644, opened in 1992, makes the same beers, root beer and ales as its Summit County cousin. Pub fare is served, and there's beer drinking and billiards late into the evening (and early into the morning). Tuesday evenings are set aside for a blues jam.

Gate 12, 2301 Blake Street, 292-2212, bills itself as a "billiards nightclub and sports bar." Situated almost directly across the street from the new Coors Field, Gate 12 draws a big after-the-game crowd. There are two dance floors downstairs, one with alternative rock and the other featuring '70s classics and Top 40.

A new restaurant and gathering spot that's been getting good word-of-mouth for its pizza and hamburgers, **Wazoo's on Wazee**, 1819 Wazee Street, 297-8500, has nine pool tables, two bars, 13 TVs and an outdoor patio that's within cheering distance of Coors Field. There's a nightclub upstairs with dance music Thursday through Saturday.

Comedy Clubs

Chicken Lips Comedy Theater, 1360 17th Street, 534-4440, hosts improvisational comedy Friday and Saturday evenings. Ticket prices average $10, and advance reservations are suggested. Chicken Lips differs from the other comedy clubs listed here in that it is an all-ages, nonsmoking club that doesn't serve alcohol. Improvisational comedy classes are offered; call for information.

A mainstay of the Greater Denver comedy scene, **George McKelvey's Comedy Club**, 10015 E. Hampden Avenue, 368-8900, is open Wednesday through Sunday and features three stand-up comedians per night. Expect to see anything from up-and-coming performers to national and touring headliners. Admission is $5 Wednesday, Thursday and Sunday and $8 Friday and Saturday. Reservations are recommended; ages 21 and older only.

Insiders' Tips

If you're going to Central City or Black Hawk for an evening of gambling, you'll probably enjoy yourself more if you use a shuttle service rather than driving yourself.

The Great American Beer Festival is an annual fall event, but Denver brewpubs have their best spirits available year round.

Roseanne (formerly Barr and Arnold) is among the many comics who made an appearance early in her career at **Comedy Works**, 1226 15th Street, 595-3637. Tuesday night is new talent night; Wednesday through Sunday nights are for established performers. Ticket prices vary; $13 is about the upper limit. Reservations are recommended; ages 21 and older only. Ask about nonsmoking performances.

Movies

Denver's finest art movie house is the **Mayan**, at First Avenue and Broadway, 744-6796. This 1930s-era movie house is decorated on every inch of its wall and ceiling surface with weird and wonderful Mayan figures and other designs. Everything is classy here: the decor, the audience, the films, even the espresso and pastries served in the second-floor cafe. There's one large screen on the main level, two smaller ones above. The **Chez Artiste Cinema**, at 2800 S. Colorado Boulevard, 757-7161; and the **Esquire Theater**, 733-5757, at Sixth Avenue and Downing Street; are owned by the same company. Discounted

multiple admission tickets are available that can be used at all three locations. The cult classic, *The Rocky Horror Picture Show*, plays every Saturday at midnight at the Esquire.

Other movie theaters worth mentioning are the **12-plex**, 790-4262, at the Tivoli (the primary site of the Denver International Film Festival each October) and the huge, 900-seat **Continental** at I-25 and Hampden Avenue, 758-2345. And, as they say in the TV commercials, check the yellow pages for theaters near you.

Gambling

Since gambling was legalized in 1991, several casinos have sprouted up in the historic mining towns of Central City and Black Hawk, a little more than 30 miles from downtown Denver. To get there, take U.S. Highway 6 west through Clear Creek Canyon to Colo. Highway 119 and follow the signs, or take I-70 westbound to the Central City/Highway 119 Exit and head north. Better yet, let someone else do the driving. If you're just visiting, ask at your hotel about transportation, or check the Yel-

Photo: Daily Camera/David P. Gilkey

Red Rocks natural ampitheater is a beautiful setting for an outdoor concert.

low Pages under "Buses — Charter and Rental" for the names of companies that offer roundtrip bus and shuttle service.

Three shuttle services you might look into are the **Black Hawk and Central City ACE Express**, 421-2780, **People's Choice**, 936-1117 and **Queen City Bullride**, 937-8170.

Once you get there, one casino is pretty much the same as the next. The biggest decision is whether to stay in Black Hawk, which is right on Highway 119, or turn in on the spur road and travel 1 mile farther to Central City. Shuttle buses connect the two, but if you're only up for the evening you probably won't want to spend your time going back and forth. If you'd like to mix your gambling with a little history, head into Central City. It's been tarted-up a lot since its mining days, but you can still get a sense of what it used to be like.

Limited stakes gambling is the rule here, with $5 being the maximum bet. Only poker, blackjack and lots of one-armed bandits are allowed at the nearly 40 parlors that operate between 8 AM and 2 AM.

The **Gilpin County Chamber of Commerce**, (800) 331-LUCK, and the

Central City Information Center, (800) 542-2999 or 582-0889, can help you pick out a casino that has the kinds of games and amenities you want. *The Colorado Gambler*, a free newspaper, is also a good guide. It's widely available in the gambling towns and often in Denver, too, especially at hotels.

Otto's, 260 Gregory Street in Black Hawk, 582-0150 or 642-0415 direct from Denver, is kind of a mom-and-pop casino with blackjack and slot machines. For 36 years, this was a five-star restaurant, the Black Forest Inn. The owners have expanded into gambling with Otto's and the Rohling Inn.

The **Gilpin Hotel**, 111 Main Street in Black Hawk, 582-1133 or 278-1114 direct from Denver, has poker tables, which not all casinos do. Its Mineshaft Bar long predates gambling — it has been a local hangout for 100 years.

Harrah's has two casinos, the **Glory Hole**, 129 Main Street in Central City, 582-1171 or 777-1111 direct from Denver, and **Harrah's**, on 131 Main Street in Black Hawk (same phone). The Glory Hole includes a beautiful old bar that dates back to 1864 and one of the area's best restaurants, Emily's. In addition to some 500 slot machines and nine blackjack tables, the Glory Hole has a video arcade for kids. The Black Hawk Harrah's is more of a Las Vegas-style casino, and it, too, is well supplied with slot machines, blackjack and poker tables.

As for entertainment in addition to gambling, well, this ain't Vegas by a long shot. Harrah's and the Glory Hole have live music in the evenings (weekends only), as does the Gilpin Hotel.

Photo: Daily Camera/Lourie Zipf

Denver's 16th Street Mall offers pedestrian-friendly shopping.

Inside
Shopping

For years newcomers to Greater Denver from the East and West Coasts bemoaned the lack of good shopping. The local department stores were no match for the Saks Fifth Avenue, Nieman Marcus and Williams-Sonoma stores they'd left behind; trips to New York or Dallas were excuses for shopping binges. But as with so many other things, Denver has caught up with and in some cases surpassed the rest of the country in retail offerings. The Tattered Cover, one of the very best bookstores anywhere, has become a much-loved Denver institution that rates coverage in *Time* magazine and the *New York Times*.

The swanky new Cherry Creek Shopping Center attracts 16 million visitors a year and is in the top 2 percent of all shopping centers in the United States in sales per square foot. In fact, the Cherry Creek mall is the area's No. 1 attraction, outdrawing the U.S. Mint, Coors Brewery and the Denver museums.

As in many other cities, large department stores left Denver's downtown in the 1970s and '80s as malls were built in outlying areas. Smaller specialty stores moved in instead on downtown's major shopping thoroughfare, 16th Street, and Tabor Center, an urban mini-mall, now anchors the lower end of 16th Street. Larimer Square remains one of the city's best shopping meccas, with interesting boutiques and restaurants in this historically rich area. To the north and west of Larimer Square, in what's called LoDo (Lower Downtown), are many galleries, restaurants and sports bars.

South Broadway is the site for dozens

of antique and folk-art stores, and of course, there are islands of delight scattered throughout the city and its suburbs.

In this chapter we've focused on three major shopping areas that have a great concentration and variety of stores: Cherry Creek Shopping Center and Cherry Creek North; Downtown and Larimer Square; and South Broadway. The Cherry Creek and Larimer Square areas are small enough to walk around and that's how we've written those sections, with directions from one place to the next. South Broadway is more spread out — we survey the shops from north to south, but you'll want to travel by car or bus rather than on foot to cover the whole span.

To finish off your introduction to Denver shopping, we've included a roundup of where to go for arts and crafts, books, clothes, food and gourmet cooking supplies, furniture, gifts and outlet and bargain stores.

Most stores are open daily and accept credit cards, but call ahead to be sure.

But first, the basics: department and grocery stores. Major department stores with more than one location in Greater Denver include Foley's, Joslins, JCPenney and Mervyn's. For Western wear, both Miller Stockman and Sheplers have locations throughout the metro area. Gart Brothers, Recreational Equipment Inc. (REI) and Eastern Mountain Sports (EMS) stores supply Denverites with camping, hiking, biking, rafting and other outdoor stuff.

New to the Denver area is **Denver Sports**, which has opened two 60,000-square-foot megastores in Littleton and Westminster. Denver Sports offers a comprehensive selection of brand name sporting goods at discount prices, as well as equipment and clothing for tennis, golf, fishing, hunting, scuba diving, team sports and just about anything you can think of. The south store is at 7848 County Line Road in Littleton and the north store is at 9219 N. Sheridan Boulevard.

A top source for consumer electronics, including stereos, televisions, VCRs and cellular phones, is **SoundTrack**. There are several SoundTrack stores throughout the metro area. You'll find their Denver location at 1370 S. Colorado Boulevard.

The big supermarket chains include **King Soopers**, **Safeway** and **Albertsons**. For natural foods, visit any of the several **Alfalfa's** or **Wild Oats** markets.

Major Shopping Areas

Cherry Creek
Shopping Center

Anchored by **Lord & Taylor**, **Saks Fifth Avenue**, **Nieman Marcus** and **Foley's**, the 130 specialty stores in the Cherry Creek Shopping Center tend to be on the high end: **Louis Vuitton**, **Bally of Switzerland**, **Abercrombie & Fitch**, **F.A.O. Schwarz**. Even the restroom is above average: clad in marble, with automatic fixtures; it was written up in *Time* magazine!

Insiders' Tips

The crowds line up for Sniagrab, Gart Brothers' annual preseason ski sale held each September. As any longtime Denverite can tell you, "Sniagrab" is "bargains" spelled backward.

A street musician serenades shoppers in downtown Denver.

There is talk of developing the "old" Cherry Creek shopping center, which sits to the west of its fancy new neighbor, and indeed some large chain restaurants have moved in. Other buildings remain vacant, and the final mix of parking, shops and office buildings has yet to be determined.

Got a question about the shopping center? Call 388-3900.

The Cherry Creek Shopping Center is off First Avenue just east of University Boulevard and can be reached by public transportation; call RTD at 299-6000 for bus information.

Cherry Creek North

The neighborhood directly to the north of the mall, Cherry Creek North, is a delightful melange of interesting shops, galleries and restaurants. The showpiece here is the **Tattered Cover Book Store**, 2955 E. First Avenue. With three floors of books, thousands of titles in stock at any given time, cozy armchairs for undisturbed reading and great service, the Tattered Cover is the bookstore of your dreams. The Tattered Cover stocks many out-of-state newspapers and foreign magazines as well as hard-to-find literary journals. Watch the Sunday papers or call 322-1965 ext. 7446 for information on book signings and other special events. The Tattered Cover also has a branch in Lower Downtown Denver, at 1628 16th Street (at Wynkoop), near Union Station.

Down the block at the corner of Milwaukee Street and Second Avenue are two furniture stores, each with a different emphasis. At **Roche-Bobois International Design Center**, 201 Milwaukee Street, the look is sleek and European. Across the street at **Expressions**, 3007 E. Second Avenue, a custom furniture store, there's more fabric and less leather. If you're looking for something to hang above the sofa, **Saks Galleries**, 3019 E. Second Avenue, carries 19th- and 20th-century representational art.

Tired of buying compact discs because you've heard one song on the radio, only to find out the rest of the album stinks? You need never have that experience again if you shop at **Disky Business**, 2960 E. Second Avenue (at the corner of Milwaukee Street and Second Avenue), where it's possible to listen to every compact disc or tape in the store before making a purchase. The store has about a dozen comfortable listening areas.

Pismo Contemporary Art Glass, 235 Fillmore Street, stocks an unmatched selection of art glass by Coloradans Brian Maytum, Kit Karbler and internationally known glass artist Dale Chihuly in its luxurious gallery. More art glass can be found at **International Villa**, 262 Fillmore Street.

Some of Colorado's best crafts artists exhibit their works at **Panache**, 315 Columbine Street. Here you'll find feather necklaces, handmade jewelry, award-winning ceramics by Steve Schrepferman and larger-than-life-size papier-mâché and mixed-media critters by local artist DeDe Larue. **Show of Hands**, 2610 E. Third Avenue, and **Artisan Center**, 2757 E. Third Avenue, have more utilitarian crafts.

The belts and jewelry at **Body Art**, 250 Fillmore Street, are expensive but unusual and classy. For young, up-to-the-minute designer clothing for women, visit **Ma Lex**, 2825 E. Third Avenue. The store also carries a small selection of men's wear. **Tapestry**, 286 Fillmore Street, has women's clothing, jewelry and accessories with an ethnic flair. Some items are one-of-a-kind. Another source for funky clothing and inexpensive jewelry for men and women is **Eccentricity**, 2440 E. Third Avenue. The highlights at **Applause**, 2827 E. Third Avenue, are the unique selection of kids' clothing and the handpainted children's furniture.

More kid stuff can be found at **The Wizard's Chest**, 230 Fillmore Street, which in addition to children's toys carries grown-up games and an attic full of costumes and masks. **Kazoo & Company**, 2930 E. Second Avenue, has educational games and toys. They have a branch in the mall, too.

Gardeners will love the **Smith & Hawken** store at 268 Detroit Street. Shop for high-quality gardening tools, workwear, containers, plants and garden furniture. **The Urban Gardener**, 3039 E. Third Avenue, also stocks gardening equipment, but most of their merchandise has more to do with decorating than with grubbing around in the dirt. Owned by an interior designer, the store changes with the seasons and carries everything from clothing to cosmetics to bed linens.

Hermitage Antiquarian Bookshop, 290 Fillmore Street, is a pleasant spot with neat library stacks of first editions and other rare or old books. And **Shalako East**, 3023 E. Second Avenue, has a fine selection of Native American arts and jewelry.

Downtown and Larimer Square

Traditionally downtown Denver's main shopping thoroughfare, 16th Street was transformed into a tree-lined pedestrian mall in 1980 through 1982. Free shuttle buses run the length of the mall, connecting Lower Downtown with the Civic Center area. Many of the stores along 16th Street are touristy, but it's worth strolling the mile-long stretch to see what's here. A relatively new arrival, **MediaPlay**, at the corner of 16th and California streets, has a

Check out the museum shops at the Denver Art Museum, the Denver Museum of Natural History and the Arvada Center for the Arts and Humanities, among others, for unusual and handcrafted gifts.

Insiders' Tips

large selection of discounted books and music. Restaurants along the mall often have outdoor seating — great for people-watching — and there are shaded benches for those who've brought their own lunch. If you haven't planned ahead, buy a to-go lunch from a street vendor or fast-food restaurant. One of our favorite sidewalk vendors is the guy with the hot dog cart at 16th Street and Glenarm Place who keeps an opera tape playing.

The best shopping takes place at the glass-enclosed, three-story **Tabor Center**, 572-6868, which extends along 16th Street from Arapahoe to Larimer. The more than 65 stores here range from card and coffee boutiques to a branch of **Brooks Brothers** and Colorado's only **Sharper Image** store, which carries high-tech gizmos and gadgets you didn't know you needed until you saw them. **Africa House** has wonderful African arts and crafts including fine textiles. There's a food court here, too, should you feel a little peckish.

The heart of Larimer Square is Larimer Street between 15th and 14th streets. From Tabor Center, walk one block south through the cluster of stores and restaurants called **Writer Square**, and you'll be standing on the spot where Denver got its start in 1858. It was on this block that Denver's first bank, bookstore, photographer and dry-goods store were located. The original buildings were made of wood and destroyed in a fire in 1863; the brick structures that now line the street were erected

for the most part in the 1870s to '90s, and the entire area was renovated in the mid-1970s. Interested visitors can pick up a walking-tour brochure and information on the individual buildings at the kiosk on the east side of the street. (It's open 8 AM to 5 PM daily.)

Larimer Square has a nice mix of shops and restaurants, including a very upscale shoe store, **Garbarini**; a hip women's clothing store, **Max**; and branches of **Talbot's**, **Ann Taylor**, **Laura Ashley** and **Williams-Sonoma**. **Gibson's Bookstore**, 1404 Larimer Street, is an independent bookstore with an emphasis on literature and a knowledgeable staff. The store carries both new and used textbooks. **Cry Baby Ranch** has Western furnishings and trinkets while the **Squash Blossom Gallery** is known for its outstanding selection of Southwestern jewelry and crafts. **J. Howell Gallery** spotlights fine crafts by Coloradans, and **The Market** has an exhaustive selection of gourmet goodies, as well as coffee, deli and bakery items to take out or eat on the premises. **Z Gallerie**, on the corner of 15th and Larimer Streets, has contemporary home furnishings and accessories.

American Costume at 1526 Blake Street has over 10,000 costumes in stock. Whether you're looking for something offbeat for Halloween, or are slated to play Santa at the office party, they'll suit you up. At this point you're just a few blocks from the **Tattered Cover Bookstore**'s LoDo branch, at 16th and Wynkoop streets.

Insiders' Tips

The historic old business district of downtown Littleton, centered on W. Main Street and packed with shops and restaurants, celebrates three major annual events: the River Festival in June, Western Welcome Week in August and the Candlelight Walk in November. For more information call Virginia Morrison, 798-1142.

The Cherry Creek Shopping Center has some big-name department stores and 130 specialty shops.

A few blocks to the north, across the street from the Market Street RTD Station, is a fine representational art gallery, the **Merrill Gallery of Fine Art Ltd.**, formerly Carol Siple, at 1401 17th Street. Down the block at 1510 17th Street is the **Persian Rug Co.**, which stocks investment-quality Persian rugs and imports.

The 1700 block of Wazee Street (coming up on your right) was once the heart of Denver's contemporary art district; it still is, in a sense, although closures and additions have shifted the emphasis away from the avant-garde. We write more about that in the Arts chapter. For shoppers, the places to keep in mind are the **Allure Rug Studio** and the **Art of Craft**.

Allure Rug Studio, 1719 Wazee Street, has distinctive modern rugs that average $35 to $40 a square foot. The studio will design a rug to your specifications, working from a photograph or description and using whatever colors you choose. They also have rugs of their own design in stock, all made on the premises.

The Art of Craft, 1736 Wazee, has fine

crafts from the functional to the decorative in an elegant gallery space as well as some paintings.

A bit farther uptown, collectors of Native-American crafts head for one of the two Denver outlets of the **Mudhead Gallery**, in the Hyatt Regency Hotel, 555 17th Street, or the Brown Palace Hotel, 321 17th Street.

The **Native American Trading Company**, a fine source for pots, textiles and Edward S. Curtis photogravures, is across from the Denver Art Museum at 1301 Bannock Street. Next door is **Chamisa Company**, 215 W. 13th Avenue, which displays its rustic Southwestern furniture, accessories and antiques in a two-story, homelike setting. Both stores are closed on Mondays.

On the upper, southern edge of downtown is one of Denver's most venerable stores. **Gart Brothers Sporting Goods** is at 10th Avenue and Broadway, in a wildly extravagant building known as the Sportscastle. This seven-level store stocks everything including tents, cameras, bicycles and tennis shoes. Gart Brothers has dozens of other locations throughout the state, but none so architecturally distinctive as this one.

A few blocks away at 1109 Lincoln Street is the **Denver Buffalo Company**, a sort of mini-mall that includes a trading post, art gallery, food market, deli and restaurant. You can find anything from cowboy-hat bottle openers to Western clothing to fine traditional and contemporary Western art. There's even a teepee inside the store. The food market stocks such indigenous delicacies as buffalo sticks and hickory-smoked bison jerky.

South Broadway

Because Broadway runs one-way from north to south until it becomes a two-way street south of the I-25 interchange, we've arranged our selections from north to south — the way a car or bus would travel the route.

Manos Folk Art, 101 Broadway (across the street from the Mayan Theatre), has a magical selection of Ocumicho devil ceramics, Zapotec rugs, and all kinds of masks, mirrors and furniture from Mexico and Latin America.

Fish Head Soup, 238 S. Broadway, advertises itself as carrying "contemporary folk art at working man's prices." The store's selection is eclectic and international, ranging from African carvings to painted wood figures and panels by noted self-taught artist Rev. Howard Finster.

Sheptons Antiques, 389 S. Broadway, also has an international selection of furniture and salvaged architectural elements including carved wood doors and portions of wrought-iron fences.

At **Popular Culture**, 1150 S. Broadway, the "antiques" are younger than many people alive today: the store focuses on deco moderne and other mid-20th-century

Insiders' Tips

Quaint older areas tucked throughout the city — sometimes only a block or two long — such as S. Pearl Street, Old S. Gaylord Street, Olde Town Arvada and downtown Littleton, are pleasant places to discover interesting shops and get a bite to eat.

Photo: Daily Camera/Jay Quadracci

Free shuttle buses stop at every block in the 16th Street Mall.

styles. This shop is noted for its collection of 1950s furniture and Russel Wright dinnerware.

The entire block of South Broadway between Arizona and Louisiana Avenues is lined with antique stores. The **Antique Market**, 1212 S. Broadway, and **The Antique Guild**, 1298 S. Broadway, consolidate the wares of many dealers under one roof.

A few blocks farther south is **Hooked on Glass**, 1407 S. Broadway, which specializes in Depression glass and other collectibles.

Shopping Malls

Following are the locations and phone numbers of the major outlying shopping malls.

AURORA

Aurora Mall
Off I-225 at Alameda Ave.
(Corner of Sable Blvd.)   344-4120

SOUTH DENVER

Buckingham Square
Havana St. and Mississippi Ave.   755-3232

Tamarac Square
Hampden Ave. and Tamarac Dr.   745-0055

Tiffany Plaza
Hampden Ave. and Tamarac Dr. (across the street from Tamarac Square)   771-8210

University Hills Mall
S. Colorado Blvd. and Yale Ave.   757-6787

LAKEWOOD

Villa Italia
Wadsworth Blvd. and Alameda Ave. 936-7424

Lakeside Mall
Off I-70 between Sheridan Blvd. and Harlan St.
Exits (entrance on 44th Ave.) 455-7072

LITTLETON
Southglenn Mall
University Blvd. and Arapahoe St. 795-0856

Southwest Plaza
Wadsworth Blvd. and
W. Bowles Ave. 973-5300

NORTHGLENN
Northglenn Mall
Off I-25 at 104th Ave. W. 452-5683

THORNTON
Town Center Mall
Off I-25 at 104th Ave. E. 252-0007

WESTMINSTER
Westminster Mall
Sheridan Blvd. and 88th Ave. 428-5634

Antiques

The South Broadway area, described earlier in this chapter, has the greatest concentration of antique stores in the Greater Denver area. In addition to the stores we mention by name, you're sure to find more, especially continuing farther south. Here are a few other destinations you'll want to explore:

The **Olde Town Arvada** business district is crammed with antique stores. **Elegant Glass Antiques**, 7501 Grandview Avenue, has glass and china. At **Olde Wadsworth Antiques**, 7511 Grandview Avenue, there are lots of smaller items, including toys. **Conestoga Antiques and Collectibles,** 5601 Olde Wadsworth Boulevard, has great old cookie jars and teapots. The **Arvada Antique Emporium**, 7519 Grandview Avenue, has a large and varied assortment of antiques. A stroll through this historic district will turn up even more antique stores. To get there from

central Denver, take I-70 west to Wadsworth Boulevard and exit to the north. Turn left onto Grandview Avenue just past the railroad tracks, where a sign directs traffic to "Olde Town Arvada."

The **Antique Mall of Lakewood**, 9635 W. Colfax Avenue (one block east of Kipling Street) has about 200 dealers under one roof, plus a bookstore and cafe. The general phone number is 238-6940.

Niwot has a two-block main street filled with antique shops. Auctions are sometimes held on Sundays. To get there, take I-25 north to Highway 52 west to connect with Highway 119. Niwot is about 1 mile north of the intersection of Colo. highways 52 and 119.

Our final suggestion is even farther afield: the town of **Lyons**, which lies at the mouth of St. Vrain Canyon on the way to Estes Park, about 45 minutes from downtown Denver. Antique stores dot both sides of the old-fashioned Main Street. You'll find a few that specialize in Western memorabilia. To get there from central Denver, take I-25 north to the Colo. Highway 66 Exit, then go west about 17 miles.

Arts and Crafts

For arts and crafts, make Cherry Creek North your first stop. (See Major Shopping Areas at the beginning of this chapter.)

Additional resources include:

Akente Express, 919 Park Avenue W., is an African-American heritage shop that stocks original fabrics from Africa, handmade clothing, jewelry, artwork, sculpture and all-natural, alcohol-free essential oils. **The Clay Pigeon**, 601 Ogden Street, is Denver's oldest gallery specializing exclusively in handmade works of clay, including both stoneware and porcelain.

Galeria Mexicana, 3615 W. 32nd Avenue, specializes in Latin American crafts and collectibles. **Off Center Gallery**, 7505 Grandview Avenue, Arvada, is an artists' cooperative in Olde Town Arvada that shows a range of media including cast paper, porcelain and paintings in a range of styles. You'll find both traditional and cutting-edge work here. The prices are excellent, and the gallery is in a cute neighborhood. Hours are limited, so call 467-0640 before heading out.

Old Santa Fe Pottery, 2485 S. Santa Fe Drive, houses two rows of shops filled with Oaxacan wood carvings, painted Talavera ceramics, furniture, rugs and all sorts of pottery. You'll enjoy a pretty central courtyard reminiscent of a Mexican village. **Pearls & Jewels**, 1457 S. Pearl Street, is a nifty little bead store that also offers classes in everything from basic bead-stringing to drum-making.

Skyloom Fibres, 1705 S. Pearl Street, the largest weaving, knitting, yarn, basketry and bead store in the Rocky Mountain area, is also a friendly, mellow place with a 20-page catalog of classes. It's easy to find in summer: just look for the overgrown garden that takes up the entire front yard.

Touch of Santa Fe, 6574 S. Broadway, Littleton, attracts many serious collectors of American-Indian arts and crafts who consider this the best source in Greater Denver.

Books

The behemoth **Tattered Cover Bookstore**, with its Cherry Creek and LoDo branches, dominates Greater Denver's literary scene, but Denver's readers are avid enough to support more than one general-interest bookstore. Large chains such as **Waldenbooks** and **B. Dalton Bookseller** have branches in many regional shopping malls. **Hatch's Book Stores** can be found at the University Hills and Lakeside malls, as well as in downtown Golden at 807 13th Street. Another good all-around bookstore, the **Book Rack**, has locations in Denver at 2382 S. Colorado Blvd. and in Lakewood at 1535 S. Kipling Parkway. **Doubleday** has a store in the Cherry Creek Shopping Center, among other locations.

Then there are the specialty bookstores, a few of which we list here.

Culpin's Antiquarian Bookshop, 3827 W. 32nd Avenue, housed in an old brick carriage house at the rear of the main property, has one of Greater Denver's largest selections of used and rare books, including an excellent selection of books of regional interest. They also provide an international book search service.

Cultural Legacy Bookstore, 3633 W. 32nd Avenue, is the only bookstore in Colorado to specialize in Latino literature, with Spanish, English and bilingual books and magazines for children and adults. Ask about book signings and other special events.

The **Hue-Man Experience**, 911 Park Avenue W., is an African-American bookstore that also sells African cards, jewelry and fabrics.

Murder by the Book, 1574 S. Pearl Street, a cozy store in a former home, specializes in new and used mystery novels, including a selection for children.

Reel Books, 1512 Larimer, has a vast selection of books on tape, for adults and children, to buy or rent.

Clothing

See our Cherry Creek and Larimer Square sections earlier in the chapter for a good overall roundup of clothing stores. Here are some more options to consider:

Auer's, 210 St. Paul Street, offers classic and designer fashions for women. **Barbara & Company**, 7777 E. Hampden Avenue, specializes in young-at-heart clothing and accessories, with a mix of classic and contemporary styles. It's in Tamarac Square.

The **Garment District**, 2595 S. Colorado Boulevard, offers an interesting and unusual, if somewhat pricey, selection of men's and women's contemporary clothing. At **Iris Fields**, 1099 S. Gaylord Street, you'll find very contemporary women's clothing and accessories.

Food and Gourmet Cooking Supplies

Don't forget the Market in Larimer Square. But keep in mind these other spots as well.

Many Asian food markets are along S. Federal Boulevard (many Asian restaurants are, too). Unusual fruits and vegetables, imported brands of soy sauce, fish oil and exotic herbs and spices are some of the hard-to-find items that are available here. The **Asian Center** is a two-story shopping center at the intersection of Alameda Avenue and Federal Boulevard with markets, restaurants, travel agencies and other Asian businesses; enter through the gate off Federal. One worthwhile stop here is the **Asian Market**, 333 S. Federal Boulevard, a good all-around source for produce, teas and noodles.

Farther south are **Indochina Enterprises**, 1045 S. Federal Boulevard, and the **Tan Phat Oriental Market**, 1001 S. Federal Boulevard. **Xuan Trang**, 1095 S. Federal, has tea sets and kitchen utensils as well as Asian ingredients.

Cook's Mart, 3000 E. Third Avenue, has an enormous selection of pots, pans, casseroles, whisks, imported knives and just about everything you could think of to set up a fully equipped semiprofessional kitchen.

Le Bakery Sensual, Sixth Avenue and

Grant Street, specializes in adults-only cakes that you won't find at the supermarket. This store is definitely not for everyone.

Pacific Mercantile Co., 1925 Lawrence Street, offers an astonishing selection of Asian foods, many of which will be unrecognizable to the average American cook. For chefs looking for a specific, hard-to-find ingredient, this is a tremendous resource as well as a cultural minivacation.

Stephany's Chocolates, with several locations, are a Colorado tradition and a popular gift for visitors to take back home. (They're readily available at the airport.) The Denver Mints — get it? — are a big seller. Stephany's has stores in the Tabor Center and the Cherry Creek Shopping Center, among other locations.

Serious foodies will devour Susan Permut's book, *Adventures in Eating* (The Garlic Press), which lists ethnic markets, bakeries and gourmet food stores throughout Greater Denver.

Furniture

A number of furniture warehouses, including **Colorado Living Furniture**, 5639 N. Broadway, and **Weberg Furniture**, 5333 N. Bannock Street, are along the west side of I-25 (take the 58th Avenue Exit and go south). Quality and prices vary, but it's worth stopping to at least comparison shop the offerings. We've also mentioned a few furniture stores in our Cherry Creek section.

Decor Southwest, 9100 W. Sixth Avenue, Lakewood, specializes in handcrafted Southwestern furniture and accessories; other styles are available as well. **Howard Lorton Galleries**, 12 E. 12th Avenue (at Broadway), is a well-established purveyor of high-end, classic home furnishings. **Lakewood Furniture**, 8990 W. Colfax Av-

enue, Lakewood, features a funky mishmash ranging from cowboy-style lodgepole pine to futons and traditional furniture, custom-made or ready-to-finish. **Whitney's of Cherry Hills**, 5910 S. University Boulevard, Littleton, features traditional but not stuffy home furnishings in the grand manner.

Gifts

In a sense, this category exists for stores we couldn't fit anyplace else, because at this point in the chapter, we've listed dozens of places to buy gifts — from gourmet food stores to arts and crafts cooperatives. But here are six more of our favorites that you won't want to miss.

Colorado in a Basket, 6005 E. Evans Avenue No. 101, is the place to look for that quintessential Colorado gift. This company prepares a variety of baskets filled with Colorado products, or you can make up your own selection. Prices begin at $25. Stop by the showroom, or call 756-4778 for a brochure.

Kobun Sha, 1255 19th Street, is in colorful Sakura Square. Kobun Sha carries futons, Japanese shoji screens, lamps, ukiyo-e print postcards and cards, dolls, kites, tea sets and other Japanese gift items, as well as an extensive line of English-language books on Japanese subjects.

The Perfect Setting, 4992 E. Hampden Avenue, in the Happy Canyon Shopping Center, specializes in classy wedding gifts. **Thistle & Shamrock**, 407 17th Street, features Scottish and Irish imports, including clothing, jewelry, fine china and assorted collectibles.

Treasures and Trifles, 8350 Washington Street in Thornton, has books, antiques, and gifts. It's a good place to know about if you live or shop up north.

For collectors of figurines (Hummel,

Armani, Royal Doulton, Swarovski crystal and many others), **Kathie's Import Chalet**, 3971 S. Broadway in Englewood, is a treasure trove. They also stock music boxes, cuckoo clocks, dolls, nutcrackers and Christmans ornaments.

Outlet and Bargain Shopping

Off-price retailers with multiple locations throughout the Greater Denver area include **Marshall's** and **TJ Maxx**. **The Snob Shop**, a consignment store at 2804 E. Sixth Avenue, has long been a "secret" source for designer clothing and shoes for men and women. **Loehmann's**, 7400 E. Hampden Avenue at Tiffany Plaza is primarily women's clothing.

The **Castle Rock Factory Shops**, Exit 184, Meadow Parkway, 688-2800, off I-25 south of Denver, are open seven days a week. Among the stores here are housewares (**Corning Revere**, **Farberware**), clothing (**Levi's, Guess, Geoffrey Beene**), shoe outlets (**Bass, Etienne Aigner**) and electronics (**Sony**).

Boyer's, a Denver-based coffee roaster and packager, offers its coffee and related items at lower-than-supermarket prices at three factory outlets in Greater Denver. There are stores at 747 S. Colorado Boulevard and 6820 S. University Avenue and 7295 N. Washington Street in Northglenn.

Those who know no greater pleasure in life than finding a bargain will want a copy of Lori Clark's *The Denver Bargain Hunter's Guide: Shopping in the 90's* (Consumer Wise Publications).

Inside
Tours and Attractions

In this chapter we've rounded up our favorite museums, gardens and historic houses. What Greater Denver has to offer in this category may surprise newcomers: The Natural History Museum is the fifth-largest of its kind in the country, and the Denver Art Museum is the largest such institution between Kansas City and the West Coast. Denver's Zoo and its Botanic Gardens are both highly respected, and the city is full of special-interest museums devoted to such diverse subjects as firefighters, railroads, African Americans in the West, dolls and the English painter J.M.W. Turner. Among the most popular tourist attractions in Greater Denver are the tours at the United States Mint and Coors Brewery in Golden.

We've organized this chapter by category, listing first museums; then historic houses and other historic sites; parks and gardens; and finally, tours. Readers with a particular interest in the arts may also want to check our Arts chapter, as community art centers and galleries are listed there. At the end of the chapter, we suggest ways of combining visits to different sites that are near each other, or that tie in thematically (for example, if you want to spend a day immersing yourself in Western history).

Hours and admission prices are subject to change. Also, be aware that some Greater Denver attractions either have shorter hours or are closed during winter. Please call before planning a visit.

RTD runs a Cultural Connection trol-

Photo: Daily Camera/Crissy Pascual

Klondike and Snow, polar bear cubs, enchanted Denver Zoo visitors in 1995.

ley that stops every half-hour at or near more than a dozen of Greater Denver's most popular cultural attractions, including the Denver Museum of Natural History and the Denver Botanic Gardens as well as sites downtown. For $3 a day, you can get on and off as often as you like. You can buy tickets and pick up a map at the Visitors' Information Center at 225 W. Colfax Avenue, the downtown RTD stations at Market Street and Civic Center or on the bus itself (exact change required). Make sure to pick up a map that shows the route, or call 299-6000 for up-to-date schedule information. The trolley operates from mid-May through Labor Day weekend, seven days a week, between 9:30 AM and 6:30 PM. And, your trolley pass is also good on local buses and light rail.

Attractions listed below that are on the Cultural Connection trolley route are indicated by the notation "CC trolley stop." In some cases attractions aren't directly on the route but are within walking distance, so we've provided directions.

Museums

THE DENVER
MUSEUM OF NATURAL HISTORY

2001 Colorado Blvd. (in City Park, at Colorado Blvd. and Montview)   *322-7009*
(Hearing impaired TDD)   *370-8257*

The Denver Museum of Natural History is the largest cultural attraction in the Rocky Mountain region, with an average of 1.5 million visitors annually. In addition to more than 90 dioramas depicting animals from around the world, the museum's permanent exhibitions include a Hall of Life devoted to studying the human body, a planetarium and a fine gem and mineral collection that includes examples of Colorado gold and the largest rhodochrosite gem

in the world. Other highlights include the Hall of Ancient Peoples, which deals with early man and early civilizations. Don't forget to take a look at the mummy.

In fall 1995, the museum opened one of the most impressive dinosaur exhibits in America, the $7.7 million "Prehistoric Journey." It includes walk-through "enviroramas" complete with controlled lighting and temperatures, sounds, vegetation and even bugs!

Special exhibitions at the museum range from artistic and archaeological blockbusters such as *Ramses II* and *Aztec: The World of Moctezuma* to entertaining fare such as 1994's interactive *Star Trek: Federation Science* and 1995's interactive *Science of Sport.*

The museum also houses the Gates Planetarium and an IMAX theater. The planetarium features changing star programs and laser-light shows (combined with rock music), with separate admission of $2.50 to $6. Call the recorded information line at 322-7009 or 370-6357 for details.

Recent shows at the IMAX theater — with its four-story-high screen — have included films on Africa's Serengeti and the exploration of the wreck of the *Titanic*. Admission is $5 for adults, $4 for seniors and kids ages 4 to 12. Call for show times and more information.

The museum is open every day except Christmas from 9 AM to 5 PM and until 9 PM on Fridays. Admission is $4.50 for adults, $2.50 seniors and children 4 to 12. Combination museum and planetarium or IMAX theater tickets are available; call or ask at the museum for more information. Also, some special exhibitions require an additional charge and advance reservations. The museum has a cafeteria-style restaurant and deli. (CC trolley stop)

See you at the zoo.

denver ZOO
OPEN EVERY DAY

THE DENVER ART MUSEUM

100 W. 14th Ave. Pkwy.	640-4433
recorded information	640-2793

The Denver Art Museum is the largest art museum between Kansas City and the West Coast and is especially noted for its superb collections of Native American, pre-Columbian and Spanish colonial art. Its six floors also house impressive displays of American, Asian and contemporary art, and galleries devoted to design, graphics and architecture.

The museum building itself, completed in 1971, is artistically noteworthy. Designed by Milan architect Gio Ponti in association with Denver architect James Sudler, the fortress-like seven-level building has a 28-sided tiled exterior with uniquely shaped windows. Most of the collections have been re-installed in recent years as part of an ongoing renovation. By 1997, the museum will

have a new entrance onto Acoma Plaza, an underground connection with the new Central Library, and permanent exhibition space for its European and textile collections.

In addition to its permanent collections, the museum hosts many traveling exhibitions, some of which travel to very few venues in the United States. *Mongolia: The Legacy of Chinggis Khan*, exhibited at the museum in fall/winter 1995-96, visited only San Francisco, Denver and Washington, D.C. Check newspaper listings, or call for a schedule of current and upcoming shows.

Choice Tours are free with admission and are scheduled daily at 1:30 PM with an additional tour Saturday at 11 AM. Tours can be scheduled at other times, so call ahead. Family programs are held every Saturday. The museum has a shop and cafe, but these facilities may be closed at times

Photo: Denver Metro Convention & Visitors Bureau

The Denver Museum of Natural History is one of the area's top attractions.

during the two-year renovation that began in earnest in mid-1995. The museum is open Tuesday through Saturday from 10 AM to 5 PM and Sundays from noon to 5 PM; it's closed Mondays and major holidays. As we went to press, the museum was experimenting with extended hours (until 9 PM) Wednesday nights. Admission is $3 adults, $1.50 seniors and students with ID, $1.50 ages 6 to 18 and free for children 5 and younger. Saturdays are free, thanks to funding provided by the Scientific and Cultural Facilities District. (CC trolley stop)

THE MUSEUM OF WESTERN ART
1727 Tremont Pl.   *296-1880*

The Museum of Western Art is housed in the Victorian-era Navarre Building, once a fancy downtown bordello and gambling hall (visitors can peek at a secret tunnel between the building and the Brown Palace Hotel, across the street). Artists exhibited include Frederic Remington, Charles Russell, Georgia O'Keeffe, Thomas Moran, Albert Bierstadt and Norman Rockwell. The museum is open Tuesday through Saturday from 10 AM to 4:30 PM. Admission is $3 adults, $2 students and seniors, and free for children younger than 7. Group and guided tours are available. The museum shop stocks books, jewelry, artifacts and art prints.

(CC trolley stop — get off at 15th and Welton streets, walk back two blocks, turn left on Tremont and walk three blocks.)

MUSEUM OF OUTDOOR ARTS
7600 E. Orchard Rd.
Englewood   *741-3609*

More than 50 outdoor sculptures comprise this "museum without walls" in the 400-acre Greenwood Plaza Business Park in the Denver Tech Center area. You can do a self-guided tour, or call to schedule a guided group tour. We recommend the children's art classes, offered year round. Visitors can view the art on their own during daylight hours for free; for guided tours, the cost is $3 adults, $1 children 17 and younger.

THE TURNER MUSEUM
773 Downing St.   *832-0924*

This unexpected treasure trove devoted to the works of English painter J.M.W. Turner has been ranked by *The Atlantic Monthly* as one of the 99 finest museums in the United States. Its impressive collection of roughly 3,000 Turner objects includes 700 of the 800 prints Turner is known to have made. There are also works on paper by Turner's American admirer Thomas Moran, the great 19th-century landscape painter. Hours are 2 to 5 PM every day except Saturday, or by appointment. The admission fee of $7.50 includes a personalized tour by the curator, Dou-

---

Those with a taste for the macabre can visit the grave of Alferd Packer in the Littleton Cemetery, 6155 S. Prince Street. Colorado's most famous convicted cannibal, Mr. Packer went into the mountains with his party of prospectors in the winter of 1874 and emerged alone the following spring. Seems he had survived by eating his companions. He died in 1907, a year after getting out of prison.

Insiders' Tips

glas Graham. Or, guests may come for breakfast, lunch, high tea or a candlelight dinner on a donation basis ($10 to $25). To appeal to yet another of the five senses, the museum hosts about 10 concerts of classical music each year.

Please note that the museum expects to move in April 1996 but doesn't know where. Call first if you're planning a visit after this date.

COLORADO HISTORY MUSEUM

1300 Broadway   *866-3682*

The Colorado History Museum offers permanent and changing exhibitions about state history. The museum has an outstanding collection of William Henry Jackson photos, a large diorama of Denver as it appeared in 1860 and a comprehensive research library that is free and open to the public Tuesday through Saturday from 10 AM to 4:30 PM. Special exhibits have included everything from photography retrospectives to a display of Vatican treasures that coincided with Pope John Paul II's visit to Denver in 1993. As part of what is called the Civic Center Cultural Complex, the history museum, the library and the art museum are collaborating on programs and sharing resources. The first collaborative exhibition is *Colorado: One Land, Many Visions*, in the spring of 1996. A different portion of the exhibition will be at each of the three locations. The museum is open Monday through Saturday from 10 AM to 4:30 PM and Sundays from noon to 4:30 PM. Admission is $3 adults, $2.50 for seniors 65 and older and for students with ID, $1.50 for kids 6 to 16 and free for children younger than 6. (CC trolley stop)

THE BLACK AMERICAN WEST MUSEUM AND HERITAGE CENTER

3091 California St.   *292-2566*

The Black American West Museum is a small but fascinating place that sets a lot of records straight and provides a long-buried picture of the role played by black Americans on the frontier. For example, few people know that the first black mayor of a major American city was Francisco Reyes, owner of the San Fernando Valley until he sold it in the 1790s and became the mayor of Los Angeles. The 1950 Van Heflin movie *Tomahawk* featured white actor Jack Okie playing explorer Jim Beckwourth, who discovered Beckwourth Pass through the Sierras. The movie's only problem is, Beckwourth was black, as were up to one-third of all cowboys in the early West. The museum is housed in the former home of Dr. Justina L. Ford, Colorado's first licensed African-American female doctor. It is open Monday through Friday 10 AM to 5 PM, Saturday and Sunday noon to 5 PM. Admission is $3 adults, $2 seniors and students, 75¢ for students ages 13 to 17 and 50¢ for children 4 to 12.

MUSEO DE LAS AMERICAS

861 Santa Fe Dr.   *571-4401*

Denver's newest museum is the first in the Rocky Mountain region dedicated to Latin-American art, history and culture. Officially opened in July 1994, the Museo de las Americas showcases art from all the Americas, including the Caribbean, in changing exhibitions. The museum supplements its temporary exhibitions with lectures, workshops and other educational programs and intends to build a small permanent collection. It has twice shown an exhibition jointly with the Denver Art Museum, with some of the material at the art museum and some at the museo: in 1994, with a folk art exhibition, and in 1995-96, with a large-scale traveling show of Latin-American women artists. Hours and admission charges are still being determined; call first, and be sure to ask about current

African-American Cowboys Tamed and Defined the West

"The greatest sweat and dirt cowhand that ever lived — bar none." That's how Bill Pickett was described by the owner of one of Oklahoma's biggest ranches. Pickett was a black cowboy. By some estimates, as many as a third of all cowboys may have been black men back when the West was still wild.

"Among the cowboys of the last frontier, five thousand black men helped drive cattle up the Chisholm Trail after the Civil War," writes William Loren Katz in his eye-opening book, *The Black West*. "The typical trail crew of eight usually included two black cowboys."

Pickett is probably the most famous black cowboy, having virtually invented the sport of bulldogging, leaping from a horse to wrestle a steer to the ground. Pickett added the flourish of biting the steer's upper lip and dragging it down with nothing but his teeth. Pickett became a rodeo star, and among his early assistants were Will Rogers and Tom Mix before they went on to careers of their own. He was the first black man elected to the Cowboy Hall of Fame in Oklahoma City, and his name lives today in the Bill Pickett Rodeo.

But Pickett, of course, was just one of the many black cowboys valued on the frontier, where a man's skill, courage and industry still counted more than the color of his skin.

"There was a dignity, a cleanliness and a reliability about him that was wonderful," said Charles Goodnight, founder of the Goodnight-Loving Trail, of Bose Ikard, one of his black cowboys. "I have trusted him farther

Photo: Denver Metro Convention & Visitors Center

Paul Stewart curates the Black American West Museum in Denver.

than any living man. He was my detective, banker, and everything else in Colorado, New Mexico, and any other wild country I was in."

As civilization closed in with its institutionalized racism, however, the era of the black cowboy waned. Nat Love, for example, was widely known as Deadwood Dick after he won a number of rodeo events in the Dakota Territory's Deadwood City in 1876. An ex-slave who was adopted by an Indian tribe and counted Bat Masterson, a famous Dodge City sheriff, among his friends, Love led an action-filled life of cattle drives, gun battles and colorful adventures. As age advanced and the 20th Century dawned, however, Love ended his career as a Pullman porter.

programming. As a general rule, the museo is open Tuesday through Saturday 10 AM to 5 PM and charges $2 adults, $1 seniors and students age 10 and older and is free for members and children younger than 10. It's easy to get there on light rail; check a map or call RTD at 299-6000 for instructions.

COLORADO RAILROAD MUSEUM
17155 W. 44th Ave.
Golden   *279-4591*

One of our personal favorites, this museum houses more than 50 historic locomotives and cars, as well as additional exhibits, in a 12-acre outdoor setting. Don't miss the D&RG Engine *No. 346*, the oldest operating locomotive in Colorado. The museum is open daily from 9 AM to 5 PM (until 6 PM June through August). Admission is $3.50 adults, $3 seniors older than 60, $1.75 for kids younger than 16. Family admission is $7.50 (two parents and children younger than 16). To get to the museum, take Exit 265 off I-70 westbound and follow the signs. The No. 17 bus stops at the museum hourly on weekdays only; call RTD at 299-6000 for schedule information.

FORNEY TRANSPORTATION MUSEUM
1416 Platte St.   *433-3643*

Located in a former streetcar powerhouse building, the Forney Transportation Museum displays all kinds of old vehicles, including a number of one-of-a-kinds. Of special interest are the world's largest steam locomotive, Prince Aly Khan's Rolls Royce Phantom I and an original McCormick reaper. The museum, which has both indoor and outdoor exhibits, is open Monday through Saturday 9 AM to 5 PM May through September; Monday through Saturday 10 AM to 5 PM October through April; and Sundays from 11 AM to 5 PM year round. It's closed on Christmas, Thanksgiving and New Year's Day. Admission is $4 adults, $2 ages 12 to 18 and $1 ages 5 to 11.

BUFFALO BILL
MEMORIAL MUSEUM AND GRAVE
987½ Lookout Mountain Rd.
Golden   *526-0747*

Dramatically located on top of Lookout Mountain, this fascinating museum is filled with memorabilia honoring the famous frontier scout, showman and Pony Express rider William F. Cody, colloquially known as Buffalo Bill. Included are gun collections, costumes and posters from the Wild West show and a collection of dime novels. The grave site affords an expansive view of the plains to the east and mountains to the west (and, less attractively, the rampant construction of large houses on the nearby hillsides). The museum is

Photo: Denver Metro Convention & Visitors Bureau

The Colorado Railroad Museum has attractions for all ages.

open daily 9 AM to 5 PM May through October; 9 AM to 4 PM the rest of the year. It's closed Mondays in the winter. Admission is $2 adults, $1.50 seniors, $1 for children 6 to 15 and free for children younger than 6.

DENVER FIREFIGHTERS MUSEUM

1326 Tremont Pl.   892-1436

Housed in Station No. 1, which was built in 1909, the museum has a collection of original hand-drawn firefighting equipment, two engines from the 1920s and various antique firefighting memorabilia, including helmets, uniforms and trophies. The museum is open from 10 AM to 2 PM Monday through Friday. Admission is $2 adults, $1 children 12 and younger.

(CC trolley stop — get off at 14th and California streets at the Colorado Convention Center and walk two blocks ahead (east); turn right on Tremont.)

DENVER MUSEUM OF MINIATURES, DOLLS AND TOYS

Pearce-McAllister Cottage
1880 N. Gaylord St.   322-3704

The two-story Pearce-McAllister Cottage, built in 1899, is of interest both for its architecture and original decor and for its changing displays of vintage dolls, dollhouses, toys and miniatures housed on the second floor. The museum is open 10 AM to 4 PM Tuesday through Saturday and 1 to 4 PM Sundays (closed major holidays). Admission is $3 adults, $2 senior citizens and $2 ages 2 to 16, and includes a tour of both the cottage and museum. A group discount rate is available. (CC trolley stop)

MIZEL MUSEUM OF JUDAICA

560 S. Monaco Pkwy.   333-4156

This, the Rocky Mountain region's only

If you're planning to take in a lot of sights in one day, consider an RTD day pass. For $3 you can get on and off local buses as often as you like.

Insiders' Tips

museum of Judaica, was established in 1982. Special programs, workshops, speakers, seminars and films are designed to complement the museum's changing exhibitions, whether drawn from its own collection or borrowed from such prestigious institutions as the Israel Museum and the Smithsonian Institution. Hours are Tuesday to Thursday 10 AM to 4 PM, Friday 10 AM to 3 PM and Sunday 10 AM to noon. Closed Monday and Saturday. Admission is free.

ROCKY MOUNTAIN QUILT MUSEUM
1111 Washington Ave.
Golden   *277-0377*

As much a resource center for quilters as a museum, the tiny Rocky Mountain Quilt Museum has more than 150 old and new quilts in its collection. Exhibits change every two months. Quilts and other needlework are offered for sale at the museum, which also conducts classes and outreach programs. The museum is open 10 AM to 4 PM Tuesday through Saturday. Admission is $1 for adults and free for children younger than 16.

Historic Houses/Museums and Other Historic Sites

BYERS-EVANS HOUSE AND DENVER HISTORY MUSEUM
1310 Bannock St.   *620-4933*

John Evans was Colorado's second territorial governor. William Byers founded the *Rocky Mountain News*. Both men and their families were prominent during Denver's early years, and their names appear on avenues and mountain peaks. This house, built by Byers in 1883 and sold to Evans' son in 1889, has been restored to the 1912-24 period. The two rooms at the entrance (the former service wing) now house the Denver History Museum and its

interactive video displays. The house and museum are open Tuesday through Sunday from 11 AM to 3 PM. Admission is $3 adults, $2.50 seniors and $1.50 for kids 6 to 16. Combination tickets including entrance to the Colorado History Museum are $5 adults, $4 seniors and $2 for kids 6 to 16. (CC trolley stop)

MOLLY BROWN HOUSE MUSEUM
1340 Pennsylvania St.   *832-4092*

Only Baby Doe Tabor can match Molly Brown for name recognition among turn-of-the-century Denver women. Each has had her life memorialized in song: Baby Doe, in the opera *The Ballad of Baby Doe*, and Molly Brown, in the Broadway musical *The Unsinkable Molly Brown*. Molly was one of early Denver's more flamboyant characters, who achieved true heroine status for her actions during the sinking of the *Titanic*, which she survived. Her Victorian home has been restored and furnished in period style with many personal mementos and possessions. The museum is open at different hours depending on the season and closed on holidays, so call first. Admission is $3.50 adults, $2.50 seniors, $1.50 for kids 6 to 12 and free for children younger than 6. Prices are expected to rise in 1996. A number of special dinners, teas, readings and workshops are scheduled throughout the year; call 832-4092 for more information. (CC trolley stop)

COLORADO STATE CAPITOL
Broadway and Colfax Ave.   *866-2604*

The Colorado State Capitol stands exactly 1 mile above sea level. On the 15th step there's a carving stating the elevation as 5,280 feet high, but a small brass plaque on the 18th step corrects the carving and proclaims itself the true mile-high marker. Inside the capitol building, free tours are given weekdays and in the summer on Saturdays, too (from 9:30 AM to 2:30 PM). Tours start at the entrance north of Colfax, last about 45 minutes and leave between 9:15 AM and 3 PM weekdays, depending on demand. Those with strong legs and lungs can climb the 93 steps to the top of the gold-plated dome for a view over the plains and mountains. Although the gold on the outside of the dome tends to receive more attention from casual passersby, the real precious mineral is on the inside of the building, where rose-colored Colorado onyx was used as wainscoting. The onyx came from a small quarry in Beulah, Colorado, and has never been mined elsewhere. (CC trolley stop)

COLORADO GOVERNOR'S MANSION
400 E. Eighth Ave. 837-8350
(tours) 866-3682

Completed in 1907, the governor's mansion was originally the private residence of the Walter Scott Cheesman family. In 1927 the house was sold to the Boettcher family, and in 1960 the Boettcher Foundation gave the property to the state to use as the governor's mansion. The Colonial Revival structure contains artwork from all around the world and a Waterford chandelier that once hung in the White House. The mansion can be visited on Tuesday afternoons between 1 and 3 PM from May through August. Tours leave every 10 minutes. Two twilight tours are offered, one in late June, the other in July. The mansion is open to the public for a week during December when it's decorated for Christmas. Call for dates, as these vary every year.

FOUR MILE HISTORIC PARK
715 S. Forest St. 399-1859

Designated a Denver Landmark in 1968, Four Mile Historic Park commemorates the site of a former stagestop and contains the oldest home still standing in Denver. In addition to the 1859 log home, visitors can tour the living history farmstead and, on nice days, have a picnic here. Stagecoach rides are available every weekend between 11 AM and 2 PM, for $1 a person. Special events days are held about six times a year and include horsedrawn wagon rides and demonstrations of blacksmithing, butter churning and other chores. There are living history re-enactments of Civil War events during the spring and summer.

Photo: Denver Metro Convention & Visitors Bureau

The Littleton Historical Museum is a real working turn-of-the-century farm.

Hours are Wednesday through Sunday from 10 AM to 4 PM, April through September. Admission is $3.50 adults, $2 seniors and students 6 to 15 and free for children younger than 6. The park recently added winter hours; call for information.

FAIRMOUNT CEMETERY

430 S. Quebec Ave.   399-0692

This 360-acre privately owned cemetery dates back to 1890 and is the final resting place for many former mayors, socialites, gunfighters, madams and Civil War veterans. An infamous "resident" is Col. John M. Chivington, responsible for the massacre of defenseless Indians at Sand Creek in 1864. The grounds contain more than 200 types of trees, and tours are given twice a year by the Denver Botanic Gardens for those interested in this aspect of the cemetery. Self-guided tours are possible anytime (a guidebook can be purchased at the site), and free guided tours are conducted from 10 AM to noon on Saturdays after Memorial Day and continuing through October. Call ahead to reserve a spot on the tour.

RIVERSIDE CEMETERY

5201 Brighton Blvd.
Commerce City   293-2466

Denver's oldest cemetery, founded in 1876, contains the graves of three Civil War medal-of-honor winners; Augusta Tabor, the first wife of turn-of-the-century silver baron Horace Tabor; and Colorado's first black ballplayer, Oliver E. Marcel. Visitors can pick up a booklet and map for $2 during office hours, 8:30 AM to 4:30 PM Monday through Thursday and 10 AM to 4:30 PM Friday. The office is closed weekends. The cemetery is on Brighton Boulevard about 2 miles north of I-70.

LITTLETON HISTORICAL MUSEUM

6028 S. Gallup St.
Littleton   795-3950

This living history museum consists of a reconstructed 1860s homestead and a turn-of-the-century farm that re-create pioneer life. Among the original buildings on the 14-acre site are a 1910 ice house, a sheep and goat shelter originally built as a settler's cabin in the 1860s, an 1890s farmhouse and the first schoolhouse in Littleton. Three galleries in the main museum building feature changing exhibits. Outdoors, costumed staff and volunteers care for the chickens and livestock and go about the business of tending a 19th-century farm. They're not too busy to stop and explain things to visitors, however. Admission is free (large groups are charged a small fee and should call first). The museum is open Tuesday through Friday 8 AM to 5 PM, Saturday from 10 AM to 5 PM and Sundays from 1 to 5 PM; it's closed Mondays and major holidays.

BELMAR VILLAGE

797 S. Wadsworth Blvd.
Lakewood   987-7850

A historic site and museum with several structures, including an 1880s farm house and a 1920s schoolhouse, Belmar Village also has a barn gallery with changing exhibits. The visitors center has a permanent exhibit on May Bonfils, daughter of one of the founders of *The Denver Post*, and exhibits of work by local artists that change monthly. Admission is free and includes a tour. Hours are 10 AM to 4 PM Monday through Friday and 1 to 5 PM Saturday (10 AM to 5 PM in summer); it's closed Sundays and holidays. Ask about special children's programs. Groups of five or more should make reservations.

Parks and Gardens

THE DENVER ZOO

City Park, E. 23rd Ave. and Steele St.
(near Natural History Museum)   *331-4100*

Easily combined with a trip to the Natural History Museum, the Denver Zoo has the usual complement of lions and tigers and (polar) bears, as well as monkeys and birds, in a mix of enclosed and open habitat areas. Its newest attraction, the $10 million Tropical Discovery exhibit, opened in late 1993 and is designed to re-create a rain-forest habitat inside a glass-enclosed pyramid. More than 240 animal species live here, nearly double what the zoo had previously. There is a separate nursery area where new arrivals needing human help get their first taste of what it's like to be in the public eye. Primate Panorama, a five-acre, all-natural habitat, is slated to open in late summer 1996 (the zoo's centennial year), to be followed by a new education building in fall 1996. The zoo is open daily from 9 AM to 6 PM in summer, 10 AM to 5 PM in winter, with some exhibits closing earlier. Admission is $6 adults, $3 seniors and children ages 4 to 12, and free for children 3 and younger. About seven free days for Colorado residents are scheduled throughout the year; call for exact dates. (CC trolley stop)

DENVER BOTANIC GARDENS

1005 York St.   *331-4000*

One of Greater Denver's most lovely refuges, the Botanic Gardens encompasses 21 acres and includes a rose garden, herb garden and other specialty gardens. The 1-acre rock alpine garden is considered one of the finest in the country. Our personal favorite is the lovely Japanese Shofu-en (Garden of Pine Wind) designed by America's foremost Japanese landscaper, Koichi Kawana. It is complete with an authentic teahouse. Local residents look to the water-saving xeriscape demonstration garden and the home demonstration garden for ideas they can put into use in their own yards. A tropical conservatory and pavilion houses orchids, bromeliads and other warmth-loving species. Outdoor concerts are held here in the summer; come early and bring a picnic dinner.

The Botanic Gardens are open daily from 9 AM to 5 PM and until 8 PM on selected summer evenings. Summer admission (May through September) is $4 adults, $2 for seniors and students with ID, $2 for ages 6 to 15 and free for children younger than 6 when accompanied by an adult. Reduced admission prices apply October through April. (CC trolley stop)

ELITCH GARDENS

I-25 and Speer Blvd. (Exit 212 A)   *595-4386*

For over 100 years, Elitch Gardens was a west Denver tradition. Opened in May 1890 as Elitch Zoological Gardens by John and Mary Elitch, it boasted three thrilling roller coasters: the Wildcat, the wooden Twister and the Sidewinder.

In the spring of 1995, Elitch's reopened in a larger, 68-acre location in the Central Platte River Valley just off the Speer Boulevard Exit from I-25. (At night, all lit up, it's a beautiful and memorable sight for any-

When Denver's dry winter weather chaps your cheeks and lips, sneak off and spend a restorative hour or two in the warm, humid, fragrant environment of the Botanic Gardens conservatory.

Insiders' Tips

one driving through Denver on the interstate.) A rebuilt, 100-foot-high Twister II is one of the top attractions. There are 23 major rides in all, including a new water ride, plus a 300-foot high observation tower and Kiddieland. The 1925 carousel made the move downtown, and in time there'll be a multipurpose building for theater, dance and special events.

It's best to call first for information about prices and park hours, as these vary with the seasons. In general, Elitch's is open daily from 10 AM until at least 8 PM from Memorial Day through Labor Day. Admission (including all rides and entertainment) is $19.95 adults; $15.50 children ages 5 and older; $7.75 children 3 and 4 years of age. Height figures into the price, and taller-than-average kids may find themselves in the adult category. Admission is free for kids 2 and younger and there's a discount price for seniors. Parking is $3 per vehicle.

LAKESIDE AMUSEMENT PARK
4601 Sheridan Blvd.
(I-70 and Sheridan) 477-1621

An all-ages amusement park, Lakeside has a merry-go-round, a Ferris wheel, a roller coaster and other exciting rides. One of the best things to do at Lakeside is to ride the train around the lake after dark. The park is open from May through Labor Day weekend. In May, the park is open on weekends only; starting in mid-June and continuing through mid-August, Lakeside is open seven days a week, reverting to the weekends-only schedule at the end of the summer. Kids younger than 8 are welcome in the kiddie playland from 1 PM on weekdays, but the major rides don't begin operating until 6 PM weekdays and noon on weekends. Gate admission is $1.50 a person. An unlimited ride ticket costs $9.75 a person weekdays; $11.25 Saturdays, Sundays and holidays. Individual ride coupons

can also be purchased. Prices are the same for adults and children.

Tours

UNITED STATES MINT
320 W. Colfax Ave. 844-3582

One of Denver's most popular tourist attractions, the Mint produces 10 billion coins each year. Free tours are conducted weekdays from 8 AM to 2:45 PM except for the last day of each month when tours begin at 9 AM. The 15-minute tours are first-come, first-served and leave every 15 to 20 minutes from the Cherokee Street entrance. Children younger than 14 must be accompanied by an adult. Wheelchairs are OK but cameras are not: no photos can be taken inside the building. Hours for coin sales are the same as tour hours. The Mint is closed on all legal holidays and for one week in summer, usually in late June, for inventory. (CC trolley stop: get off at Visitor's Bureau; the Mint building is visible across Colfax Avenue)

COORS BREWERY
13th Ave. and Ford St.
Golden 277-BEER

Colorado is the second-largest producer of beer in the United States, and most of it comes from the Coors Brewery in Golden, the world's largest single-site brewing facility. The free tour and tasting ranks as one of Greater Denver's top tourist attractions; more than 10 million people have taken the 30-minute tour. Tours run from 10 AM to 4 PM Monday through Saturday.

HAKUSHIKA SAKE
U.S.A. CORPORATION
4414 Table Mountain Dr.
Golden 279-7253

Tours at Golden's newest brewing facility—the first brewery outside Japan for this

Photo: Rick Wicker, Courtesy of Denver Museum of Natural History

The skull of a Tyrannosaurus rex is one of seven dinosaur skulls featured in the new permanent Prehistoric Journey exhibition at the Denver Museum of Natural History.

300-year-old company — illustrate the process of making sake, but many people take the tour just to see the company's gorgeous collection of Japanese art, including 19th-century woodblock prints. Advance reservations are necessary; call one to two days ahead. Tours last about 45 minutes and are conducted every hour between 10 AM and 4 PM Monday through Friday, except noon.

Suggested Outings

ONE-DAY FAMILY OUTING . . .

Visit the Denver Museum of Natural History and the Denver Zoo. Take in a show at either the Gates planetarium or the IMAX theater. Then, if you have time, the Denver Museum of Miniatures, Dolls and Toys isn't far away.

WITHIN WALKING DISTANCE DOWNTOWN . . .

The Denver Art Museum, the Museum of Western Art, the Colorado History Museum, the U.S. Mint, the Colorado State Capitol, the Molly Brown House, the Firefighters Museum and the Denver History Museum (Byers-Evans House) are all within walking distance of each other downtown. Don't try to see all these sights in one day, but pick the ones that interest you most; plot a route and save the rest for another afternoon.

FOR ART LOVERS . . .

The Denver Art Museum and the Western Art Museum can be visited in one day if you don't try to see the whole art museum (save the non-American art galleries for another day). If you're at the Denver Art Museum at lunchtime, eat in their cafe. If you're over by the Western Art Museum, try the Trinity Grille next door at 1801 Broadway, 293-2288. Or, if it's getting late, stop in at the Brown Palace Hotel across the street for afternoon tea in their elegant lobby.

TRAINS AND AUTOMOBILES . . .

Greater Denver has three museums of special interest in this category: the Forney Transportation Museum, the Colorado Railroad Museum and the Denver Firefighters Museum. With a car, all could be visited in one day.

ONE-DAY OUTING IN GOLDEN . . .

Start with a tour of the Coors Brewery (or end here if you're afraid the free beer samples will make you too sleepy to enjoy what comes next). Then drive up to the Buffalo Bill Memorial Museum and Grave and, if it interests you, nearby is the Mother Cabrini Shrine, which honors the first American saint. Please see our Places of Worship chapter for more information. For lunch, take a picnic to Red Rocks Park if the weather's nice or eat Southwestern food at Silverheels Southwest Grill, 1122 Washington Avenue, in downtown Golden. In the afternoon, visit the Colorado Railroad Museum or, for the more artistically inclined, the Foothills Art Center, a small community arts center at 809 15th Street. We've fully described the arts center in our Arts chapter. You may also want to visit the Rocky Mountain Quilt Museum, 1111 Washington Avenue.

HISTORY BUFFS . . .

Don't miss the Black American West Museum. A visit there combines well with visits to the Colorado History Museum and/ or the Denver History Museum. Another possible combination is with the Western Art Museum.

ETHNIC HERITAGE TOUR (HALF-DAY). . .

Divide your time between the Black American West Museum and the Museo de las Americas. Grab a snack at the Panaderia and Pastelaria Santa Fe, 750 Santa Fe Drive — it's recommended by the Museo staff for authentic Mexican pastries.

ART AND GARDEN TOUR . . .

Spend half the day at the Denver Art Museum, the rest at the Denver Botanic Gardens (via CC trolley).

FAUNA AND FLORA . . .

Spend half the day at the Denver Zoo, the rest at the Denver Botanic Gardens. Take the CC trolley.

PLATTE RIVER TOUR . . .

Divide your day between the Forney Transportation Museum and the Children's Museum (described in the Kidstuff chapter), using the Platte Valley Trolley to get back and forth. For trolley information, call 458-6255.

WALKING TOURS . . .

A booklet of six downtown walking tours collectively called *The Mile High Trail* is available for $1.50 at the Greater Denver Chamber of Commerce, 1445 Market Street, 534-8500, or the Denver Visitors Information Center, 225 W. Colfax, 892-1112. The information booth at Larimer Square can provide historical and architectural information about buildings in the 1400 block of Larimer Street. Historic Denver, 534-1858, used to conduct walking tours on a regular basis but has cut down to once or twice a year. "Discover Denver" classes that include guided walking tours

Photo: Denver Metro Convention & Visitors Bureau

Early Denver society snubbed Molly Brown, but tourists flock to see the house of the unsinkable woman who survived early Denver and the sinking of the Titanic.

are offered several times a year through Colorado Free University, 399-0093. Despite the school's name, the classes aren't free of charge — but prices are quite reasonable.

PUBLIC ART TOUR . . .

The Mayor's Office of Art, Film and Culture, 280 14th Street, 640-2696, can provide a brochure identifying public art throughout the city. The brochure contains a suggested walking tour and driving tour. Don't miss the outdoor murals on the 15th Street viaduct and Barbara Jo Revelle's vast tile mural of photographic images of people from Colorado's history, at the Colorado Convention Center (Welton Street side). The brochure is also available at the Denver Visitors Information Center, 225 W. Colfax Avenue, 892-1112, and at public libraries in the Greater Denver area.

GART sports

The Rocky Mountain Region's Sporting Goods Headquarters

When you think about sports in the Rocky Mountain Region, you think about Gart Sports.

- Saloman
- Remington
- Wilson
- Rawlings
- Speedo
- Rossignol
- Slumberjack
- Winchester
- The North Face

- Louisville Slugger
- Avia
- Nike
- Daiwa
- KHS
- Kelty
- Obermeyer
- Nordica
- The Game
- Easton

- Descente
- Reebok
- Silstar
- Starter
- Browning
- Spalding
- Jansport
- Dunlop
- Marker

Gart Sports is everywhere in Colorado, with over 30 locations to serve your sports shopping needs. Our locations include the incredible Denver Sportscastle® Store, 3 NEW Superstores in Aurora, Arvada and Southwest Denver, plus we have stores in Vail and Glenwood Springs.

Gart Sports IS sports in the Rocky Mountain Region!

Book your Sports Travel with Gart Sports travel Agency, located in the SportsCastle® Store, 10th and Broadway 303-861-2212

SPO66

Inside
Recreation

Denver is a health-conscious place, if measured only by the yardstick of having 92 health clubs, according to the February 1994 issue of *Allure* magazine. But there are plenty of other yardsticks as well. You can find organizations, facilities, rentals, tour guides and landscape aplenty for everything from bicycling, climbing, fishing, hunting, running, Rollerblading, water sports, participatory team sports, sailing and water-skiing to horseback riding and ranges for skeet, trap, pistols and rifles. Skiing, of course, is probably Colorado's most popular and famous form of recreation, as well as one of the state's biggest money-earners. In addition to some brief tips in this chapter, we've given skiing a chapter of its own called Ski Country.

Golf

Nothing enhances a golf game like beautiful scenery, and in Greater Denver you always have the mountains for a backdrop. No matter where you live or stay, you're always near a golf course because Greater Denver has more than 50 of them, and more are on the way. As of mid-1995, the *Denver Business Journal* counted 32 new golf courses under construction or planned in Colorado, 16 of those in Greater Denver. Good thing, too, because the National Golf Foundation counted 17,000 more golfers in Colorado in 1994 than in 1993.

The most prestigious courses are those at Cherry Hills Country Club in Cherry Hills Village and Castle Pines in Dou-

Photo: Denver Metro Convention & Visitors Bureau

Denver's City Park golf course offers both urban and natural views.

glas County. Unfortunately, those are private clubs; unless you've got connections and/or a membership, forget about it.

You *can* enjoy Castle Pines as a spectator each summer at the International, Colorado's biggest pro golfing event. And the Colorado Open takes place each July at the Inverness Golf Course near the Denver Tech Center; it's really one of the better state "opens" in the nation.

But playing is more fun than watching. The main thing you have to know, if you're coming to Colorado as a visitor and want to play golf, is that you need a tee time in advance because the courses are jammed. Unfortunately, an outsider can't just waltz in and get an advance tee time at many local golf courses because Denver and Aurora golf courses operate according to a computerized reservation system. You need a pre-purchased $10 reservation access card with an individual code to use these systems. If you call in and try to make a reservation without a pre-authorized code, the computer will thank you nicely and hang up.

If you're in town for more than a fast swing-through, go ahead and get a card, because Denver has eight fine courses including a par 3 and an executive course. Call **Denver's Golf Line**, 964-2563, for details.

Of course, you certainly don't have to confine yourself to Denver and Aurora. There are plenty of other courses around the area that don't have this reservation card requirement.

Even with a reservation card, you're typically not allowed to make a reservation at most golf courses more than a couple of days ahead of time. Unfortunately, during the summer, a lot of the more prestigious golf courses are locked up a week or two in advance. A real golfer is not going to go on vacation without tee times locked in up-

front. One suggestion, if you're coming for a vacation from outside Colorado and you're interested only in golf in the mountains, is to call the **Colorado Golf Resort Association**, 699-GOLF. The Colorado Golf Resort Association also has a *Colorado Golf Vacation Guide* that is aimed strictly at destination vacationers. It's mailed only out of state. You can't get it in state. It lists all the courses in Colorado with greens fees, yardages, information on hotels and tee time preferences, etc.

The same phone number, 699-GOLF, is also the phone number for the *Colorado Golfer Newspaper*. The newspaper sells an annual guide issue that has listings and fees of all the courses in Colorado. A subscription to the *Colorado Golfer Newspaper* costs $6 for a year of six issues, including the annual guide.

Another golfing organization you might want to know about is the **Colorado Golf Association**, 779-4653. It's an organization for amateurs with some 40,000 members, and it serves as an information clearinghouse for all the amateur tournament events in the state. It also has a fine publication informally known as its "SHAG book" and formally known as the *Schedule Handicap and Association Guidebook*. This booklet is a golf course directory with information covering all the courses in Colorado, including handicap information, tournament schedules and other features such as handicap conversion tables. It lists golfing organizations, and also has maps of Colorado and a blowup map of Greater Denver showing you where all the courses are located. To get it, you really need to be a member, but if you contact the CGA early in the year before all the booklets have been mailed out, you may be able to get one even if you're not a member.

Another excellent publication is *The Guide to Golf in the Rockies*, which gives you a color photo, description and information on fees, yardages, slopes and other features for the best golf courses in the mountains and on the Front Range. This book is published by Breckenridge Publishing Company, (970) 453-5512.

We can't tell you all the great places to golf around Greater Denver; there are just too many of them. But here are a few hot tips.

Arrowhead, 10850 W. Sundown Trail in Littleton, 973-9614, designed by Robert Trent Jones, winds through a landscape of scrub oak and towering red sandstone rocks. *Golf Digest* ranks it among the state's top-20 courses. To get there, don't go to Littleton; that's just the mailing address. It is actually in unincorporated Douglas County, right next to Roxborough State Park, and that's a clue that the scenery is spectacular. Take Exit C-470 south on Santa Fe Drive to Titan Road; go west on Titan Road for about 8 miles; the course entrance will be on the left. Another golf course ranked as one of Colorado's top-20 courses by *Golf Digest* is **Fox Hollow at Lakewood,** 13410 W. Morrison Road, Lakewood, 986-7888. Fox Hollow has become a real hit since it opened in 1993. This 27-hole course, consisting of three nines, is a nice place to play because it's well-designed. You have everything from high-up greens with wonderful views over the whole area, to low-down play among the trees, ponds, lakes and meadows.

Guests of the Inverness Hotel in Englewood or guests of the club's members may play at the **Inverness Golf Club,** 200 Inverness Drive W., Englewood, 397-7878. The private/resort club features a park-style course designed by Press Maxwell.

For the feel of a country-club course with lots of water and sand traps and a challenging variety of terrain, **Legacy Ridge,** 10801 Legacy Ridge Parkway in Westminster, 438-8997, is a good course to try. The 18-hole course opened in September 1994 and was designed by Arthur Hills, a big-name course designer based in Toledo, Ohio. It's just off 104th Avenue between Sheridan and Federal boulevards.

Commonly esteemed as a good place to play, **Meridian Golf Club,** 9742 S. Meridian, Englewood, 799-4043, is a links-style course designed by Jack Nicklaus. It's also the home of the Meridian Golf Learning Center, run by the famed teaching pro Mike McGetrick.

Formerly a private country club but now under the South Suburban Recreation District is **Lone Tree,** 9801 Sunningdale Boulevard, Littleton, 799-9940. Littleton is the mailing address; the course is actually in Douglas County. Take I-25 south past C-470 to Lincoln Avenue, then exit west on Lincoln Avenue. Less than 2 miles of driving will take you to the course. This Arnold Palmer/Ed Seay design, built in 1984, is a links-style course out in the open with a minimum of trees. Fitting right in with those public courses that seem like private courses is the links-style **Plum Creek Golf Club**, 331 Players Club Drive, Castle Rock, 688-2611. Prior to going public, it was a tournament players' course and used to be owned by the PGA tour.

Just below the City of Denver's southwest corner lies the 18-hole **Raccoon Creek**, 7301 W. Bowles Avenue, Jefferson County, 973-4653. The course was designed by Dick Phelps, a well-known course designer based in Evergreen. It's fun, interesting, challenging and pretty. **Riverdale**, 13300 Riverdale Road, Brighton, 659-4700, also known as Riverdale Dunes, is a wonderfully challenging links-style course designed by Pete Dye. It was the site of the USGA Public Links Championship in 1993. *Golf Digest* places it among Colorado's top 20 courses. You may need a little more than the above address to find it: Take I-25 north to 120th Avenue, then go east to Colorado Boulevard, left on Colorado to 128th Avenue, then east until 128th ends at Riverdale Road, turn left and go a half-mile to the clubhouse. If you're coming from U.S. Highway 85, exit west on 124th Avenue to Riverdale Road, turn right and drive 1 mile to the clubhouse.

The **Thorncreek Golf Course,** 13555 Washington Street, Thornton, 450-7055, is not exactly links-style or park-style. It's a pro-level 18-hole course and a public course that feels like a country-club course. Another one of those public courses with a private, country-club layout is the **Westwoods Golf Club,** 6655 Quaker Street, in Golden, 424-3334. Also known as the Westwoods Ranch, this 18-holer opened in June 1994. The terrain gets pretty high, and it's esteemed for its spectacular views.

Tennis

Greater Denver has plenty of tennis facilities. **Gates Tennis Center,** for example, at 100 S. Adams Street in Denver, 355-4461, just south of the Cherry Creek mall, is rated consistently as one of the top public tennis facilities in the country. You don't need a membership, court times are reasonable and lessons are competitively priced. It has one of the nation's largest tennis ladders, a challenge arrangement in which you sign up at a certain level and begin to play and move up and down the ladder. Gates has more than 1,000 people on its computerized ladder, enough to offer specialized ladders for singles, doubles, etc. There's even a coed ladder that is reputed as a good place for singles to meet. It's a 20-court facility complete with clubhouse,

locker room and pro shop. Pros will teach you, and ball machines will test you.

A lot of clubs and other organizations offer leagues, tournaments, tennis camps, junior tennis camps and private, group and semiprivate lessons around Greater Denver. **Denver Parks and Recreation,** 331-4047, runs junior programs and adult lesson programs throughout the Denver area. **Aurora Parks and Recreation,** 695-7200, has a good public tennis program. The **Chatfield/Columbine YMCA,** 979-3707, has a lot of programs and six outdoor courts in a pretty setting at 10393 W. Alamo Place in Littleton. Overall, Jefferson County has perhaps the strongest tennis programs, including the **Holly Tennis Center** at 6651 S. Krameria Way in Englewood, 771-3654; and the community center in **Ken Caryl Ranch,** 1 Club Drive, Littleton, 979-2233. Ken Caryl has four indoor courts and six outdoor courts. You won't find prettier surroundings; the Ken Caryl Ranch community is located in the red-rock moonscape of the valley hidden behind the Hogback Formation that runs north/south along C-470. The facility is actually owned by Jefferson County Open Space. On the northwest side, the **Arvada Tennis Center,** 420-1210, at the corner of 64th and Miller streets, has a fine public facility with eight courts. If you want to take to the courts, we suggest making reservations in advance, when possible. Greater Denver's central tennis resource is the **Colorado Tennis Association,** 695-4116. If you're looking for courts or you're interested in finding out how to get into organized tennis leagues or sanctioned tournaments, the CTA can help steer you to the right place. They also have copies of tournament schedules for adults and juniors as well as general information brochures. They're the local branch of the U.S. Tennis Association as well, so you can get USTA memberships and publications through the CTA.

Of course, you don't have to contact any organizations or join any leagues to play tennis. You can find courts in just about any city park; in Denver try **Washington Park**, between S. Franklin Street and S. Downing Street just north of I-25; and City Park, between Colorado Boulevard and York Street, two blocks north of E. Colfax Avenue.

Pavement Bicycling

The City of Denver isn't the only city that has put a lot of effort into making nice parks and trail systems. The bike path greenbelt along Cherry Creek is well known as a good continuous bike route from Confluence Park through downtown Denver all the way to Denver's southeastern corner. Not as well known is the **Arapahoe Greenway Trail** in Littleton, a part of the bike path system that runs past Confluence Park and down through Littleton with lots of spurs going off into the community. One of Littleton's natural areas is the **South Platte Park** nature preserve. In the 1970s, the U.S. Army Corps of Engineers was preparing to channelize the Platte River in Littleton, and the city went to Congress and got an act passed to preserve the area in its pristine state. Now it's a 630-acre natural area with a lot of wetlands and wildlife. The **Highline Canal** is another Littleton highlight. Built in the 1880s, it is now lined by huge cottonwoods in what amounts to a river of ancient trees through the city, and it also has a bike path. Access to this greenbelt is often at the top of the list for reasons why people live in that part of Littleton.

Other cities and unincorporated areas have the same kinds of amenities, such as the **Clear Creek bike path** that runs from Lowell Boulevard in Denver west along Clear Creek all the way to Golden. If only it connected from Lowell Boulevard to Confluence Park, so bicyclists wouldn't have to ride city streets in between. Greater Denver is distinguished by its many greenbelt bicycle paths, and that's one of the reasons why urban bicycling is among the city's most popular recreational activities. Bicycling is also one of the ways you can enjoy some local lakes and reservoirs. The **Chatfield State Recreation Area**, where you can rent bicycles if you don't have your own, has created some lovely bike paths around the Chatfield Reservoir and through the wooded glades along the South Platte River. **Cherry Creek Reservoir** also has miles of bike trails near Cherry Creek Lake and away to the south through the nature preserve upstream along Cherry Creek. **Aurora Reservoir** has 8.5 miles of bicycle trails. Many of the smaller lakes are circled by bike paths. **Sloan Lake**, in Sloan Lake Park on Denver's western edge, is one example. **Crown Hill Lake**, in Wheat Ridge's Crown Hill Park, is another.

The state has urban trail maps for four different areas of the state, and one of those is for the metropolitan Denver area: *Urban Trails in Colorado, Denver Metro*

Call the Colorado State Highway Patrol's road condition report, 639-1111, to check road conditions within two hours of Denver, particularly if you're planning to go over a high mountain pass in questionable weather.

Insiders' Tips

Photo: Daily Camera

Hiking/biking trails abound in the cities and open spaces of Greater Denver.

Area. The state also has a very useful *Colorado Trails Resource Guide*. These references are available free if you stop by or write: Trails Guides, 1313 Sherman Avenue, Room 618, Denver, Colorado 80203. Provide a self-addressed, stamped return envelope with six first-class stamps; the envelope should measure at least 6 by 9 inches. Some bike shops will have urban trail maps available as well.

A nonprofit group called **Bicycle Colorado**, 756-2535, is perhaps the biggest single source of bicycling information. They have a general guide to public-lands trails and other tips, and they also have a beautiful publication called *Bicycle Colorado Magazine*. Among the other bicycling resources that may be helpful are **The Denver Bicycle Touring Club**, 756-7240; **Team Evergreen**, 674-6048, one of the friendlier of local bicycle clubs, with about 700 members, weekly road-bike and mountain-bike rides, its own newsletter and other attractions; the **Colorado Bicycle Coalition**, 355-5451; and the **Bicycle Racing Association of Colorado**, 440-5366.

Mountain Biking

If any outdoor sport could be said to define Colorado, mountain biking would probably run a close second to skiing. Hikers are still the primary users of Colorado back country, but increasingly they are having to share the path with mountain bikers. Mountain bikes are a return to sanity, rather like the fat-tire bikes we older people had as kids before skinny-wheel bikes became the norm. Of course, mountain bikes are a quantum leap ahead of the old fat-tire bikes, with super-light frames and gearing low enough to ride up the steepest hills.

Mountain bikers can pretty much go on any hiking trail, and off-trail as well. Well, we have to qualify that. Since the mountain bikes have become a boom sport, a lot of hikers and horseback riders have begun to feel the same revulsion when they see a mountain bike coming that they often feel when they see a motorized "dirt bike." It's not as noisy, but mountain bikers do tend to race toward and past hikers at breakneck speed. Some narrow-minded hikers or horse people will glare and act surly or superior in the

presence of even the most polite mountain bikers. Polite bikers are those who slow when passing hikers, or get off the trail for people on horses; maybe saying, "Beg pardon," or, "Howdy." In fact, consideration for others is among the International Mountain Biking Association's official Rules of the Trail: 1) Ride on open trails only, 2) Leave no trace, 3) Control your bicycle, 4) Always yield the trail, 5) Never spook animals, and 6) Plan ahead.

Unfortunately, too many mountain bikers come barreling by as though others in the trail have a moral obligation to scatter like chickens. It's become a controversy that often pops up through letters of denunciation from one side or the other on local newspaper editorial pages.

We love this most joyous and accessible of outdoor sports, however, and it must be said that the majority of hikers and bikers can enjoy the trails in harmony.

And the vast majority of trails in Colorado are open to mountain biking.

Where trails are closed specifically to mountain biking, in places like Boulder Mountain Parks, it's most likely because mountain bikes in excessive numbers are viewed as destructors of trails. Mountain bikes don't drop road apples all over the trails, but they supposedly erode trails in ways that horses do not. At any rate, you can't mountain bike in Roxborough State Park, in City of Boulder open space or on about half the trails in Golden Gate State Park. Then again, the other half of the trails in Golden Gate are open to bikes, as are virtually all national forests along the Front Range, nearby areas over the Continental Divide and, as of 1995, all Jefferson County parks and open spaces. In late 1995, however, new rules were being pushed to close some of Jefferson County Open Space to mountain biking due to conflicts on the trails. "Bikers are going faster and coming up behind the hikers, who have to jump off the trail," said one Open Space manager. Generally, if you don't see a sign prohibiting mountain biking, you can take to the trails.

A lot of great mountain-biking rides are available right in Jefferson County on Denver's immediate west side, wonderful places for their terrain, scenery and/or technical aspects. All of them are accessible to anyone with reasonable lungs and legs. **Waterton Canyon** is one. Take Wadsworth Boulevard south from its junction with C-470, 4 miles to the Waterton Canyon Recreation Area sign, and turn left to park. You are now at the South Platte River just upstream from Chatfield Recreation Area; there are also lovely and gentle trails around the recreation area. But up the canyon, it gets a little more dramatic. No dogs are allowed; there's a herd of big-

horn sheep up this canyon. A 6-mile dirt road heads up past Cottonwood Gulch, Mill Gulch and Stevens Gulch to the Colorado Trail. You can keep going on the Colorado Trail if you want to, but the 6-mile stretch is technically intermediate as far as bike handling skills and average as far as lungs and legs. Some people like to go about a mile beyond Stevens Gulch and turn left on the Roxborough Loop, which can take you around and back down to Waterton Canyon Road.

Another great mountain-bike ride is **Mount Falcon**, a 10-mile ride that you reach by taking U.S. 285 south to Colo. Highway 8, for about a mile to Forest Avenue; turn left and drive to Mount Falcon Park. From the Morrison Trailhead, you can head up the Castle Trail to the pavilion at the Walker's Dream Shelter. You can ride a lot of loops above this point, with moderate technical skills and high exertion.

Matthews/Winter Park, Dakota Ridge, Apex Park, White Ranch, Elk Meadow Park, Chatfield State Park and Recreation Area — these are just a few of the other great opportunities right in Jefferson County. New in 1995 is the **Deer Creek Park Trail**, about 4 miles up Deer Creek Canyon from Wadsworth Boulevard, in Jefferson County Open Space. One of the best overall references for these and other rides is a book, *The Best of Colorado Biking Trails*, published by Outdoor Books & Maps Inc., of Denver, and available in many local bookstores, bike shops and outing stores. Other good mountain-biker references include: *Denverides, The Mountain Biking Guide to Denver, Colorado*, by Dave Rich; *Mountain Bike Rides in The Colorado Front Range*, by William L. Stoehr; *Bicycling the Backcountry*, also by Stoehr; *Bike With a View*, by Mark Dowling; *Ride Guide*, by *Rocky Moun-*

tain News columnist David Nelson; and *Colorado Gonzo Rides*, by Michael Merrifield.

Skiing

You'd expect skiing to be the top entry in any guide to Greater Denver recreation, but we're placing it down here because it's well-covered in our Ski Country chapter. That chapter gives you an abundance of information on all the major ski areas near Denver, along with plenty of tips on tickets, lessons and the ski season.

Skiing is certainly recreation, however, and if you're a beginner or a want-to-be beginner, you may want to know about a couple of the information sources that can help you get into the sport.

Colorado Ski Country USA, 837-0793, a trade association for all the ski resorts in the state, publishes the *Colorado Ski Country Consumer Guide*. Within about 130 pages, it contains a lot of the information you want to know about skiing in Colorado. Colorado Ski Country USA will mail it to you free if you give them a call and ask for it. Colorado Ski Country USA also sponsors a major consumer show every fall at one of Denver's big convention spaces, where you can find out about the latest in gear, apparel and accessories.

You may also want to know about Sniagrab (bargains spelled backward), the big annual ski equipment and apparel sale held every year by Gart Brothers Sporting Goods outlets around Greater Denver. It starts on the Saturday before Labor Day and runs through much of September. You can find some fine deals on new and used equipment there.

One of the best ways to get into skiing is to link up with a ski club. It's not only a social event, but a way of letting the more experienced take you under their wing via group outings to local ski areas where all you have to do is show up, get on the bus and have a good time. A lot of health clubs and recreation districts have ski clubs, and it's not unlikely that you'll find a ski club at your place of employment. But if you want the best overall source of local ski clubs, try the *National Ski Club News*. This is a newsletter about ski clubs nationwide, and it's published in Denver. To get a list of local ski clubs, all you have to do is send your request and a self-addressed, stamped envelope to National Ski Club News, P.O. Box 17385, Denver, Colorado 80217.

When on the slopes, always be conscious of what is coming from above you. Often, it's someone coming faster than they should and intending to pass closer than they should. If you're skiing with children, ski behind and uphill from them to shield them with your body. It seems like somebody gets killed every year — and certainly, large numbers of people get hurt — when they get slammed by hot-dogging idiots. It's really sad when the victim is a small and easily-smashed child. We've seen many bad collisions, and been hit ourselves. Ski defensively. The Colorado Legislature has severely limited the amount for which anyone can sue a ski area. When someone gets hurt in a collision, they are now more likely to sue the person they collided with. That can be bad even for the victims. As a friend of ours tells it, an out-of-control skier hit him and together they flew downslope and struck and injured a third party. The out-of-control clown jumped up and sped away. Our friend stayed with the third party until medical help arrived. Since the clown was gone, the third party thanked our friend by suing him.

Running

Runners are everywhere in Greater Denver, in the streets of the downtown and the suburbs, in the city parks and greenbelts and along the mountain paths. You can run anywhere. Most people run in their own neighborhoods. But there are some popular running venues for those who want to run where others are running, in pleasant settings and on motorist-free trails.

Washington Park, between S. Franklin and S. Downing streets just north of I-25, probably has Denver's highest runner density. That may be because it's one of Denver's biggest and most pleasant parks, or it may be because it's in an area with a lot of upscale empty-nesters who believe in exercise and don't have to get it by pushing their kids on the park's swings. Closer in, **City Park**, between Colorado Boulevard and York Street, two blocks north of E. Colfax Avenue, is another popular running area where folks can get away from cars and run through some semblance of foliated quietude. Greenbelts, including the popular **Highline Canal** in Littleton, the **Cherry Creek Bike Path** and the **South Platte River trails** in Chatfield Reservoir are particularly nice places to run for that same aesthetic. If you like running on natural terrain, which is healthier because it avoids the repetitive, one-dimensional joint-pounding of flat terrain, you may want to try the many fine trails along the Front Range. See some of our suggested mountain biking trails outlined in our Mountain Biking entry.

A lot of runners are solitary souls. You see them at dawn while you're driving to work, and you see them in the evening when you're coming home, running alone and happy about it. But for those who enjoy the group experience, there are plenty of events and clubs. Greater Denver's largest yearly running events include the 5-mile **Cherry Creek Sneak** in April, 394-5152; the **Governor's Cup 5K** in September, 727-8700; the **Run for the Zoo**, a 5K and 10K in October, 331-5800; the **Race for the Cure 5K** in October, 727-8700; and the 4-mile **Turkey Trot** on Thanksgiving morning, 433-8383.

Among the larger running clubs are the **Colorado Masters**, for the older than 30 crowd, 751-4284 or 232-1308; and the **Rocky Mountain Road Runners**, 871-8366. Don't forget that walkers have found increasing acceptance in the area's big running events. **The Front Range Walkers**, 377-0576, is perhaps the area's biggest walking club. Some running stores also serve as information clearinghouses on running clubs, events and race series, as well as places where you can sign up for races. These include **Mongoose Runners Den**, 8877 Harlan Street, Westminster, 657-0225; and **Runners Roost Ltd.**, 1685 S. Colorado Boulevard, Denver, 759-8455. A store called **Fleet Feet** has outlets around the Greater Denver area, but its main information and race sign-up center is Fleet Feet's Cherry Creek North store at 2760 E. Second Avenue, 320-0750.

Boating and Windsurfing

Boaters and windsurfers have a lot of lakes and reservoirs to choose from around Greater Denver, but if you're into power boating there are only a few select places that are either large enough or allow enough horsepower to do more than putt from one fishing spot to the next.

The most popular lakes are the big boys, **Cherry Creek Lake** and **Chatfield Reservoir**, the focuses, respectively, of Cherry Creek Reservoir State Recreation Area and Chatfield State Recreation Area. Both of

The Bay is an outdoor water park run by the Broomfield recreation department.

them are big reservoirs and, as part of state recreation areas, are just nice environments in which to split the water. You can find more general descriptions of these recreation areas in our State Parks and Recreation Areas entry later in this chapter, but boaters will be interested to know that both of them have extensive marinas offering a lot of rentals.

The **Cherry Creek Marina**, 779-6144, has slips, water access and rentals of canoes, motorboats, sailboards, Jet Skis, rowboats, pontoon boats and bicycles. This marina also has a little restaurant.

Chatfield Reservoir's boating center is the **Chatfield Marina**, 791-5555, which includes a store with boating and fishing supplies, groceries and take-out food. It's Denver's only on-the-water grill and deli restaurant with patio and observation deck, nearby restrooms and rental for sailboats and fishing boats, paddleboats, water toys and pontoon boats. You can also charter a crewed sailboat.

Perhaps less appreciated than closer-in venues of water play is **Aurora Reservoir**, 5800 Powhatan Road, 690-1286, 7 miles east of Quincy Reservoir in Arapa-

hoe County. Powerboaters pay it little attention, since gas motors aren't allowed on the water. But the water is clean, and it's popular with sailors and windsurfers. There's a little marina with a general store, where you can rent electric motorboats, rowboats, sailboats, sailboards, paddleboats and canoes. You'll find the reservoir by driving about 2 miles east of Gun Club Road on E. Quincy Avenue and turning right at Powhatan Road.

Lakewood's **Bear Creek Lake Park**, 697-8013 (gatehouse), 697-6159 (park rangers), spreading above U.S. Highway 285 where it intersects with C-470, gets a lot less attention than the bigger areas of aquatic sporting, but it has some very nice bodies of water to offer. Bear Creek Lake is valued by many for its sailing, partly because it allows no motors greater than 10 horsepower. One can find a little more action on the park's **Soda Lakes** to the southwest. Drivers on C-470 can often see water-skiing on Little Soda Lake, a narrow body of water that lies along the highway's northeast side. But don't go down there with your boat. This is a part of the park, but it's privately run. The

Soda Lake Ski School, 697-0121, is the only boat operator allowed, and you can ski there only by using one of the school's boats. Big Soda Lake is open to the public, except for power boats and has its own Soda Lake Marina, 697-1522, where you can rent sailboats, sailboards, canoes, kayaks, paddleboats and bicycles. Reach Big Soda Lake by taking Colo. Highway 8, which runs along the north side of the park; turn right about 100 yards east of C-470; then take an immediate left to get into the park and continue to the stop sign, turn right and follow the signs to the marina.

Big Soda Lake, by the way, is the base of operations for Greater Denver's only accredited windsurfing school, **Chip Graham Windsurfing Academy**, 426-6503. Soda Lake and Aurora Reservoir are the two significant bodies of water in the area with dual advantages: You can rent sailboards, but motorboats are not allowed. Windsurfers prefer smooth water. **Standley Lake**, the big north Jefferson County lake bordered on the north and east by Westminster and on the south by Arvada, is another popular location. Motorboats are allowed there, but you need a permit for boats with more than 20 horsepower, and the number of permits is limited. Boats with less than 20 horsepower can use the lake for $10 per day. Call the City of Westminster's office at the lake, 425-1097.

On the south, windsurfers prefer the two state recreation area lakes, **Cherry Creek Lake** and **Chatfield Reservoir**. These do have the disadvantage of being crowded by motorboats, but where you go is likely to depend on both driving distance and where the winds are coming from. If it's blowing from the north, Standley Lake is probably the best. If the wind is coming from the south, Soda Lake is probably the best.

Horseback Riding

What's more quintessentially Western than an outing on the back of a horse, especially when you're riding on the prairies or mountain Foothills of the Rockies? Riding in the Denver suburbs may not compare with the more remote horse experiences in the high country and points west, but it sure beats the pants off of a canter through the Midwestern cornfields.

A lot of people around the Denver area have their own horses, but if you don't, there are some fine stables to choose from for a daily rental ride. The two state recreation areas on Greater Denver's south side are nice places to ride, simply because they have large and carefully cultivated natural areas and their own stables on site where you can pay to ride the nature trails. Try the **Paint Horse Stables**, 690-8235, at Cherry Creek Reservoir State Recreation Area; and **B&B Livery**, 933-3636, at Chatfield State Recreation Area. **Stockton's Plum Creek Stables Ltd.**, 791-1966, also has access to the 7,000 acres of Chatfield State Recreation Area via its own private entrance. Find Stockton's by going about 4 miles south of C-470 on Santa Fe Drive and turning right on Titan Road. About a half-mile west of Santa Fe, Stockton's address is 7479 W. Titan Road.

On the other side of Greater Denver's south side are a couple of stables in the town of Parker, which you can reach by taking I-25 a little more than a mile south of its intersection with C-470, then traveling east about 2.5 miles on Lincoln Avenue (Exit 193) before turning right on Parker Road. **A Worthy Ranch & Stables**, 841-

9405, offers lessons as well as riding, with miles of trails.

Old West Stables, 697-1416, at the corner of Foxton Road and U.S. Highway 285 in Morrison, offers horse rides, guided and self-guided, in the 2,700 acres of Lakewood's Bear Creek Lake Park. It also offers half-day and full-day rides in the mountain community of Conifer. Old West's Conifer rides take place on the 460 acres of Beaver Ranch, which is a children's summer camp and, in the winter, an alternative school. Old West offers horse-drawn sleigh rides at Beaver Ranch in the winter, the closest mountain sleigh rides to Denver.

In-Line Skating

Sometimes known as Rollerblading, this sport is more properly called "in-line skating" for the same reason you say "copying" instead of "Xeroxing" — because Rollerblade is a trade name. In-line skates differ from traditional roller skates in that the wheels are in a single line rather than being set four-square like the wheels of a car. This makes in-lines go a little faster than ordinary roller skates and work a little better for outdoor use, since they are better at traversing cracks and other surface glitches.

If you're a beginner, you might want to try the safe route of renting in-lines at a local indoor roller rink, where there are music, lights and other amenities. **Roller City**, 237-5622, 6803 Alameda Avenue, in Lakewood, is Colorado's biggest rink, with a pro shop, snack bar, game room, rentals

and lessons for both traditional and in-line skates. **Roller Express**, 428-5061, 8412 N. Huron Street, Thornton, is the big rink in north Greater Denver. Here, too, you can rent both in-line and traditional rollers in a safe, indoor atmosphere of neon lights and music. This rink features teen nights, adult nights and family nights.

Outdoors is a different story; it's where you go when you want to get a little more serious about in-line skating. Outdoors, there's the temptation to go faster, which in-lines can do, and the tendency to fall harder with rougher landings. One friend of ours, an ultimate sports dude fanatically active in numerous sports and healthy until he happened on in-lines, fell while in-line skating and tore a ligament in his knee. Then again, you can fall in the bathtub.

One place that's "totally happening," according to one in-liner jock, is the bike path that follows C-470 along its eastern side in Jefferson County. It has good up-hills and downhills, sharp corners and a smooth surface built for speed. The most popular in-liner locus of all is Denver's downtown, according to the jocks, because it's just one big concrete playground; and the 16th Street Mall is everybody's favorite place, but unfortunately, it's illegal to blade there, even on days when bicycles are allowed.

There are plenty of places around Greater Denver where in-lining can be slow and easy, where people of all experience levels can enjoy the sport. Check our Bi-

Insiders' Tips

cycle section earlier in this chapter, and Denver's city bicycle maps, for the city bike paths where the Rollerblading is good. If it's a good pavement biking path, then it's a good blading path. The **Cherry Creek greenbelt path** that runs from downtown through the Cherry Creek neighborhood to the east side of town and down to C-470 is one of the most esteemed blading zones due to its pleasant and fashionable location, smooth surface and the many connecting bike paths along its length. The streets of Cherry Creek itself have a great reputation: It's a cool place to be, and the streets tend to be new and smooth. The paved paths along the **South Platte River**, from downtown Denver through Littleton, are also renowned. **Washington Park**, between S. Franklin and S. Downing streets just north of I-25, is a popular blading zone, partly because it has a couple of lakes and beautiful trails and partly because a lot of people in that part of town are outdoors people. A lot of them tend to ski. When you try in-line skates, you find that the stance and motion is similar to that of skiing. **Crown Hill Park** on the east side of Kipling Street between 32nd and 26th avenues in Wheat Ridge, is popular for the seamless concrete path surrounding Crown Hill Lake. And of course, the paved trails in **Cherry Creek Reservoir State Recreation Area**, south of I-225 between the east end of Greenwood Village and the south tip of Aurora, and **Chatfield State Recreation Area**, just south of C-470 and east of Wadsworth Boulevard, are also popular. In-line skating rentals can be found in every area of town. **Ski Tech**, 777-3380, a store at 700 S. Pearl Street, in Denver, rents to a lot of Washington Park skaters. So does **Sports Plus**, 777-6613, 1055 S. Gaylord, Denver. **The Skate Shop,** formerly Platte River Roller Sports, 730-1344, 5050 S. Federal, No. 6,

Englewood, rents largely to skaters on the South Platte River and Cherry Creek trails. The Skate Shop has another store in Aurora, 755-3774, 10890 E. Dartmouth Avenue, Suite B, renting a good deal of its blades to people using the Cherry Creek greenbelt path and the paths of the Cherry Creek Reservoir State Recreation Area. **Grand West Outfitters**, 825-0300, 801 Broadway, Denver, is an outdoors store that rents a lot of in-lines to people skating on the Cherry Creek greenbelt path. **Pederson Ski and Sports**, 650-5967, in the Westminster Mall at Sheridan Boulevard and 88th Avenue, rents to people who use the park and greenbelt paths on the west and north sides of the metro area, as well as downtown.

Climbing

Training is a good idea. Every year, the papers periodically carry news items about someone killed while climbing. Tragedy hits even those who have some experience. We know one fine young man whose leg had to be rebuilt after it was smashed by a rock, a rock that had just struck the head of his friend farther up the rope, killing the friend.

Climbing is inherently dangerous, but you can make the risk reasonable by taking advantage of the many learning and practicing opportunities available right in the urban area. A number of businesses and recreation centers have their own in-house climbing walls.

Paradise Rock Gym, 6260 N. Washington Street, No. 5, 286-8168, is a health club built around technical climbing, with 6,000 square feet of climbing wall and structure as well as lessons, a small amount of climbing accessory retail and cross-training facilities such as weight machines, stationary bicycles and stair machines.

Thrillseekers Inc., 1912 S. Broadway, 733-8810, is a climbing gym with its own climbing walls, lessons and a substantial climbing equipment retail section.

Recreational Equipment Inc., more familiar to many as simply REI, has a climbing wall and offers lessons at its store at 4100 E. Mexico Avenue, 756-3100; at its store at 8991 Harlan Street, Westminster, 429-1800, just west of the Westminster Mall; and at its store at 5375 S. Wadsworth Boulevard, Lakewood, 932-0600.

Aurora Parks and Recreation Department, through its Outdoor Adventures Program, 366-1718, conducts climbing classes in the mountains, with preliminary lessons on the rock wall at REI's Mexico Avenue store in Denver. Note, however, that this program took a hiatus in 1995, and it's not yet absolutely certain that it will take place in 1996. But it probably will. Call and ask.

City Park Recreation Center, 10455 Sheridan Avenue, Westminster, 460-9690, has its own climbing wall in its gymnasium, where people can practice climbing or take climbing lessons while the basketballs bounce behind them.

Finally, technical climbing instruction is available from the grandfather of Colorado mountaineering organizations, the Colorado Mountain Club, 710 10th Street, No. 200, Golden, 279-3080. But only once a year, in the spring; basic rock climbing is offered in May and intermediate rock climbing in April.

Public Recreation Centers and Programs

Public parks and recreation departments are your greatest resource for year-round recreation, so use them often. Their public recreation centers, ubiquitous throughout Greater Denver, are your best bets for finding swimming pools outdoors in summer and indoors in winter. No matter where you are, there is more than one nearby. If you're a member of the community, the cost is minimal. If you come from another community, the cost is not much higher. Parks and recreation departments are also your best bet for youth team sports ranging from basketball to soccer, and if they don't run their own programs in some sport — T-ball for the kiddies, for example — they will certainly be able to refer you to the nearest local organizations that do.

Denver

Denver Parks and Recreation Department, 964-2500

Adams County

Adams County Parks and Community Resources Department, 659-3666

Aurora Parks and Recreation Department, 695-7200

Brighton Recreation Center, 659-7088

Commerce City Parks and Recreation Department, 289-3779

Hyland Hills Park and Recreation District, Federal Heights, 428-7488

Northglenn Parks and Recreation Department, 450-8721

Thornton Parks and Recreation Department, 538-7300

Arapahoe County

Arapahoe Park and Recreation District, 730-6109

Aurora Parks and Recreation Department, 695-7200

Cherry Creek Vista Park and Recreation District, 779-4525

Englewood Parks Department, 762-2520

South Suburban Park and Recreation District (also covers a small area of Douglas County), 798-5131

Douglas County

Castle Rock Recreation, 660-1036
Parker Recreation Center, 841-7191

Jefferson County

Arvada Parks and Recreation Department, recreation handled by North Jeffco Park and Recreation District (below), 424-7733

Broomfield Recreation Center, 469-5351

Edgewater Recreation Center, 274-6280

Foothills Park and Recreation District, 987-3602

Golden Recreation and Parks Department, 279-3331 or 384-8100

Lakewood Recreation Department, 987-7800

North Jeffco Park and Recreation District, 424-7733

Westminster Parks and Recreation Department, 430-2400 Ext. 2192

Wheat Ridge Parks and Recreation Department, Anderson Community Building, 421-0700

Urban Parks

City and county parks and recreation departments are much more than fabricated facilities and structured activities. The parks themselves offer pleasant havens everywhere you look in Greater Denver's urban fabric; havens of greenery, playing fields and playgrounds; and surfaces for running, biking, skating and whatever your imagination can unleash. We've mentioned

several of the area's parks in relation to activities described previously.

The city parks offer a lot more than we sometimes suspect. Denver Parks and Recreation, for example, is the responsible agency for such widely varied facilities as the Denver Zoo, Mile High Stadium, the city's golf courses and 100 miles of foliated center strips on major streets. Denver has about 250 parks ranging from small triangles to enormous open spaces, as well as a trail system guesstimated at about 130 miles. As of 1995, the city was maintaining about 3,950 acres of parks, although other city park property is often maintained by neighborhoods and business groups. And, of course, there are the 14,000 acres of Denver Mountain Parks, including a variety of named and about 25 unnamed parcels of natural area.

You also have a lot of gem-like little nature places that stand in a class of their own. **The Plains Conservation Center** is one of these, a 1,900-acre Colorado Prairie Natural Area just east of (so far) the eastern edge of the urban fabric of Aurora. Get off I-225 northeast of Cherry Creek Lake, onto Parker Road south, then turn east on Hampden Avenue. A few miles down you come suddenly to the end of the housing developments; the road turns to gravel, and in a few miles you find the center on top of a ridge to the left. They have a museum, monthly moonlight walks, Saturday night wagon rides from June through September, and other attractions. But you need reservations to go out there and reservations for their activities. Call 693-3621.

Another little gem is the **Chatfield Arboretum**, operated by the Denver Botanic Gardens and offering historic sites, trails and naturalist guides. It's a great place for a picnic, and the traditional playground next to the historic schoolhouse is fun for kids. Down the path along Deer Creek you can see the foundation where the schoolhouse was located before they moved it. Look for the piece of chain on one of the cottonwood branches above the path, the remnant of the swing where kids played 100 years ago. Chatfield Arboretum is just off Wadsworth Boulevard south of C-470. Call for information, 973-3705.

You might also check out **Dinosaur Ridge**, exposed dinosaur bones and tracks along with plant and other fossils where West Alameda Parkway skirts the southwest shoulder of Green Mountain in Jefferson County. The best way for most people to get there is to take I-70 west to the Morrison exit, and head south on Colo. Highway 26. A couple of miles downhill, you'll see the right turn that takes you to Red Rocks. Don't take that! We're offering it only as a landmark to help you identify the turnoff across the road (which will be a turnoff to the left) on West Alameda Parkway. At that left turnoff, there will also be a sign that says Natural National Landmark, and that landmark is Dinosaur Ridge. The road swings uphill, and on the north side of the road, you'll see a stone building and barn. That's the Dinosaur Ridge visitor center, 697-DINO, where you can get information about Dinosaur Ridge hours, tours and directions, as well as buy T-shirts, books, casts of dinosaur footprints and other dinosaur-relevant things. Dinosaur Ridge is essentially an outdoor experience, however. Continuing east on West Alameda Parkway, you'll find on the uphill slope exposed dinosaur bones in the hillside. This is where the first dinosaur bones in the Western United States were found in 1887. It's wheelchair accessible. Over the hill and starting down, you come to another display, this one of exposed dinosaur footprints. It can be a little irritating visiting this display, because usually you have to park and walk along a narrow ditch beside a narrow road where cars are whizzing by. You stand in the ditch and look at the footprints. It's particularly scary when you have small children along, because they tend to jump around erratically and bolt in unexpected directions. However, the Friends of Dinosaur Ridge hold "Open Ridge Day" one Saturday each month from April through October, when the road is closed to cars and volunteers station themselves at the various stops along the road to tell you what you're looking at. You can also join one of the Dinosaur Ridge guided tours. Again, call the visitor center, 697-DINO, for information.

As long as you're out there, you may want to combine your Dinosaur Ridge visit with a visit to the **Morrison Natural History Museum**, where they have some of the original bones that were taken out of the first dinosaur dig site as well as other exhibits. To get to the museum, get back on Colo. Highway 26 and go south into the town of Morrison, turn right in the center of town at the intersection by the Morrison Inn (a great place to stop for American-Mexican food, by the way; see our restaurants section), go about a half-mile to the last stoplight and turn left onto Colo. Highway 8 and go about a half-mile to the museum. You'll see it on your right, a log cabin structure.

State Parks and Recreation Areas

Moving farther out from the urban area, you encounter county park and open space systems. Jefferson County has the largest, but Adams, Douglas and Arapahoe also have their county park systems.

As you get into the mountains, you also encounter the Denver Mountain Parks system, 14,000 acres of mountain parks scattered through four counties. **Red Rocks Park** is one of these, as is **Echo Lake Park**, on the way from Idaho Springs to Mount Evans. So is the **Winter Park** ski area.

When people want to enjoy the great outdoors without driving way into the mountains, the first places they often think about are the four state parks and two state recreation areas right in Greater Denver. We've already mentioned two of them — Chatfield State Recreation Area and Cherry Creek Reservoir State Recreation Area — in relation to a number of activities covered above. But they're all exceptionally fine, and you can get more information by calling ·each park or by contacting the Colorado Division of Parks and Outdoor Recreation's Metro Region office, 791-1957.

Barr Lake State Park near Brighton is a 2,600-acre state park surrounding a 1,900-acre prairie reservoir. Decades ago, the reservoir used to be something of a sewage dump, and people would roll up their car windows when they drove past on I-76. But please, that was long ago. Today it's a charming and tranquil place with more than 300 species of birds. It's the greatest place around here to watch eagles that hunt around the lake and nest in the trees of the lake's southern half, which is designated as a wildlife refuge. It's also the biggest lake in the Denver area where you can canoe, kayak or otherwise go boating without being buzzed by Jet Skis, powerboats and water-skiers. The only boats allowed on the lake are sailboats, hand-propelled craft and boats with electric trolling motors or gas engines of 10 horsepower or less. Hiking here is pleasant because the lakeshore is lined with cottonwoods. There are plenty

of aquatic plants and marshes, where it's always fun to watch the big carp rooting and sucking. On both the north and south ends of the lake you can walk out on wooden boardwalks extending into the lake and watch wildlife from the gazebo at the end. Bring a telescope or binoculars; it's fun to watch the eagles from the southern gazebo. To get there, take I-76 northeast out of Denver about 20 miles to Exit 22, Bromley Lane, east to Picadilly Road and south to the park entrance. There's also a nature center with displays and information and a bookstore. Call the park and/or nature center at 659-6005.

Castlewood Canyon State Park is one of those delightful discoveries that people often make only after years or decades of living in the area. To those used to thinking of Colorado as a mountainous place, this may seem more like some hidden natural gorge refuge on the far plains of Kansas. Part of Colorado's Black Forest, it's a popular place for short- and medium-range hiking and bird-watching. There are viewpoints and hiking trails aplenty. You can follow Cherry Creek along its scenic cut in the landscape. You can visit the old stone ruins of Castlewood Canyon Dam, which look like something left over from the Egyptians. There's also a nifty trail that leads up to a cave, a small cave, but very delightful for kids. Take I-25 south to Castle Rock, go west on Colo. Highway 86, turn south just before Franktown on Douglas County Road 51, and you'll see the park entrance after about 3 miles. Call the park at 688-5242. **Chatfield State Recreation Area** has Greater Denver's widest range of outdoor experiences from powerboating to appreciating nature in remote surroundings. The northern end is the reservoir, a place popular with boaters, water-skiers, swimmers and anglers. At any rate, it's probably the area's great-

Photo: Daily Camera/David P. Gilkey

Colorado may not have an ocean, but lakes and reservoirs offer opportunities for water recreation.

est general recreational resource in terms of variety and scenery. As you get toward the south end, where the South Platte River flows into the reservoir, and head on south from there, you're in the nature part of the park. The South Platte Valley along here is heavily wooded beneath a striking canopy of old-growth, riverbottom cottonwoods. People bike, hike and horseback-ride on the paths following the river, and the river here is also a charming place to cast a line. On the west side, between the river and U.S. Highway 75, the Chatfield Wetlands is a newly created area with ponds and flora engineered to be a natural Colorado wetland. There are lots of waterfowl and animals. You can walk the wetlands from either side. There's a viewing platform just off U.S. Highway 75 on the west side. And if you keep on U.S. Highway 75 farther south, you get to the **Waterton Canyon Recreation Area,** about 4 miles south of C-470. You can take a trail up the canyon, where there are lots of nature observation opportunities (including the canyon's own bighorn sheep herd), picnic spots, fishing, historic spots and

ultimately a connection into the Colorado Trail, which goes all the way to Durango.

The north end of Chatfield, however, is where you'll find the more civilized activities concentrated. The swimming beach is large and first-rate. The campgrounds have more than 150 sites with all the amenities, but we would sure suggest reservations, 470-1144. The **Chatfield Marina**, 791-5555, has extensive facilities and extensive capacity for renting boats, as outlined in our Boating and Windsurfing entry above. You can also rent paddleboats, water toys and pontoon boats there, and you can ride on a hot-air balloon that takes off near the swimming beach. The U.S. Army Corps of Engineers has also been offering summer tours of the Chatfield Dam.

The **B&B Livery**, 933-3636, offers horseback riding. Note that dogs are not allowed in Waterton Canyon Recreation Area. Dogs are allowed in Chatfield on a leash not longer than 6 feet, and there is a dog exercise area where they're allowed off-leash on the north side of the dam, in Chatfield State Recreation Area. To get to Chatfield, take I-25 or I-70 to C-470, and C-470 to the Wadsworth Boulevard Exit, or just take Wadsworth Boulevard south, if you're near it on the west side. Just south of C-470 on Wadsworth, you'll see the park entrance on the left. For more information on all of this, call the Chatfield State Recreation Area's office, 791-7275.

Cherry Creek State Recreation Area is, like Chatfield, based on the existence of a large reservoir, in this case Cherry Creek Lake. It's less nature-oriented and more activity-oriented than Chatfield. However, there are wetlands, including beaver ponds that kids can enjoy by seeing the beaver pop up out of the water now and then. The recreation area gets a lot of school groups for its trails and guided nature walks. The south end is the most nature-oriented, where Cherry Creek and Cottonwood Creek flow into the reservoir. There is a mountain-bike trail and a lot of cottonwood trees and aspens. Along the trail systems you may see mule deer and whitetail deer, owls, coyotes, foxes and the like.

One of the big advantages of this recreation area is that it's so centrally located. It's right off of I-225, surrounded by Aurora, Denver, the Denver Technological Center and Centennial Airport. A lot of people coming here to visit friends or family opt to stay at the recreation area where they can camp or park their RVs. Cherry Creek Lake is not much smaller than Chatfield Reservoir, and the folks at Cherry Creek Rec think their campground is nicer. Call 470-1144 for camping reservations. Their swimming beach is free, unlike Chatfield's. It has 102 campsites on five loops, and most of them are shaded by trees. It has a marina, 779-6144, which we described in our Boating and Windsurfing entry above. Cherry Creek

Rec has riding stables, 690-8235, and a gun club, 693-1765. Call the Cherry Creek State Recreation Area office, 690-1166 or 699-3860. The recreation area is 1 mile south of I-225 on Parker Road.

Golden Gate Canyon State Park is the mountainous one among Greater Denver's six nearby state parks and recreation areas. It's where you go for vistas, and it's real heavy on the aspens, which means you're not likely to find a nearby place with better viewing of the autumn gold — from Panorama Point especially, on the top of the park at its northern edge. A lot of folks like to drive up to Panorama Point on those autumn days of blue skies and green and gold mountains. A little path from the parking lot and picnic area leads to a multilevel, mega-gazebo on the brim of a westward-sloping mountainside, where you can look across deep valleys and up to more than 100 miles of snowcapped peaks along the Continental Divide. The park's 14,000 acres range from 7,600 to 10,400 feet in altitude, and it has 35 miles of trails for foot and hoof, 275 picnic sites and more than 140 campsites as well as backcountry shelters and tent sites. Your first stop is always at the visitors center on the park's lower east end, where there's a pond full of big, tame trout to watch and a museum to browse through. Right outside the visitors center is a nature trail designed for accessibility to the physically impaired. Call Golden Gate's office at 592-1502. You can reach the park by turning west off of Colo. Highway 93 onto Golden Gate Canyon Road and driving about 15 winding miles to the park.

Roxborough State Park is the most natural of Greater Denver's local state parks. It was Colorado's first state park to be designated both a Colorado Natural Area and a National Natural Landmark.

There is only one building, the visitors center. Camping, rock climbing and pets aren't allowed. What you do have is the opportunity to take a number of really lovely hikes/walks through some dramatic and unique natural terrain. Geology-wise, it's spectacular. The Dakota Hogback runs north/south along the west side of the metro area. The park hides behind it to the west with the spectacular red-rock moonscape of the Fountain Formation. You can see this more easily to the north by driving through the Ken Caryl Ranch development north of Deer Creek Canyon, but you can see it in the undeveloped natural state here. There has been some controversy about new housing developments going up just outside the boundaries of Roxborough that destroy the sense of being in a remote place. You can't really see the development from the bulk of the park; the way the park is sequestered behind the Dakota Hogback makes it one of those special places where you can feel remote even though you're close to the metro area. The park is in a transition zone between mountains and plains and has an interesting mixture of mountain and prairie species. You have scrub oak, prairie grass, wet meadows, cottonwoods and box-elders. You'll find some aspen groves, ponderosa pine and Douglas fir on Carpenter Peak. The highest point in the park, Carpenter Peak is one of the trails and offers some great views. The Fountain Valley Loop and the South Rim Trail are also wonderful ways to spend a good part of your day. Bring a backpack with a picnic lunch, and, of course, plenty of water. There are numerous guided nature hikes and nature programs. The park also has an "extended golf cart" ride, known as The Rocks Ride, that can cover some of the trails, available to people who can't hike because of

health reasons or handicaps. But it has a limited schedule, and reservations are required. So call ahead. Reach Roxborough by U.S. Highway 85 (Santa Fe Drive) south from Denver to Titan Road, take a right on Titan and go 3.5 miles. Follow Titan Road left onto Rampart Range Road. Go 3 miles, and turn left onto Roxborough Park Road; then take an immediate right onto the park access road. Call the park, 973-3959, for more information.

Fishing

One-third of the state's land area is open to public hunting and fishing. Colorado is a national destination for these activities, the kind of place where people come from the Midwest and both coasts to hunt elk in the high country, to hunt pronghorn antelope on the prairies or to cast a fly in the mountain streams.

Fishing in Colorado, of course, isn't just a matter of mountain trout streams. The state has flatland rivers, large lakes and reservoirs aplenty. The state's 6,000-plus miles of streams and 2,000-plus lakes and reservoirs open to public fishing include high-country fishing for cutthroat, brook, brown, lake and rainbow trout; but there's also a lot of warm-water quarry such as walleye, largemouth and smallmouth bass, catfish, crappies, yellow perch, wipers, bluegill and muskie. A lot of warmwater fishing is available right in Greater Denver, and, in fact, the state's record tiger muskie at 27 pounds was caught in Quincy Reservoir in Aurora.

Trout enthusiasts may want to try Colorado's Gold Medal waters, so designated because they have a high-quality aquatic habitat, a high percentage of trout 14 inches or longer and a high potential for trophy fish. The Colorado Division of Wildlife has a booklet they can send you on the state's 10 Gold Medal waters; call 297-1192. They have another booklet, *Colorado's Fishing Hot Spots*, featuring a number of hot spots right around Denver, including Aurora Reservoir, Chatfield Reservoir, Cherry Creek Reservoir, Quincy Reservoir, the South Platte River and Bear Creek.

Recorded information on fishing is available 24 hours a day from the Division of Wildlife, 291-7533; for information on fishing conditions, call 291-7534.

Licenses are required; you can get yours at most major sports and outdoors stores. Prices range from $20.25 for Colorado residents to $40.25 for nonresidents for a yearly license; less for a one- or five-day pass. There are discounts for senior citizens and handicapped persons and children younger than 16 do not need a license.

Hunting

Hunting in Colorado offers even more extensive choices of quarry than fishing. There are both gun and bow-and-arrow seasons. Big game is what the state is most famous for, of course, including elk, mountain lion, black bear, mule deer, bighorn sheep, mountain goat, white-tailed deer and pronghorn antelope. But 105 of the state's 113 species of sport game are small game, including ducks and geese, wild turkey, ring-necked pheasant, mourning dove, band-tailed pigeon, quail, grouse, rabbit and coyote. There's a lot of winter trapping as well for beaver, muskrat, bobcat, weasel, marten, mink, badger and fox. The Division of Wildlife has a number of 24-hour, recorded-information lines for hunters: big game hunting, 291-7529; small game, 291-7546; game birds, 291-7547; and waterfowl, 291-7548.

While hunting wildlife is more traditional, recent years have seen a tremendous growth in the stalking of wildlife either to photograph it or just for the joy of seeing it as close as is possible or safe. Again, the Division of Wildlife has a number of publications that promote and assist this pastime, as well as a watchable wildlife information line, 291-7518.

The Colorado Division of Wildlife's main number for information and publications on hunting, fishing, wildlife watching and other outdoor information and opportunities is 297-1192.

Licenses are required; you can get yours at most major sports and outdoors stores. License prices vary greatly, from $15.25 for some small game to almost $1,000 for some big game. Call the Division of Wildlife for a complete list of prices.

Inside
The Great Outdoors

What kind of geography offers more opportunity for outdoor adventure — the seashore, the mountains or the plains? Well, put it this way: The seashore is a line; the plains are a plane; the mountains are a three-dimensional universe. And if it's water you want, the mountains have rivers, lakes and wetlands aplenty, and more trails, mountainsides and hidden valleys than anyone could explore in a lifetime.

Add the state park and recreation areas to the city and county parks, then throw in Rocky Mountain National Park (mentioned in our Daytrips chapter) and the state's federal lands, and you have a lot of open country to bop around in close to Denver.

More than one-third of Colorado's land area is owned by and is available to the public, including 8.3 million acres of Bureau of Land Management tracts and 14.3 million acres of national forest. There are 11 national forests in Colorado, covering major parts of the state. One can't point to specific attractions in the national forests as easily as one can in the state parks and recreation areas, because the national forests are basically undeveloped areas where you can hike, fish, hunt, ride and camp just about anywhere. They are also where the vast majority of wilderness can be found, and if you want to hike to some remote and beautiful backcountry refuge anywhere in the United States, the likelihood is that you'll hike in a national forest.

Photo: Ski the Summit/Carl Scofield

Arapaho National Forest is one of many wilderness areas near Greater Denver.

THE GREAT OUTDOORS

National Forests

While national forests are open generally to timber sales, mining and other activities that purists might find at odds with the idea of a natural setting, wilderness areas are those set aside specifically under the 1964 Wilderness Act, allowing no permanent roads, structures, timber sales or mining other than those that already exist. These areas are wild country, accessible only by trail and closed to motorized transport.

Three of Colorado's national forests are located immediately to the west, northwest and southwest of Greater Denver: Pike National Forest, Arapaho National Forest and Roosevelt National Forest. You can seek information on these from the National Forest Service's Denver Regional Office, 275-5350, or call each National Forest office itself.

Arapaho and Roosevelt National Forests

Arapaho and Roosevelt National Forests, 498-1100, are a combined jurisdiction that span the Continental Divide from the Wyoming border to just south of I-70, west of Denver. Roughly speaking, the Roosevelt National Forest comprises that section east of the Continental Divide. The Arapaho National Forest lies west of the Continental Divide, although the Arapaho National Forest comes east to cover the area south of I-70 to mid-Jefferson County.

Together they make up some 1.3 million acres in the Rocky Mountains and Foothills, wrapping around Rocky Mountain National Park and including 47 National Forest campgrounds and a number of wilderness areas such as the Rawah Wilderness on the Wyoming border, the Indian Peaks Wilderness west of Boulder

and the Cache La Poudre Wilderness around the Cache La Poudre River that flows through Roosevelt National Forest and down to Fort Collins.

Pike and San Isabel National Forests

Another combined jurisdiction, the Pike and San Isabel National Forests, (719) 545-8737, consist of 2.3 million acres. The San Isabel is, at its closest, about 100 miles of winding, two-lane U.S. Highway 285 away from Denver; at its farthest, winding south almost to New Mexico.

The Pike National Forest, at 1.1 million acres, is Greater Denver's national forest neighbor south of I-70 and west of I-25, reaching to the southwest of Colorado Springs (Pikes Peak is part of this national forest.) It contains several converging sources of Greater Denver's South Platte River, as well as that river's most scenic stretches before it reaches the Flatlands. It has a half-dozen of the state's peaks higher than 14,000 feet, sharing Mount Evans with Arapaho National Forest. Its vegetation is drier than Arapaho and Roosevelt, with more juniper, oak brush and bristlecone pine. Its major wilderness area is the Lost Creek Wilderness, 106,000 acres where Pikes Peak granite has been eroded into domes, spires, turrets and crests, with a lot of big-boulder slopes. Lost Creek is less popular than Indian Peaks and the other big wilderness areas to the north, and it's a good place to backpack and find a bit of solitude. One unique feature of the Pike is 118 miles of motorcycling trails in a designated area around Sedalia.

Hiking

Hiking — with backpack, daypack, no pack or leading a laden llama — is the most common way of enjoying the backcountry. Wherever you hike, things get more beautiful the higher you get. You will probably start climbing in the lower forests of aspen and ponderosa pines or dark, moody groves of spruce and fir, but eventually, as you rise, the forest will break open into the "krummholz," or crooked wood zone, where trees stunted by altitude and twisted by relentless winds make a border before the alpine meadows above. When you're "above treeline," you're in alpine meadows, and you're also in the heights of drastic weather.

After advising you not to drink the river water without using disinfectant pills or passing it through a disinfectant pump, the second piece of advice that mountain-savvy folks will give you is to dress in layers. When you start hiking down low, shorts and T-shirt are probably what you'll want to be wearing. But there are few things more miserable than someone who takes nothing warmer or drier and reaches 14,000 feet as the weather moves in, dropping temperatures into the 40s or lower with high winds, sometimes a cold rain, or snow, and usually a good afternoon lightning storm. In a sizeable backpack, if you're hiking high, bring a long-sleeved shirt to put over the T-shirt, something warm such as wool or flannel. Bring a sweater or sweatshirt to put over that, and a windbreaker/raincoat to put over that. A hood is always nice, but you should at least have a knit cap and warm gloves. Bring trousers, or at least sweatpants, to put on over or instead of the shorts. Those are the minimum pieces of

clothing you'll need, along with a sizeable water bottle, water disinfectant tablets and some snacks in case you get weak at high altitude. And don't forget hiking boots if you plan a lengthy hike. Wear double socks, thick socks, to prevent blistering. With two pairs of socks, the socks rub against each other instead of the shoe rubbing through one sock against your foot.

We always hear stories about people who started hiking, miserable with the heat, and wound up huddling in a snowstorm on some alpine boulder field, unable to go on or back because the snow had made the boulders too slippery, thanking their lucky stars that they had brought enough clothes, or cursing their luck that they hadn't.

Another piece of advice you hear from the medical community is to drink a lot of water. Dehydration seems to be a contributing factor in whether or not someone will get altitude sickness, and how badly. Altitude sickness can be deadly; at the very least it's miserable for the sufferer and ruins the day for companions. After eight solid hours of assault on Longs Peak, we've had to turn back just short of the top to shepherd and half-carry a cramping, shaking, nauseated and gasping victim of altitude sickness down to richer oxygen. There's about half as much oxygen at 14,000 feet as at sea level. Consequently, Coloradans have a lot more red blood cells than people living lower.

Also, make sure to get a map, a good map. Get yourself one of those "quadrangle" maps on a 1:24,000 scale, where an inch equals about 0.4 miles. You may

Bring mosquito repellent on those backpacking trips. It makes a big difference in your level of enjoyment.

Insiders' Tips

Photo: Daily Camera

Volunteers work each summer on the Colorado Trail, a recreational path through the high country.

need more than one of them to cover the area of your interest. Another great resource is the *Colorado Atlas & Gazetteer*, a road-atlas-sized book that consists of topo maps of the entire state. Here the scale is more like 1 inch equals 2.5 miles, but you still get good detail, contour lines and trail routes. You can find quadrangle maps and the *Colorado Atlas & Gazetteer* in well-stocked outdoor/camping stores, bookstores and even some gas stations. You can also get maps from the Bureau of Land Management in Lakewood, 239-3600, or from the U.S. Geological Service at the Denver Federal Center in Lakewood, Map and Book Sales, 202-4700.

You need topo maps if you're hiking far off-road. On the rainswept alpine heights of the San Juan National Forest in southwestern Colorado, we once encountered a Boy Scout troop from Texas, hopelessly lost three days into a seven-day tour, the weather worsening and dark falling. They had brought inadequate, large-scale maps, expecting to find signs at trail junctions. There are, of course, few or no signs.

While few things are grander than the mountains in the varying moods of daytime, even fewer things are more eerie or romantic than hiking by moonlight. Plan a hike for a night that's close to a full moon. You may not want to do any hiking off-trail, but where there are trails, it's a beautiful way to spend a night, and a morning. We've done the full-moon hike of Longs Peak, beginning before midnight and climbing the last rock slopes while the first orange sunbeams were making the mountains glow like neon. Another advantage is that, by reaching the top in the early morning, you avoid the more common experience of reaching the top from midday to afternoon, when the thunderclouds often close in.

One-way, long-distance hiking is a lot of fun. Drive two cars to the "trailhead" at one end of some trail of choice that crosses, say, a mountain range. Then both drivers, or as many more as are in the group, get into the other car and drive around to the other side of the mountain range. You get a good hike in without having to retrace your steps.

One of the most impressive places in which to try this maneuver is **Rocky Mountain National Park**. From Bear Lake on the east side of the park to the city of Grand Lake on the west side is about 18 miles. You'll want to get a map of Rocky Mountain National Park, and the park map should be sufficient for this one. It's fun to be able to say you did this, hiking across the entire national park in one day, and it's easier than it sounds. You spend the early part of the day doing about 4.5 miles of steep uphill to the Continental Divide on Flattop Mountain; the rest of the day is an easy downhill amble. The only problem with this hike is that you may overestimate it, and wind up in Grand Lake too early for your dinner reservations. At least one group of senior citizens makes this hike an annual social event.

Another good hike of this kind is through the **Indian Peaks Wilderness** of Arapaho National Forest, just south of Rocky Mountain National Park. Start at scenic Brainard Lake, which you reach via a turnoff to the west from Colo. Highway 72 just north of Ward. Head west from Brainard Lake on the South St. Vrain Creek trail, up and over the Continental Divide, and down to Lake Granby's Arapahoe Bay. Say two couples want to do this hike. Both can drive their cars to Brainard Lake. Couple No. 1 does the hike west to east while couple No. 2 splits up and drives both cars around through Rocky Mountain National Park. Everybody has a camping vacation at the wonderful campground at Arapahoe Bay, or stays at any of the more civilized accommodations in the area. Going back, couple No. 1 drives the cars while couple No. 2 gets to do the hike back to Brainard Lake.

You don't have to be a "technical climber," with ropes and "beaners" and ice axes and all the other gear and specialized knowledge to mount most of the highest peaks in Colorado. You can certainly take any of the many courses available around the area if you want to do technical climbing. A lot of gyms and recreation centers nowadays have their own climbing walls (simulated rock faces) to practice on.

Most people, however, just want to climb mountains, not scale them. You can do it the easy way on any of Colorado's 500 or so peaks higher than 12,000 feet (56 of them higher than 14,000 feet). People feel themselves part of a special club when they have done all of Colorado's "fourteeners." The average person can do many of them, and there are some relatively easy ones close to Denver.

Grays Peak and Torreys Peak are two very accessible fourteeners near Denver. Grays Peak, at 14,270, is the state's ninth-highest mountain, and Torreys Peak, at 14,267, is the 11th-highest. The hike to the top of either peak is about 4 miles. The two peaks are also just a half-mile apart, separated by an easily walkable saddle, so this is really a good opportunity to do two fourteeners in one day. On this, like many high-altitude hikes, you're likely to encounter mountain goats along your path. To find the hike, take I-70 about 6 miles west of Georgetown to the Bakerville Exit; take the road south for about 3 miles up Stevens Gulch to the Stevens Mine. You'll probably see cars parked up ahead, other hikers on the same trail. Cross the creek from where the cars are parked, and you'll find the trail heading 4 miles uphill to Grays and Torreys.

The easiest way to do a fourteener, as we mention in our Daytrips chapter, is to simply drive up to the top of **Mount Evans** from Idaho Springs. If you like to hop boulders as well as walk on trails, one of the most fun excursions you can have in Colorado is to drive to the top of Mount Evans and then hike from there to the top of neighboring **Mount Bierstadt** and back. Like Grays and Torreys, the two mountaintops are quite close, and the sawtooth ridge saddle between them is quite negotiable. It's a wonderful way to enjoy the top of the world. We've made it from the top of Mount Evans to the top of Mount Bierstadt in less than 1½ hours. On the way back, however, we were charmed to see a lovely cloud bank floating toward us until it arrived and closed us in a dense, deathly-chill fog that soaked, turned to snow and covered the boulders with ice. We got so exhausted from the struggle and so cold that we began imagining ourselves succumbing to hypothermia. As we say, come prepared. And watch those cliffs; not just on Mount Evans but everywhere in the mountains. "Quite negotiable" is a relative term, and each year somebody last seen on what should have been an easy hike is found dead by searchers at the bottom of a cliff that should have been approached more carefully, and a lot of others are injured. Here, for example, is the first sentence of a story from the *Denver Post* (July 18,

1995): "A hiker from Minnesota was in critical condition at a Denver hospital last night after falling off a ledge on Mount Evans and sustaining head injuries."

Bierstadt is perhaps a more traditional climb from the parking area at **Guanella Pass**, 3 miles of trail. You reach Guanella Pass by driving south from Georgetown on the Guanella Pass Scenic Byway.

Longs Peak is the most famous fourteener hike, easily reached by trail. That is, it's easy in that the trail is easy to follow, but the climb is a long one. You gain 4,800 feet over 8 miles to the top, and then, of course, you have to hike 8 miles back down. It's truly amazing how many people you encounter up there. Longs Peak is the big one that people point to from Denver. It's probably the most famous and popular big hike in Colorado, and it's close to Estes Park, the tourist city that everyone drives through on their way to Rocky Mountain National Park. To start your hike, drive 10 miles south from Estes Park on Colo. Highway 7, then turn west to the Longs Peak campground and ranger station, where you can start hiking. Typically, the best time is late July and early August. The rest of the year, snow and ice make Longs a technical climb. You might want to check with the rangers at Rocky Mountain National Park before heading out.

For other hiking opportunities, read *A Climbing Guide to Colorado's Fourteeners*, by Walter R. Borneman and Lyndon J. Lampert. Fourteeners aren't the only mountains around, of course, and there are plenty of thirteeners and twelvers that put you at the top of the world. We've always been fond of the hike to the top of **Mount Audubon**, a 13,223-footer that's about a 4-mile slog uphill from Brainard Lake, just off of Colo. Highway 72 north of Ward. The last long slope of this climb is

A 19th-century Perspective of Denver

In 1873, British traveler Isabella Bird spent some time in Denver and other areas of Colorado. Her account of her travels, *A Lady's Life in the Rocky Mountains*, is still in print today and easy to find at Denver bookstores and libraries.

Isabella was an intrepid traveler and a keen observer. She came to town after passing a summer in Estes Park, a summer that included a dramatic climb up 14,255-foot-high Longs Peak in what is now Rocky Mountain National Park. The peak had been scaled for the first time only five years before Isabella was hauled up it by a true character named Rocky Mountain Jim. Isabella missed being the first woman to stand on its summit by about three weeks. American writer and orator Anna Dickinson got credit for that.

Isabella was surprised by Denver, which she called a "great, braggart city." Here, as recounted with permission from the biography *Amazing Traveler: Isabella Bird*, is her description of the streets of Denver:

British traveler Isabella Bird visited Denver in 1873.

Photo: Denver Public Library - Western History Dept.

"Hunters and trappers in buckskin clothing; men of the Plains with belts and revolvers, in great blue cloaks, relics of the war; horsemen in fur coats and caps and buffalo-hide boots with the hair outside; Broadway dandies in light kid gloves; rich English sporting tourists, clean, comely and supercilious-looking; and hundreds of Indians on their small ponies, the men wearing buckskin suits sewn with beads, and red blankets, with faces painted vermilion, and hair hanging lank and straight, and squaws much bundled up riding astride with furs over their saddles."

Readers interested in learning more about Isabella Bird and her adventures are directed to *A Lady's Life in the Rocky Mountains* and also to *Amazing Traveler: Isabella Bird*, by Evelyn Kaye (Blue Penguin Publications, 1994.)

---

pure boulder-hopping, but at the top it's a beautiful view into the Lake Granby/Grand Lake area to the west, not to mention everything else for 70 miles in every other direction. For adventures such as this, Walter R. Borneman wrote a worthwhile book, *Colorado's Other Mountains: A Climbing Guide to Selected Peaks Under 14,000 Feet.*

You don't have to confine yourself

to one-day peak assaults, since the bulk of the state's trails wind along the shoulders of mountains, through their valleys and over the passes between them. *Hiking Trails of Central Colorado* by Bob Martin and *Northern Colorado Hiking Trails* by Don and Roberta Lowe highlight a lot of opportunities not far from Denver. One other book we mentioned in our Kidstuff chapter that bears mentioning again here is *Best Hikes With Children in Colorado* by Maureen Keilty. It has a lot of nice, easy but scenic and enjoyable hikes close to Denver, and it's not just for kids. Adults will enjoy it, too. A popular approach to hiking or horsepacking in the mountains is the get-high/stay-high philosophy. If you're going to gain a lot of altitude, you want to stay up there a while and not go way down and have to hike back up. You may want to camp at some high mountain lake and spend a few days exploring the neighboring peaks and valleys; or you may want to move from one high mountain lake to another. Some people do the latter by taking the trail down from the lake until it intersects another trail to another lake, and then hiking back up. A more scenic way, which is easy if you have a topo map, is to simply hike over the ridges between the lakes. A week spent ridge-hopping from lake to lake along a mountain range is memorable indeed. Among our favorite high mountain camping areas along the central/northern Front Range are the **Rawah Wilderness** west of Fort Collins; the **Never-Summer Range** just east of Rocky Mountain National Park's northern end; and the **Indian Peaks Wilderness**, along the Continental Divide just south of Rocky Mountain National Park. A very lovely area for backpacking to the heights is the **Collegiate Peaks** area, uphill to the west from the city of Buena Vista, about 120 miles southwest of Denver on U.S. Highway 285.

Don't think just in terms of summertime hiking. The trails of summer are the cross-country ski trails of winter. Lisa Stanton's *Colorado Cross-Country Skiing* will be a valuable reference for those of you who take on the winter trails.

Camping

A lot of people want an overnight or longer stay in the mountains, without having to backpack in, and that's no problem. Colorado has car campgrounds nearly everywhere. The only trouble is, it's a little more difficult to make sure you'll have a campsite. The national forests are where most of the camping is, but Colorado is a popular place in the summer. One thing you can do is get there early and take your chances at cruising around looking for an empty space or finding somebody who looks like they are about to leave. The national forests have an toll-free number, and in any part of Colorado a certain percentage of the forest service campgrounds are part of that reservation system. Call (800) 280-2267, but make sure to have ready not just the name of the campground you want but also a selection of other campgrounds in the vicinity. Many times they'll tell you that the one you want is not open to reservations but operates on a first-come, first-camp basis. The person you're talking to on that 800 number is actually sitting in Cumberland, Maryland, where Biospherics, the company that has the contract with the federal government, is located. If you ask the reservationists at Biospherics to suggest another reservations-accessible campground nearby, they will know as much about Colorado campgrounds as they do about campgrounds in Australia.

You should also know that Biospherics in 1995 replaced another company, this one in California, that was handling national forests through a different 800 number in 1994.

If you should call the Biospherics number in 1996 and find it's no longer working, then call the National Forest Service's Denver Regional Office at 275-5350, and ask for the most recent 800 number.

Following is a helpful list, by name, of national forest campgrounds in Colorado that are under the Biospherics reservation system. Note that a road atlas or Colorado state map is likely to have a little tree symbol representing each campground, but no name. The *Colorado Atlas & Gazetteer* often has the name of a lake or creek that coincides with the nearby tent symbol indicating a campground. But there's one resource that names each campground on the map, and that's the National Forest visitor map, one for each national forest, produced by the National Forest Service itself and selling for $3. You can get such maps from the National Forest Service's Denver Regional Office. You can either call them at 275-5350 and ask that they fax or send you an order form, or you can drop in to the Regional Office at 740 Simms St., Lakewood, and pick up the map(s) of your choice. You can also find these maps selling at some outing stores. Call the outing stores in your area first, to make sure they have the maps you need.

ARAPAHO/ROOSEVELT NATIONAL FOREST

(970) 498-2770

Boulder Ranger District

Boulder   444-6600

Campgrounds:
Kelly Dahl
Olive Ridge
Pawnee

Clear Creek Ranger District

Idaho Springs   567-2901

Campgrounds:
Cold Springs
Echo Lake
Guanella Pass
West Chicago Creek
Pickle Gulch (Group Campground)

Estes-Poudre Ranger District

Fort Collins   (970) 498-2770

Campgrounds:
Mountain Park

Redfeather Ranger District

Fort Collins   (970) 498-2770

Campgrounds:
Chambers Lake
Dowdy Lake
West Lake

Sulphur Ranger District

Granby   (970) 887-3331

Campgrounds:
Arapahoe Bay
Green Ridge
Stillwater

Backpacking or car camping, don't forget to bring a fishing pole if you like to fish. Nothing is more aggravating than seeing a limpid lake or exquisite trout pools in a mountain stream and realizing, "Oh no! I didn't bring my pole!" Don't forget your fishing license either.

Insiders' Tips

PIKE NATIONAL FOREST
(719) 546-8737

Pikes Peak Ranger District
Colorado Springs   (719) 636-1602
Campgrounds:
Meadow Ridge
Thunder Ridge
Pike Community (Group Campground)
Red Rocks (Group Campground)

South Platte Ranger District
Morrison   275-5610
Campgrounds:
Buffalo
Kelsey
Lone Rock
Meadows (Group Campground)

South Park Ranger District
Fairplay   (719) 836-2031
Campgrounds:
Aspen
Jefferson Creek
Lodgepole

Just in case you venture farther west than the immediate Greater Denver vicinity, we've included the following listing of other national campsites available through Biospherics in Colorado.

WHITE RIVER NATIONAL FOREST
(970) 945-2521

Aspen Ranger District
Aspen   (970) 925-3445
Campgrounds:
Difficult
Maroon Lake
Silver Bar
Silver Bell
Silver Queen
Difficult Group (Group Campground)

Dillon Ranger District
Silverthorne   (970) 468-5400
Campgrounds:
Heaton Bay
Peak One
Windy Point

Holy Cross Ranger District
Minturn   (970) 827-5715
Campgrounds:
Camp Hale Memorial

Sopris Ranger District
Carbondale   (970) 963-2266
Campgrounds:
Bogan Flats
Chapman
Mollie B
Bogan Flats Group (Group Campground)
Chapman Group (Group Campground)

SAN ISABEL NATIONAL FOREST
(719) 545-8737

Leadville Ranger District
Leadville   (719) 486-0749
Campgrounds:
Baby Doe
Father Dyer
Lakeview
Molly Brown
Silver Dollar
Tabor
Printerboy

Salida Ranger District
Salida   (719) 539-3591
Campgrounds:
Cascade
Chalk Lake
Collegiate Peaks
Mount Princeton
O'Haver Lake
Angel of Shavano Group (Group Campground)

San Carlos Ranger District
Cañon City   (719) 275-4119
Campgrounds:
Lake Isabel South Side
Lake Isabel La Vista
Lake Isabel St. Charles
Ponderosa
Spruce

GUNNISON NATIONAL FOREST
(970) 874-7691

Taylor River Ranger District
Gunnison   (970) 641-0471
Campgrounds:
Dinner Station

Canyons and cliffs of the Rocky Mountain Foothills draw rock climbers.

Photo: Daily Camera/David P. Gilkey

Lake Irwin
Lakeview
Lodgepole
One Mile
Rosy Lane

RIO GRANDE NATIONAL FOREST
(719) 852-5941
Conejos Peak Ranger District
La Jara   (719) 274-8971
Campgrounds:
Aspen Glade
Elk Creek
Lake Fork
Mogote

Del Norte Ranger District
Del Norte   (719) 657-3323
Campground:
Big Meadows

ROUTT NATIONAL FOREST
(970) 879-1722
Hahns Peak Ranger District
Steamboat Springs (970) 879-1870
Campground:
Hahns Peak Lake

North Park Ranger District
Walden   (970) 723-8204
Campground:
Big Creek Lake

SAN JUAN NATIONAL FOREST
(970) 247-4874

Columbine Ranger District
Durango   (970) 274-4874
Campgrounds:
Haviland Lake
Chris Park

Columbine Ranger District
Bayfield   (970) 884-2512
Campgrounds:
Florida
Transfer Park
Florida Group (Group Campground)

Dolores Ranger District
Dolores   (970) 882-7296
Campgrounds:
House Creek
McPhee
House Creek Group (Group Campground)
McPhee Group (Group Campground)

Mancos Ranger District
Mancos   (970) 533-7716
Campground:
Transfer

Pagosa Ranger District
Pagosa Springs (970) 264-2268
Campground:
Williams Creek

Uncompahgre National Forest
(970) 874-7691
Ouray Ranger District
Montrose   (970) 249-3711
Campground:
Amphitheatre

One further note on national forest campgrounds: When one counts those that work on a first-come basis, as well as those on the reservation system, there are a lot of them. For a full list of *all* campgrounds, by national forest, you can call the National Forest Service's Denver Regional Office at 275-5350. They'll mail you the free brochure, "Rocky Mountain Region Campgrounds." Not only does it list all the campgrounds in Colorado, but it also lists campgrounds in national forest and national grasslands in Wyoming, Kansas, Nebraska and South Dakota. This brochure also indicates which campgrounds are in the reservation system, and it also carries the reservations 800 number. It's a good idea to get it, because the campgrounds covered by the reservations system can change from year to year.

You can find a lot of books about camping, but a good basic reference is *The Complete Colorado Campground Guide*, by Outdoor Books Inc. of Denver, available at local bookstores and outing stores.

Resources

There are umpteen books on how to enjoy Colorado's recreational, scenic and natural opportunities. A pass through a major bookstore will load you down with more than you need. Following are a few other informational resources.

Colorado State Parks
Camping, boating and recreation, 866-3437

Colorado Campgrounds
Cabins and Lodge Association, 499-9343

Colorado Division of Wildlife
Headquarters, Denver, 297-1192
Central Region, Denver, 291-7230
Northeast Region, Fort Collins, (970) 484-2836
Northwest Region, Grand Junction, (970) 248-7175
Southeast Region, Colorado Springs, (719) 473-2945
Southwest Region, Montrose, (970) 249-3431

Colorado Dude and Guest Ranch Directory Service
Serving Colorado exclusively, (970) 887-31281

Dude Ranchers Association
Serving all western states including Colorado, (970) 223-8440

Colorado Mountain Club
279-5643

Denver Audubon Society
696-0877

Colorado Dept. of Regulatory Agencies
Outfitters registration office for hunting and fishing, 894-7778

COLORADO OUTFITTERS ASSOCIATION
841-7760

"Lakes of Colorado" is a set of two one-hour videos oriented toward family vacations. They cover 40 lakes and provide relevant information on things such as camping and fishing. Produced by Tenderfoot Productions, 45 Plainsview Road, Boulder, 444-7780, the videos cost $19.95 each or $35 for the set. They're available at local Gart Brothers and other outing stores, or by calling (800) 484-2458.

Photo: Daily Camera/Jay Quadracci

Skiers have their choice of runs or trails within a few hours' drive of Denver.

Inside
Ski Country

Although Denver is on the plains, it's only a little more than an hour or so away from some of the best skiing on the continent. In good snow years (and with the help of snowmaking) the ski season stretches from mid-October through June. Remember, snow can be falling like crazy in the mountains while it's 60 degrees and sunny in Denver. One of the great pleasures of Greater Denver for outdoor enthusiasts is the ability to ski on Saturday and play golf on Sunday — in the same weekend.

At last count, Colorado had 26 ski areas, ranging from little more than hills with rope-tows to world-famous resorts such as Aspen and Steamboat Springs. Seven major areas are daytrips from Denver, including Vail, one of the country's premier ski resorts.

All the big ski areas offer adult and child lessons, child care and specialized lessons; call the general information number given for each resort for prices and special packages. We've given prices for the 1995-96 season whenever possible; the tendency has been for lift tickets to go up $1-$2 every year. Discounted lift tickets are sold at Front Range King Soopers, Albertsons, Safeways, Total gasoline stations and REI sporting goods stores. Availability varies, so call ahead.

If, despite all the wide-eyed descriptions of champagne powder and unbelievable scenery, downhill skiing just isn't your thing, don't despair. The resorts have realized that not everybody skis, and they've come up with winter activities for non-skiers. Sans skis, you can ride the chairlift up to the Lodge at Sunspot at Winter Park simply to enjoy the view and have lunch, then ride back down again. Other widely available winter activities include ice skating, snowmobiling, snowshoeing, horse-drawn sleigh rides and dogsledding.

Cross-country skiing is very popular and getting more so. Groomed cross-country tracks are available at most downhill areas and many backcountry trailheads — including some that connect with the 10th Mountain Trail Association Hut System, which was built to train the U.S. elite ski corps for World War II alpine assault. Some of these are within a few hours' drive from Denver.

Buy reduced-price lift tickets at Greater Denver locations including King Soopers, Albertsons and Safeway supermarkets, Total gasoline stations and REI sporting goods stores.

Insiders' Tips

The fun doesn't stop when the snow melts. During the past 10 years or so, most of Colorado's destination ski areas have concentrated on becoming year-round resorts. They've developed golf courses and have established annual festivals and events such as the annual WestFest at Copper Mountain and A Taste of Vail. Drifting over the Vail Valley in a hot-air balloon ride is a great way to spend the afternoon. And the more than 50 miles of paved bike paths that extend from Breckenridge to Vail are unsurpassed. Joggers, parents with strollers and in-line skaters like it too.

It's crucial to take altitude into consideration when traveling to the mountains. Even folks accustomed to Denver's 5,280 feet above sea level can get dizzy after a high-speed chairlift ride to 12,000 feet. Drink plenty of water, give yourself time to adjust, and slow down if you get a headache or nauseated.

Also, no one should set out on backcountry trails, either on foot or on skis, without sound knowledge of avalanche awareness, direction-finding skills and adequate clothing, food and water. Ideally, even people going on daytrips should be prepared to spend a night outside, as weather conditions in the mountains change extremely. Local bookstores are filled with trail guides; buy one that has basic safety information as well as backcountry routes. And always let someone know where you're going and when you expect to be back. If you want to enjoy the great outdoors when the snow is gone, see our Great Outdoors chapter for hiking, mountain biking and climbing information.

We've listed and described below some ski areas that make feasible daytrips from Denver. We've included information about winter and summer activities, dining, shopping and accommodations, should you decide to extend your daytrip into a weekend or longer. For more information on skiing and ski clubs, see our Sports and Recreation chapter. We've given resource phone numbers at the end of each section and at the end of the chapter as well. Most phone numbers are in the new (970) area code, although a few resorts retain Denver direct-dial numbers and some have toll-free (800) numbers. In general, for activities on the ski mountain itself, call the resort; for lodging, dining and other activities, call the chamber of commerce.

Loveland

The closest major ski area to Denver, Loveland is at the Eisenhower Tunnel, an easy hour's drive west on I-70. Take Exit 216, just before the tunnel entrance. Loveland, the ski area (as opposed to the town, which isn't even close by) is strictly for skiing; there's no lodging or shopping here to speak of, and there's very little in the way of restaurants. Still, with an average annual snowfall of 385 inches, 60 runs, 10 lifts and lower prices than the other close-in areas, there are plenty of reasons to pull off the highway. Snowboarders enjoy a snowboard-only park. One-day lift tickets are $32 adult, suggested Front Range discount price $29. The direct-dial phone number from Denver is 571-5580.

Winter Park

Although it's 70 miles away from Denver, Winter Park is a City of Denver park — hence its name. The resort (Colorado's fifth-largest in skier visits) was developed in the '40s and doubled its capacity in the '70s; the 1992 opening of Parsenn Bowl, a treeless, sunny alpine expanse of largely ungroomed terrain, added another 200 acres.

Photo: Ski The Summit/Bob Winsett

Colorado's ski country resorts offer winter sleigh rides.

Skiing

The town of Winter Park has grown up alongside the resort, but both town and ski area remain casual and low-key. Snowboarding is permitted. Nonskiers can ride the *Zephyr* Express lift to the top of Winter Park ski area and meet the rest of the group for lunch at the beautiful Lodge at Sunspot. One-day lift tickets are $40 adult (1994-95 price), suggested discount price $33 (1995-96 price).

Winter Park is renowned for its handicapped ski program. The National Sports Center for the Disabled is located here. Its 38 full-time staff members and more than 1,000 volunteers can handle the needs of more than 40 different disabilities.

Getting There

To get to Winter Park from Denver, drive West on I-70; exit onto U.S. Highway 40 West at Empire; and continue over Berthoud Pass. There are two entrances to the ski area. Expert skiers turn off at Mary Jane to tackle its challenging mogul runs, while beginners and intermediates start the day at the main Winter Park base. The town of Winter Park is another few miles down the road; the town of Fraser is 5 miles farther. Virtually all lodging, dining and shopping is situated along Highway 40 and visible from the road.

If you balk at driving over a pass, you can make the trip by train. On weekends, the Denver Rio Grande ski train departs Denver's Union Station at 7:15 AM, dropping skiers within walking distance of the lifts, and leaves Winter Park at 4:15 PM just after the lifts close. The trip takes two hours each way and passes through the Moffat Tunnel. Originally, trains traveled over the Continental Divide via the Rollins Pass Road over Corona Pass. The 6.2-mile Moffat Tunnel was completed in 1927, drastically shortening travel time between Denver and the mountains. Cost is $35 same-day roundtrip for adults, $50 in first-class. Discounted lift tickets are available on the train. For information and reservations call 296-I-SKI.

CROSS-COUNTRY SKIING

Downvalley from the downhill area is a top-notch cross-country center called **Devil's Thumb Ranch**, (970) 726-8231 or (800) 933-4339. Skate-skiers love the 85 kilometers of wide flat trails at Devil's Thumb, which fan out into the forest from an expansive meadow. To get there, drive west from Winter Park to the town of Fraser and turn right onto County Road 83. Tickets are $8 adult, $5 ages 7 to 12 and seniors 60 and older, free for children 6 and younger. Lessons and equipment rental are available. Devil's Thumb Ranch is open year round, with hearty dining in the Ranch House Restaurant & Saloon, and private or bunkhouse-style accommodations available. Ask about moonlight sleigh rides and dogsled rides in the winter, and about horseback riding and trout fishing in the summer.

Backcountry skiers like the trails on top of Berthoud Pass and the Jim Creek Trail that begins directly across from the Winter Park ski area. As mentioned in the introduction to this chapter, no one should set out on these trails without a knowledge of avalanche awareness, adequate clothing and a trail guide or maps.

DOGSLED RIDES AND OTHER WINTER ACTIVITIES

Dogsled rides are a newly popular winter activity in Winter Park. **Dog Sled Rides of Winter Park**, (970) 726-8326, charges $90 for two people for a one-hour ride; a child can accompany you for another $10. If you'd rather be pulled by horses than dogs, **Jim's Sleigh Rides**, 726-5527, takes up to 20 bundled-up guests per sleigh past the historic Cozens Ranch, along the Fraser River, with a stop in the woods for refreshments. Cost is $14 adults, $11 ages 12 and younger. Toddlers 2 and younger ride free. Winter Park also has a free public ice-skating rink (rentals can be arranged at a nearby store). Winter Park Resort and the Winter Park/Fraser Valley Chamber of Commerce can provide the names of companies that offer snowcat and snowmobile tours and rentals.

SUMMER FUN

Every summer the green slopes of Winter Park are the site of acclaimed musical events. The **American Music Festival** has featured such popular performers as Bonnie Raitt, John Prine and the Nitty Gritty Dirt Band, while the **Winter Park Jazz Festival** attracts an equally stellar lineup of great jazz musicians. You might see performers enjoying Winter Park's alpine slide or human maze during a break. In 1994, the events were combined for the first time, and in 1995 the jazz festival was canceled — but two country/folk music performances filled the gap. Just what the balance will be in the future remains to be seen; the best bet is to call Winter Park Resort for the most up-to-date information.

MOUNTAIN BIKING

Winter Park has worked hard to attract mountain bikers. More than 600 miles of marked, mapped and maintained trails wind through the Fraser Valley. At the ski area itself, riders can take the easy way up via the Zephyr Express chairlift to connect with another 45 miles of steep, exciting trails. Pick up a trail map at local bike stores or the Chamber of Commerce Visitor Center on the east side of U.S. Highway 40 downtown. The Chamber is open daily from 8 AM to 5 PM and until 7 PM during peak tourist times.

GOLF

Golfers will enjoy the beautiful 18-hole **Pole Creek Golf Club**, about 10 miles northwest of Winter Park in the town of Tabernash, (970) 726-8847. Everyone else can choose among fishing, hiking, horseback riding, jeeping and rafting. Much of the Fraser Valley that isn't privately owned falls within the boundaries of the Arapaho National Forest. The Winter Park/Fraser Valley Chamber of Commerce can provide more information, or contact the National Forest Service in Denver at 275-5350.

DINING

Winter Park has traditionally been a day-use area for Denver families and doesn't have the range of restaurants and stores that the Summit County areas or Vail can offer. But things are picking up. **Dinner at the Barn Sleighrides** provides more than a meal: a horse-drawn sleigh ride through the woods and meadows of an 80-acre ranch, where dinner — with linens and china — is eaten by a kerosene lantern in the horse stalls. After dinner there's live musical entertainment (guitars, harmonica, washboard, banjo). In summer, you make the trip by horse-drawn show wagon. Advance reservations are required. Cost is $45 adult, $30 ages 4 to 12, $5 lap fee for ages 1 to 3 and free for those younger than 1. Prices are slightly higher with a credit card, lower in the summer and don't include tip. Group discounts are available. Call (970) 726-4923.

Gasthaus Eichler, in downtown Winter Park on U.S. Highway 40, (970) 726-5133, is noted for its Austrian and German specialties, while **Chalet Lucerne**, on the opposite side of the highway, serves Swiss food, including fondue, (970) 726-8105. Reservations are suggested at either place. For more casual dining and nightlife, there's the **Crooked Creek Saloon & Eatery** in Fraser (970) 726-9250, which serves Mexican and American food and no small amount of beer. The **Last Waltz Restaurant**, (970) 726-4877, also on Highway 40, has great green chili and other Mexican specialties, as well as a continental menu and killer desserts baked by owner Nancy Waltz. A particularly considerate touch is the senior citizen's menu, with reduced prices for older folk.

SHOPPING

The stores in Winter Park can provide essentials if you've forgotten your hat or goggles or want to rent skates, snowshoes or a mountain bike. There's a nifty little bookstore, **Curiosity Books**, and a sweet bakery, **Carver's** (tucked near the back of Cooper Square). And that's about it. If neat boutiques are what you're looking for, you'd better head to Breckenridge or Vail.

ACCOMMODATIONS

Accommodations in Winter Park range from condominiums on the mountainside to bed and breakfasts in town. **Winter Park Central Reservations**, (800) 729-5813 or 447-0588 (direct dial from Greater Denver) can arrange lodging in more than 50 condominiums, motels, hotels, lodges, inns and bed and breakfasts.

Engelmann Pines, (800) 992-9512 or (970) 726-4632, a bed and breakfast run by a friendly couple, is pleasant and moder-

The luxury hotel at Vail or Beaver Creek that's way out of your price range in the winter may not be so in the summer — rates can drop substantially.

Insiders' Tips

ately priced ($65 to $115 double). Heinz and Margaret Engel have furnished the place with heirloom furniture brought from Europe, and they offer guests a separate kitchen and reading/TV room. If ski-from-the-room convenience is what you're after, check into the full-service **Vintage Hotel**, (800) 472-7017. Its restaurant, Winston's, is known for Beef Wellington and creative pasta dishes (you don't have to stay there to eat there, either). The bulk of available lodgings are condominiums in larger complexes; **Beaver Village Resort** is one well-run and centrally located, although not lavish, choice: (800) 666-0281.

USEFUL NUMBERS

Winter Park Resort, (970) 726-5514, direct dial from Greater Denver, 892-0961

Snow Conditions, 572-SNOW

Winter Park/Fraser Valley Chamber of Commerce, (970)726-4118, direct dial from Greater Denver, 422-0666

Summit County

The Summit County ski areas include **Breckenridge, Keystone, Arapahoe Basin** and **Copper Mountain**. Collectively, these four areas attract more skiers than any other ski destination in North America — and why not? There's tremendous variety, good shopping and restaurants, dependably fine snow and easy access from Greater Denver. Lift tickets are interchangeable among Breckenridge, Keystone and Arapahoe Basin. Ticket cost is $43 adult one-day. A one-day adult lift ticket at Copper Mountain will set you back $42. If you plan to be a frequent user, check out the Ski 3 card (available at Christy Sports stores in the Front Range and Frisco), or the Copper Card (800) 458-8386.

Summit County is about 1½ hours west of Denver on I-70. The Eisenhower Tunnel, opened in 1973, saves motorists 10 miles of driving over Loveland Pass on U.S. Highway 6, a steep, twisting road. Still, U.S. 6 is hard to beat for sheer scenic grandeur, as it crosses the Continental Divide and drops down past Arapahoe Basin before flattening out as it heads toward Keystone and the towns of Dillon and Silverthorne. When time permits and road conditions are favorable, this is a recommended alternate route and the most direct approach to Arapahoe Basin.

The crowds have been coming to Summit County in the summer in record numbers. Among other things, they come for the more than 50 miles of well-marked, paved bike path that winds through Summit County from Breckenridge to Frisco to Copper Mountain and beyond. It is an unmatched public amenity in Summit County, luring even daytrippers from Denver with its motor vehicle-free lanes and grand mountain scenery.

If you're planning a trip to Summit County, you might find it worth your while to read through the entire Summit County section that follows. We've treated each Summit County area separately, listing first ski information, then other winter and summer activities, and finally restaurants, shopping and lodging. But things are close enough so that a person might ski at Breckenridge, eat in Dillon and stay overnight in Frisco. An excellent free public transportation system, the Summit Stage, makes getting around without a car easy; pick up a schedule at the Visitors Center in Frisco, 011 S. Summit Boulevard (at the intersection of Summit Boulevard and Main Street) or Dillon, on U.S. Highway 6 about 1 mile south of I-70 at the Dillon Dam Road. The visitors centers are open daily year round.

Breckenridge

GETTING THERE

To get to Breckenridge, take the Frisco exit from I-70 and drive south on Colo. Highway 9 for 9 miles.

SKIING

Breckenridge, the oldest and largest of the Summit County communities, is an old mining town that got its start when gold was discovered nearby in 1859. A national historic district, Breckenridge boasts a Main Street lined with handsome Victorian buildings that now house great shops, art galleries and restaurants. Breckenridge has 135 trails and 17 lifts spread over four distinct peaks. It is the second-most popular ski mountain in North America. Snowboarding is permitted. There's close-in pay parking near the Peak 9 base, but most skiers park in one of the town's public lots and take the free shuttle to the slopes.

CROSS-COUNTRY SKIING AND OTHER WINTER ACTIVITIES

There is a Nordic skiing center adjacent to the ski area; call (970) 453-6855 for more information. Other winter activities in Breckenridge include the usual — sleigh rides, snowmobiling, ice skating — and the unusual: the annual Baileys International Snow Sculpture Championships every January.

SUMMER FUN

In summer, there's hiking in the Arapaho National Forest and outstanding golf at the only Jack Nicklaus-designed municipal course in America, the **Breckenridge Golf Club**. In 1991, *Golf Digest* named the Breckenridge Golf Club the top public course in Colorado. Call (970) 453-9104.

The **Breckenridge Recreation Center** at 880 Airport Road, (970) 453-1734, is open every day and has indoor and outdoor tennis courts, a pool, racquetball courts, a steam room, a hot tub and separate locker room facilities for men and women. Visitors can purchase a daily admission.

If you'd like to see the Tenmile Range of the Rockies from the back of a horse rather than on foot, **Breckenridge Stables**, (970) 453-4438, prides itself on its gentle horses.

The Blue River, which runs through Breckenridge, is a favorite fly-fishing locale. Fishing licenses can be purchased at various locations in town. A water activity in Breckenridge that's fun for the whole family is paddleboating on Maggie Pond in The Village at Breckenridge.

DINING

Breckenridge has superb dining and shopping. Among the fine restaurants in town are the **St. Bernard Inn**, 103 S. Main Street, (970) 453-2572, for northern Italian food; **Pierre's Restaurant**, 111 S. Main Street, (970) 453-0989, the creation of a French-trained chef; and **Cafe Alpine**, 106 Adams Street, (970) 453-8218, noted for its tapas bar. Reservations are strongly suggested at all of these places. One of the state's first brewpubs, **Breckenridge Brewery & Pub**, is located at 600 S. Main Street, (970) 453-1550 — try the Avalanche Ale or their pub-brewed root beer. Locals favor the **Blue Moose Restaurant**, 540 S. Main Street, (970) 453-4859, for its affordable natural food and friendly atmosphere; and **Mi Casa Mexican Restaurant & Cantina**, 600 Park Avenue, (970) 453-2071, for its Mexican dinners (no reservations).

Greater Denver health clubs and recreation centers offer conditioning classes for skiers.

SHOPPING

Breckenridge's shopping also rates superlatives. A few hours spent walking up and down Main Street will acquaint you with the best the town has to offer. Two galleries that would stand out anywhere are **Hibberd McGrath**, 101 N. Main Street, for fine crafts; and **Kinkopf Gallery**, 320 S. Main Street, for contemporary fine art, including paintings, sculpture, glasswork and pottery. You can get a complete list of local galleries at the Visitor Information Center, 309 N. Main Street.

A few shops that you won't want to miss are **Amazonia's Sweaters**, at Bell Tower Square, 555 S. Columbine and Town Square, 100 N. Main Street. These shops stock a large selection of hand-knitted sweaters at excellent prices. **World Beat Planet Imports**, 100 S. Main Street, offers an interesting collection of clothing, jewelry and accessories from around the world.

Breckenridge also has a first-rate small bookstore, **Morris' Books**, 100 N. Main Street. For Western apparel, visit **The Twisted Pine**, 411 S. Main Street, for men's clothing and hats. For women's gear, check out their shop at 100 S. Main Street.

Blue Harry, 421 S. Main Street, is a unique clothing store that offers unisex jackets, belts, jewelry and other accessories, including their own exclusive shirts. Their men's and women's clothing has a distinctive Western, outdoorsy look. They also have a store in Vail. For a free catalog, call (800) 548-0480.

ACCOMMODATIONS

Accommodations in Breckenridge range from luxury condominiums to Victorian-style bed and breakfasts in historic homes. The **Williams House Bed & Breakfast**, 303 N. Main Street, is an especially well-appointed 19th-century home with period furniture and antiques, but guests also enjoy the modern pleasure of an outdoor hot tub. A wheelchair-accessible Victorian cottage with Jacuzzi, fireplace and sitting area is also available. Winter rates range from $89 to $200; you can reach the innkeepers at (970) 453-2975. Nonsmoking adults only. The Breckenridge Resort Chamber can provide information about the other bed and breakfasts in town or book a condominium or hotel room. **The Village at Breckenridge** is a huge complex with athletic facilities, (970) 453-2000.

USEFUL PHONE NUMBERS

Snow Conditions, (970) 453-6118

Breckenridge Ski Resort General Information, (970) 453-5000 or (800) 789-SNOW

Breckenridge Outdoor Education Center (Disabled Skiing), (970) 453-6422

Breckenridge Resort Chamber, (800) 221-1091 or (970) 453-6018

Breckenridge Resort Chamber Guest Services & Activities, (970) 453-5579

Town of Breckenridge Trolley Information, (970) 453-2251

Keystone and Arapahoe Basin
Frisco, Dillon, Silverthorne

GETTING THERE

The exits for Dillon and Frisco are directly off I-70. For Keystone and Arapahoe Basin, exit onto U.S. Highway 6 at the Dillon/Silverthorne Exit 205. Keystone is 6 miles down the road, and Arapahoe Basin is 5 miles farther.

SKIING

Keystone is a self-contained resort, but what contains it are the municipalities of Dillon, Silverthorne and Frisco. When Keystone opened for business in 1969-70 it was widely considered a good spot for be-

ginners and intermediates but not challenging enough for experts. The addition of steep and bumpy North Peak in 1984 and the expansion into the powder-filled glades of The Outback and The Outback Bowls in the '90s have greatly changed the character of the area and made it more attractive to advanced skiers. Keystone is noted for its snowmaking capability, which often allows it to open earlier than its neighbors. It is also the only ski area in Summit County to offer night skiing, until 9 PM. Snowboarding is not permitted here — an important distinction between Keystone and all the other ski areas close to Greater Denver.

Keystone is in the midst of a $400 million base area development that will add hundreds of residences, shops and a planned 250-room grand hotel. Called the Village at River Run, the multiphase project will include five different residential communities and facilities such as a library and community center.

Technically part of Keystone but situated 5 miles away at a (gasp) base altitude of 10,800 feet above sea level, Arapahoe Basin is where Insiders head for unbeatable spring skiing. In 1992-93, a phenomenal snow year throughout the state, Arapahoe Basin stayed open until July 4, and in 1995 — when late-season snows piled up — Arapahoe Basin was open until August 10, its latest closing date ever. It's not unusual late in the season to see skiers in shorts and T-shirts. A-Basin, as it's universally called, is characterized by tough terrain and tough weather conditions — but a good day here is a great day. Don't forget the sunscreen.

CROSS-COUNTRY SKIING AND OTHER WINTER ACTIVITIES

A Nordic center at Keystone provides 18 kilometers of groomed trails and access to 57 kilometers of backcountry trails in the Arapaho National Forest. Rentals, lessons and tours are offered, including a full-moon tour with après-ski beverage. **The Keystone Cross Country Center** is located 2.2 miles east of Keystone on Montezuma Road next to the Ski Tip Lodge. The **Keystone Activities Center** can provide more detailed information. There is a Nordic center, designed by Olympic silver-medalist Bill Koch, in Frisco, too, with 35 kilometers of trails near Dillon Reservoir. Call (970) 668-0866 for prices and rental information.

If you'd rather strike out on your own, some of the best cross-country skiing in Summit County is found by continuing along the road to Montezuma past the Ski Tip Lodge. Peru Creek (for beginners) and St. Johns and Wild Irishman Mine (for intermediates) are favorite tours for Front Range skiers. Remember to take precautions; let someone know where you're going and when you expect to return.

As for other winter activities, Keystone is home to the largest maintained outdoor skating lake in the country. Sleigh rides and snowmobiling can be arranged by calling the Keystone Activities Center.

SUMMER FUN

In summer, Dillon Reservoir — locally known as Lake Dillon — provides landlocked Coloradans with one of the state's greatest recreational assets, a 3,000-acre reservoir (the country's highest) ringed by mountains. The lake can accommodate sailboats, kayaks and fishing boats; char-

ters are available. Weather and water level permitting, the marina is open from the end of May through the last weekend in October. For information, call the **Dillon Marina** at (970) 468-5100.

There's golf at the **Keystone Ranch Golf Course**, designed by Robert Trent Jones Jr., (800) 451-5930, and at the more mountainous **Eagles Nest Golf Club** in Silverthorne, 468-0681.

The main fishing artery in Summit County is the Blue River, where anglers hope for trout. Contact a local fishing shop or the Colorado Division of Wildlife for more information, 291-7533.

DINING

The **Alpenglow Stube**, atop Keystone's North Peak, serves Bavarian-accented contemporary cuisine for lunch and dinner and is reached via enclosed gondola chairlift. The Stube is closed during the spring and autumn shoulder seasons, when the gondola doesn't operate. The rustic **Keystone Ranch** is another very classy place to eat: a restored ranch with a AAA Four Diamond rating and six-course dinners. It's open year round. To make a reservation at either restaurant (required), call **Keystone's Dining & Activities Center**, (800) 451-5930 or (970) 468-4130.

The **Old Dillon Inn**, (970) 468-2791, on Colo. Highway 9 in Silverthorne, is always packed on weekends with skiers who come for the Mexican food and margaritas, the impressive 19th-century bar and the rollicking music. For a quieter evening, cook your own steaks on the grill at **The Mint** in Silverthorne, 341 Blue River Parkway, (970) 468-5247. In one of the oldest buildings in Summit County, The Mint is a fun-for-the-whole-family dining spot. For a hearty pre-ski or pre-sail breakfast, take your appetite to the **Arapahoe Cafe**, 626

Lake Dillon Drive, Dillon, (970) 468-0873. The **Snake River Saloon**, 23074 U.S. Highway 6 in Dillon, (970) 468-2788, is locally famous for its spirited après-ski and late-night entertainment.

SHOPPING

The factory outlet stores in Silverthorne are reason enough to drive up from Denver. Clustered in three malls just off I-70 at Exit 205 are bargain outlets for 80 well-known manufacturers, including **Bass Shoes, Liz Claiborne, Starter Sports, Nike, OshKosh B'Gosh** and **Miller Stockman Western Wear**. The stores are open seven days a week and claim a 40-percent average savings over retail. For information, call (970) 468-9440.

ACCOMMODATIONS

Accommodations in Keystone include the luxurious **Keystone Lodge** and the truly deluxe **Chateaux d'Mont**. There are also condominiums of all sizes and private homes available for rental. Contact **Keystone Reservations**, (800) 222-0188 or (970) 468-4242.

Simpler but charming and comfortable lodging can be found in Frisco, Dillon and Silverthorne. The **Galena Street Mountain Inn**, (800) 248-9138 or (970) 668-3224, is a pretty, modern bed and breakfast in Frisco, tucked half a block back from Main Street and near the bike path. Rooms are $80 to $150, depending on the season. Summit County Central Reservations can provide more possibilities.

The **Best Western Ptarmigan Lodge**, (800) 842-5939 or (970) 468-2341, is on Lake Dillon at 652 Lake Dillon Drive (take Exit 205 off I-70). The lodge has deluxe motel accommodations, kitchenettes, condominiums with fireplaces and serves continental breakfast year round. Rates vary, depending on the season and type of accommodation selected, but are generally mid-range for this area. Kids younger than 12 stay free. In the height of ski season, a five-night minimum stay may be required. Newly remodeled to be more wheelchair-accessible, the lodge now has a hot tub, sauna and more cable TV channels.

There is a second Best Western lodge in Summit County, the **Best Western Lake Dillon Lodge**, at 1202 N. Summit Boulevard in Frisco, (800) 727-0607 or (970) 668-5094. More of a full-service hotel than the Ptarmigan Lodge, it has large rooms, an indoor pool, a hot tub, a restaurant, a ski shop and a lounge on-site. It also has family rooms available with three double beds. Kids 18 and younger stay free. Again, rates vary tremendously, but are moderate for the area and comparable with the Holiday Inn, described below.

The 215-room **Holiday Inn**, at 1129 N. Summit Boulevard in Frisco (across the street from the Best Western Lake Dillon Lodge), provides comfortable overnight accommodations in a location just off I-70 that's more convenient than scenic. There's an indoor pool, sauna, hot tub, restaurant, lounge, gift shop and ski shop on the premises, and you are also within walking distance of Frisco shops and res-

Lift tickets are usually cheaper the first and last few weeks of the ski season. Check local newspapers or call the ski areas to find out what deals are available.

taurants. Rooms can cost anywhere from $59 to $175, depending on the season. Kids 18 and younger stay free. For reservations, call (800) 782-7669, or from Denver, 573-6345. The local phone number is (970) 668-5000.

Both the Best Western Lake Dillon Lodge and the Holiday Inn are close to the bike path and a Summit Stage bus stop. To reach either hotel, take Exit 203 off I-70.

USEFUL PHONE NUMBERS

Snow Conditions, (970) 468-4111, direct dial from Greater Denver, 733-0191

General Information, (800) 222-0188

Keystone Resort & Keystone Reservations, (800)789-SNOW, (970) 468-2316 or (970) 468-4242

Keystone Activities & Dining Center, (800) 451-5930 or (970) 468-4130

Summit County Chamber of Commerce general information, (970) 668-5800

Summit County Chamber of Commerce, Dillon Visitors Center, (970) 668-3671

Summit County Central Reservations, (800) 365-6365 or (970) 468-6222

Copper Mountain

GETTING THERE

Copper Mountain is about 75 miles west of Denver. To get there, take I-70 west and get off at Exit 195.

SKIING

Copper Mountain was constructed as a self-contained resort in the early 1970s. It is the home of Club Med's first North American ski center and a very enticing place for intermediate and expert skiers, as more than half the trails are rated advanced. Copper has also put a great deal of effort into its ski school program, so beginners will feel comfortable here as well — sometimes Copper even offers free skiing on its easiest lifts. Actually, the mountain divides itself rather nicely between harder and easier skiing. Still, Copper has a reputation as a prime destination for serious skiers who are looking to maximize time on the slopes and are turned off by the glamorous atmosphere of Vail. Snowboarding is permitted. A one-day adult lift ticket to Copper Mountain costs $42, suggested discount price $34.

In January 1996, Copper is expected to complete construction of a new double lift that will serve the 700-acre Copper Bowl. The expansion makes Copper the biggest ski area in Summit County.

CROSS-COUNTRY SKIING AND OTHER WINTER ACTIVITIES

The cross-country skiing tracks at Copper Mountain begin near the Union Creek base area and branch off into the rolling, wooded valleys of the Arapaho

---

Insiders' Tips

If you'd like to hike or ride a mountain bike into the wilderness around the Holy Cross Wilderness area near Vail, Aspen or Copper Mountain, but aren't keen on sleeping in tents, the 10th Mountain Division Hut Association huts are open in the summer from July 1 through Sept. 30. Call (970) 925-5775 for more information or to make reservations.

Photo: Rio Grande

The Rio Grande Ski Train runs from Denver to Winter Park, Denver's ski area.

National Forest. You can book rentals, lessons and overnight hut trips by calling (970) 968-2882.

SUMMER FUN

The **Copper Creek Golf Club** is the highest altitude championship golf course in America (elevation is 9,650 feet, meaning your ball will fly 15 to 20 percent farther than at sea level). Hikers, backpackers and horseback riders will enjoy challenging themselves on the Wheeler-Dillon Pack Trail, which begins across the highway from Copper Mountain and climbs rapidly into the rugged Gore Range in the Arapaho National Forest. You can arrange pack trips through Copper Mountain Stables. The Colorado Trail, a 469-mile trail that extends from Denver to Durango, passes near Copper Mountain, too. During Labor Day weekend, Copper Mountain hosts the **Michael Martin Murphey WestFest**, with three days of country-and-western music, crafts and food. For information about any summer activity at Copper Mountain, call Copper Mountain Resort, (800) 458-8386.

DINING

O'Shea's, (970) 968-2882, ex. 6504, in the Copper Junction Building at the base of the American Eagle lift, has been satisfying hungry skiers with its nachos, burritos and hamburgers for years. It's closed during the summer. Locals also like **Farley's Prime and Chop House**, 104 Wheeler, for steaks, ribs and seafood, (970) 968-2577.

SHOPPING

While Copper Mountain has enough shops to provide the necessities and a few that provide delight, its offerings are eclipsed by what Vail, just a half-hour away, has to offer.

ACCOMMODATIONS

Virtually all the overnight lodging at Copper Mountain is in condominiums. Call **Copper Mountain Resort**, (800) 458-8386, for rental information.

USEFUL PHONE NUMBERS

Snow Report, (800) 789-7609 or (970) 968-2100

Copper Mountain Resort general information, (800) 458-8386 or (970) 968-2882

Vail Valley

GETTING THERE

Vail is along I-70 about 100 miles west of Denver; Beaver Creek is 11 miles farther west.

SKIING

Many Front Range residents have a love-hate relationship with Vail. They love the skiing — acres and acres of varied, magnificently designed slopes — but hate the crowds, glitz and high prices. Driving to Vail from Denver also means navigating Vail Pass, which can be treacherous in bad weather and an incentive to exit at Copper Mountain, or sooner. Still, every self-respecting skier should try Vail at least once. It's the largest single ski-mountain complex in North America: three base areas, more high-speed quadruple chairlifts than any other ski area and vast powder-filled back bowls that spread out over 2,700 acres of spectacular alpine terrain. China Bowl alone is as large as many ski areas. Intermediates especially can ski all day and never go down the same run twice.

What's more, a ticket at Vail is interchangeable with one at Beaver Creek, Vail's little (but even richer and more exclusive) sister 11 miles farther west on I-70. First opened in 1980-81, elegant Beaver Creek attracts an international elite clientele as well as local skiers who praise the area for its spectacular natural beauty, lack of crowds, free parking and intimate feel. About 80 percent of the runs at Beaver Creek are intermediate or advanced. Snowboarding is permitted at Vail and Beaver Creek.

One-day adult lift tickets are $49. Kids do not ski free here: a child ticket for ages 12 and younger is a hefty $35. Parking can add another $10 to your tab, so carpool if you can. Still, with more than 4,000 acres of trails, and only 100 miles from Denver, Vail remains a top destination for serious skiers. Its international clientele means that you never know who might be in the gondola with you — a neighbor from Denver or a visitor from Europe or Mexico.

Modeled after a Tyrolean village, Vail is a charming town that caters to pedestrians. Free buses link all the base areas. Vail is also home to the **Colorado Ski Museum**, at the Vail Transportation Center, (970) 476-1876, and the frequent site of World Cup ski races.

CROSS-COUNTRY SKIING AND OTHER WINTER ACTIVITIES

Vail and Beaver Creek operate three cross-country ski centers: a **Nordic center** at the Vail Golf Course, (970) 479-4391, for track skiing and skating; the **Golden Peak Cross Country Ski Touring Center**, (970) 845-5313, at Vail with backcountry access to Vail Mountain and the White River National Forest; and the **Beaver Creek Cross Country Ski Center**, (970) 845-5313, at the bottom of Strawberry Park lift (chair 12). At Beaver Creek, skiers ride the lift up to McCoy Park, which sports a 32K system of groomed trails. Equipment rentals, tours (including snowshoe tours) and lessons are available at all three areas. On Thursdays you can take an all-day nature tour from Golden Peak that includes a gourmet lunch (about $65); advance reservations are required.

There are abundant opportunities for backcountry touring throughout the Vail Valley; the summit of Vail Pass itself is often the first ski tour of the year for many Denver backcountry enthusiasts, as it receives plentiful early snow. The town of Vail and Vail Pass are the starting or ending points for several overnight tours to 10th Mountain Trail Association huts, including the luxurious (well, for a hut) **Shrine Mountain Inn**. Reservations are essential; call the **10th Mountain Trail Association**, (970) 925-5775.

The bobsled run at Vail is a thrilling ride. Snowmobile and sleigh rides can be booked through local companies, and Vail's world-class **John A. Dobson Ice Arena** is open for public skating (admission: $4 adults, $3 for children younger than 12 and $2 for skate rentals). Children 4 and younger admitted free. Call (970) 479-2271.

SUMMER FUN

Summer is glorious in the Vail Valley. Hikers and backpackers can explore a large network of trails, either on foot or on horseback. Most of these trails lead rather rapidly up to the Continental Divide and are fairly steep, but the many lakes and waterfalls provide lots of resting and picnic spots. Much of the land around Vail is part of the White River National Forest; call or visit the Holy Cross Ranger District Office (off the West Vail exit ramp) for suggested routes and maps, (970) 827-5715.

There are several public and private golf courses in the Vail Valley, the most touted of which is the **Beaver Creek Resort Golf Club**, (970) 949-7123, a Robert Trent Jones Jr. course.

DINING

Two of the finest restaurants in the state are located in Vail: **Sweet Basil**, 193 E. Gore Creek Drive, (970) 476-0125, and the **Wildflower Inn**, 174 E. Gore Creek Drive in the Lodge at Vail, (970) 476-5011. Both are expensive but well worth it for special occasions; reservations recommended. Sweet Basil serves inventive American cuisine in a pretty spot by Gore Creek. The Wildflower Inn offers up superbly creative American cuisine in an elegant setting.

Dining in Beaver Creek is even more heavily tilted toward the expensive than in Vail, and reservations are de rigueur. **Mirabelle**, located in a former home at 55 Village Road, (970) 949-7728, receives high praise for its romantic ambiance, excellent service and French cuisine with a twist. It's closed briefly during the spring and fall, between ski season and summer. Up on the slopes of Beaver Creek, **Beano's Cabin** is more than just a meal: reached by sleighride, this elegant log-and-glass lodge offers six-course gourmet meals for adults and children, as well as entertainment. In the summer, you can get there via horseback or horse-drawn wagon (about a one-hour trip) or by shuttle van (a 10-minute trip). Naturally, an experience like this doesn't come cheap: adults pay $75 (tax, tip and alcoholic beverages extra); children 12 and younger, $46. For reservations call (970) 949-9090.

Eldora Mountain Resort in Nederland, 440-8700, is a great little ski area in Boulder County that you can get to without sitting in the middle of I-70 traffic. It has nine lifts, 1,400 feet of vertical gain, beautiful Continental Divide views, rentals and lessons, cross-country tracks and night skiing.

Insiders' Tips

For more casual, less expensive meals, head to **Chili Willy's**, 101 Main Street, in Minturn (7 miles west on I-70, 2 miles south on U.S. Highway 24). You'll find great Tex-Mex fajitas, margaritas and a fun atmosphere, (970) 827-5887.

SHOPPING

Vail and Beaver Creek are known for their fine selection of shops and galleries. For colorful, contemporary regional art, visit **Vail Village Art**, 194 E. Gore Creek Drive. The Vail Valley Gallery Association publishes a guide to area galleries that you can pick up at any member gallery, or call (970) 949-1626. Ask about their Saturday evening gallery walks in the summer.

Vail and Beaver Creek offer resort town shopping at its finest. **The Golden Bear**, 286 Bridge Street, has ladies' clothing and men's and ladies' jewelry, including earrings, pendants, bracelets and other accessories featuring its trademark golden bear (available in sterling silver, too). **Gorsuch Ltd.**, 263 E. Gore Creek Drive, has been supplying Vail Valley residents and visitors with ski clothing and other sportswear — including biking and fly-fishing gear for the summer — for more than 30 years. **Pepi Sports** at 231 Bridge Street, is another longtime source for outerwear and sportswear, as well as ski, bike and Rollerblade rental. There's also **True North**, at 100 E. Meadow Drive, which stocks an array of Canadian-designed outerwear, sweaters, pants and boots. **Slifer Collection**, 230 Bridge Street, carries gorgeous furniture and home furnishings, including the Ralph Lauren Home Collection.

ACCOMMODATIONS

A reasonably priced room can be hard to come by in the Vail Valley. When money is no object, grand lodges and luxury hotels such as **The Lodge at Vail**, (800) 331-5634 or (970) 476-5011; **Beaver Creek Lodge**, (800) 732-6777 or (970) 845-9800; and the truly special **Lodge at Cordillera**, (800) 548-2721 or (970) 926-2200; are happy to oblige. A bed and breakfast somewhat off the beaten track is the **Eagle River Inn**, 145 N. Main Street in Minturn, (800) 344-1750 or (970) 827-5621, an enchanting Santa Fe-style hostelry with 12 rooms ranging in price from $95 to $200. U.S. Highway 24 runs right through Minturn. Many hotels offer greatly reduced rates in summer. Check the Denver newspapers for special packages, or call **Vail/Beaver Creek Reservations**, (800) 525-2257.

USEFUL PHONE NUMBERS

Vail Associates/Ski Area information, (970) 476-5601

Snow Report, (970) 476-4888

Vail/Beaver Creek Reservations, (800) 525-2257 or (970) 845-5745

Vail Valley Tourism & Convention Bureau, (800) 525-3875 or (970) 476-1000

Ski Country Resources

COLORADO
CROSS-COUNTRY SKI ASSOCIATION

For brochures on cross-country centers, (800) 869-4560

COLORADO SKI COUNTRY

Daily Ski Conditions/Reports (statewide), 825-7669

NATIONAL WEATHER SERVICE

Denver and central mountains, 398-3964

Road Conditions within 2 hours of Denver, 639-1111

NATIONAL FOREST SERVICE
Denver Regional Office, 740 Simms, Lakewood, 275-5350

ARAPAHO NATIONAL FOREST
Dillon District Office, 680 Blue River Pkwy., Silverthorne, (970) 468-5400

WHITE RIVER NATIONAL FOREST
Holy Cross Ranger District Office, 24747 U.S. Highway 24, Minturn, 827-5715

COLORADO DIVISION OF WILDLIFE
Fishing information, 291-7533

10TH MOUNTAIN DIVISION HUT ASSOCIATION
Aspen, (970) 925-5775

U.S. GEOLOGICAL SURVEY
Topographical maps, 202-4700

Recommended Guidebooks

Rocky Mountain Skiing by Claire Walter (Fulcrum Publishing)

Skiing Colorado's Backcountry by Brian Litz and Kurt Lankford (Fulcrum Publishing)

The Hiker's Guide to Colorado by Caryn and Peter Boddie (Falcon Press)

Watch out for wenches at the Colorado Renaissance Festival,
held each summer at Larkspur.

Inside
Annual Festivals and Events

Exactly what constitutes a festival or annual event?

Nature puts on its own festivals and annual events, like the festival of golden glory that you can enjoy when the mountains stage their annual event of aspen trees in autumn colors. The bugling of elk, an eerie piercing serenade that sounds a lot like the singing of whales, is certainly an annual event you may enjoy experiencing in numerous mountain valleys. Around and in close proximity to Greater Denver, both the natural and human worlds present continuous menus of festivals and annual events ranging from the large to the minuscule.

This list should be viewed as a practical guide to those staged human festivals and events with a designated date and location, but a few words of warning: Dates can change from year to year, often well after this guide is published, so an event listed below as being in September, for example, may actually turn out to be in October; telephone numbers can also change after this guide has been published, although the old number can usually steer you to the new number. A good

hedge against late changes in dates and information phone numbers, and just a useful thing to acquire anyway, is the "Denver Events Guide 1996" (updated annually) available from the Denver Metro Convention & Visitors Bureau, 892-1505. Or if you find that one of our information phone numbers has gone bad by the time you try to use it, just call the Bureau and ask for the correct number. They may have it.

While the Bureau's events guide is not as extensive as the listings below, it has one significant advantage. Our listings include only annual events, those that happen every year. The Bureau's guide includes many events that happen just once, such as a performance by a specific musical or dance group.

A lot of the events below are not one of a kind, and similar events can be found throughout the year. Between the City of Golden, the Buffalo Bill Memorial Museum and the Buckhorn Exchange, for example, you can find enough Buffalo Bill events to keep you buffalo crazy all year. There are mountains of mountainman rendezvous. Nearly every community has its own yearly celebration, from the Carnation Festival in Wheat Ridge to Western Welcome Week in Littleton. Mountain communities and ski areas, ditto. Remember that whenever you go to an event in some community or ski area, you're also placing yourself in a position to enjoy the other attractions there and nearby.

Some festivals and events, such as the Bolder Boulder 10K run, are one-shot deals. Others, such as the "World's Largest Christmas Lighting Display" at the Denver City and County Building, may stretch out over weeks.

For the most part, this list is confined to the Greater Denver area, but you'll notice that we've also covered events during the year at nearby ski areas and mountain communities. This list goes as far afield as Cheyenne, Wyoming; Estes Park and Colorado Springs, all easy daytrips.

In some cases, you can expect to experience exactly what we have described in the following entries. We can't guarantee that a festival or event will be exactly the same every year, but we can tell you what to expect based either on promises by the organizers or on the experiences of past years.

And once again, we certainly haven't covered everything there is to do. On the Fourth of July, for example, communities and organizations all over Greater Denver and the surrounding landscape have fireworks shows. Looking out across the plains from the mountains, the entire landscape seems to be erupting in fireworks. We recommend driving up in the evening to any Foothills road with an east-facing view, parking and enjoying the show.

And of course, if you're looking for festivals and events, you may want to go beyond those annual events that a book like this can clearly provide. Many of the organizations and communities listed here have events that are not repeated every year, and many other organizations and communities have the same. Take the **Colorado Rockies** baseball team for one example. They're playing constantly from spring to fall. The **Centro Cultural Mexicano**, 830-0708, every month presents art exhibits, storytelling, and featured Hispanic artists. Fashionable **Cherry Creek** has what it calls summer strolls from June through August and gallery walks in February, May, September and December. The **Colorado Railroad Museum** at several points throughout the year has what it calls "steam ups," in which it fires up and moves Colorado's oldest locomotive, No. 346. The **Denver Botanic Gardens** has a wonderful series of concerts during the summer, too many to list individually here. These are just a few of countless sources of entertainment.

Beyond this list, the best advice we can give is that you should check your Friday weekend sections of *The Denver Post*, *Rocky Mountain News* and the Boulder *Daily Camera*, where the goings-on are listed in considerable detail. And don't miss the impressive events and activities section each week in *Westword*, Denver's leading weekly newspaper available free in newspaper dispensers all over Greater Denver beginning on Wednesday and continuing until the dispensers are empty.

Use this list and take this advice, and you'll have more events and festivities than you could attend if you split into 10 copies of yourself and every danged one of you spent the year at a dead run in pursuit of fun.

January

DENVER BOAT SHOW

The Colorado Convention Center
700 W. 14th St.
Convention Center or Currigan Exhibition Hall
1324 Champa St.
Denver   892-1505

Boathead heaven in January. The year's big boat show usually lasts four days, spanning a weekend and jammed with aquatic craft, rubber rafts, gear and accessories fore and aft. It's great fun to goggle at the huge luxury boats.

CHEF'S CUP RACE AND BENEFIT DINNER DANCE

West Portal Station at the base of Winter Park Ski Area
Winter Park   892-0961

Ski competition followed by gastronomy in early January. The West Portal Station is where the Moffat (train) Tunnel under the Continental Divide comes out on the west side, right by the base lodge of Winter Park. You can watch the ski racing from the base lodge, and that's where the dinner dance is held. Each of the featured chefs from around the Fraser Valley (the region from Winter Park to Fraser) prepares one specialty dish, and visitors can thereby get a sampling of the regional fare.

ULLR FEST

Breckenridge   (970) 453-6018
Usually the third full week of Jan.

Pronounced "oo-ler." Helmets with horns on them are the height of fashion at this festival in honor of Ullr, the Norse god of snow. If you don't have a horned helmet, it will be a miracle if you can't find somebody selling them. (They are handed out free at the parade.) Ullr Fest starts on a Monday and runs into the following weekend. It includes a parade, fireworks on the mountainside near the ski area and a variety of different events daily. There are World Cup Championship freestyle competitions at the ski area, including events in ski ballet, mogul skiing and aerial jumping. Other activities include the opportunity for kids to go ice skating with cartoon characters and concerts. A dating game is hosted by Biff America. And the Ullympics feature coed teams competing in crazy events throughout the week.

NATIONAL WESTERN STOCK SHOW & RODEO

Denver Coliseum
4600 Humboldt St.
National Western Complex
4655 Humboldt (Take Brighton Blvd. Exit off I-70), Denver   297-1166
Starting on a weekend in early January and running through the next two weekends.

Get out of Dodge and get into Denver for this one. Everybody else does, or at least what seems like half the population of the American West. At nearly 90 years of age, the National Western is the largest annual event in Denver and growing. You'll be in the company of more than 580,000 people, but the National Western is spaced over 16 days, so there's plenty of room and time to tour the show competitions of everything from horses, sheep and cattle to chickens and rabbits in more variety than you dreamed existed on the planet. Rodeo events go on every day, with the nation's top horse and bull riders, calf ropers, you name it, competing for nearly $500,000 in prizes. Between the big events, you can see all kinds of oddball fun: Western battle recreations (cover the kids' ears if loud noises scare them), a sheepdog herding sheep with a monkey in a cowboy suit riding on its back, rodeo clowns, chuckwagon races. The National Western begins with a colorful parade through downtown Denver.

You might also want to check out what

Photo: Daily Camera/Eugene Tanner

The National Western Stock Show & Rodeo starts in January with a big parade through downtown Denver.

Denver calls the world's largest display of Christmas Lights at the City and County Building downtown. The lights are on from late November to the end of December, but they turn them on at night during the stock show as well.

THE DENVER SPORTSMEN'S SHOW
The Colorado Convention Center
700 W. 14th St.
Denver   *(800) 343-6973*
Mid- to late Jan.

Not just for sportsmen, mind you, but a family-oriented trade show with hundreds of exhibitors in outdoors activities including hunting, fishing, camping, hiking, horseback riding, boating and recreational vehicles. It's heavy on the hunting and fishing.

THE ANNUAL COLORADO COWBOY POETRY GATHERING
The Arvada Center for the Arts and Humanities
6901 Wadsworth Blvd.
Arvada   *431-3939*
1996 event, Jan. 11-14, and usually the second week of Jan.

Tales grow tall under a wide open sky, and nobody spends more time under a wider sky than cowboys and cowgirls. Once a year the poetic cream of the ranching and cowpunching community brings its Western oral tradition of tales and humor to Arvada from Colorado and beyond. Expect about 40 poets performing in three evening sessions, as well as daytime events in which the public is sometimes invited to join in. There are also performances by cowboy musicians.

COLORADO INDIAN MARKET & WESTERN ART ROUNDUP
Usually Currigan Hall
14th & Stout sts.
Denver   *447-9967*
Typically mid-Jan.

Mainly an art fair, with probably around 400 contemporary and traditional artists, visual and performing, who bring their own work and set their own prices. It's not limited to Indian art, but it's heavily weighted in that direction. Entertainment is usually Native American tribal dancers, but in past years it has included Eskimo dancers, Maoris from New Zealand and native Hawaiian dancers, as well as New Orleans Jazz.

INTERNATIONAL
SNOW SCULPTURE CHAMPIONSHIPS

Breckenridge (970) 453-6018
Second week in Jan.

The City of Breckenridge lends its front-end loaders to fill wooden forms with 20-ton blocks of snow. Four-person sculpting teams from around the world climb on top and tromp and stomp until the snow is packed tight. The forms are removed, and what happens to each big block of snow is up to the contestants, who use only hand tools. Sculptures run the gamut from geometric to free-form to recognizable shapes and scenes. The sculptures can last up to 10 days, depending on the weather.

COLORADO RV
ADVENTURE TRAVEL SHOW

Currigan Exhibition Hall
1324 Champa St.
Denver 892-6800
Late Jan.

Greater Denver's version of hog heaven for the recreational-vehicle enthusiast. Admire and wander through the shining state of the art in anywhere from 100 to 200 new recreational vehicles, see the latest in RV accessories and meet exhibitors from lodges and resorts that cater to the RV crowd.

February

REGISTRATION FOR RIDE THE ROCKIES

See the June entry, Ride the Rockies, for more on the largest and longest public group bicycling tour of the year, but right now is when you need to register if you're interested in taking part. It's a lottery, and you need to get on the stick if you want in. *The Denver Post*, sponsor of the ride, usually makes applications available in the first week of February, and they're due by the last week of February. Call 820-1338 for information.

ANNUAL FIRST INTERSTATE BANK CUP

Winter Park Ski Area 892-0961
Usually the first weekend in Feb.

Winter Park bills this as the longest continuous professional ski event in the country. Actually consisting of a number of events that visitors can enjoy from the base area over a three-day period, along with evening functions, it is a fund raiser for the National Sports Center for the Disabled (NSCD), also located in Winter Park. Events vary somewhat from year to year, but typically expect to see pro slalom and giant slalom races as well as the occasional downhill race. Other events include the Pro HandiCup, in which some of the pro skiers put on the outriggers that disabled skiers use and compete with disabled skiers who train at the NSCD; the Bronco

On the Fourth of July, you can see fireworks in many parts of the metro area. The Denver Country Club, just west of the Cherry Creek Shopping Center on First Avenue, puts on a wonderful fireworks show and opens its gates to the masses on the Fourth. You may also want to drive and/or climb to innumerable positions on the Foothills before dusk. From up there, you can watch fireworks going up from Boulder County on the north and Douglas County on the south.

Insiders' Tips

Alumni Challenge, in which former Denver Broncos football players compete with each other; and another racing competition between 20 and 30 teams each composed of four amateur racers and one pro racer.

SENIOR GAMES

Breckenridge Ski Area and
Breckenridge Nordic Center (970) 668-5486
First part of Feb.

Open to anybody older than 55. The Games feature competitions in Nordic events, alpine events, ice skating, snowshoeing, biathlon, and there's usually a welcoming dinner. If you're not in the competition, you can watch.

DENVER AUTO SHOW

The Colorado Convention Center
700 W. 14th St.
Denver   831-1691
Late Feb. or early March

Shop among, or just enjoy looking at, all the new cars under one roof. (No driving from lot to lot and being stalked by salespeople.) The show includes imports and domestics, sometimes exotics, futuristics and prototypes. Attendance at this five-day affair has exceeded 170,000.

INTERNATIONAL SPORTSMAN'S EXPO

Currigan Exhibition Hall
1324 Champa St.
Denver   (800) 545-6100
Early to mid-Feb., starting on a Wed. and running through the following Sun.

This is a pure hunting and fishing show that features products and services from archery and firearms and fishing paraphernalia. This is a how-to show with a lot of educational aspects geared toward stimulating you to hunt and fish. You can sit in a U-shaped theater-seating section, for example, to watch a presenter on stage explaining as he ties flies or wraps fishing rods. Video monitors allow you to see the small work. Top-name seminar speakers from magazines such as *Field and Stream* or *Outdoor Life* will be here. Expect around 350 exhibitors and crowds in the low 30,000s.

CHSAA STATE
WRESTLING CHAMPIONSHIPS

McNichols Sports Arena
1635 Clay St.
Denver   344-5050
Mid- to late Feb., Thurs., Fri. and Sat.

Don't expect to see bellowing mesomorphs in outlandish costumes. Do expect to see real mainstream wrestling, as the top high school contenders square off for the state titles. At any one time, you will be able to see simultaneous contests on 10 different mats.

COLUMBIA CREST CUP

Lower Hughes Ski Run
Winter Park   892-0964
Usually late Feb. or early Mar.

Part of the National Handicapped Sports Qualifications Series, this is a three-day qualifying race for disabled skiers working their way up the competitive ladder toward the U.S. national championships. See some of the best disabled skiers in the Rocky Mountain region in the super giant slalom, the giant slalom and the slalom. Benefits the National Sports Center for the Disabled.

FAT TUESDAY CELEBRATION

Bars and Restaurants around town
Breckenridge   (970) 453-6018
On Fat Tuesday, which is usually in late Feb.

Breckenridge has a modest version of Mardi Gras, which consists of ceremonies around the village. Beads, costumes and seafood abound.

KBCO CARDBOARD
DOWNHILL DERBY

Arapahoe Basin Ski Area   444-5226
Usually the last Sat. in Feb.

This is one of those fun, flaky ski-area

events that provide comic relief in the Warren Miller ski films. People build crafts out of cardboard, string, tape, paper and glue, and then they ride them down a ski slope at the Downhill Derby. Not infrequently, the crafts disintegrate before they stop moving. It's not a race. Judging is based on originality, theme, costumes and engineering. Past derby themes have included takeoffs on the Pope's 1993 visit to Denver and Lorena Bobbitt. "A-Basin," as the locals like to call it, has discounted skiing for this event. You can ski and stop to watch the antics in early afternoon. Afterward there's an award ceremony and live band.

BUFFALO BILL'S BIRTHDAY

The Buckhorn Exchange
1000 Osage St.
Denver   *534-9505*
Usually the last Sat. of Feb.

This is the first of Greater Denver's many annual celebrations of Buffalo Bill, a celebrated local citizen. The Mountain Man Association descends in full costume in the Buckhorn Exchange, Denver's oldest restaurant, to celebrate Bill's February 26 birthday. Everybody at the restaurant dresses in costume too. The costumes are around pretty much all day. You can come for lunch or dinner, enjoy the color, and enjoy staged gunfights on the hour during the afternoon. Reservations are suggested for supper, if you want to get a table.

BUFFALO BILL'S BIRTHDAY CELEBRATION

The Buffalo Bill Memorial Museum on Lookout Mountain
987½ Lookout Mountain Rd.
Golden   *526-0744*
On a weekend close to Bill's Feb. 26 birthday

This celebration takes place on the grounds of the Buffalo Bill Museum on Lookout Mountain, where the Buffalo meister's grave is located. Past celebrations

have included bluegrass music, free ice cream and cake and a birthday ceremony. Buffalo Bill lookalikes lend atmosphere and give talks about Bill's early years. In past celebrations, they've even had a guy who remembered Bill.

Take I-70 west to Exit 256, where the sign says "Lookout Mountain" and "Buffalo Bill's Grave," and follow the very good signs to the top of Lookout Mountain.

March

COLORADO RV, SPORTS, BOAT AND TRAVEL SHOW

The National Western Complex
4655 Humboldt St.
Denver   *892-6800*
First week of March

This is a general outdoor product show featuring hunting, fishing, boating, camping, whitewater rafting and travel.

CHSAA STATE BASKETBALL TOURNAMENT

Second full weekend in March
Locations vary, but typically it has taken place at:
McNichols Sports Arena
1635 Clay St. (for the big schools)
Denver Coliseum (for the smaller schools)
CU-Boulder
Colorado State University
Fort Collins High School
Fort Collins   *344-5050*

See the final competitions of Colorado's high school basketball season.

ST. PATRICK'S DAY PARADE

Streets of downtown Denver   *399-9226*
Sat. before March 17

This is big, folks, the second-largest St. Patrick's Day parade in the country (New York City is first). The divil you say. Yes, it's true. It never seems to end. Past parades have taken more than four hours for 250 floats, bands and other colorful entrants to pass as clowns and leprechauns and vendors ply the awesome crowds of spectators. There are ancillary events during the entire week, actually, Irish entertainment at various pubs and other locations.

ANNUAL SPRING HOME & PATIO SHOW

The National Western Complex
4655 Humboldt St.
Denver 892-6800
Wed. through Sun., third week of March

There's nothing like a nice trade show to get you in the mood for whatever slice of life they're selling. So get in the mood for the spring cleaning and summer grooming of house and yard by visiting the 300 exhibitors of home and garden products and services.

DENVER MARCH POW-WOW

The Denver Coliseum
4600 Humboldt St. (Take the Brighton Blvd. Exit off I-70)
Denver Pow-Wow
Denver Coliseum Box Office 295-4444
Mid- to late March

Don't miss this one. More than 1,000 Native Americans of tribes from most of the U.S. states as well as Canada dancing simultaneously in full costume will stuff your eyes with enough technicolor spectacle to last all year. At the edges of the dancing, groups of men surround huge drums and make the whole Coliseum vibrate. The big en masse dancing, the Grand Entry, happens Friday and Saturday at noon and 7 PM, and Sunday at noon, with other activities scattered throughout those days. And, you'll get plenty of opportunities to see the costumes close up: The seats around you will be filled with Native American families who contribute the dancers,

and costumed competitors will be sitting next to you and walking past you. That's one of the reasons why this event is such a find. It hasn't been "discovered" yet by the kinds of crowds who attend the National Western Stock Show & Rodeo, so you feel more completely immersed in authenticity. Kids love it. There's a modest Native American market downstairs. Expect between 40 and 50 drum groups to be at the Pow-Wow, along with representatives of 60 to 70 tribes and a total three-day crowd in the neighborhood of 80,000 (not including children younger than 6 and adults older than 60, who get in free).

April

BRECKENRIDGE BEACH DAZE

Breckenridge (970) 453-6018
Usually the whole month of April

No, there's no beach, but the month of April is usually pretty warm, and this is a chance to enjoy the spring skiing and discounted lodging and lift tickets in the context of daily Beach Daze events. A parade, volleyball, a crawfish festival, races and what Breckenridge calls the world's highest Easter egg hunt. Some 2,000 eggs containing prizes are hidden around the ski mountain and the town on Easter weekend.

TASTE OF BRECKENRIDGE

City of Breckenridge
Breckenridge (970) 453-5970
First Sat. in April

Chefs from the best restaurants in the Breckenridge area each prepare one of their specialties. The idea is to go and taste the food (and wine). Participants vote for their favorite restaurant and hotel restaurant. The charge has been $30 per person in the past.

Place your bets on the racing pigs at the Colorado State Fair.

EASTER SUNRISE SERVICE

Red Rocks Amphitheater (North of Morrison on Hogback Rd. Take I-70 E. to the Morrison Exit, then south)
Sunrise on Easter Sunday

One of the most inspirational places you'll ever find for an Easter sunrise service is this gargantuan natural amphitheater of red sandstone facing east over the plains. It's nondenominational, free and open to the public.

ROCKY MOUNTAIN HOME SHOW

Currigan Exhibition Hall
1324 Champa St.
Denver   778-1400
April, dates vary, Thurs. through Sun.

Domestic engineers take note. This regional trade show and its 300-some exhibitors feature the latest home-building and remodeling products and materials. You'll find interior design, energy conservation and about 50 seminars for your illumination.

ROCKY MOUNTAIN
TROPHY SERIES FINALE

Winter Park Ski Area   892-0961
Early to mid-April (Not held some years)

Top racers in the Rocky Mountain states

turn out for this two-day event: usually a giant slalom for men one day and women the next day. On the second day is the super giant slalom (or "Super G," as the in-crowd puts it). This one is faster with fewer turns and offers men's and women's events. Watching the races is about all you can do if you're not in them, but that can still be fun. You might want to bring binoculars. This is an opportunity to see some of the up-and-coming athletes of the U.S. Ski Team.

SPRING SPLASH/CLOSING DAY

Winter Park Ski Area   892-0961
Always on the closing Sun. of the season, which varies but is typically mid-April

This is one of those events that public relations people love because they get to use the word "zany." If you've ever seen the part of a Warren Miller ski movie where the sun is out, everybody wears sunglasses, and ski-babes in bikinis and ski-bozos in goofy costumes come barreling down the hill trying to hydroplane across a puddle of ice water and belly flop with a big splash — you've been looking at Spring Splash in Winter Park. It has become one of the quintessential Colorado images — kind of an outdoor spectacle that

• 193

people try to get a good view of by jockeying for position on the balconies of the base lodge.

EARTHFEST

Larimer Square
Between 14th and 15th streets on Larimer St.
Also in Writer Square on Larimer St.
Denver   *534-2367*
Late April

Started in 1993, this has been an annual environmental festival. It features 70 or more environmental organizations with booths, entertainment, children's craft workshops, free RTD bus transfers and free bike checks for people who come by bicycle.

CHILDREN'S DAY CELEBRATION

The Aztlan Recreation Center
4435 Navajo St.
Denver   *830-0708*
Last Sat. in April

Children's Day is an old Mexican tradition, like Father's Day or Mother's Day in the United States. In Mexico the date is April 30, but here it's on the last Saturday in April. In Mexico, they take kids on field trips and have other festivities at school. Here, you can come and enjoy entertainment for kids including clowns, piñatas, prizes, balloons, puppet shows, booths and mechanical games. Entrance is free, but some rides and booths have moderate costs.

May

DENVER BOTANIC
GARDENS PLANT AND BOOK SALE

The Denver Botanic Gardens
1005 York St.
Denver   *331-4000*
Usually Mother's Day weekend

Plants and books are for sale, and proceeds benefit the DBG library. You can buy thousands of flowers, herbs and vegetables. There are speakers and demonstra-

tions going on in appropriate parts of the gardens: a bonsai-tree demonstration is in the bonsai section, for example, an expert on roses would hold forth in the rose garden.

THE KBCO/BUDWEISER
KINETIC SCULPTURE CHALLENGE

The Boulder Reservoir (The parade on the previous Sat. is in downtown Boulder.)
Boulder   *442-5226*
First Sat. of May; Rain date the following Sat.

This has become one of the biggest and most colorful annual events in the Denver area, and it's certainly the looniest event of its size. The hijinks at the Boulder Reservoir pulled around 18,000 in attendance in 1995. The kinetic conveyances, sometimes called kinetic sculptures, are crafts powered by human muscle. They must be capable of going on land and water; and at the Challenge, they are required to go through a mud pit as well. The competition is judged not just on speed but also on creativity, team costumes and team spirit. There's also a beach volleyball tournament, live music and a food court. A warning: big crowd, small access roads, limited parking. Car pooling is a good idea. An even better idea is to park somewhere nearby, or even in Boulder, and bicycle the rest of the way. The festival now has two locations (University of Colorado Campus and Crossroads Mall in 1995) where you can park and ride a shuttle bus for $2. Bring binoculars, since a lot of the race takes place way out on the reservoir.

SPRING MOUNTAIN
MAN RENDEZVOUS

The Fort Restaurant
19192 Colo. Hwy. 8
Morrison   *697-4771*
Usually a Sun. in early May

This event features re-enactors of the 1830s and 1840s, dressed in buckskins and behaving like mountain men. There are competitions for best costume, tomahawk and knife throwing, black-powder target shooting, fire-starting with flint and steel and survival skills. There's also a mountain-man run. Check out Native-American trading tables where you can buy and trade for the works of Colorado Native-American artisans.

HISTORIC DENVER WEEK

Larimer Square
Larimer St. between 14th and 15th sts.
Denver   534-1858
Early May

A week-long salute to historic Denver and historic Larimer Square, this festival has a variety of activities. There are historic preservation awards and historic walking tours (East Colfax, the South Platte Valley, etc.), as well as a bus tour of historic police and fire department facilities. There is always a "Box City" where elementary school students build a city out of donated boxes. There's also a Queen for a Day event at the Molly Brown House Museum, where tea is served with scones and cream and preserves.

CINCO DE MAYO ON SANTA FE

Santa Fe Dr., extending about six blocks from
W. Sixth Ave. north to 12th Ave.
Denver, Contact: Isabella Beason, 534-8342
Around May 5

This is Denver's celebration of its enormous Hispanic heritage. Many confuse this with Mexican Independence Day, which is on September 16. Cinco de Mayo is actually a big celebration that has grown from a small event, although the event had big meaning: la Batalla de Puebla, the Battle of Ciudad Puebla, which took place during the Mexican battle for independence from France.

Mexicans, equipped with little more than farm implements, whipped one of the greatest armies on Earth, although the French came back five days later and made up for it. Still, it's a spiritual moment for Mexico and a big holiday in Denver. It starts with the Celebrate Culture parade, intended to celebrate diversity, and a traditional Mariachi mass. Past celebrations have included about 200 different booths with arts and foods, entertainment on six stages, ethnic-fashionwear showings, and Latin, jazz, rap and contemporary music. There's also a children's area with stage including clowns, rides, dancing, a petting zoo and all that jolly kid stuff.

COPA MEXICO CINCO DE MAYO

1996 games in the Fort Logan Mental Health
Facility, Oxford St. and Federal Blvd., Lakewood,
with the final game at Mile High Stadium
2755 W. 17th St.
Denver   830-0708, 832-0050
Around May 5

Copa Mexico means trophy Mexico. The best Hispanic soccer teams in Colorado participate in this tournament, and the two playoff finalists square off in Mile High Stadium. After the championship game, Mile High hosts a game between the Colorado Foxes and a professional soccer team from another country.

Festivals and events any time of year are a great opportunity to get the jump on Christmas shopping. They often feature the work of local artists and craftspeople.

Insiders' Tips

Photo: Daily Camera

Cinco de Mayo (Fifth of May) is a Mexican holiday joyously celebrated all over Greater Denver.

CINCO DE MILES

City Park
Colorado Blvd.
Denver   727-8700, 978-1698
May 5th weekend

Part of Greater Denver's general Cinco de Mayo festivities, this is a 5-mile and 5K run, a 5K walk and a 1-mile family fun run.

CENTRAL CITY OPERA GALA

Usually the Brown Palace Hotel
312 17th St.
Denver   292-6700
Mid-May

The historic opera house in Central City doesn't start its season until summer, but it likes to remind people early on that there's some good singing to come. This is an evening of dancing, cocktails, dinner, silent auction and, of course, a preview of the season through performances by some of the opera's singers.

KOPS 'N KIDS
East High School and City Park
Across 17th St. from City Park
Denver 863-1633
Third Sun. in May

This is a law-enforcement expo and family entertainment benefiting the children of officers killed in the line of duty. There are five events: a 10K run, a 5K run/walk, a 1K fun run, a 15-mile bike ride, a 50-mile bike ride and the Iron Mouse Biathlon, an event that combines the 15-mile bike ride with the 1K fun run. The bike rides are not competitions; they're recreational rides. Along with food and beverage vendors, law enforcement people put together fun things to see and take part in, such as canine exhibitions.

BOULDER CREEK FESTIVAL
Downtown Boulder, Colorado Blvd. along the
Boulder Creek Path, Central Park and the
Library-Municipal Building Complex
Boulder 441-4420
Memorial Day weekend, with some events on
the previous weekend.

The Boulder Creek Festival expanded to two weekends in 1995. The weekend before Memorial Day weekend is the kick-off, with activities including the Creek Clean-Up, the Festival parade and an arts celebration. On Memorial Day weekend, activities include a Boulder Community Barbecue picnic, a rubber duck race on the creek, an International Folk Festival, five stages with free entertainment, Kids Place in the Park and other merriment. Attendance at the whole thing has been ranging over 100,000.

BOLDER BOULDER
Boulder 444-RACE
Usually the Mon. of Memorial Day weekend

No more limit on the number of runners for this 10K race as there was in previous years, and you can even enter on the day of the race. Except, there is a $5 late fee if you register after a certain date and a $10 late fee if you register on race day. If you don't register late, it's just $21 including T-shirt and $14 not including T-shirt, and a bag lunch is included in what you are buying. What you are buying mainly, however, is participation in what may be the most fun race you've ever run or spectated, of which 37,914 people took part in 1995. There's a race for pros, the "elite" race, including many of the world's leading runners. And there's a "citizens' race," in which anybody can take part. Most of the race is along small streets that go up and down through the charming small town of Boulder. It's not that small of a town anymore, but it has that feel. Secondly, the locals put on quite a show along the route. On the curbs along the course is a never-ending succession of string quartets, jazz bands, belly dancers, you name it, and a lot of runners and groups of runners dream up theme costumes in which to run. You can also just go to enjoy the spectacle. Get there early in the day, though, because the traffic gets horrendous. Typically, you will have to park and hike a ways to get to the race course.

THE PARADE OF THE YEARS
Loveland to Estes Park
Frank Hicks (970) 586-4407
Richard Paynter 832-6400
Four days, close to Memorial Day weekend

Antique-car buffs love this old-car rally. It commemorates the beginning of the tourist season, when people used to take their flivvers out of the barn and start using them.

This was the weekend when the Stanley Hotel opened each year, and F.O. Stanley — who invented the Stanley Steamer auto and developed an auto road up the Big Thompson Canyon in about 1908 — took cars from Estes Park down to Loveland and Lyons to pick up guests at the railroad stations. People congregate in Loveland on a Friday night for an informal get-together, then parade through Loveland on Saturday morning and stop at the railroad station, where the public can inspect the cars; then they head up the Big Thompson Canyon on U.S. Highway 34. Sunday, there's a car rally in the morning and an exhibition in the evening at the Estes Park Historical Museum. There's a banquet Sunday night and a rally Monday morning, and that's that.

ENTERTAINERS ON THE SQUARE
Larimer Square
Larimer St. between 14th and 15th sts.
Denver   *534-2367*
Memorial Day through Labor Day, every Friday from 7 PM to 11 PM, and Saturday from 11 AM to 5 PM

Enjoy a variety of street entertainment including performers, painters and character artists.

June

SYMPHONY ENSEMBLES
Larimer Square
Larimer Street between 14th and 15th sts.
Denver   *534-2367*
June, July & August

Every Sunday, 12 PM to 2 PM, see various ensembles including string quar-tets, horn ensembles and other musical combinations.

CAPITOL HILL PEOPLE'S FAIR
Civic Center Park
Between Colfax Ave. and 14th St.
Denver   *830-1651*
Usually the first weekend in June

Capitol Hill is a colorful and historic neighborhood that ranges from the funky to the aristocratic, and this is its annual celebration. They claim Colorado's largest arts and crafts festival, with about 500 exhibitors, as well as food, dance, entertainment on six stages and kids' activities such as putt-putt golf, face painting and more. Crowds have been running about 250,000.

FRESH FISH FESTIVAL
Breckenridge   *(970) 453-6018*
Early June

Held every year in conjunction with National Fishing Week and on Colorado's annual free fishing day, when all Colorado waters are open to fishing without a license. Breckenridge has fishing contests around town. The festival also features a kids' fishing derby, a 5K run they call the Trout Trot, gourmet-seafood cooking classes and fish-related movies for children.

CONSERVATION DAY
The Denver Zoo in City Park
E. 23rd Ave. and Steele St.
Denver   *331-4100*
Second Sat. in June

This is a conservation awareness day with educational activities focusing on the

Insiders' Tips

importance of conserving world wildlife and resources. The fun in past has included environmental education activities, a zoolympics course, face painting, conservation murals, a paper chain, keeper talks, live animal demonstrations, an endangered species scavenger hunt, sidewalk art, conservation murals and storytelling. They place emphasis on the Species Survival Plan, which seeks to strengthen and coordinate captive breeding programs so zoos can help preserve vanishing species.

THE ELEPHANT ROCK CENTURY BIKE TOUR

Registration at Douglas County High School
Castle Rock   688-4597 or 733-8775
First Sun. in June

Bike tours of various lengths — 15-mile, 27-mile, 32-mile, 68-mile and 100-mile — around county roads that end in a celebration with food booths in Courthouse Square. The Shimano Youth Race, on a special loop around the area, is for younger people.

ANNIVERSARY OF BUFFALO BILL'S BURIAL

The Buffalo Bill Memorial Museum on Lookout Mountain
987½ Lookout Mountain Rd. (Take I-70 west to Exit 256, where the sign says "Lookout Mountain" and "Buffalo Bill's Grave." Follow the very good signs to the top of Lookout Mountain.)
Golden   526-0744
A weekend close to June 3

This is a commemoration of Buffalo Bill's burial, one of the biggest events in Colorado history. Bill Cody died in January of 1917, but he lay in state in the Capitol Building while mourners and gawkers filed by for months. At his interment on June 3, next to what is now the Buffalo Bill Memorial Museum, 25,000 people came up the narrow Lookout Mountain road and walked and rode horses up the mountainside. Bill had once said he wanted to be buried in Cody, Wyoming, a town he founded, and the Wyomingans thought that was a good idea. There were threats of stealing the body, so Denver stationed a military tank at the gravesite. It was a colorful event, and today people make it a colorful celebration. It includes a mock funeral, with a procession of old cars and motorists who blunder into the procession and get trapped in it. The procession winds up the Lariat Trail on the east side of Lookout Mountain facing the plains. Somebody from the Masonic Temple (which handled part of the funeral for Bill) explains the funeral. A representative of Horan Funeral Home in Aurora, which embalmed and re-embalmed Bill while he lay in state, gives a talk on how the body was kept and buried. Guys in mountain-man costumes show up with horses and tepees. There's a Buffalo Bill-lookalike contest, buffalo-burger barbecue and children's activities.

FIRST FEST

The Arvada Center for the Arts and Humanities
6901 Wadsworth Blvd.
Arvada   424-0313
Usually the second Sat. of June

This is a celebration of the business communities in Arvada and Westminster, but it's not just for the business crowd. There are usually around 200 exhibits, food booths and activities for grownups and children. Police and fire departments sponsor exhibits. It also includes a 5K family fun run and live entertainment.

ESTES PARK WOOL MARKET

Estes Park Fair Grounds
Estes Park   586-6104
Second weekend of June

Sheep ranching is a big part of Colorado's history and agriculture, and here's an event dedicated to its product. You'll find: spinning and weaving classes;

dyeing classes; showings of sheep, llamas and alpacas; spinning and weaving demonstrations and contests; spinning wheels for sale, and commercial exhibits related to the wool industry.

COLORADO RENAISSANCE FESTIVAL

Take I-25 S., then take the Larkspur Exit and follow the signs.
Larkspur 688-6010
Eight weekends in June and July

Renaissance festivals are ripping good fun, and this is truly one of the most fun things you can do during the year. Spreading over a huge site beneath the greenwood trees, the festival re-creates a 16th-century marketplace filled with costumed characters and ruled by King Henry and Queen Ann. More than 200 costumed craftspersons sell hand-crafted goods. One of the main attractions is the battling and strutting and jousting by knights on foot and horseback. You'll also enjoy strolling minstrels, jesters, jugglers, medieval food, rides and games galore.

OPERA POPS PICNIC WITHOUT ANTS

Usually at the downtown Marriott Hotel
17th and California sts.
Denver 292-6700
Usually the third Thurs. in June

A benefit for the Central City Opera, this event involves a picnic in a ballroom followed by a preview of all the artists who will be performing in Central City during the summer, as well as the opera's full orchestra. This is an evening of the opera's "greatest hits." In the past, the picnic supper tickets have been $25 or $50, and the full gala has been $175.

THE BRECKENRIDGE MUSIC FESTIVAL

The Riverwalk Center
Breckenridge (970) 453-2120
Mid-June until mid-Aug.

Pretty much everyday, visitors can enjoy performances by the National Repertory Orchestra and the Breckenridge Music Institute. Some days, it's just practice, but that can be even more interesting, and you get in free.

MADAM LOU BUNCH DAY

Central City (800) 542-2999
The Sat. and Sun. of Father's Day weekend

Madam Lou Bunch was a scarlet woman who ran a herd of brazen bawds, prancing harlots and painted hussies in the mining boomtown days of Central City. The main event of this celebration is a race on Main Street between brass beds on wheels, each of which is pushed by a brace of men in period costumes and carries a woman in full strumpet regalia. There are also costume contests and other activities including music, an evening ball and trophy ceremony.

JUNETEENTH

The Five Points Business District
Welton St. between 24th and 28th sts.
Denver 388-0193
The weekend before or including June 19th

A major festivity of Denver's black community, Juneteenth stands for June 19th, which was the day that slavery ended in Texas. For about three days, there are booths with food, arts and crafts, games and other activities. There is also a baseball tournament, exhibits at the Black American West Museum, a senior luncheon, a large parade, a Sunday gospel fest and more.

THE BONSAI EXHIBITION

Denver Botanic Gardens
1005 York St.
Denver 331-4000
Father's Day weekend

An exhibition and sale, by the Rocky Mountain Bonsai society. Some of the plants are hundreds of years old, and young plants will be available for training.

Photo: Daily Camera/Glenn Asakawa

There are more mountain-man rendezvous in the Greater Denver area than you can shake a flintlock at.

SUMMER POPS CONCERTS SERIES
The Arvada Center for the Arts and Humanities
6901 Wadsworth Blvd.
Arvada 431-3939
Usually the third weekend in June to the third weekend in Aug.

For a mixture of country, Big Band, jazz and Cajun music, come to the Arvada Center's outdoor amphitheater. You can picnic on the grounds before the shows and browse the art gallery. You can bring your picnic inside for the concert. Also a musical every year, usually last week of July and first week of August.

RIDE THE ROCKIES
All over the state, a different route every year
Usually the third week of June 820-1338

If you have thighs like Tyrannosaurus Rex, Ride the Rockies is for you. Or at least you should be in shape. This event lasts six to seven days, during which time a stream of about 2,000 jolly, miserable, laughing, moaning, exuberant bicyclists push their pedals for more than 400 miles. You will go through resort towns like Steamboat Springs or Vail, and more nor-mal towns like Walsenburg, Durango and Granby. You'll be going up and down a lot, probably crossing the Continental Divide about three times and doing plenty of lesser mountain passes as well. At night, you'll probably camp on high school sports fields or in their gyms. Communities nightly provide low-cost meals and various forms of entertainment. Not everyone can take part. The event's title sponsor, *The Denver Post*, holds a lottery in February. If you win, you're in. The registration fee has been around $160, and usually includes some-thing like a cycling jacket or jersey or shorts.

CHILDREN'S AND ADULT CONCERTS
Denver Botanic Gardens
1005 York St.
Denver 331-4000
From June to Aug.

Sitting on the grass surrounded by the Denver Botanic Gardens on a summer evening is a great way to listen to music. This series of outdoor concerts is aimed at families in an informal setting. Picnics are encouraged.

SCANDINAVIAN MIDSUMMER FESTIVAL

Bond Park, downtown Estes Park
Estes Park (970) 586-2557
Usually the last Fri. and Sat. of June closest to
June 24

June 24 is midsummer in the Scandinavian countries, and their biggest celebration next to Christmas. This is a big traditional Scandinavian festival that features arts, crafts, ethnic foods, educational mini-seminars and demonstrations, and the raising of the maypole with appropriate cavorting of Scandinavian folk dancers every hour. At least one dance group usually comes all the way from Scandinavia. There's also a bonfire, which is how Norwegians celebrate midsummer.

SUMMER NIGHTS

Larimer Square
Larimer St. between 14th and 15th sts.
Denver 534-2367
Late June through late Aug.

On four nights, at varying dates during this period, Larimer Square hosts a free concert series open to the general public, featuring national talent with spirits and edibles. From 7:30 to 11 PM.

GREEK FESTIVAL

The Assumption Greek Orthodox Cathedral
4610 E. Alameda Ave.
Denver 388-9314
Usually the last full weekend in June, Thurs.
through Sun.

This cathedral, with its gold dome, is a familiar landmark. Denver's Greeks and Grecophiles convene here on the church grounds each year for "wonderful food prepared by the ladies of our church," authentic Greek food, live music and Greek dance shows done by groups ranging in age from children to adults. Calimari, Aegean beer, wine and beverages are served, and there is usually a gift shop and a small carnival area for kids. All proceeds benefit the church.

THE YELLOW ROSE BALL: OPENING NIGHT

Central City Opera House
Central City 292-6700
Late June or early July

The Central City Opera begins its season, usually with a dinner at the Teller House and a performance.

INTERNATIONAL BUSKERFEST

Larimer Square
Larimer Street between 14th and 15th sts.
Denver 534-6161
Late June

Buskers are street entertainers. This event features more than 200 lively shows by world-class jugglers, mimes, sword swallowers, magicians, tightrope artists, singers and dancers. It includes a "Buskerstop" in Noel Park, located next to Champion Brewing Co., where the buskers will perform.

AMERICAN RED CROSS FAT TIRE CLASSIC

Winter Park
Fraser Valley 722-7474
Last weekend in June

This is a two-day mountain-bike pledge tour to benefit the American Red Cross. It's not a race; it's just a tour, and it has events for all levels of riders. You should be in shape, though. Even the beginner's ride is a 15-mile off-road event. All events include additional challenges along the way for those who want more fun/pain. You'll find gourmet food, entertainment with a live band on Saturday night, prizes for different categories of riders and a raffle at this event.

LADY FOOT LOCKER 5K

City Park
Colorado Blvd.
Denver 863-1633
Usually the last Sun. in June

A benefit for SafeHouse Denver, a shelter for battered women and their children, this one-day event includes a 5K run and walk for girls and women only. Men can register and become official supporters of SafeHouse, and can choose to volunteer and/or participate in Raymond's Fun Run, which is free and open to the whole family. It's the fourth-largest women-only event in the nation, and the largest women's event in the Rocky Mountain region.

DRUMS ALONG THE ROCKIES
Probably in Mile High Stadium
2755 W. 17th St.
Denver 424-6396
Sometime Mid- to late July

This is a booming good time. This is the annual regional drum and bugle corps championships. Mile High Stadium is usually sparsely filled, mainly by alumni of the corps and friends and families of those competing, so there's plenty of room to spread out and relax. Usually about 12 of the best drum and bugle corps from the western United States and Canada compete in the Drum Corps Regional Championships, usually including four or five of the top-ranked corps in the world.

July

SUMMER NIGHTS
See June entry.

RENAISSANCE FESTIVAL
See June entry.

SUMMER POPS CONCERTS SERIES
See June entry.

CHILDREN'S AND ADULT CONCERTS
See June entry.

ENTERTAINERS ON THE SQUARE
See May entry.

SYMPHONY ENSEMBLES
See June entry.

SUMMER IN THE CITY
Larimer Square
Larimer St. between 14th and 15th sts.
Denver 534-2367
A weekend in July: Fri. evening; Sat., day and evening; and Sun., midday to afternoon

This is another of those Larimer Square activities designed to promote Larimer Square and its commercial base and provide fun for people who come to Larimer Square. This is typically a three-day affair. The street is closed off for non-stop entertainment, food and beverages.

CHERRY CREEK ARTS FESTIVAL
Cherry Creek North (an area bordered by St. Paul St. on the east and Clayton St. on the West, Second St. on the south and Third St. on the north)
Denver 355-2787
Fourth of July weekend

Pulling some 300,000 visitors for this event, Denver's upscale retail shopping area hosts a sidewalk festival featuring fine arts and fine crafts, with 200 artists from around the nation and Europe. National and international performers provide entertainment. Local chefs cook up their best for a block-long culinary arts extravaganza where food vendors line the street.

THE INDEPENDENCE DAY CELEBRATION
Four Mile Historic Park
715 S. Forest
Denver 399-1859
Fourth of July

The Four Mile Historic Park, Denver's living-history park, gives good old-fashioned Fourth of July fun in the wholesome family manner. This is a day of patriotic music, games and activities featuring re-enactments by historically costumed people, stagecoach rides and foods. The event in the past has also included historic and craft demonstrations such as blacksmithing, quilting, weaving, lacemaking and butter churning.

RACE TO THE CLOUDS

Pikes Peak
Outside Colorado Springs   (719) 685-4400
Fourth of July

You can enjoy this famous annual Pikes Peak Hill Climb even if you're not one of the top race-car drivers who come here to test their skill on one of Colorado's 14,000-foot peaks. But you do need tickets ahead of time to drive up, park and watch the race from designated areas on the mountain. There are also a whole bunch of other races and events in the weeks surrounding this big one.

FREEDOMFEST

Main St.
Central City   (800) 542-2999
Around July 4

This is Central City's patriotic celebration featuring bands playing American-style music, food booths, a beer garden, hay wagon and carriage rides, and fireworks.

DENVER BLACK ARTS FESTIVAL

City Park West
23rd Ave. and Colorado Blvd.
Denver   293-2559
Usually the second weekend in July

The festival that celebrates African-American arts and culture through visual and performing arts draws the best African-American artists of the region to Denver's City Park West. It starts with a parade. Events include audience participation, African-American cuisine, art sales and displays, Afrocentric crafts and major performances by headline acts.

NATIONAL ARCHERY MEET

The base of the Mary Jane ski area
Winter Park   322-4063
A weekend in early July

The Great Western Shootout, as it's called, brings in top archers from across the nation to meet for three days of competition.

GENUINE JAZZ IN JULY

Breckenridge   (970) 453-6018
Mid-July

Breckenridge's three-day midsummer jazz festival features Colorado artists. Evening sessions take place at local bars. Free daytime performances occur at Maggie Pond, where a stage is built over the water and spectators can sit on the shore.

OBON: GATHERING OF JOY

Sakura Square
The area bracketed by Lawrence and Larimer sts. and 19th and 20th sts.
Denver   295-1844
Usually the second Sun. of July, but the date depends on when the Colorado Rockies are playing

A gathering in honor of those who have passed away, with the OBON service being held at 4 PM every year. At 8 PM Japanese folk dancers perform, dressed in colorful traditional kimonos and yukatas. During intermissions, the kids will certainly enjoy the Taiko drummers, those guys who hammer those huge drums.

ROOFTOP RODEO

Estes Park Fairgrounds
Estes Park   (800) 44-ESTES
Second or third week of July

A rodeo plain and simple, with four days of events with a rodeo parade and six PRCA (Professional Rodeo Cowboy Association) rodeos and, along with that, Western Heritage Day including mountain-man rendezvous, an Indian village, gold panning, western entertainment on stage and so on. Other past attractions have included cowboy cartoonists and poets, a dirt dance and concerts.

BUFFALO BILL DAYS

Golden   279-3113 or 278-7789
Usually the third weekend in July

The Buffalo Bill Days Corp. hosts this western celebration, which started in Buffalo Bill's honor but is now a celebration held every year to promote the City of Golden. The event in the past has included a parade and other activities on Main Street and in Parfet Park and Clear Creek Living History Park. There has been musical entertainment, a golf tournament, country and Western dance contests, living history re-enactments, a talent contest, a burro race and the Golden Derby for Young Racers.

BUFFALO BILL DAY

The Buffalo Bill Memorial Museum on Lookout Mountain
987½ Lookout Mountain Rd. (Take I-70 west to Exit 256, where the sign says "Lookout Mountain" and "Buffalo Bill's Grave"; follow the very good signs to the top of Lookout Mountain.)
Golden   526-0747
Mid- to late July

Just can't get enough of that Buffalo Bill. The Buffalo Bill Memorial Museum celebrates its namesake with wagon rides, Indian dancers, music, an outdoor barbecue and demonstrations of old daily-life techniques such as weaving, spinning, making saddles, preparing foods, preserving foods and making bullets.

GOLD RUSH DAYS

Downtown Idaho Springs   567-2079
Third weekend in July

This event celebrates mining history. Past Gold Rush Days have included bands and other entertainment, a country-fair theme, pie-baking and chili-cookoff contests, food and crafts booths, a Sunday parade, mining demonstrations, a mucking and drilling contest, a pony express, children's games, a rodeo, dancing and antique fire equipment.

KEYSTONE
ARTS & CRAFTS CELEBRATION

Keystone Village at Keystone Resort in Summit County   (800) 451-5930
Usually the third weekend in July

This event features artists, live entertainment, booths, and it includes the Taste of Keystone, in which the local restaurants sell samples of their best.

MOLLY BROWN'S BIRTHDAY

The Molly Brown House Museum
1340 Pennsylvania St.
Denver   832-4092
On July 18, Molly's birthday

Outcast from high society though she remained, the Unsinkable Molly Brown was a celebrity, and her house is a museum. It celebrates her birthday with an authentic 19th-century summer evening ice cream social/garden party at which those serving wear period costumes and those attending are welcome to do likewise. The price of admission, $5 for adults in advance, $6 at the door; kids $2 in advance, $3 at the door, is a fund-raiser for the museum.

MOPAR PARTS
MILE-HIGH NATIONALS

Bandimere Speedway
3051 S. Rooney Rd.
Morrison   697-4870
Usually the third weekend in July

This is motorhead heaven. Between 600 and 700 cars and the nation's top racers compete in pro-stock drag racing, top fuel cars and nitro funny cars.

THEATER IN THE PARK

The historic Greek Amphitheater
Civic Center Park
Between Colfax Ave. and 14th St.
Denver 770-2106
Last two weekends in July and the first weekend in Aug.

Nine performances over three weeks, each week changing the shows. Previous shows have included the musical *Oliver, Peter and the Wolf* in pantomime, the female version of the *Odd Couple* and flamenco ballet.

WINTER PARK
AMERICAN MUSIC FESTIVAL

Winter Park Ski Area (970) 726-5514
Mid- to late July

This festival is two days of great music in a great setting. People sit on Lower Parkway, a ski run, and look down on the stage. Winter Park switches their concerts and contents around every year, but you're likely to see all or some combination of top national country, folk, Western, jazz, easy listening, instrumental, vocal, and light-rock acts. Past performers have included Hiroshima, Sara McClaughlin, David and Tab Benoit, the Brian Setzer Orchestra, the Deans, George Benson, Bonnie Raitt, Lyle Lovett, Big Head Todd and the Monsters and Little Feat. There are usually vendors of food and trinkets.

ALPINE ARTAFFAIR

Main St.
Winter Park (970) 726-4118
Usually the third weekend in July

A two-day, outdoor, judged and juried art event. Expect about 90 booths, exhibiting artists and craftspersons, photography, oil painting, pottery, jewelry and the rest. Live entertainment and craft demonstrations.

CHEYENNE FRONTIER DAYS

Frontier Park
Cheyenne, Wyo. (800) 227-6336
The last full week in July

This is a 10-day western theme event centered around rodeo events, but it also includes a carnival, evening shows by some of the biggest names in country-western music, parades, free pancake breakfasts, a chili cookoff, a performance by the Air Force Thunderbirds team and a free entertainment area with music and other acts. Cheyenne is only 100 miles from Denver, so it's a nice way to spend a day. About 300,000 people show up during the 10 days, but parking is generally no problem in the gravel lots around the Frontier Park stadium.

BIKE TO THE ZOO DAY

The Denver Zoo in City Park
E. 23rd Ave. and Steele St.
Denver 331-4100
Usually the Fourth Sun. in July

In conjunction with Denver Bike Month, everybody who rides their bike to the zoo today gets in free and receives a bike-to-the-zoo button and free valet bike parking. The Denver Police Department also does free bike registrations and safety clinics.

August

SUMMER NIGHTS

See June entry.

SUMMER POPS CONCERTS SERIES

See June entry.

CHILDREN'S AND ADULT CONCERTS

See June entry.

ENTERTAINERS ON THE SQUARE

See May entry.

SYMPHONY ENSEMBLES

See June entry.

WELD COUNTY FAIR

Island Grove Park
Greeley   (970) 356-4000, Ext. 4465
Early Aug.

County fair! Weld County, north of Adams County, ranks fourth among counties nationwide in agricultural revenues. Weld County contains the world's two largest feedlots and accounts for about a fourth of all Colorado agriculture. Its county fair does not have a carnival midway, but it does have a lot of animal showings and competitions, including about 1,400 4-H and FFA kids, with an animal-catching contest, food booths, a fun fair and a concert night.

ROCKY MOUNTAIN WINE AND FOOD FESTIVAL

Winter Park Ski Area   (970) 726-5514
First weekend of Aug.

This is mainly a weekend affair, with wine and beer tasting and food tasting of creations prepared by some of Colorado's finest chefs. But, the festival does start earlier in the week with evening events such as dinners for wine makers and wine tasters at restaurants in the valley, where winemakers representing their products provide different wines throughout the evening to go with the meals. These events are sold out ahead of time, so get on the stick if you want a reservation. There are also wine and beer seminars. A fund raiser for the National Sports Center for the Disabled.

EVERGREEN MOUNTAIN RENDEZVOUS

The grove next to the Hiwan Homestead Museum
4208 S. Timbervale Dr.
Evergreen   674-6262
First Sat. in Aug.

This is a mountain-man rendezvous, with lots of costumes and accoutrements.

Entrants and watchers alike often don costumes for the Bolder Boulder 10-K race.

Photo: Daily Camera/Jay Quadracci

There is folk and country music all day long. Mountain men have their village set up showing mountain crafts and artwork. Trading-post type items are sold and traded. There are games for kids and a "heckuva lot of food." Take part in the singing, dancing and tale-telling.

SCULPTURE IN THE PARK SHOW AND SALE

Benson Park Sculpture Garden
29th St. and Aspen Dr.
Loveland   (800) 551-1752
Second weekend in Aug.

Loveland bills this as the largest exhibition of sculpture in the United States. The Benson Park Sculpture Garden ordinarily has about 40 sculptures, but on this day it attracts about 150 artists from around the world to show and sell their pieces. The event features entertainment, demonstrations by artists, tours of local foundries where sculptures are cast, and a sculpture auction. There are also seminars, and speed-sculpting (artists who sculpt while you watch) demonstrations.

COLORADO SCOTTISH
FESTIVAL AND HIGHLAND GAMES

Highlands Heritage Park
Get off C-470 (on the south side of Denver) at
Quebec St., and go south to the intersection
with Lincoln Ave.
Highlands Ranch   238-6524
Second weekend in Aug.

Wake up and smell the heather. Enjoy bagpiping, highland athletic events, highland dancing and other events. You'll also see clan tents, drumming, food, crafts, souvenirs, and exhibitions of highland cattle, dogs and Clydesdale horses.

DOUGLAS COUNTY FAIR

Douglas County Fairgrounds
Castle Rock   688-4597
August

This is an old-fashioned county fair with rodeo, carnival and all the accoutrements of county fairdom. Simultaneously with the county fair, Castle Rock holds a community fair that includes a parade to celebrate the 4-H winners, with over 100 parade entries, and a barbecue in the Courthouse Square.

ADAMS COUNTY FAIR AND RODEO

Adams County Fairgrounds
9755 Henderson Rd.
Brighton   659-3666
First weekend in Aug.

Adams County claims the largest county fair in Colorado, and it has included such attractions as rodeos, tractor pulls, a draft horse pull, more than 150 exhibits and livestock shows, 4-H events, a children's pavilion, a petting zoo, a multicultural village, an artisans bazaar, free entertainment and top-name concerts. Past celebrity entertainers have included Alan Jackson and Mel Tillis. There's also a Latin music festival and a Charro rodeo.

NO MAN'S LAND

Breckenridge   (970) 453-6018
The second weekend in Aug.

From a fluke of history, a celebration is born. In 1936, the story goes, a local women's club discovered that Breckenridge had been left off various maps and treaties. So they had a flag-raising attended by Colorado's governor, and invested Breckenridge into the United States. Still, for four days every year, Breckenridge likes to pretend that it is not part of the United States and calls itself the Kingdom of Breckenridge. The city celebrates its independence with the International Woodcarving Competition, historic walking tours, gold-panning demonstrations, a re-enactment of the 1936 flag-raising and other eccentricities, plus concerts.

WESTERN WELCOME WEEK

Littleton's Main St., Arapahoe Community
College, Stern Park   797-5774, 730-7369
10 days beginning the second Fri. of Aug.

This is Littleton's big yearly celebration of itself. You'll find arts and crafts and continuous entertainment on Littleton's Main Street, with concerts, fireworks, barbecue, pancake breakfasts, a chili cookoff, a circus, used book sales, 5K and 15K races, a "ride-the-trails" bike ride, a grand parade and a children's parade.

KEYSTONE
ARTS & CRAFTS CELEBRATION

Keystone Village
at the Keystone Ski Area   (800) 451-5930
Usually the second weekend of Aug.

This is primarily a weekend arts and crafts show, but there is also a performance of the National Repertory Orchestra on Sunday and a fiddle contest on Saturday for anybody who wants to sign up. They've had fiddlers from age 5 to age 80.

THE JOSLINS CENTRAL CITY OPERA FASHION SHOW

The Opera House
Central City 292-6700
Mid-August

This is a preview of fall and winter fashions featuring a guest designer, and the designer always attends. Past shows have featured such luminaries as Oscar De La Renta and Victor Costa. This is a fund-raising event for the opera association. Tickets range from $30 to $200. The higher-price tickets involve lunch, preferred seating at the show and limousine rides from Denver to Central City.

SUMMERFEST JAZZ FESTIVAL

Main St.
Central City (800) 542-2999
Usually mid-Aug.

Colorado's gambling mecca gets down with a weekend featuring hot jazz by renowned jazz musicians, plus an art festival, haywagon rides, a beer garden and dancing on historic Main Street.

THE SPRINT INTERNATIONAL

Castle Pines Golf Club
1000 Hummingbird Dr.
Castle Rock 660-8000, (800) 755-1986
The third week in Aug., Mon. through Sun.

A special afterlife for golf-watchers might look something like this Colorado golf event of the year. One of the world's great courses hosts one of the most unique and challenging tournaments of the Professional Golf Association's finest. An international field presents the best golfers from around the world. You're welcome to walk the holes with the golfers, thrill to their mighty drives and stand behind ropes at each hole and clap or moan as they sink or muff their putts. You can attend golfing clinics, and if the pros are good Joes, you may even be able to talk with them and get your picture taken with them.

FAMILY ARTS FESTIVAL

Arvada Center for the Arts and Humanities
6901 Wadsworth Blvd.
Arvada 431-3939
Usually the third weekend in Aug.

Free family fun including kite flying, stunt-bike riders and performances for the family.

CARNATION FESTIVAL

Parade on 38th Ave., Harlan St. to Upham St.; Carnival in Albert E. Anderson Park at 44th Ave. and Field St.
Wheat Ridge 422-0326, 235-2806
Third weekend in Aug.

The fine community of Wheat Ridge has a jolly small-town parade in which floats are invited to cover themselves with carnations, though a lot of them don't. The carnival in the park has rides for children, and the carnival midway has food, arts and crafts, etc. There's also a rubber duck race on Clear Creek, in which you buy sponsorship of a rubber duck, a fund raiser for Family Tree, a battered-women's shelter program.

COLORADO STATE FAIR

State Fairgrounds
Pueblo, 2 hours south of Denver on I-25
(800) 444-3247
Two weeks, from late Aug. into early Sept.

The City of Pueblo is the farthest away of any listing in this guide for Annual Festivals and Events, but this is the state fair. And who wouldn't want to know about that? It's one of the state's largest annual events and a big-time Colorado tradition.

It's rather huge, so let's just say there are all the rodeo events and livestock sales and horse shows and cooking competitions and midway carnival rides and games and lots of good food that we as Americans have come to expect from this distinctive piece of Americana known as the state fair. There are also concerts with big-name country-Western singers who have in the past included Garth Brooks,

Photo: Daily Camera

The KBCO/Budweiser Kinetic Sculpture Challenge, the flatland version of the radio station's cardboard ski derby, takes place over two spring weekends in Boulder, weather and mud permitting.

George Strait and Vince Gill. There are plenty of performers of other types of music as well. Julio Iglesias even came one year. The first day of the fair is Fiesta Day, a Mexican heritage day.

CHILE HARVEST FESTIVAL
The Denver Botanic Gardens
1005 York St.
Denver   *331-4000*
Typically the last weekend in Aug.

This celebration of Hispanic culture includes Hispanic food booths, chile roasting, chile-pepper arts and crafts projects for kids, entertainment such as Hispanic bands and dance groups, and demonstrations of weaving, tinwork and adobe making. Booths will sell various Hispanic arts.

LODO BREWFEST
Lower Downtown
Between the newer downtown area and the Central Platte Valley
Denver   *964-8997*
Mid- to late Aug.

This is two days of opportunity to sample more than 30 kinds of beer from Colorado brewpubs and microbreweries, of which the festival organizers claim Colorado has more than any place in the world. Colorado boasts about 20 microbreweries and 18 brewpubs. The festivities include a street/block party with food and entertainment.

KING OF THE ROCKIES MOUNTAIN BIKE FESTIVAL
Base of the Winter Park Ski Area
Winter Park   *(970) 726-5514*
Mid- to late Aug.

This festival features races and guided mountain-biking tours for all levels of mountain bikers, as well as a mountain-bike and summer-sports expo.

ROCKY MOUNTAIN FOLKS FESTIVAL
Lyons (On the way to Estes Park)
                      (800) 624-2422
Mid-Aug.

This festival features lots of folk-music performances, which in the past have included artists such as Michelle Shocked, John Gorka, The Story, Lowen and Knavery. There are workshops and activities geared toward future musicians, and a song seminar that includes sessions on songwriting, copyrighting, bookkeeping, scoring and other elements of being a professional singer/songwriter. There are also vendors and food.

LAKEWOOD ON PARADE
Lakewood Park
Kipling St.
Lakewood   987-7800
The weekend before Labor Day weekend

The City of Lakewood's hour in the community-festival sun, this event typically combines food, a bike race, games, entertainment, a parade, a tennis tournament, a golf tournament, a car show and an art show.

September

THE FESTIVAL OF MOUNTAIN AND PLAIN: A TASTE OF COLORADO
Civic Center Park
Between Colfax Ave. and 14th St.
Denver   534-6161
Around Labor Day weekend

The Promised Land for gourmet and gourmand, and for those seeking fun, it's equally grand. Running about four days around Labor Day weekend, this is one of Denver's largest annual gatherings, attracting more than 400,000. They usually even block off a street or two. You can sample culinary delights from Greater Denver restaurants so it's a good way to find new restaurants dear to your tastes. It's also about five festivals in one: not only a food festival but also a children's festival,

an arts and crafts festival, a carnival midway, stages with live entertainment and a kaleidoscope of buskers and vendors and other jollies. The Festival of Mountain and Plain actually began in the 1800s and was named to celebrate Denver's dual personality as the Queen City of the Plains and the Monarch Metropolis of the Mountains.

BACK-TO-SCHOOL BLOCK PARTY
The Denver Zoo in City Park
E. 23rd Ave. and Steele St.
Denver   331-4100
Last Sunday in August, Noon to 6 PM

Enjoy a variety of family activities and entertainment at the zoo's annual back-to-school block party cosponsored by the Denver Police Chief's Youth Council.

COLORADO SPRINGS CABLEVISION BALLOON CLASSIC
Memorial Park
Pikes Peak Ave. and Union Blvd.
Colorado Springs   (719) 471-4833
Labor Day weekend

This is a grand spectacle. Typically about 150 hot-air balloons from around the nation ascend en masse at 7 AM on Saturday, Sunday and Monday. They are preceded by the "dawn patrol," about five balloons going up at 5:30 AM and dangling strobe lights, just to let folks know that the big event is coming. About 50 balloons light up Saturday night in the "Balloon Glo." Albuquerque trademarked the name "Balloon Glow," so the folks in the Springs had to drop the "w." In 1995 the festival added a new event, the Sunday night "glo" over the downtown area.

Find specifics on festivals and events each week by looking at the Friday sections of *The Denver Post, Rocky Mountain News* and *Daily Camera*. Also check the activities/events listings in Denver's weekly newspaper, *Westword*.

Insiders' Tips

Kiwanis Country Breakfast is served in a big tent from 5:30 to 9:30 each morning. There is a model hot-air balloon competition. A hang glider is launched from a balloon. Sky divers jump onto the site every morning and Saturday evening. Past years have included cloggers, an orchestra and a children's chorale. Plus, there's a concert on Saturday night by Flash Cadillac.

WINTER PARK FAMOUS FLAMETHROWER HIGH ALTITUDE CHILI COOKOFF
Winter Park (970) 726-5514
Labor Day weekend

A hot prospect. This is a one-day opportunity to sample different types of chili and salsa produced by a regional competition among costumed chili chefs for the Flamethrower title and the opportunity to represent the Rocky Mountain Region in the World Chili Cookoff. It has been held concurrently with the **Fraser Valley Railroad Days Festival**, which takes place on six levels of Winter Park's West Portal Station Cafeteria (so named because it's located right where trains from Denver come out of the tunnel under the Continental Divide). The railroad festival features model trains and you'll see a lot of model-train setups and vendors selling model-train products. Special presenters talk about model-train subjects and the history of trains.

LONGS PEAK SCOTTISH HIGHLAND FESTIVAL
Different parts of Estes Park (800) 44-ESTES
The weekend after Labor Day

The Celtic tradition goes bananas for four straight days: Thursday night through Sunday night with performances and competitions by bagpipe bands, highland dancers, Irish step dancers, highland dogs herding sheep, and Scottish athletes throwing the hammer and the caber.

There is a parade, medieval re-enactments and folk concerts, performances on the Celtic harp and fiddle and tin-whistle contests. There will be a seminar on tartans and other necessities of the Celtic aesthetic.

THE TASTE OF CENTRAL CITY
Main St.
Central City (800) 542-2999
Usually early Sept.

The outstanding chefs of Central City's casinos prepare casino cuisine, including a dessert-tasting booth. There are also comedians and live music which, in 1995, came from the bands Firefall and Ozark Mountain Daredevils.

FALL FEST
Downtown Golden 279-3113
Early to mid-Sept.

This used to be Oktoberfest, but they decided to broaden the scope. It's two days of food, entertainment, arts and crafts, a farmers' market, kids' activities, games, a mini-carnival and rides. And a hometown parade.

CASTLE ROCK ARTFEST
Old Courthouse Square
Castle Rock 688-4597
The weekend after Labor Day

This is an arts festival with family entertainment, continuing musical performances, children's entertainment and food. It features artists displaying, selling and working in the full range of media.

ARVADA HARVEST FESTIVAL
Olde Town Arvada
West of Wadsworth Blvd. between 56th and 58th aves.
Arvada 431-3928
The first weekend after Labor Day

This event celebrates the harvest festival with a parade, carnival, food and entertainment. The midway has booths from local service clubs and businesses. Arvada claims it's the oldest continually run festival in the West. A part of it is now the Visions West Art Show and Sale, which is held concurrently in Olde Town Arvada, the quaint and small-town center of what is now one of Greater Denver's biggest and fastest-growing suburbs.

SENIOR CITIZENS' DAY AT THE ZOO
The Denver Zoo in City Park
E. 23rd Ave. and Steele St.
Denver   331-4100
The second Tues. of Sept.

All seniors 55 and older get in free, with special entertainment and tours and free refreshments.

SUMMERSET FESTIVAL
Clement Park
Bowles Ave. and Pierce St.
South Jefferson County   973-9155
Second weekend after Labor Day

This is an end-of-summer outdoor celebration that has in the past included a parade, hot-air balloon rides, a pancake breakfast and other food, a volleyball tournament, entertainment, booths, games, an arts and crafts show, a golf tournament, a softball tournament, a concert-in-the-park picnic, a 5K run and a fishing derby.

GATEWAY TO THE
ROCKIES PARADE AND FESTIVAL
Colfax Ave. between Dayton and Florence sts.
Aurora   361-6169
Mid-Sept.

This is Aurora's party. Folks on the west side of Denver like to think of Jefferson County as the gateway to the Rockies, but Aurora also makes that claim. Aurora's reason is that East Colfax Avenue is the original U.S. 40 into the Rocky Mountain area, and until I-70 was built, Aurora was the first city that westbound travelers hit on their way into Greater Denver. The party has in the past included a parade, a farmers' market, arts and crafts, food booths with

Colorado produce, on-stage entertainment, clowns, face painting, a petting zoo and pony rides.

MINIATURES, DOLLS & TOYS
FALL SHOW AND SALE
Location varies   322-1053
Denver
Usually Sept.

This is a benefit for the Denver Museum of Miniatures, Dolls & Toys, though the show and sale is never held there. Usually it's at some place with conference-room space. It typically includes more than 100 national artists who specialize in making miniatures, dolls, teddy bears and toys. They display and sell their wares during a two-day weekend. There are also workshops Wednesday through Sunday, which you can attend but you have to preregister.

THE GILPIN COUNTY HISTORICAL
SOCIETY'S ANNUAL CEMETERY CRAWL
Historic Cemetery
Central City   (800) 542-2999
Usually mid-Sept.

Lend an ear to the living dead at this entertaining and educational event portraying the life of Gilpin County 100 years ago. Members and friends of the Historical Society transform into "spirits" of former residents, leaders and movers and shakers of the period. The spirits will share their stories as visitors walk through the historic cemetery.

MEXICAN INDEPENDENCE DAY
Civic Center Park
Between Colfax Ave. and 14th St.
Denver   534-8342 or 830-0708
A weekend close to Sept. 16

Held in conjunction with the Mexican consulate, this event celebrates Mexican Independence Day, which is September 16. There are Latino entertainments including continuous live music, dancers, artists and food vendors. Performances are on the Civic Center's Greek Theater stage, usually cranking up around 6 PM. Past events have also included a 5K run.

COLORFEST

Keystone Village   *(800) 354-4386*
Third weekend of Sept.

This includes the Taste of Keystone — food booths from all the Keystone restaurants — along with a raffle and musical entertainment, all on Saturday, with a golf tournament on Sunday.

ORGANIC FAIR

Four Mile Historic Park
715 S. Forest St.
Denver   *399-1859*
Mid-Sept.

Here, organic farmers peddle natural foods from around Colorado. This is more an organic farmers fair than a farmers market. Some booths don't sell anything, instead they offer free tastes of their products. Four Mile Historic Park is a good place for an organic farmers market/fair, whatever it is, because it's a living-history park. There are also historic and craft demonstrations, which in the past have included blacksmithing, quilting, weaving, lacemaking and butter churning. There's also music.

BRECKENRIDGE FESTIVAL OF FILM

Breckenridge   *(970) 453-2600*
Mid-Sept.

This three-day fest includes premieres of documentaries, feature films and children's features, as well as parties in local clubs and bars. Past years have seen visits by James Earl Jones, Mary Steenburgen, Elliott Gould and Angie Dickinson.

FALL FEST

Winter Park, downtown   *(970) 726-4118*
Mid-Sept.

A celebration marking the logging history of the Fraser Valley and the changing of the aspens as the scenic mountain community enters into the fall season. A weekend highlight is the Scheer's Lumberjack Show of Champions, and you can take part in other activities such as mountain biking, hiking and golf. Most events are free or nominal in cost.

OKTOBERFEST

Larimer Square
Larimer St. between 14th and 15th sts.
Denver   *534-2367*
Two weekends in mid-Sept.; Fri., Sat. and Sun.

Denver's main bow to the famous harvest festival of Munich is filled with polka bands and beer-drinking and sausage-eating fun. You'll see plenty of jolly Germanic costumes. This is one of the highlights of Larimer Square's festival year.

It includes Kinderplatz, a kid's area that has included "Prince Ludwig's castle" where kids can enjoy the Black Forest Maze and German storytellers, and "the world's shortest parade."

ROCKY MOUNTAIN SNOWMOBILE WINTER RECREATION EXHIBITION

The National Western Stock Show Complex
4600 Humboldt St. (take the Humboldt St. Exit off I-70)
Denver   *892-6800*
Typically the third weekend of Sept.; Sat. and Sun. only

If Greater Denver hasn't had at least a trace of snow by this time, it's an unusual year. And if you don't make a point of enjoying snow, you won't enjoy winter. Snowmobiles are one way of enjoying snow, so you may want to check out the latest in snowmobiles and accessories, snowmobile services and snowmobile travel destinations.

FALL FESTIVAL
Northridge Park & Recreation Center
Highlands Ranch   791-8958
Late Sept.

At this crafts show, with more than 100 crafters, you'll find a crafts bazaar, entertainers and exhibitors, a pumpkin-carving contest, food and kid activities.

October

ROCKY MOUNTAIN BOOK FESTIVAL
Currigan Exhibition Hall
1324 Champa St.
Denver   273-5933
A Fri. and Sat. in Oct.

About 200 exhibitors sell books, and more than 200 authors come in to read from or talk about their books. There are panel discussions and activities for kids that include a kids' performance stage. Previous literary celebrities have included Judy Blume, Ivan Doig, Barbara Kingsolver and a lot of Colorado authors.

COLORADO PERFORMING
ARTS FESTIVAL
Denver Performing Arts Complex
Speer Blvd. and Arapahoe St.
Denver   640-2758
Usually the first weekend of Oct.

Sample the performing arts in this free festival, outside the buildings and inside the theaters of the Denver Performing Arts Complex. There is a day-long theater marathon of nonstop theater, music, dance, cowboy poets and kids' entertainment. Performers from around the state attend and sponsor hands-on art activities on the grounds for kids. You can also see free performances at an "annex" stage in Larimer Square (Larimer Street between 14th and 15th streets).

CIDER DAYS HARVEST FESTIVAL
Lakewood's Historical Belmar Village
797 S. Wadsworth Blvd.
Lakewood   987-7850
First weekend in Oct.

Craftspersons recreate historic farm and domestic activities. You'll see antique farm machinery, a vintage tractor-pull competition, food vendors and live music.

GREAT AMERICAN BEER FESTIVAL
Location varies
Denver   447-0816

This is America's biggest beer bash. Bring a designated driver, because there are more than 1,600 beers to taste, the product of some 300-plus American breweries, microbreweries and brewpubs.

CHATFIELD ARBORETUM
PUMPKIN FESTIVAL
Chatfield Arboretum (Take Wadsworth Blvd. just south of C-470, go west on Deer Creek Canyon Rd. for about 1/3 mile.)
Unincorporated Jefferson Co.   973-3705
Generally the second Sat. of Oct.

Pick your own pumpkin from the pumpkin patch, and take part in pumpkin-carving and pumpkin-painting contests. Enjoy demonstrations of corn grinding, apple crushing and sometimes plowing. There are also hayrack rides, booths, crafts and food.

FALL MOUNTAIN MAN RENDEZVOUS
The Fort Restaurant
19192 Colo. Hwy. 8
Morrison   697-4771
Usually in the first week of Oct.

Re-enactors of the 1830s and 1840s dress in buckskins and behave like mountain men. You'll watch competitions for best costume and tomahawk, knife-throwing contests, black-powder target shooting, fire-starting with flint and steel and survival-skills demonstrations. There's a mountain-man run. Stop by Native-American trading tables where you can buy and trade for the works of Colorado artisans.

DENVER INTERNATIONAL FILM FESTIVAL

Various locations   595-3456
Usually the second week in Oct.

The late Raymond Burr didn't just shoot all those Perry Mason TV movies in Denver because he liked the local sausage. Denver has an impressive community of film companies, technicians, artists, etc., and this is that community's finest annual hour. The festival showcases more than 120 top feature, documentary and short films from around the world, screened at the Tivoli Theaters (Ninth Street and Auraria Parkway). The festival draws a host of actors, directors and producers. Celebrities roam the streets like cattle. Previous festivals have drawn celebrities such as Robert Altman, Geena Davis, Lillian Gish, Peter Bogdonavich, Stockard Channing, John Sayles and Gena Rowlands. After some film showings, enjoy a question-and-answer session with the director, producer, actors or others involved in the film's genesis. Often, there are seminars for interested regular Joes and Janes on subjects such as screenwriting.

ANNUAL SKI SWAP EXTRAVAGANZA

Winter Park, exact location determined a month before the event   (970) 726-5514
Mid-Oct.

Winter is knocking at the door. Here's a chance to get that new equipment, clothing and accessories — anything related to skiing or snowboarding — and a chance to dump your old stuff. Ski shops from around the Rocky Mountain region put their goods on sale. "Outstanding bargains," says Winter Park, "with prices reduced up to 60 percent." Guys and gals just like you will be selling their own equipment, and you can

do it too. You just have to check in several days before the sale starts.

SCUBA EXTASEA

Denver Coliseum
46th and Humboldt sts.
Denver   892-6800
Third week in Oct.

Denver has more divers than any landlocked area in the country, claims the local dive community. Here's a chance to dive into Denver's biggest annual diving show, with the latest in scuba equipment along with exhibitions by diving-destination companies from around the world.

RUN FOR THE ZOO

City Park
E. 23rd Ave. and Steele St.
Denver   727-8700
Third Sun. in Oct.

In the past this has included a 5K and a 10K run, and a 5K fitness walk to benefit a special project of the Denver Zoo. Sometimes people wear costumes. There is a costume contest and a "centipede" category, for people who run linked together in some kind of costume, and there is live music and refreshments. All participants receive a commemorative long-sleeved T-shirt, a free admission pass to the zoo and a chance to win post-race drawings for prizes.

SPIRITS OF THE PAST

Four Mile Historic Park
715 S. Forest St. (East of Colorado Blvd. and south of Leetsdale Dr., on the Cherry Creek Bike Path)
Denver   399-1859
Usually the third weekend in Oct.

This is a Halloween event in Four Mile Historic Park. Denver's oldest house, dating from 1859 and spookily decorated, emits a ghostly aura with historically dressed re-enactors in several of the rooms posing as ghosts and doing skits to demon-

KBCO's Cardboard Downhill Derby challenges entrants to find alternative transportation down the slopes of Arapahoe Basin Ski Area.

strate historic lifestyles. Other attractions include a bonfire, hayrides, stagecoach rides, music and the demonstrations of archaic lifestyles that make the Historic Park a fun place to hang. Out, that is. In the past this has included blacksmithing, quilting, spinning, weaving, lacemaking and butter churning.

THE HARVEST FESTIVAL

Main St.
Central City   (800) 542-2999
Usually late Oct.

Central City rings in the fall with a harvest festival that includes a baking contest, with recipes made exclusively from apples and pumpkins. You can also enjoy a haunted house tour, a wine and beer tasting highlighting Colorado wineries and breweries, and (the ever-popular) "much more."

WITCHES WALK

Larimer Square
Larimer St. between 14th and 15th sts.
Denver   534-2367
Late Oct.

This is a Larimer Square promotion for kids of all ages, in which they can show off their costumes in a safe setting with free entertainment and goodies.

VICTORIA HORRORS

Molly Brown House Museum
1340 Pennsylvania St.
Denver   832-4092
Last weekend in Oct.

A nice way to see the museum. As visitors go through the house, they encounter costumed characters reading selected bits from old horror writers like Mary Shelley, Bram Stoker and Edgar Allen Poe. There are refreshments in the carriage house.

BOO AT THE ZOO

Denver Zoo in City Park
E. 23rd Ave. and Steele St.
Denver   331-4110
The last Sat. of Oct.

Celebrate Halloween at the zoo; all kids 12 and younger who wear a costume get in free, but they must be accompanied by a paying adult. Trick-or-treat doors are set up throughout the zoo, and kids get a food or toy item at each door. The zoo sets up a medieval village offering storytelling and face painting.

November

DIA DE MUERTOS

Mexican Cultural Center
707 Washington St.
Denver   830-0708

The Day of the Dead is an old Mexican tradition celebrating death and the de-

parted, and here in Denver it's an exhibition of morbid arts and crafts and rituals. That doesn't mean morbid in a negative sense, because the Mexicans have a lot of fun with it. Although you really have to see it in Mexico to enjoy the full festive force of the occasion, you can have a lot of fun with it in Denver too.

BOTANIC GARDENS HOLIDAY SALE

Denver Botanic Gardens
1005 York St.
Denver   331-4000
Usually the weekend before Thanksgiving

This is a sale of the organic and the inorganic. Plants are for sale as well as herbs, oils and vinegars that volunteers have been producing all year long. Ornaments are crafted and purchased. You'll also find books on gardening, tools and other botany-related subjects.

STARLIGHTING

Old Courthouse Square, with chili dinner indoors
Castle Rock   688-4597
The Sat. before Thanksgiving

The annual lighting of the Christmas star on top of Castle Rock, the monolith that towers above the City of Castle Rock, is a Saturday evening event that's been going on since 1936. It goes along with a ceremony in Courthouse Square, including carolers, Santa, and hot chocolate, followed by a fire-department-sponsored chili supper and dance.

CONTINENTAL DIVIDE
HOT AIR BALLOON FESTIVAL

Breckenridge   (970) 453-6018
Thanksgiving weekend

Hot-air balloons from all over the nation fill the early morning skies in competition; then they fill the evening skies in a spectacular luminary event. That is, they are lighted. Along with the balloons goes a town street party to kick off the ski season. The party features live entertainment for all ages, food booths and sampling of microbrewery products.

COME-CATCH-THE-GLOW CHRISTMAS PARADE

Downtown Estes Park   (800) 44-ESTES
The Fri. after Thanksgiving

Christmas season starts early in the mountains. Start off this event by visiting with Santa and various character animals, then watch the evening light parade.

CHRISTMAS IN THE BROWNS' NEIGHBORHOOD

Molly Brown House Museum
1340 Pennsylvania St.
Denver   832-4092
Last Sun. in Nov.

Called an architectural history tour, really it's a walking tour of Molly's neighborhood in which you see three different Victorian homes or businesses, including Molly's. Tickets have previously cost $10.

WORLD'S LARGEST CHRISTMAS LIGHTING DISPLAY

The City and County Building, across from Civic Center Park
Between Colfax Ave. and 14th St.
Denver   935-0037
Late Nov. to Dec. 31, (They're turned on again during the National Western Stock Show in Jan.)

If light were music, the Denver City and County Building would be the world's largest pipe organ. About 20,000 colored spotlights turn this huge government building into one big neon sign. It has become a Denver holiday tradition, and it's a delight to go walk around and ogle on a frosty winter evening. Bundle up the kids.

CHRISTMAS WALK

Larimer Square
Larimer St. between 14th and 15th sts.
Denver   534-2367
Late Nov. until the night before Christmas

Larimer Square wants to pump you up for Christmas with entertainment and atmosphere, strolling carolers, roasting chestnuts, Father Christmas, etc. The majority of the entertainment is local, such as high-school and church groups of singers, bands, dancing groups and so on.

December

WORLD'S LARGEST CHRISTMAS LIGHTING DISPLAY

See November entry.

CHRISTMAS WALK

See November entry.

OLDE GOLDEN CHRISTMAS

Downtown Golden   279-3113
First Fri. in Dec., and first three Sats. in Dec.

Golden may be spreading out a bit, but it's still one of the last of the Greater Denver communities with a real small-town feel about it, and here's an old-fashioned, small-town Christmas festival. Golden is a charming location for holiday festivities that begin with candlelight walks through downtown Golden, in which everybody carries a candle and files down to Clear Creek to see the tree lights ignited. Santa Claus shows up. In the past, they've had a dance troupe clogging, and kids dancing. Then everybody troops over to the Coors Hospitality Center where there's a train exhibit, angel display, Christmas carolers, sleigh rides and other festivities, as well as hot chocolate, cookies and candy. On that day and on the first three Saturdays in December, other events include snow sculpting, children's igloo contests, wagon rides, cookie decorating, carolers, and kids sometimes get to make their own Christmas ornaments. Over at the Clear Creek Living History Ranch in restored old cabins from the turn of the century, they serve cowboy beans, doughnut holes, coffee and entertainment. At the Pioneer Museum, 911 10th St., there's live musical entertainment, hot cider, cookies and a big bonfire across the creek.

PARADE OF LIGHTS

Streets of downtown Denver   534-6161
The first Fri. and Sat. night of Dec.

This is truly one of the great public events of Denver's calendar: a night parade that lasts more than an hour and features floats, clowns, marching bands, giant balloon figures and other parade elements, all of them lit up or festooned with lights. Greater Denver has a number of big parades during the year, but this one has a special magic by virtue of being at night in the holiday season with everybody bundled up, with steamy breath and rosy cheeks. The whole event is one big Roman candle of multicolored holiday illumination. You might consider bringing extra wraps, blankets and a thermos of something hot and comforting. And as with all parades, if you want to position a folding chair for a front row seat, get there an hour before the show.

REINDEER DASH

Downtown Denver   534-6161
Immediately preceding the Parade of Lights described above.

This is a 2-mile family fun run through the streets of downtown Denver before the Parade of Lights. It's open to everybody.

HANDEL'S MESSIAH

Boettcher Concert Hall
905 13th St.
Denver   98-MUSIC
Typically the first weekend of Dec.

Holiday music lovers love this one: classic Christmas music with the Colorado Symphony Orchestra and the Colorado Symphony Chorus performing Handel's *Messiah*. There are Friday and Saturday evening performances where you just listen. On Sunday afternoon is the big one, where the audience is invited to participate in the performance. What you do is get a copy of the sheet music for the *Messiah* from any respectable music store. But call the Colorado Symphony administrative office, 595-4915, to make sure you get the right version of the *Messiah*. Even if you're not musical, the sheet music should have the words, and you can join the general caterwauling of fellow amateurs and/or just enjoy the spectacle of *Messiah* buffs around you singing away.

CANDLELIGHT TOURS

Molly Brown House Museum
1340 Pennsylvania St.
Denver   832-4092
Usually the first week of Dec.

Join the Browns as they celebrate Christmas in 1903. See a Victorian dinner party in progress, meet Santa Claus and sing Christmas carols.

CANDLELIGHT TOURS

Denver Museum of Miniatures, Dolls & Toys
1880 Gaylord St.
Denver   322-3704, 322-1053
Early Dec.

In a house built in 1899 that is decorated for the holidays, the museum has a nice old-time Christmas atmosphere in which to take a tour by candlelight. Volunteers provide entertainment, which includes Christmas music and food is donated by local businesses.

BUFFALO BILL'S
HOLIDAY CELEBRATION

The Buffalo Bill Memorial Museum on Lookout Mountain, 987½ Lookout Mountain Rd. (Take I-70 west to Exit 256, where the sign says "Lookout Mountain" and "Buffalo Bill's Grave;" follow the signs to the top of Lookout Mountain)
Golden   526-0744
Mid-Dec.

This is the museum's Christmas event. Past years have included bell ringers, Girl Scouts singing Christmas carols, high-school choirs, food and drink, and a Buffalo Bill lookalike playing Santa Claus.

HOLIDAY OPEN HOUSE

Four Mile Historic Park
715 S. Forest St.
Denver   399-1859
Mid-Dec.

Find an old-fashioned, Christmas atmosphere at Four Mile Historic Park during this two-day affair. St. Nick or Father Christmas will be there; Christmas music will be performed; and sleigh rides (if snow conditions permit) will be offered along with the Park's usual offerings of stagecoach rides and demonstrations of antique arts.

WILD LIGHTS

The Denver Zoo in City Park
E. 23rd Ave. and Steele St.
Denver   331-4110
Usually from the second Sat. in Dec. through Dec. 31, 6 to 9 PM

This is a family outing that is memorable on any of its many nights in December. Thousands of sparkling lights are strung on trees and used to create Christmas light sculptures of colored animals. There's nightly entertainment, storytelling, holiday refreshments and a nightly appearance by Santa Claus (through Christmas). Amid all the lights, it's fun to visit the animals and see what they do with their time on a winter night. Be warned that some of the animals are not out, but the seals and sea lions are a real scream playing on the ice.

BLOSSOMS OF LIGHTS

The Denver Botanic Gardens
1005 York St.
Denver   331-4000
Early Dec. to Dec. 31

Have you seen the lights? The Denver Botanic Gardens does for plants in its Blossoms of Lights what the Denver Zoo does for animals in its Wild Lights (See listing above). There are giant flowers of Christmas lights and lights draped all over plants and other objects. There's nothing more invigorating than a stroll through a wonderland of lights on a frosty evening, and it's a different way of seeing Denver's beloved Botanic Gardens. And nightly entertainment is included, along with holiday refreshments.

TEDDY BEAR TEAS

The Denver Botanic Gardens
1005 York St.
Denver   331-4000
Two Sats. in Dec.

Children share the English high-tea experience with a favorite teddy bear. A Barbie or a Power Ranger would probably not be turned away, but it would certainly clash with the ambiance, so go for the teddy bear.

Some parents and grandparents tend to dress their kids like little ladies and gentlemen for these teas. There are also snacks and assorted entertainments such as a storyteller and magician. It takes place during the Blossoms of Lights (see above), so there's another attraction.

HOLIDAY CONCERTS

The Denver Botanic Gardens
1005 York St.
Denver   331-4000
Tuesdays and Thursdays in Dec.

Holiday concerts at the Botanic Gardens range from 16-piece bands to blues and other types of music. Concerts are held inside during the evenings. Outside, you can see the Blossoms of Lights (see above).

CHRISTMAS POPS CONCERT

Boettcher Concert Hall
905 13th St.
Denver   986-8742
Usually the third weekend in Dec., Thurs. through Sun.

This is a benchmark in our year, our

favorite way to inaugurate the Christmas season as being officially under full steam. The concert features The Colorado Symphony Orchestra, the Colorado Symphony Chorus and the Colorado Children's Chorale.

CHRISTMAS EVE TORCHLIGHT PARADE

Winter Park Resort   (970) 726-5514
Christmas Eve, starting at dusk

Watch from the base of Winter Park ski area as skiers weave a trail of light down the slopes and then create a Christmas-related formation such as a Christmas tree or star. Fireworks and religious services follow.

FIRST NIGHT COLORADO

Various locations
Downtown Denver   399-9005
New Year's Eve

From noon into the evening, downtown Denver celebrates New Year's Eve with family entertainment, music, dance, storytelling, theater, visual displays and the like. Fireworks light up the evening sky. The indoor program, which is most of it, costs $7 for a First Night button. A 5K run in the afternoon requires an added entry fee.

Inside
The Arts

Denver's reputation as a cowtown without culture is like Denver's reputation as a place where there's snow on the ground six months of the year: It's just not true. Fact is, more tickets are sold to arts events than to professional sports events in Denver, according to the Denver Metro Convention and Visitors Bureau. Denver has the second-largest performing arts complex in the country (only New York City's Lincoln Center has more seats), as well as nationally recognized dance, music and theater companies. Denverites are avid moviegoers who flock to the Denver International Film Festival each October.

There's a large section on art galleries in this chapter, but for descriptions of museums, see the Tours and Attractions chap-

ter. And given that one person's definition of culture may overlap with another person's idea of popular entertainment, check our Nightlife chapter, too. In general, we've put concert venues, both indoor and outdoor, where you sit and listen and buy tickets in advance, in this chapter. Movie houses and bars and restaurants with music or other kinds of entertainment are in the Nightlife chapter.

In this section we begin by describing the Denver Performing Arts Complex, its theaters and resident performing groups. Next we describe other performing groups, theaters, theater companies and dinner theaters. The following section covers popular music concert venues, and then we move on to community art centers, the most sig-

Photo: Denver Metro Convention & Visitors Bureau

The Denver Art Museum's distinctive building is located in the Civic Center downtown.

nificant of which, the Arvada Center for the Arts and Humanities, is a leader in both performing arts and visual arts programming. Finally, we describe Greater Denver's art galleries.

Denver Performing Arts Complex

The Theaters

Extending over the space of four downtown city blocks, the Denver Performing Arts Complex has 9,000-plus seats and is home to several of Denver's most prominent performing companies, including the Denver Center Theatre Company, the Colorado Symphony Orchestra, the Colorado Ballet and Opera Colorado.

The newest and largest theater in the complex is the **Temple Hoyne Buell Theatre**, which opened in 1991. The theater has 2,800 seats. **Boettcher Concert Hall**, a unique 2,600-seat concert hall-in-the-round, dates from 1978. The **Auditorium Theatre** is a grand old (1908) neoclassical proscenium house with 2,200 seats.

The **Helen Bonfils Theatre Complex**, built in 1979, houses four smaller theaters. The Stage (700 seats) is a thrust theater; the Space is theater-in-the-round (well, it's actually more of a pentagon) with 450 seats; the Ricketson Theatre is a 195-seat informal proscenium; and the Source, with only 150 seats, is an intimate experimental thrust stage.

Also in the complex is the **Garner Galleria Theatre**, which presents cabaret shows.

At intermission, patrons spill out into the high, arched, glass-ceilinged galleria to stretch their legs and get some fresh air (or, conversely, to smoke a cigarette).

The Companies

Robert Garner Center Attractions brings in touring Broadway shows to the Buell or Auditorium theaters. The **Denver Center Theatre Company** is the resident troupe, with a season running from September to June. For tickets or information, call the box office at 893-4100 or stop in; it's on 14th Street at Curtis Street and open 10 AM to 6 PM Monday through Saturday. To avoid a service charge, purchase tickets at the box office. Tickets are also available by phone through TicketMaster at 830-TIXS (830-8497) and at TicketMaster outlets throughout Greater Denver, including the Ticket Bus at 16th and Curtis streets (cash only).

The **Colorado Symphony Orchestra**, 98-MUSIC, is a successful regrouping of musicians from the former Denver Symphony Orchestra, which ceased to operate in 1989. The principal conductor is Marin Alsop. The CSO plays classical music and "popular classics" in Boettcher Hall during its regular season, which lasts from September to May. Each season there are also about six low-priced "casual classics" concerts, one-hour performances of a masterwork concert with informal dialogue from the podium. In 1992 the orchestra added a summer season of outdoor performances, which has proved to be very popular.

The **Colorado Ballet**, 837-8888, was established as the Colorado Concert Ballet in 1961. The resident company of 25 dancers is under the artistic direction of Martin Fredmann and is the only dance company in the state to perform with a live orchestra. The repertoire includes full-length classical and one-act ballets. Performances are held in either the Buell or Auditorium theater, from fall through spring. In 1993, the company made its exciting New York debut and was praised by *New York Times* dance critic Anna Kisselgoff for its "surprising maturity, presence and solid technique of its performers."

Opera Colorado, 98-MUSIC, presents three grand operas each winter and spring, two in the round at Boettcher Concert Hall and one on the traditional proscenium stage in the Buell Theatre. It is the only company in the United States producing grand opera in the round. Performances are sung in the original language, with English translations projected onto screens above and around the stage. Opera Colorado director Nathaniel Merrill was resident stage director at the Metropolitan Opera for 28 seasons. Opera Colorado also performs at special holiday concerts and summer festivals throughout the state. The Opera Colorado for Children program includes children's opera workshops, matinee performances for students and an in-school puppet opera.

Other regular presenters at the Denver Performing Arts Complex include:

The **Colorado Children's Chorale**, 892-5600: This 400-member chorus, which tours nationally and internationally, celebrated its 20th anniversary in 1994. Each year it joins the Colorado Symphony Orchestra for a very special, very popular holiday concert.

The **Denver Young Artists Orchestra**, 571-1935: Formed in 1977 as a means for Colorado's talented young musicians to rehearse and perform under professional standards, the Young Artists Orchestra plays three concerts each year in Boettcher Concert Hall, including a free joint concert with the Colorado Symphony. Top admission price at the other two concerts is only $5.

Other Performing Companies

Music

Formed in 1981, the 12-member **Denver Brass**, 832-4676, is one of very few symphonic brass ensembles in the country. Concerts feature "something for everyone," from splendid brass fanfares to big-band music. Performances, including an annual Christmas concert, are held at Bethany Lutheran Church, 4500 E. Hampden Avenue, and Montview Boulevard Presbyterian Church, 1980 Dahlia Street.

Also under the same management, and reached at the same phone number as the Denver Brass, is **Aries Brass Quintet**. Founded in 1976, Aries has toured the United States, Europe and South America; performed its fresh and vibrant renditions of chamber music live on National Public Radio; and recorded several albums. Aries is a resident company at St. John's Episcopal Cathedral in Denver, 1313 Clarkson Street.

Dance

Cleo Parker Robinson Dance, 295-1759, is a multicultural performing arts institution with a professional modern dance company and a dance school based in the historic African Methodist Episcopal

Photo: Colorado Ballet

The Colorado Ballet is creating a national reputation for high-quality dance.

Church at 119 Park Avenue W. The ensemble performs regularly in Denver and extensively around the country and is one of Denver's best-known exports in the arts field. It celebrated its 25th anniversary in 1995.

David Taylor Dance Theatre, 797-6944, which marked its 16th season in 1995, is Denver's foremost professional contemporary ballet company. They are, in addition, one of the region's major presenters of *The Nutcracker*, which is performed annually at the Arvada Center and on tour throughout the state and the Northwest. The main focus of the company, however, is original contemporary works. Although the company is headquartered at 2539 W. Main Street in Littleton, where they offer ballet classes for children and adults, they perform in different venues throughout Greater Denver from September through May.

Kim Robards Dance, 825-4847, was established in 1987 as Colorado Repertory Dance Company and is an important center for modern dance in Colorado. The dynamic collection of works in KRD's repertoire includes pieces by artistic director Kim Robards along with works by selected international guest choreographers. The professional touring company, which consists of six to eight dancers, has performed in New York and California, among other places. Locally, the company presents a winter and spring season at different venues in metro Denver, along with an educational outreach program. The KRD school at 821 Acoma Street, established in 1990,

offers classes for beginners (children must be at least 6 years old) and professionals.

Theaters: Variety

The historic **Joseph B. Gould Family Paramount Theatre**, 1631 Glenarm Place, has more than once been on the verge of falling to the wrecker's ball. Built in 1930 by Temple Hoyne Buell, a prominent Denver architect, the theater is the epitome of art deco style and has one of only two Mighty Wurlitzer organs in the country (the other is at Radio City Music Hall in New York City). During the summer of 1994 — under new management yet again — the Paramount underwent extensive remodeling. The Paramount presents a mixed bag of theater, comedy, pop music, children's programming and ballet. The box office number is 534-8336.

The **Bluebird Theater**, 3317 E. Colfax Avenue, 322-2308, is Denver's newest old movie theater to offer a variety of musical and other programming. Built in 1914 and originally used to show silent films, the Bluebird fell upon hard times and closed in the late 1980s. The newly restored theater reopened in fall 1994. On Sunday nights, the Bluebird shows cult movie classics and music movies, and on Wednesday through Saturday nights there's a wide variety of live music: rock, reggae, Latin, jazz, folk, and blues. An espresso bar upstairs and a bar are on hand to quench a thirst. Questions? Call 322-2308.

A vaudeville-era theater that later became a moviehouse, **The Ogden Theatre's**

Half-price theater tickets are sometimes available at the Ticket Bus, 16th and Curtis streets. Hours are 10 AM to 6 PM Monday through Friday and 10 AM to 3 PM Saturday; you must pay in cash.

Insiders' Tips

newest incarnation is as a concert hall presenting a wide variety of local and national acts. The Ogden is at 935 E. Colfax, and the box-office number is 830-2525.

Theaters and Theater Companies

Denver

The **Ad Hoc Theatre** presents plays by Shakespeare, Chekhov and other classics at the new 225-seat Acoma City Center at 1080 Acoma Street. The company also performs at an intimate 45-seat theater at 416 E. 20th Avenue. Call 820-2544 for information and tickets.

The award-winning **Avenue Theatre**, 2119 E. 17th Avenue, 321-5925, is an intimate space next to Mike Berardi's and Juanita's Uptown restaurants. Producer John Ashton offers an eclectic schedule of performances: often comedies, but not always. They perform the perennially popular *Murder Most Fowl* — Denver's longest-running play — every holiday season, from Thanksgiving to mid-January.

City Stage Ensemble, 433-8082, is in its 10th season at Jack's Theatre, 1553 Platte Street in Lower Downtown, an intimate, $^3/_4$-round theater. They perform plays by Moliere, Shaw and Shakespeare, with a focus on works that address the issues of our times. They also do one original play each season and have a resident playwright.

El Centro Su Teatro was formed in 1971 by students at the University of Colorado at Denver as a forum for those interested in the Chicano movement. It has grown into a multidisciplinary cultural-arts center that sponsors concerts, drama, performance art, dance, festivals, workshops and art exhibitions. Theater performances emphasize original works by Chicano and Latino playwrights, including Su Teatro's director Tony Garcia. El Centro Su Teatro is housed in a former elementary school at 4725 High Street in Denver and can be reached at 296-0219.

The **Changing Scene**, 1527½ Champa Street, 893-5775, is the oldest independent theater in Denver and presents only world premieres, some of which continue on to New York and Europe. In addition to original dramas, Changing Scene hosts dance, music, film, performance art and events in its small theater — "anything new and fresh," says director Al Brooks.

Compass Theatre Company, 398-7578, formed in the early 1990s, does primarily the classics, including a great deal of Shakespeare. It was named as Best New Theater Company by the local weekly *Westword* in 1993. Most performances are held at the Denver Civic Theatre. Established in 1985, the **Denver Civic Theatre**, 595-3800, has been in its present location at 721 Santa Fe Drive since 1991. Under the guidance of Henry Lowenstein, who spent 30 years as a producer at the old Bonfils Theatre on Colfax Avenue (now called the Lowenstein Theatre), the Denver Civic Theatre stages well-known plays, including Broadway musicals, and original works from September through June. The theater building was originally built in 1923 as a movie theater and over the years has been used for many different purposes; it was a meatpacking plant in the '50s and '60s and later a photographer's studio. Now it houses two theaters: a main stage proscenium with 340 seats and an intimate black box theater that seats 104. Continuing programs at the Denver Civic Theatre include a theater series for children, a Latino theater series and a school touring program.

The **Denver Victorian Playhouse**, 4201 Hooker Street, 433-4343, in northwest

Denver, is a restored and refurbished 1911 house with a 74-seat theater. Classical music, children's shows, a full range of adult comedies, dramas and musicals are performed here year round.

Founded in 1982, Eulipions' mission is to foster, promote and encourage artistic expression of Denver's diverse cultural communities, with an emphasis on the African-American community. Performances are held at the **Eulipions Theatre**, 2425 Welton Street, in the Five Points neighborhood. Eulipions has received a mayor's award for excellence in the arts, and in 1989 their production of *Ma Rainey's Black Bottom* won a Denver Critics Circle Award for best theater production. Sometime in 1996, Eulipions plans to move its base of operations to a historic red sandstone building at 1770 Sherman Street. For a schedule or ticket information, call 295-6814.

Germinal Stage Denver, 455-7108, was founded by four Denver actors in 1973, making it one of the longest-living small theaters in the region. Performances are held in a fully air-conditioned, 100-seat converted storefront at 2450 W. 44th Avenue, five blocks east of Federal Boulevard. The repertoire includes everything from traditional to more arcane and experimental plays.

Hunger Artists Ensemble Theatre, 893-5438, is a successful 15-year-old acting ensemble that in 1994 became the resident theater company at the University of Denver. They produce about four plays a year, one per season. An eclectic company, they do primarily contemporary pieces bordering on experimental with some forays into the classics, although with the move to DU they anticipate increasing their classical work. Performances are held in the 250-seat Harry Richie Theater on the DU campus in Margery Reed Hall.

The **Industrial Arts Theatre Company,** known for its stagings of classic and contemporary plays, is going through a transitional period. They hope to begin performances again in mid-1996. In the meantime, they're offering workshops. Call 832-3037.

RiverTree Theatre, at 1124 Santa Fe Drive, produces classic and contemporary American and British plays year round, as well as some original work, in its 99-seat proscenium theater. Call 825-8150.

The **Theatre on Broadway** (recorded information, 777-3292) presents Denver premieres of new Broadway and off-Broadway shows in a small black-box theater at 13 S. Broadway. The season generally runs from September through July. The box office number is 860-9360.

The **Physically Handicapped Amateur Musical Actors League** (PHAMALy) gives physically handicapped actors a chance to perform and physically handicapped members of the public a chance to enjoy theater. This group does only one musical a year, which in recent years has been staged during the summer at the Denver Performing Arts Complex. Performances are always wheelchair-accessible, and arrangements are made to provide assistance to hearing-impaired and visually-impaired audience members. Call 575-0005

More than two dozen Lower Downtown galleries stay open until 9 PM on the first Friday of each month. Some serve refreshments. Pick up a map at a participating gallery, or call 321-1510 for information.

Insiders' Tips

Germinal Stage Denver

Ed Baierlein played to perfection the buffoon role of Major Petkoff in George Bernard Shaw's comedy, *Arms and the Man*, scowling and bellowing, gaping and grinning and lolling his tongue, his face a writhing parade of expressions so foolish that the audience sometimes laughed loudest when he was saying nothing at all.

"That's some play you're running," a fan told him over the telephone one night an hour before the curtain went up. "You're quite a comedian."

"Well thanks," Baierlein said. "We're doing pretty well. You wanted how many reservations now? Would that be Visa or MasterCard?"

More than a comedian, Baierlein, 53, is also one of the Denver area's most respected serious actors, but that doesn't mean he is above taking reservations, cleaning the theater, maintaining the mailing lists and doing the books at the Germinal Stage Denver theater in northwest Denver.

"The thing that makes Ed unusual is that he's in a category that's almost gone," said Jackie Campbell, theater critic at the *Rocky Mountain News*. "He's manager, producer, director and actor. Because he is all of those things, his theater has his stamp very clearly."

So does Greater Denver. Since its founding in 1973, Germinal Stage has built a faithful audience with more than 130 plays including everything from experimental, first-run productions to Ibsen, Shaw and Shakespeare. Those plays have earned the theater a reputation and influence all out of proportion to its 100-seat facility in an old 5,000-square-foot building.

"The smaller theaters are where the vital theater wells up in any town," says Campbell. "Germinal Stage is certainly the definitive smaller theater in town."

While the large theaters of the Denver Performing Arts Complex are a point of pride and a focus of entertainment on Denver's cultural landscape, Germinal Stage and the more than a dozen other smaller local theaters perhaps provide a truer measure of that landscape's cultural depth.

"In the smaller theaters," Baierlein says, "the artists tend to be in primary control. They tend to be more eclectic, with a more specialized audience and repertoire. The problems today are fairly similar to what they were when we started out — on the one hand, maintaining the integrity of our repertoire, and on the other hand, being popular enough so that people will pay to see your next failure."

Baierlein and Sallie Diamond, 52, his wife and partner in the nonprofit Germinal Stage and one of the area's most versatile and respected actresses, are among the many who came to Denver by chance and stayed by choice.

"I was in the Air Force and was shipped here in 1968 and spent most of my time in the service at Lowry Air Force Base," Baierlein said. "My wife and I decided this was the nicest place we had ever lived. My philosophy is, find a place where you like to live and then make the work happen there."

Photo: Stacker Edwards

Denver's several small performance theaters, such as the Germinal Stage Denver, have attracted faithful audiences of Denverites based on their ability to present a variety of productions from experimental first-runs to Shakespeare.

It was the city that attracted them, Baierlein said. The city is where they and their son Thaddeus, who was born here in 1980, spend most of their time. From their home just a block away from the theater, they take periodic trips to Glenwood Springs, a three-hour drive to the west, to enjoy the world's largest outdoor hot pool.

"That's our favorite vacation, just to let the city seep out of us in the pools," Baierlein said. "We're not great outdoors people. We don't ski and we don't camp."

Even so, Baierlein said they try to get to the mountains as much as possible, just to enjoy the unearthly beauty and solitude that are never far away from the lives and thoughts of even the most urbane of Greater Denverites.

"When you're away from here for any period of time," he said, "you really miss just the presence of the mountains. There's no other place I know where you can have the amenities of a big city and still, in half an hour, be absolutely isolated in a place where you feel nobody has ever been before."

or watch the DPAC schedule for performances.

The **Mirror Players**, 430-4862, is another group that only presents one play a year—and sometimes not even that! Their renditions of Shakespeare are very well thought of by local critics.

Aurora

From fall to spring, the **Aurora Fox Arts Center**, 9900 E. Colfax Avenue, Aurora, 361-2910, is home to three performing arts groups: the **Aurora Theatre Company**, which puts on three plays and a musical each year; and the **Aurora Singers** and the **Aurora Symphony**, each of which gives four performances in the center's 250-seat theater. In the summer there's a children's theater program, performed for and by children.

Arvada

There's plenty of history behind the **Festival Playhouse**, 5665 Olde Wadsworth Boulevard, 422-4090. The **Denver Players Guild**, formed in 1936, stages eight plays a year — primarily Broadway comedies — in this converted Grange building in Olde Town Arvada. The Players Guild believes it is the oldest community theater group in the country under the same family management, and the theater is even older: Built in 1874, it's the second-oldest standing Grange hall in Colorado and the oldest building in the city of Arvada.

Dinner Theaters

Country Dinner Playhouse, 6875 S. Clinton Street, Englewood, 799-1410: An Equity theater that presents Broadway hits and family entertainment year round, with a buffet dinner preceding the show. There are Saturday and Sunday matinees.

Heritage Square Music Hall and Dinner Theater, U.S. Highway 40 in Golden (18301 W. Colfax Ave.), 279-7800: A Victorian-style theater with original comic melodramas and musical revues. A buffet dinner precedes the show, but it's possible to buy a ticket for the performance only. Performances are Wednesday through Sunday evenings, with Sunday matinees.

Popular Music Concerts

Outdoor rock and other popular music concerts are held at McNichols Arena, Mile High Stadium, Fiddler's Green Ampitheatre and Red Rocks Ampitheatre. Indoor venues include the Ogden Theatre and the Paramount Theatre, which are described above under "theaters" as they're not limited to popular musical events. Tickets for all concerts at virtually all venues are most conveniently purchased at TicketMaster outlets (cash only) or by calling TicketMaster at 830-TIXS (830-8497), but a trip to the box office can generally (though not always) save you from paying a service charge.

Red Rocks and Fiddler's Green are the venues for the **"Summer of Stars"** series, which brings major recording artists in for concerts during the summer.

Fiddler's Green Amphitheatre, 6350 Greenwood Plaza Boulevard in Englewood, is a huge new 18,000-seat amphitheater just west of I-25 between Arapahoe and Orchard roads. The box office, 770-2222, is only open on show days, from 10 AM to 9 PM; tickets purchased here are slightly less expensive than through TicketMaster.

Red Rocks Ampitheatre is one of the most spectacular settings anywhere for a concert. About half the size of Fiddler's

Photo: Arvada Center for the Arts and Humanities

The Arvada Center for the Arts and Humanities offers performances, classes and gallery shows.

Green, Red Rocks is a natural red sandstone ampitheater set deep into the Foothills on Hogback Road near Morrison (take I-70 west to the Morrison Exit, and follow the signs). For recorded information about upcoming events, call 640-7334. You can avoid a service charge by purchasing tickets at the TicketMaster advance ticket window at McNichols Arena from Monday through Friday 11 AM to 6 PM and Saturdays from 10 AM to 3 PM (cash only).

The venerable **Swallow Hill Music Hall**, 777-1003, is Denver's center for folk and traditional acoustic music. All concerts at their intimate 1905 S. Pearl Street location are nonsmoking, all-ages events. Swallow Hill also presents concerts elsewhere in the city.

Community Art Centers

The major contender in this category is the **Arvada Center for the Arts and Humanities**, 6901 Wadsworth Boulevard in Arvada, 431-3939. The Arvada Center has two galleries, which display changing exhibits of contemporary art, folk art, design and crafts, with a strong regional empha-

sis. There's also a small historical museum. In addition, the Center has both an indoor 500-seat auditorium and an outdoor amphitheater with 1,200 seats (600 covered, 600 on the lawn).

The Arvada Center keeps up an impressive schedule of performing arts programming that includes children's and adult professional theater, dance and music concerts. One resident company calls the Arvada Center home: the **Arvada Center Chorale**, but many groups perform here. It's the site each winter of a cowboy-poetry gathering, and a day each spring is devoted to a celebration of female experiences. A highly regarded deaf-access program makes many programs accessible to the hearing-impaired.

In 1992, the Arvada Center underwent a $10.5-million expansion that added more than 59,000 gross square feet, more than doubling its previous size. At this time they installed a controversial "dirt wall" by New York artist Vito Acconci that wends its way through the building.

The **Foothills Art Center**, 809 15th Street in Golden, 279-3922, is much smaller than the Arvada Center and does not offer a performing arts program. However, the center is home to two prestigious annual national exhibitions, *The North American Sculpture Exhibition* and the *Rocky Mountain National Watermedia Exhibition*, as well as the statewide annual *Colorado Clay* exhibition. The remainder of the center's schedule is composed of changing exhibits of national and regional arts and fine crafts.

Art Galleries

Downtown

Greater Denver's contemporary art galleries are clustered in the Lower Downtown area (LoDo), although with the construction of Coors Field and the corresponding influx of sports bars, brewpubs and such, it's unclear whether the fledging arts district will be able to hold its own. Working on the assumption that there's strength in numbers, the LoDo galleries have banded together to form a **Lower Downtown Arts District** and to coordinate openings and other special events. The most significant program to come out of this cooperative effort is First Fridays, in which more than two dozen LoDo galleries stay open until 9 PM the first Friday of each month. Especially in the summer, there's kind of a street festival atmosphere as patrons go from one gallery to the next, stopping to compare notes with friends on the sidewalk. For more information about LDAD and LDAD membership, call 321-1510.

Gallery openings are usually held on Fridays and are, with rare exceptions, free and open to the public. Check *Westword* or the Friday editions of *The Denver Post*, *Rocky Mountain News* and *Daily Cam-*

era for a list of openings and current exhibit information. Most galleries close on Mondays, but this varies, so call ahead to be sure.

Think of art galleries as a wonderful free smorgasbord of exciting things to see. Of course, the bottom line is that galleries must sell art to stay in business, but unlike art dealers in some cities, Denver dealers are notably low-key and happy to educate browsers without pressuring them to buy. Dealers know that the best way to develop customers is to make people feel comfortable, and high-pressure sales tactics aren't going to do that.

On the other hand, if you are a serious buyer, you should be aware that virtually every gallery in town adds the phrase "and by appointment" to its set hours. This may be especially important to visitors whose time in the city is limited.

The heart of Denver's avant-garde arts district is the 1700 block of Wazee Street. Here you'll find **Robischon Gallery**, at 1740 Wazee Street, 298-7788, Denver's premier gallery for abstract painting and sculpture. They show representational art, too. Next door at 1734 Wazee Street is **Sandy Carson Gallery**, 297-8585, which shows contemporary painting, sculpture and photography, as well as ceramics and glass. **The Art of Craft**, 1736 Wazee Street, 292-5564, exhibits fine crafts.

Across the street at 1743 Wazee is the **Opicka Gallery**, 291-1014, a representational art and photography gallery. The **1/1 Gallery** (say "one over one") at 1715 Wazee Street, 298-9284, specializes in monotypes, which are one-of-a-kind prints, but it also displays painting, generally by regional artists. On the corner of Wazee and 17th streets is the **Metropolitan State College of Denver Center for the Visual Arts**, 294-5207. Technically a university gallery, Metro seldom shows student work, but rather, puts on some of the best and most provocative exhibitions in town. Recent exhibitions have included African-American quilts, contemporary Chinese painting and baseball paraphernalia from local collections.

The **Sloane Gallery of Art**, 1612 17th Street, 595-4230, is devoted exclusively to contemporary Russian art. **Core New Art Space**, a cutting-edge gallery that primarily features local artists, is a few blocks farther south at 1412 Wazee Street, 571-4831, and is open Thursday through Sunday noon to 5 PM and Fridays from noon to 10 PM.

More traditional LoDo galleries include the **Merrill Gallery of Fine Art Ltd.** (formerly the Carol Siple Gallery), 1401 17th Street, 292-1401, an excellent representational art gallery; and the **William Matthews Gallery**, 1617 Wazee Street, 534-1300, which exhibits the Western watercolors of William Matthews. The **J. Howell Gallery**, 1420 Larimer Street, 820-3925, exhibits fine clay, both sculptural and functional, plus two-dimensional art, mostly by Coloradans. There's a second branch in Tamarac Square, 7777 E. Hampden Ave. The large **Third Canyon Gallery**, 1512 Larimer Street at Writer Square, 893-3936, has contemporary Southwestern painting and sculpture, plus traditional and contemporary Indian jewelry. **Knox Gallery**, 1632 Market Street, 820-2324, specializes in realistic bronze sculpture.

A little farther to the north, at 1936 Market Street, is the **Grant Gallery**, 296-3071, which began as a contemporary and vintage photography gallery but now alternates photography shows with contemporary abstract painting and printmaking exhibits. The **Denver Center for Fine Photography**, 295-7548, is located in the rear of the Grant Gallery. DCFP offers a full schedule of classes and darkroom rental and has a darkroom equipped with 15 enlargers.

Over by the Platte River, at 1535 Platte Street, is **Spark Gallery**, 455-4435, an artists' cooperative (Denver's oldest) that's only open weekends.

Near the Denver Art Museum at 1309 Bannock is **Camera Obscura Gallery**, 623-4059, devoted exclusively to photography. Owner Hal Gould is supremely knowledgeable; spend a little time talking with him, and he'll show you the vintage treasures he keeps upstairs.

Inkfish Gallery, 949 Broadway, 825-6727, is the last holdout in what used to be an entire block of galleries. Inkfish shows contemporary art by established local and international artists. The gallery is one of Denver's old-timers — it's been in business 20 years.

Cherry Creek and Other Central Denver Galleries

Most of the galleries in Cherry Creek are more commercial and more geared toward Santa Fe-style art than those downtown. For this reason, we've listed many of them in our Shopping chapter rather than

---

The early bird may get the worm (and the two on-the-aisle seats), but spontaneous theatergoers might be interested to know that any remaining tickets for Denver Center Theatre Company productions go on sale at the box office for $10 (regular price is at least $17) 10 minutes before the curtain goes up.

Insiders' Tips

here. One exception is the **Ginny Williams Family Foundation**, 299 Fillmore Street, 321-4077. The gallery recently changed its format and now exhibits about four shows a year from Ginny Williams' estimable collection of photography, sculpture and other artwork.

Cherry Creek is the site of a hugely popular arts festival every July Fourth weekend. Started in 1991, the **Cherry Creek Arts Festival** has been astonishingly successful in attaining national recognition. See our Annual Festivals and Events chapter for details.

Artyard, 1251 S. Pearl Street, 777-3219, is a wonderful, out-of-the-way place that feels like a discovery even when you've been there a dozen times. The indoor space doubles as a studio for acclaimed kinetic artist Robert Mangold as well as gallery space for a variety of artists; outdoors is a large sculpture garden that features changing exhibitions of sculpture by well-known artists. It's open Wednesday through Saturday afternoons.

The peripatetic **Rule Modern and Contemporary** gallery, which used to be on Wazee Street, then on Wynkoop, recently moved into new quarters at 111 Broadway across from the Mayan Theater. Call 777-9473.

The glass-topped galleria is part of the Denver Performing Arts Complex.

dios from the Platte River area to the area just west of I-25. In this transitional neighborhood you'll also find the **Mackey Gallery**, 2900 W. 25th Avenue, 455-1157, which shows contemporary art and photography by up-and-coming and established artists. **Pirate, A Contemporary Art Oasis** at 3659 Navajo Street, 458-6058, has what are generally regarded as the hippest openings in town. Pirate is only open on weekends, and shows change frequently. The same is true for **Edge Gallery**, across the street at 3658 Navajo, 477-7173.

The buzz is good on **The Bug**, a renovated movie house at 3654 Navajo Street that's now an avant-garde showcase for emerging artists and their artwork, includ-

Westside Galleries

As LoDo has changed, and rents have gone up, many artists have moved their stuing poetry, music, film and new media. Call the Bugline at 477-5977 to find out what's coming.

CHAC, the Chicano Arts and Humanities Council, has a gallery at 4130 Tejon Street that is open by appointment only. In addition, CHAC sponsors a number of special events and programs through-out the city, including Cinco de Mayo celebrations in May, a Chile Harvest Festival every August at the Denver Botanic Gardens, a Day of the Dead exhibition and related programming in October and November and Las Posadas at the gallery during December. Call 477-7733 for more information.

Photo: Daily Camera/Spence Michael Wilson

The Twister is the highlight ride at Elitch Gardens Amusement Park.

Inside
Kidstuff

One of the first pieces of advice anyone in Greater Denver should heed to find ways for kids to have fun: Take them out to play with Mother Nature. It doesn't matter what trail or mountainside you take them to; short hikes or climbs for smaller kids are found in the same places where adults and older kids go to get serious. There is an abundance of trails and natural beauty close to Greater Denver. Go to a local bookstore and pick up a copy of *Best Hikes with Children in Colorado*, by Maureen Keilty, and you can get good directions to a lot of kid hikes on the edge of the metro area. When hiking, make sure to protect yourself and your kids by using sunscreen.

Mother Nature is only one of the juvenile attractions around Greater Denver. Check the other chapters of this book for ideas, especially Tours and Attractions, Spectator Sports, Annual Festivals and Events, Recreation and Daytrips.

Our listing that follows is limited to a reasonable number of unique attractions aimed at the younger set, but there are others that are too numerous to mention. Many of the following entries are generally desirable for all ages and only incidentally for kids. Take them fishing at any of the many reservoirs and rivers along the Front Range and in the nearby mountains. Take them horseback riding at any of the stables around Greater Denver. Walk or ride bicycles on trails, usually along creeks, rivers, canals and lakeshores that thread the greenbelts of Greater Denver.

Call nearby public libraries about story hours and other child-oriented activities. Call city and county departments of parks and recreation in your area to see about kid activities ranging from soccer and baseball to art classes. Telephone numbers for public libraries in the area are listed in the Community Services chapter of this book; departments of parks and recreation are listed in the Recreation chapter.

Ice- and roller-skating rinks abound in Greater Denver. Among the big roller-skating opportunities are those mentioned in our Recreation chapter: **Roller City**, 6803 Alameda Avenue, in Lakewood, 237-5622; and **Roller Express**, 8412 N. Huron Street, Thornton, 428-5061. For ice-skating, you can choose from a number of nice indoor rinks including the **Hyland Hills Ice Arena**, 4201 W. 94th Avenue, Westminster, 426-8912; the popular **North Jeffco Ice Arena**, 9101 Ralston Road, Arvada, 421-1774; the **Pioneeer Ice Arena**, 3601 S. Monaco Parkway, Denver, 758-8019; and the **South Suburban Ice Arena**, 6580 S. Vine, Littleton, 794-6522. Check the Yellow Pages under "Skating Rinks" for a complete listing of skating opportunities.

There are swimming pools all over the place and some of them go the extra mile to be kid-friendly. A good example is the indoor pool complex at **City Park Recreation Center**, 10455 Sheridan Avenue, Westminster, 460-9690. It has a large children's pool with a tile beach sloping gently at one end, a fountain and a slide just for kids. The main pool for lap swimmers bulges out at one side and under a waterfall. You can go behind the waterfall and look through windows to get an underwater view of the next pool, one floor above and dedicated entirely to swinging out on and dropping from a rope fastened at the ceiling three stories up. Above the rope-swing pool is the beginning of a water slide that ends with a splash in the main pool.

Another fun kid pool worth mentioning is **The Bay Aquatic Center**, 250 Community Park Road, Broomfield, 469-5825. This outdoor city facility is strictly for kids; there's no lap pool like there is at the City Park Recreation Center. But kids will surely enjoy it. The tot pool has straight slides. The main pool has larger straight slides and spiral slides, and it also has a jungle gym in the water where kids can climb around and release sprays of water by pulling on ropes. This pool never gets deeper than 5 feet, and the jungle gym is in less than 1 foot of water. **The Thornton Recreation Center**,

11151 Colorado Boulevard, Thornton, 252-1600, opened a fantastic new 15,000-square-foot aquatics center in October 1994, which includes artificially generated waves, lap swimming, a raindrop play area with waterfall and Jacuzzi, a lazy river and a water slide. **The Golden Community Center**, 1470 10th Street, Golden, 384-8100, has another pool that kids will love, with a raindrop play area, water slide and hot tub as well as its lap pool and leisure pool.

There are a lot of fun restaurants that combine dining with fun and games, the most well-known being **Chuck E Cheese's** restaurants in Arvada, 425-5925; and Englewood, 761-8636. Chuck E Cheese is actually more of a fun emporium than a restaurant, and it's one of those places like Jungle Jim's and Funtastic Fun (referenced below) that can seem to parents like hellish madhouses, but kids love them. There are also a number of more mainstream restaurants, however, which have features interesting to kids. Kids love the two-story slide that empties onto the hardwood dance floor at the **Trail Dust Steak Houses** in Westminster, 427-1446, and Englewood, 790-2420. Kids enjoy the unbelievable array of mounted fish and birds and animal heads on the walls of both floors of the **Buckhorn Exchange**, 1000 Osage Street, Denver, 534-9505, Denver's oldest restaurant. We've featured a few interesting dining choices and other options in our list of kid activities.

One of your best comprehensive local resources to kid activities is *A Colorado Parent Directory*, available at local bookstores for $4.95. This annual directory is a comprehensive family resource guide and has just about everything a parent would want to know about the area; it's a good place to go for entertainment as well. It's produced by *Colorado Parent Magazine*,

County fairs are treats for kids all summer long.

320-1000, a free monthly publication that can be found at 800 locations ranging from bookstores and libraries to doctors' offices and day-care centers.

Just out with a first edition in 1995 is another great kid reference: ***Kids Discover Denver and Boulder,*** by Sara Goodman Zimet. At $12.95 and more than 200 pages, it's full of suggestions about playgrounds, entertainment centers, amusement parks, wildlife watching, museums, arts, sports, story reading and storytelling, and it also has a calendar of kid-friendly events. You should be able to find it at local bookstores, but you can also order it from Discovery Press Publications, P.O. Box 201502, Denver, 80220-7502; 355-9689.

Places to go With Children in Colorado, by Patti Thorn and Marty Meitus, is another good reference. It covers a range of opportunities from museums and fun parks to whitewater rafting and dude ranches. About $^{1}/_{4}$ to $^{1}/_{3}$ of the information covers opportunities specifically in Greater Denver. You should be able to find it near our book in most significant Greater Denver bookstores, for $10.95.

BOARDWALK USA

6601 W. Colfax Ave.
Lakewood   238-7811
2802 S. Havana St.
Aurora   745-7529
151 W. Mineral Ave.
Littleton   745-7529

Boardwalk USA builds on the video arcade concept by adding virtual reality, laser tag, bumper cars, indoor go-carts at the Lakewood outlet and miniature golf at the Aurora outlet. An all-day play pass is $7; $5 buys an hour of play or an evening of play after 6 PM Sunday through Thursday. Boardwalk USA is open 11 AM to 10 PM Monday through Thursday, 11 AM to midnight on Friday, 9 AM to midnight on Saturday, and 9 AM to 10 PM on Sunday.

CASA BONITA

6715 W. Colfax Ave.
Denver   232-5115

Rising from the JCRS Shopping Center in Lakewood, the distinctive steeple of Casa Bonita has become a Greater Denver landmark. Although this is a perfectly good Mexican restaurant with American dishes too, people come here more for the play than for the food. It's like eating in a cave with huge chambers and a complex labyrinth of tunnels and hidden nooks, with strolling mariachis and other features. Kids love Black Bart's cave, a series of creepy scares in tunnels sized for kids. There's a video arcade and other entertainments. The crowning glory is the 30-foot waterfall, where divers plunge into a pool below while performances at the top of the waterfall involve cowboy gunfights and explorers tangling with a gorilla. Every performance ends with somebody falling 30 feet into the pool. It's a popular place for kid birthday parties and for parents who want to kick back while their kids run wild. Admission is the price of a meal, which for adults ranges from $5.49 to $8.49 with an $8.39 all-you-can-eat binge. Children younger than 12 can get $2.99 meals. Hours are 11 AM to 9:30 PM Sunday through Thursday, 11 AM to 10 PM Friday and Saturday.

CLUB 22
Northglenn Recreation Center
11701 Community Center Dr.
Northglenn   **450-8800**

"Club 22" stands for "2 old for a sitter and 2 young to drive." This is safe and supervised nightlife for adolescents of middle-school age. Parents check their kids in, and the kids don't leave until the parents check them out. In between, there's music and dancing, swimming and other activities, such as volleyball and wallyball in the Rec Center's athletic facilities. There are con-

tests, food and beverage concessions and always some sort of special event, such as a movie or an entertainer or demonstrator. Admission is $4 per night. Club 22 takes place on the first and third Saturdays of each month, from 7 to 10:30 PM.

COLORADO RAILROAD MUSEUM
17155 W. 44th Ave.
Golden   **279-4591**

A lot of Western city parks used to have trains that kids could climb around on, but now they're mostly surrounded by fences to keep the kids out. None of that nonsense here! The Colorado Railroad Museum is mentioned in our Tours and Attractions chapter, but at 12.5 acres, with more than 50 pieces of "rolling stock," it's so fantastic for kids that it bears repeating. Kids can climb up and walk through the antique railway cars, climb into the cupolas of the cabooses to look out the windows and climb up on the big engine right outside the museum building and pull the rope and ring the awesome bell. You have to be a bit older to appreciate most of the two floors of memorabilia inside the museum building, but kids love the enormous model train setup in the basement, which you can run by plugging in a quarter. Several times a year the museum fires up and runs the state's oldest railway engine. The first week of December, Santa Claus parks inside a caboose and receives children between the hours of 10 AM and 4 PM. Admission is

---

One kid activity you can never go wrong with is swimming. Denver's indoor and outdoor pools are sure to have opportunities near you year round. Check city and county recreation districts (listed in our Recreation chapter), as well as the "special districts," all in the blue-edged government pages in the front of the phone book.

Insiders' Tips

$3.50 for adults, $1.75 for kids younger than 16 accompanied by a parent, $3 for people over 60 and $7.50 for a family, which the museum defines as two adults and children under 16. Hours are 9 AM to 6 PM every day of the week from Memorial Day through the end of September, and 9 AM to 5 PM the rest of the year.

THE DENVER ART MUSEUM
100 W. 14th Ave. Pkwy.
Denver   640-2793

The Denver Art Museum features family workshops in which kids can explore the galleries while learning and creating, as well as all-the-time features such as "eye spy" games on every floor. Available every second, fourth and fifth Saturday of the month is a free Family Backpack, which is a backpack that kids can check out, containing games and activities relating to exhibits. There's Kids Corner on the main-floor lobby, but a lot of kids, of course, will also be interested by the museum itself. See our Tours and Attractions chapter for more on this great museum. Call 640-7577 for specific information on children and family programs.

DENVER BOTANIC GARDENS
1005 York St.
Denver   331-4010

Kids of all ages enjoy these lovely gardens and the tropical conservatory. We've described the gardens in detail in our Tours and Attractions chapter. Most likely, however, children will be more interested in the changing menu of year-round kid activities, such as the Halloween jack-o'-lantern show and the summer evening concerts listed in our Annual Events and Festivals chapter. It's also a pretty place to run around, with a couple of grassy knolls that small kids love to climb on and roll down. It's a nice place for a picnic, like being out in the country when you're in the city.

DENVER CHILDREN'S MUSEUM
2121 Children's Museum Dr.
Denver   433-7433

There's a wealth of things to do here, all of it aimed specifically at kids and all of it educationally oriented. There's a miniature grocery store, where kids can shop or be the checkout person, and a Denver Nuggets exhibit, where kids can compare their sizes to basketball players' sizes, shoot baskets, etc. There are laboratories where kids can work with earth sciences and natural phenomena and play educational games on computers. You'll find a light room and sound room, plant and animal exhibits, woodworking and a traveling exhibit that changes every three months. Play Partners is a special toddler play area set up like The Three Bears' house. Kids can ski year round on the KidsSlope, although reservations are recommended. It's a great museum, but a very busy one that's often crowded. The museum recommends coming between 2 and 5 PM on weekdays, when it's least crowded. Admission is free for kids younger than 2, $4 for ages 2 to 59, and $1.50 if you're 60 or older. Hours are 10 AM to 5 PM Tuesday through Saturday, noon to 5 PM on Sunday, and 10 AM to 5 PM on Mondays throughout the summer.

Worthy of note is the museum's annual Halloween party, "Trick-or-Treat Street," which runs for nearly a week including Halloween. The museum is converted into a haunted house. Multitudes of kids show up in costumes to pass through the many spooking sections and receive candy from people hiding behind spooky scenery, although they want you to know that it's a "non-scary" event including pumpkin carving, a petting zoo and other activities.

The museum can be a little tricky to reach, so here are some directions: It's right off 23rd Avenue and I-25. If you exit from I-25, go east on 23rd and take the first right,

*Of course the buildings are little at Tiny Town,
but even the working railroad is child-size.*

on Seventh Street, and then an immediate right onto Children's Museum Drive.

THE DENVER MUSEUM OF NATURAL HISTORY

2001 Colorado Blvd.
(in City Park, at Colorado Blvd. and Montview)
Denver 370-6357

See our Tours and Attractions chapter for more detail on this museum, but don't forget it's one of the greatest places around for kids. We know one woman from Montana who recalls the museum as a favorite childhood memory from the time her family came down specifically to visit it. From the time you walk under the claws of the huge Tyrannosaurus Rex skeleton as you enter the front door you know you've entered a place of wonder. Sure, kids have to be older to appreciate a lot of things here, but the exhibits of dinosaurs and Pleistocene megafauna, such as the two saber-toothed tigers attacking the giant sloth, are sure winners. So are the many dioramas showing different kinds of fauna in exquisitely crafted natural settings that blend so flawlessly into exquisitely painted backdrops that you really feel like you're on a mountain top with the eagle family or at the seashore with the sea lions. A number of the woodland backdrops have elves painted into them or elf figurines hiding in the foreground foliage or under rocks or logs. A real challenge is trying to find the elves; we've only managed to spot a couple of them. The IMAX theater with its four-story-high screen is a treat some Denverites enjoy taking their kids to frequently. The museum also has some great children's educational programs, although they fill up frighteningly fast once their scheduling becomes public knowledge.

THE DENVER ZOO

City Park, E. 23rd Ave. and Steele St.
(near Natural History Museum)
Denver 331-4100

You can't miss with a zoo, and The Denver Zoo may well be Greater Denver's most popular kid place of all. For more on this wonderful place, see our Tours and Attractions chapter and also our Annual Festivals and Events Chapter. The Zoo has some wonderful special events around the seasons, including one that's not really an event because it happens every day from Memorial Day weekend to Labor Day Weekend, but it's a kiddie delight. Three times daily, at 11:30 AM and 1:00 and 3:30 PM, there's a 20-minute Free Flight Bird Show at the Zoo's Event Meadow, with birds of prey that fly out over the audience; some reptiles are featured as well. The Event Meadow's seating is limited to 600, and zoo gurus advise arriving early.

DISCOVERY ZONE

14281 E. Exposition Ave.
Aurora   340-1619
7510 Parkway Drive
Littleton   649-1831
8100 W. Crestline Ave.
Building D
Littleton   879-7938
9110 Wadsworth Parkway
Westminster   420-1450

Discovery Zones are designed for kids ages 18 months to 12 years. They feature an obstacle course, slides and nets and bins of plastic balls connected by human-sized gerbil tunnels. A separate play area for babies and toddlers makes sure they won't get trampled by the big kids. The game room includes 26 games such as whack-an-alligator, skee ball and basketball. Right next to the games is a cafe, with food and drink of the pizza/hot dog variety and tables. Since our last edition, the Discovery Zones have eliminated the quiet room, surrounded by windows, where parents used to be able to get away from the noise. All-

day admission is $5.95 for kids, and parents get in free. Hours are 9 AM to 8 PM Monday through Thursday, 9 AM to 10 PM Friday and Saturday and 9 AM to 7 PM Sunday.

ELITCH GARDENS AMUSEMENT PARK

I-25 and Speer Blvd.
Denver   595-4386

Elitch Gardens is Denver's oldest fun park, dating from 1890 when it began as a botanical and zoological gardens and had no mechanical rides. Since then, it has become Denver's flashiest amusement park. Now it's even bigger, expanding in 1995 from its old 28-acre site to a new 68-acre site along the South Platte River across from the Children's Museum. It's one of the wonders of the renascent Central Platte Valley of downtown Denver. The new Elitch has more than 20 rides, not counting its Kiddieland, which is bigger than the old Kiddieland. It's got 80,000 square feet of gardens, and has most of the old park's rides as well as many new ones. Among the new rides is an absolute horror called the Avalanche, in which rows of strapped-in riders are carried several stories into the air and turned upside down and flipped around. It's a nightmare from hell. Disaster Canyon is another beauty, a raft ride on white water and through a spray tunnel that will soak you. One of the great new features is the Total Tower, which reminds one of Seattle's Space Needle. It's 300 feet high with a 360-degree viewing platform.

There are plenty of other wonderful features including six performance stages and plenty of restaurants. The trees are just starting to grow, however, so unlike the pleasant shady walks of the old Elitch Gardens, it's mostly out in the hot sun. Also unlike the old Elitch Gardens, you can't bring in your own food for picnics. By 1996, however, they're supposed to have completed a park on the Platte River just outside the park, where people can picnic. You can't ride the Kiddieland rides unless you're under 52 inches in height, and you can't ride the grownup rides unless you're over 52 inches, although on some you can ride them accompanied by a parent if you're over 36 inches. Passes to the park are $19.95 for adults; $15.50 for children older than 5 and under 52 inches in height; $7.75 for 3- and 4-year-olds; free for kids 2 and younger and seniors 70 and older, and $14 for seniors 55 to 69 years of age. Parking is $3.

Getting to Elitch Gardens is no problem, since it now has its own exit from the Speer Boulevard viaduct, with its own traffic light intersection on Speer. Coming across the viaduct toward downtown Denver, it will be a right turn. Coming from Downtown, it will be a left turn. There is also an access from 15th Street.

FOUR MILE HISTORIC PARK
715 S. Forest St.
Denver   399-1859

This museum is covered in our Tours and Attractions section but should be noted here as well. Kids enjoy walking through the living history farmstead, where they can see old machinery, reconstructed barns, outhouses (not for use, and odor-free), root cellars, chickens, ducks, calves and horses. Older kids may also enjoy the tour of Denver's oldest house, led by costumed tour guides. In 1995, the park added a guided tour of itself via stagecoach on weekends

only. During special events, there are more kid attractions such as demonstrations of blacksmithing, butter churning and other crafts of yesteryear, as well as horse-drawn wagon rides. The number of events annually varies, but the museum has five standard events: an opening event with varying themes in April; a July Fourth old-fashioned family picnic; a September "organic fair" to which organic farmers bring their produce and where health-food stores set up booths; two spooky theme nights on the weekend before Halloween; and the holiday open house in December. Admission is $3.50 for adults, $2 for kids and seniors, and free for kids younger than 6. The park also does special programming with special rates for groups of 10 or more.

In 1995 for the first time, the park went to year-round operation. Summer hours are still 10 AM to 4 PM, Wednesday through Sunday. Call the park for winter hours.

FRIDAY NIGHT LIVE
Westminster City Park Recreation Center
10455 Sheridan Blvd.
Westminster   322-9317
Goodson Recreation Center
6315 S. University Ave.
Littleton   322-9317
Highlands Ranch Recreation Center
8801 S. Broadway
Highlands Ranch   322-9317
Louisville Recreation Center
900 W. Via Appia
Louisville   322-9317
Harvard Gulch Recreation Center
550 E. Iliff
Denver   322-9317

Friday Night Live features safe and supervised weekend nightlife for adolescents ages 9 to 14. Depending on where one attends, it may be on Saturday instead of Friday. The phone number above is for Friday Night Live of Colorado, the franchisor for the program at the different rec centers. It's turned out to be a popular program.

Roller hockey is a favorite pastime for urban kids.

Only two rec centers had it in 1994, and by the fall school season of 1995 there were five. It typically takes place during the school year, although in areas where schooling goes on year round, you may find it open in the summer as well.

You'll typically find games, dancing and music with a live DJ; a gym is open for such activities as basketball, dodgeball, wallyball and volleyball; concessions for pizza and soft drinks; movies, contests and special guests. There is one adult counselor for every 25 kids, a uniformed policeman on hand at all times and parental check-in and check-out. Admission in 1995 was $6 for all the rec centers. Hours vary among the rec centers, but Friday Night Live programs open as early as 6:30 PM and close as late as midnight.

FUNPLEX

9670 Coal Mine Ave.
Littleton   972-4344

This is a 3½-acre indoor fun center for all ages. Activities include 40 lanes of bowling, roller-skating, two 18-hole miniature golf courses, more than 170 video games, two restaurants, an ice-cream shop, a sports bar and Laser Storm, a light tag game. There's also Kids Corner, with a pool of balls, a big bouncer and three rides just for tykes. There's no admission fee; you pay by activity, which ranges from $2 to $5. Thursday is a bargain day when you get each activity for $1.99, including rentals necessary for things like skating and bowling.

Hours begin at 11 AM daily in the summer and 4 PM the rest of the year. Closing varies from 10 PM to 1 AM, depending on the day of the week.

FUNTASTIC FUN
3085 S. Broadway
Englewood   *761-8701*

This used to be called Funtastic Nathan's when it was located in the Cinderella City mall, but in 1994 it moved and changed its name. It's popular among kids of Greater Denver's south side. This fun center includes a Ferris wheel, a carousel, a train, swings, a cave, an air castle and a lot of things kids can do on their own such as a room of plastic balls with slides and nets connected by gerbil tunnels and games such as skee ball and air hockey. They also have such a room for younger kids, which includes a smaller air castle, so the squirts don't get roughhoused by the bigger kids. Individual admission is $5.95 for all day, except on Tuesdays and Wednesdays, when it's $2.95. The group rate is $2.95 per head every day. Hours are 10 AM to 9 PM daily.

GUNTHER TOODY'S
4500 E. Alameda Ave.
Glendale   *399-1959*
9220 E. Arapahoe Rd.
Englewood   *799-1958*
7355 Ralston Rd.
Arvada   *422-1954*

The help all dress like characters from *Grease* at this 1950s-concept restaurant, and they usually do such a good job of acting their sassy, gum-chewing parts that there must be a Gunther Toody's acting school somewhere. The only games are a few classic pinball machines, and it's not exclusively a kid restaurant like Chuck E Cheese's. But that's why we're mentioning it here, because it deserves wider recognition as a great, non-arcade dining place for kids and their families. Entrees mostly range between $5 and $7, although prices go as high

as $11.75 for the full rack of ribs. Hours are 6 AM to 11 PM Sunday through Thursday and 6 AM to midnight on Friday and Saturday.

HERITAGE SQUARE
Intersection of U.S. Hwys. 40 and 93
Golden   *279-2789*

Out in the open all by itself, up against the Foothills, Heritage Square is a great place to go for family entertainment. It's what appears to be a small Western town, with porticoed boardwalks along the front of retail stores, restaurants and entertainment options lining its streets. The hill on the west side of town has an Alpine slide that operates in summer, and it's just the greatest fun; except that all too often, if you don't go fast enough, some gung-ho geek comes racing up behind you with a bump. Heritage Square claims more than 40 attractions counting stores, restaurants and amusement rides. It has bumper boats, go-carts and a family arcade. The Heritage Square Music Hall usually has a fun show to offer, and you can rent the town hall and wedding chapel for parties. You might also want to check out The Lazy H Chuckwagon Show and Dinner, a dinner show and hayrack ride that costs $15 for adults, $10 for kids ages 3 to 10 and nothing for little pardners younger than 3.

Admission to Heritage Square is free, as is the parking. It's fun just to stroll around. Hours are 10 AM to 9 PM every day, during the summer. Spring, fall and winter hours are 10 AM to 6 PM every day but Sunday, when it's noon to 6 PM.

JUNGLE JIM'S PLAYLAND
13686 E. Alameda Ave.
Aurora   *360-5333*
8055 Sheridan Blvd.
Arvada   *427-3200*

Really one of the best playlands around Greater Denver, Jungle Jim's has an excellent complex of human gerbil tunnels and slides, nets, obstacles and rooms filled with plastic balls. And it has a great indoor kiddie land of carnival rides including a carousel, bumper cars, flying jets, spinning tops, a roller coaster and kiddie jeeps. It has a good selection of non-video games such as air hockey. There's also a concession with pizza and the like. You can get unlimited rides for birthday-party kids, but otherwise they sell ride tickets for 75 cents apiece, and the more you buy the cheaper they get. Adults ride free. During summer, hours are 11 AM to 8 PM on Sunday, 11 AM to 9 PM Monday through Thursday, and 10 AM to 10 PM on Friday and Saturday. The rest of the year, they open 11 AM to 8 PM Sunday through Thursday and 10 AM to 9 PM Friday and Saturday.

LAKESIDE AMUSEMENT PARK
Just south of I-70, 4601 Sheridan Ave.
Lakeside   *477-1621*

Amid the grand hoopla of Elitch Garden's whopping new amusement park that opened in 1995, don't forget Lakeside. It remains an old-fashioned amusement park, with a lot of art deco that marks it as having changed little since the 1940s, although, of course, it has more recent rides. Denver City Councilman Dennis Gallagher, who has been visiting Lakeside since he was a kid, told a local newspaper last year, "I love Lakeside. It's like a moment frozen in time." Among the sentimental favorites of Greater Denveroids are the little trains that run around the lake, and everybody likes to scream when they go

through the funky old tunnel. It has an extensive kiddieland with rides sized for the tots. Lakeside still lets you bring in your own food for a picnic, and you don't have to pay big bucks to get in. Admission is $1.50. Once inside, you pay 25 cents per coupon, and it takes two to five coupons per ride. Sometimes we just like to swing in for a ride on the Cyclone, the big roller coaster, and then call it a day. If you're a parent who wants to take your kid in for a few rides or an evening in kiddieland, and you don't want to do any rides yourself, your entry cost is only $1.50. Unlimited ride passes are $9.75 during the week and $11.25 on Saturday, Sunday and holidays. It opens weekends in May and full time in June and closes after Labor Day weekend. The kiddie playland opens during the week from 1 to 10 PM and on Sundays and most Saturdays from noon to 10 PM. The rest of the park rock and rolls from 6 to 11 PM during the week and from noon to 11 PM on Sundays and most Saturdays.

LITTLETON HISTORICAL MUSEUM
6028 S. Gallup St.
Littleton   *795-3950*

This museum is well-covered in our Tours and Attractions chapter, but it's one of our favorites for kids. As a living-history museum, it's particularly fascinating to kids interested in the past. But it's also a great way to let the kids see lots of animals and explore a fantasy world of the past. It's a working homestead and farm, with sheep, oxen, pigs, cows, chickens, horses and other animals. Costumed staff and volunteers go about their antiquarian life chores, keeping to the roles and speaking in the manner of people from the late 19th century. As you walk around, you may encounter them working in a garden or barn or fields, cooking in the house, blacksmithing in the 1903 blacksmith shop or teaching in the 1860s schoolhouse. If you're lucky in the winter, you may catch them harvesting ice from the lake for the 1900 ice house, although the ice in recent years often has not been thick enough to harvest.

MILE HIGH GREYHOUND PARK
6200 Dahlia at Colorado Blvd.
Commerce City 288-1591

See our Spectator Sports chapter for details, but don't forget that this is a great place to go to entertain your kids for just $1 a head for parents, with kids younger than 18 getting in free. You don't even have to bet. Kids who love dogs will love this show, and smaller children can always take an interest in Rusty, the white mechanical bunny that never gets caught. It's a lovely outing on a warm summer evening, and its a fascinating spectacle for kids and parents alike.

PIKES PEAK COG RAILWAY
U.S. Hwy. 24 W. from Colorado Springs
to the Manitou Exit, west on Manitou Ave.
and left onto Ruxton Ave. *(719) 685-5401*

Adults become kids again during this delightful experience. We've covered this in greater detail in our Daytrips chapter than here, yet this is one of the greatest kid activities on the Front Range: a 3½-hour trip to the top of Pikes Peak on the highest cog railway in the world. All this presumes, of course, that your kids are of an age and temperament to tolerate the long ride. Reservations are required.

PLATTE VALLEY TROLLEY
2200 Seventh St.
Denver 458-6255
Park at the Denver Children's Museum listed previously; walk from the museum east to the Platte River

This turn-of-the-century streetcar tour is for all ages. Small tykes may recognize its near-exact resemblance to the streetcar on the *Mister Rogers' Neighborhood* TV show. Kids 6 years of age and younger may prefer the half-hour tour to the hour tour. You'll enjoy a narrated tour along the Platte River, with bits of history and expositions on present and future features of this area such as Mile High Stadium and Golda Meir's former residence. The hour tour goes up Lakewood Gulch, along the tracks where the interurban trolley used to run from Denver to Golden.

Admission for the half-hour tour is $2 for adults and $1 for kids and seniors. The hour tour costs $4 for adults, $3 for seniors and $2 for kids. Hours are 11 AM to 4 PM. June through September, there are tours every day; September and October, every day but Monday, weather permitting, and November through March, weekends only.

RENAISSANCE FESTIVAL
I-25 about 25 minutes south from Denver to Larkspur,
Exit 173, then follow the signs 688-6010

See our Annual Events and Festivals

chapter for more on the Renaissance Festival, but it's such a killer kid-pleaser that it cannot be omitted from this section. It's a dizzying fantasy world full of battling knights and cavorting jesters and associated monsters and grotesques, where hundreds of attractions attendants, food vendors, craftspersons and performers dress, act and speak appropriately to their setting in this recreated 16th-century village. It's an event rather than a place, however, so remember it's only around for eight weekends in June and July. Admission is $11.95 for adults; $5 for children ages 5 to 12. Kids younger than 5 get in free. Discount tickets are available at King Soopers supermarkets.

Kids cool off in the fountain of the Denver Museum of Natural History.

SOUTH SHORE WATER PARK

10750 E. Briarwood Ave.
Englewood   649-9875

This is the smaller of Greater Denver's two big water parks, but it's still sizeable at 20 acres, and it's practically new, having completed its first full season in 1993. It has all the water park features including the heart-stopping high slides, corkscrew slides and a wave pool. You'll also find volleyball courts and full concessions. Spend all day in the water (adults $10.95, kids 48 inches and under $9.95). During the park's 90-day summer season, the hours are 10 AM to 6 PM during the week and 10 AM to 7 PM on weekends.

TINY TOWN

6249 Turkey Creek Rd.
Morrison   697-6829

Hidden away in a mountain canyon southeast of Greater Denver, this is a curious and charming town of 110 miniature buildings constructed at ⅙ scale on 6 acres. Kids can actually go inside some of the buildings, but it's a place where families enjoy just walking around. You can ride a miniature train pulled by a real — but tiny — steam engine over a mile-long course. They have a snack bar, a gift shop and puppet shows on weekends. Part of the magic of this place is that it looks rather ancient, and it is. It's the oldest miniature town in the United States. George Turner was the owner of a Denver moving and storage business just after the turn of the century, and this was his mountain property. His granddaughter was chronically ill, so he built a few miniature houses in the pasture for her to play in, then kept adding to the tiny town. Turkey Creek Road was dirt then, and people would stop their cars and delight their kids with the magic little town. By the 1920s and 1930s, it was one of Colorado's major tourist attractions. After World War II, it went through several decades of decline, including a flood and a number of failed attempts to make it a profitable tourist business. Now it's operated by the Tiny Town Foundation, which donates 30 percent of the profits to charities and uses a lot of volunteers. Admission is low: $2 for adults and $1 for kids ages 3 to 12, and children younger than 3 get in free. Pay an extra $1 if you want to ride the train. It's open 10 AM to 5 PM weekends only in May, September and October; and daily Memorial Day through Labor Day. Tiny Town is closed during the winter, but on the two weekends just before Christmas they sometimes dress it up in lights. But not always. Call to check. During this time, you can't wander around and see the buildings up close, but you can stop in to ride the train and visit the gift shop, weather permitting. Take C-470 to U.S. Highway 285, travel about 4 miles southeast on 285, turn left on Turkey Creek Road, and go about .25 of a mile. You'll see Tiny Town on the right.

YOUNG AMERICANS EDUCATION FOUNDATION

311 Steele St.
Denver   *321-2954*

This foundation was launched in the late 1980s by Bill Daniels, one of Denver's most famed citizens for his role as *the* pioneer of the cable TV industry, an industry in which Denver now plays a leading role. Daniels, now chairman of Daniels Communications Inc., a broker/dealer of major cable systems around the country, started the foundation to give kids an early grounding in the business culture. Most widely known is the Young Americans Bank, a real FDIC-insured bank of which the foundation is the nonprofit holding company. Designed for ages 0-21, it's the only bank in the world exclusively for kids. They can

have their own savings and checking accounts, ATM and credit cards, and mutual funds. It emphasizes individual attention to children, with small teller booths designed with steps so kids can look the teller in the eye, and tellers who teach the kids one-on-one about deposit slips, interest and so on.

The Young Entrepreneur Society is another foundation effort. Joining this group free, kids meet monthly and make excursions to meet and talk with people who have successfully started their own businesses in the area. Be Your Own Boss is another program, started in 1994, for kids interested in starting and/or owning their own companies. Held once each year in spring/summer for kids in middle and high school, it consists of a five-day camp ($130) and a three-day junior camp ($90). Kids are taken step-by-step through the entrepreneurial process, from basic education on things like financing to the writing of their own business plans. If a business plan is approved, the Young Americans Bank may advance a loan to get the business going.

Young AmeriTowne is a nifty program, involving students role-playing in 16 different jobs and running their own town. It's accessed through schools, but parents can help by hustling their children's teachers to get their classes involved. During the school year, students learn first in their classrooms before coming in for a one-day program. Kids can also go to Young AmeriTowne on an individual basis during its summer programs ($50): the Undergraduate Program (ages 10-12), the

Girls Can Program (girls only, ages 10-12); the Executive Program (for experienced Young AmeriTowne citizens, ages 10-14), and the Junior AmeriTowne (for kids who have just completed 2nd, 3rd or 4th grades).

WATER WORLD
88th Ave. and Pecos St.
Federal Heights   427-7873

Greater Denver's bigger water park, Water World offers more than 60 acres of aquatic fun. Float down a circular series of chutes and pools on an inner tube. Ride a huge rubber raft down a torrent. Sit on a plastic sled that plunges almost straight down and builds up enough speed to aquaplane across the pool at the bottom. Water World has it all. The park also recently added a Journey to the Center of the Earth ride, in which you ride through caves where moving dinosaurs menace you. From late May to the end of summer Water World operates from 10 AM to 6 PM every day. Admission is $16.50 for adults and $15.50 for kids 4 to 12. If you're 60 and older or 3 and younger, it's free. Resident admission for people presenting a valid Highland Hills or City of Westminster resident ID card is $8.50 for adults and $7.50 for children. All eyeglasses must have safety straps.

WINGS OVER THE ROCKIES
7750 E. Irvington Pl.
Denver   360-5360

The closing of Lowry Air Force Base in the fall of 1994 was accompanied by the opening a few months later of what is now one of Greater Denver's greatest museums. Wings Over the Rockies does for aviation what the Colorado Railroad Museum does

for the railroads: puts the biggest and best of the historic hardware on very impressive display for the public. With the exception of the Space Station Module, you can't actually go inside the displays, but up close and gargantuan, they have a tremendous, visceral impact. Among the 20 aircraft on display in the museum's first months (more to be added) were big bombers, racy fighter jets and helicopters, a scan of aviation history. You've got civilian and military aircraft, models, simulations, photographs and space-related objects with hands-on activities so visitors can experience scientific discovery. Plus, since it's all contained in the vast interior of Lowry's Hangar 1, a candidate for the National Register of Historic Places, kids can run around like crazy, and some kids like to bring toy gliders to throw in the open spaces. Since it's all indoors, it's particularly nice on a winter day when outside activities are curtailed. This excepts the B-52B bomber on display outside. There are also a variety of historic aviation artifacts, a museum store and aerospace education programs for kids. Admission is free to museum members, and for others it costs $4 for adults, $2 for children ages 6 to 17 and seniors over 60, and it's free for kids 5 and younger.

From I-225, take Sixth Avenue west to Lowry Boulevard, and turn left there and proceed until you see the hangars. It's the first one to the east. Or you can take Alameda West to Fairmont Cemetery, and turn left on Rampart Way. Straight ahead you'll see the two hangars, and it's the first one to the east.

Photo: Daily Camera/Cliff Grassmick

Denver Broncos' quarterback John Elway talks to head coach Mike Shanahan.

Inside
Spectator Sports

Even when the football, baseball, basketball and hockey teams aren't winning championships, Denver fans remain loyal and enthusiastic. Bronco fans have long been a fiercely devoted group, but attendance is up at Nuggets games as well. As for the Rockies, well, in their first major-league season this National League expansion team broke just about every attendance record on the books: the all-time major league single-season attendance record, the largest opening-day crowd, largest attendance at a single game and fastest team to reach 1, 2, 3 and 4 million attendance levels. All told, almost 4.5 million tickets were sold during the 1993 season. In 1995 Denver added a national hockey league team to its major-league lineup when it was announced that the Quebec Nordiques were moving to the Mile High City to become the Colorado Avalanche.

Greater Denver also has an up-and-coming professional soccer team and several racetracks. Lots of people would consider the National Western Stock Show and Rodeo the city's premier spectator sports event, but as it only happens once a year, we've covered it in our Annual Events chapter.

Baseball

The Colorado Rockies were one of two expansion teams added to the National League in 1993; despite a losing first season, they won the hearts of Coloradans and received national media attention for the record-breaking attendance they attracted and for the player they call "the Cat," Andres Galarraga, winner of the National League batting title with a batting average of .370.

The Rockies began their 1995 season in Coors Field in Lower Downtown at Blake and 20th streets. Designed by Hellmuth Obata & Kassabaum, a Kansas City firm, Coors Field is an updated version of a classic urban ballpark. Its exterior is built of two shades of red brick, and its seats provide Rocky Mountains views. Its capacity of 50,000 has raised a few eyebrows, however, as attendance at Rockies games during their inaugural season at Mile High Stadium peaked at 80,227. And the above-average number of home runs during the first month of play had sportswriters wondering if the stadium was too small for players as well as fans.

Although many of the most desirable seats are scooped up by season-ticket holders, the Rockies insist that they will cap the

Broncos fans meet at Jackson's Hole Sports Bar at Sixth and Kipling to eat burgers, drink beer and cheer on their team on television.

Insiders' Tips

The Colorado Rockies played their 1995 season in their new ballpark, Coors Field.

Photo: Daily Camera

number of season tickets sold so that some seats are always available at every game. Single seats go on sale for all games beginning in February and range from $4 to $8. During the season, purchase tickets at the stadium at Gate C between 20th and 21st streets and Blake Street, or at Rockies Dugout Stores and King Soopers supermarkets. Handicapped seating is available. Day-of-game "Rockpile" seats go on sale at the stadium 2½ hours prior to game time and cost $4 for adults, $1 for kids 12 and younger and seniors 55 and older. For information, call 762-5437 (ROCKIES).

RTD (Regional Transportation District) provides special buses to and from Rockies games from 16 suburban park-and-rides and along Broadway. The fare is $4 round trip for express routes, $2 round trip for the Broadway shuttle. Regular service to and from Market Street Station also brings you within walking distance of the stadium, but may not be as conveniently timed for evening games. For schedules and fare information, call 299-6000 (TDD 299-6089).

Basketball

Coach Dan Issel – a former Nugget whose jersey, which now hangs in the locker room, was retired when he left the team – led the **Denver Nuggets** to a spectacular 16th season in 1993-94. In a stunning upset, the Nuggets eliminated the Seattle Supersonics from the NBA playoffs in an overtime victory. Next, they met the Utah Jazz and played seven games before being eliminated. Denver's sportswriters, with typical hyperbole, proclaimed the win over Seattle the biggest upset in the history of Denver sports. Certainly it knocked the Rockies off the sports pages for a few weeks and boosted Nuggets season-ticket sales. The Nuggets went to the playoffs again in 1994-95, but the big news of that season was Issel's surprise mid-season retirement. General manager Bernie Bickerstaff took on the duties of head coach in early 1995.

Crowd-pleasing players on the team include LaPhonso Ellis and Dikembe Mutombo, defensive player of the year. The most popular home games, against Chicago, New York and Orlando (teams the Nuggets only play once per season) sell out quickly, and the average attendance of just more than 17,000 (the Nuggets sold out every home game in 1994-95) puts the Nuggets in the top half of the league. The Nuggets play in McNichols Sports Arena, off I-25 at W. 17th Avenue (part of the same

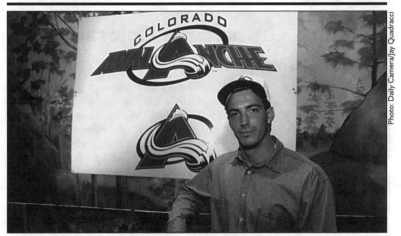

Joe Sakic is captain of the new Colorado Avalanche hockey team.

sports complex as Mile High Stadium). Tickets start at $8.50, and there are a number of special deals, such as family and youth nights, and group discounts. Handicapped seating is available on request. Nuggets tickets are available by calling 893-3865 or through TicketMaster at 830-TIXS (8497).

The Nuggets are tentatively scheduled to open their 1997 season in their new arena, the Pepsi Center, in the Platte Valley next to Elitch Gardens. However, the loss of a major investor in fall 1995 put the whole project in jeopardy, and will probably delay things a bit.

Football

If you want to get your heart broken, become a **Denver Broncos** fan. The team has been to the Super Bowl three times in recent years (1986, 1987 and 1989), only to lose each time. But Broncos fans are noted for their loyalty; they'll sit through snow and bitter cold to cheer on their team and its popular quarterback, John Elway. Virtually every home game is a sellout; call 433-7466 well in advance for tickets and information, or show up at the game and take your chances that someone in the parking lot has a ticket to sell. The Broncos play at Mile High Stadium. RTD's BroncoRide services all home games from a number of locations in Greater Denver, with special shuttles available for fans catching the BroncoRide along Federal Boulevard and at the Auraria campus. Call 299-6000 for schedules and current fare information.

Insiders know that college sports can be as exciting to watch as pro games, and they follow the various University of Denver and University of Colorado teams. Even the Air Force Academy, an hour away in Colorado Springs, isn't too far to drive for a game.

Insiders' Tips

The Unshakable Colorado Rockies and Their Die-hard Fans

Plain and simple, the Colorado Rockies are the most successful expansion team in the history of Major-League baseball.

It almost seemed like an omen when the first Colorado batter in the first-ever Rockies game stepped up to the plate at the start of the premiere 1993 season and hit a home run. Maybe it *was* an omen. Playing in the Denver Broncos' Mile High Stadium, the Rockies in 1993 won 67 games, more than any National League expansion team has ever won in its first year. Nor has any expansion team ever had a batting champion in its first year, until the Colorado Rockies. First-baseman Andres Galarraga batted .370, the best in the league for the year and the highest batting average ever for a right-hander since Joe DiMaggio 50 years before.

The Rockies reached 100 wins in record time, midway through their second season in 1994. In August 1995, late in their third season, they were in competition for a division title. Every other expansion team in its third season had been buried.

Why are they so successful? One might well argue that it's because of their fans.

The post-strike season of 1995 saw dramatic dropoffs in attendance for virtually every other Major-League team, but not for the Rockies. Despite an initial bout of post-strike ennui, only four of the 40 Rockies' home games by mid-August had failed to sell out the 50,200 seats of their new stadium, Coors Field. Even those games pulled in more than 40,000 each, followed by 32 sellouts in a row.

Pile those statistics on top of the previous two years, and you have an incomparable picture of fan loyalty. The Rockies in their first year brought 4.5 million fans to their games, breaking the record for season attendance by any team ever in Major-League history. And this in a population area many times smaller than those enjoyed by major-league teams in places like New York, Chicago and Los Angeles.

Maybe even more amazing, this was not just a first-year phenomenon of everyone wanting to see the new team at least once because it was a novelty. Rockies games attendance in 1994 was ahead of 1993 and seemed headed for yet a new season record when the strike ended that dream. By the time of the strike, the Rockies had never drawn a crowd of less than 40,000 to any game. And by the time of the 1994 strike, the Rockies had drawn crowds of more than 70,000 21 times. Compare that with a three-game series the Rockies played in 1994 against the San Diego Padres on the Padres' home turf. The Padres drew a grand total of 30,000 people in a three-game series in a population area twice the size of Denver. Meanwhile, during the 1994 season in Denver, not one Rockies game drew a crowd of less than 45,000.

Financial success of the Colorado Rockies has enabled the team to buy the best talent. During their first off-season the Rockies managed to sign up

*The Colorado Rockies have set plenty of records in their
three years as a Major League team.*

Ellis Burks, Walt Weiss and Howard Johnson, established Major-Leaguers with excellent records. Ordinarily, such players don't want to sign with an expansion team; they want to sign with a contender. But the Rockies, amazingly, were a contender. Shortly before the Major-League strike that ended the Rockies' second season in early August of 1994, the Rockies were only a half game out of first place; again, an achievement never before attained by an expansion team.

The next year saw more stellar gains as the Rockies brought in the premier free agent Larry Walker, who some sports writers hailed as the best athlete in baseball because of his ability to hit for average, hit with power, run fast and wield a terrific outfield arm and glove; and Bill Swift, a premier starting pitcher who had an excellent career with the San Francisco Giants.

To top it all, 1995 was the first year the Rockies played in their new Coors Field. Greater Denver wanted a major league baseball team so badly that it became the first metropolitan area in recent memory to vote itself a sales tax to build a ballpark, rather than depending on private investment like all other cities. What a fine investment that was. The park is an architectural beauty, and has a host of unique features such as its own brewpub. Modeled after the old ballparks such as Boston's Fenway Park and Chicago's Wrigley Field, it's built with girders and bricks rather than concrete and glass.

Fans are closer to the field on average than in any other field in the major leagues. If you're sitting in the front seats behind home plate, in fact, you're closer to the batter than the pitcher is, and that's as intimate as you can get at a ballpark. Virtually every game at this ballpark is exciting and explosive. The Rockies in 1995 had the top four home-run hitters in the National League — Dante Bichette, Andres Galarraga, Larry Walker and Vinny Castilla. By September, each of them had more than 30 home runs, a feat equalled only one other time in history when four Los Angeles Dodgers made the same milestone in 1977. The average number of home runs per game at Coors Field by August was 3.4, obliterating the previous record of 2.9 set at Wrigley Field in Los Angeles in 1961.

Contrary to popular perception, however, Coors Field is not smaller than the average ballpark. Coors Field designers intentionally made it larger than the baseball field in Mile High Stadium to avoid the cheap home runs that people complained about. It's the air, the theory holds, the thin and dry air of the Mile High City, that makes the balls fly so far.

That thin, dry air, and the form and positioning of the park, helps to give fans the most spectacular panorama of any ballpark in the country. Some fans will have their backs to the mountains, of course, but most of them can look right out at the peaks along the Continental Divide.

Hockey

By mid-1995, Denver could boast of having four major-league teams when it was announced that the company that owns the Nuggets purchased the Quebec Nordiques. The team, renamed the **Colorado Avalanche**, calls McNichols Arena home until — and if — the new Pepsi Center is built. Team coach Marc Crawford was coach of the year in 1994-95, and the

team also reaped rookie-of-the-year honors in the person of Peter Forsberg. Single game tickets go on sale in early fall, with prices ranging from $9.50 to $100; ask about group discounts. Season tickets are available. To purchase tickets, call 893-6700 or Ticketmaster, 830-8497.

Soccer

The **Colorado Foxes**, a franchise of the

Dikembe Mutombo is one of the giants of the Denver Nuggets basketball team.

American Professional Soccer League formed in 1990, have twice won the APSL championship, in 1992 and 1993, and reached the finals in 1994. In addition to A-league games in the summer, the Foxes play international matches in the spring. The Foxes moved from Lakewood to Mile High Stadium in 1994. Tickets may be purchased at the Foxes box office windows at the west side of the stadium or at TicketMaster outlets, 830-8497. Single-ticket prices range from $5 to $12. For information on special promotions or for a schedule of games, call 89-FOXES (893-6937).

Racetracks

Parimutuel greyhound races take place at **Mile High Greyhound Park**, 6200 Dahlia Street (at Colorado Boulevard) in Commerce City June through February. Matinee and evening races are scheduled throughout the week. General admission is $1; clubhouse admission is $3. Call 288-1591.

Championship drag racing events are held from April to October at **Bandimere Speedway**, 3051 S. Rooney Road in Morrison (off C-470 between Alameda Avenue and Morrison Road). Call 697-6001 or 697-4870 (24-hour information recording).

Colorado National Speedway has NASCAR and a variety of other races on a paved three-eighths of a mile oval track. Races are held Saturday nights April through September. Colorado National Speedway is in Erie, 20 minutes north of Denver off I-25, Exit 232. Call 665-4173.

Parimutuel thoroughbred, quarter horse and other races take place Thursdays through Sundays and holiday Mondays from May through early September at the **Arapahoe Park Racetrack**, 26000 E. Quincy, just east of Gun Club Road. General admission is $1, clubhouse admission, $4. Call 690-2400.

Photo: Daily Camera

Photo: Daily Camera

Many Rocky Mountain cities have balloon festivals.

Inside
Daytrips

Just to keep things reasonable, our daytrips are destinations within about 100 miles of Denver. Using the old pi-r² rule, however, that still forces you to choose from more than 3,000 square miles of opportunities. Our recommendations tend to concentrate in the mountains and up and down the Front Range along I-25. That's not a prejudice against the plains; simply a result of the fact that the Front Range and the mountains to the west have historically focused a lot more energy on tourism, and that's where the tourists tend to go. And for most people who come to Denver, a ride to see the scenery seems automatically to mean heading into the mountains.

Anyone who loves the Great Plains knows that few landscapes are more tranquilizing or tremendous than the endless rolling prairie, and few things are more magnificent than 180 degrees of sky. Towns and cities on the plains, furthermore, retain much more of their original historic feel because they haven't been so relentlessly populated by newcomers or so dolled-up to attract the tourist trade.

That being said, however, our recommendations are heavily weighted westward, wherein lie attractions on a larger scale connected by drives through flamboyantly awesome scenery. The landscape itself is a daytrip. Anywhere you go in the mountains, you can get out of your car and take a walk. Parking at the top of Berthoud Pass on U.S. Highway 40 between Empire and Winter Park, for example, you may just want to hike eastward up the windswept slope to the top of Colorado Mines Peak for some great views and landscape. Loveland Pass or any other mountain pass in the state offers a similar opportunity to go to great heights and wonderful views from a high-altitude parking spot. As we said, the landscape itself is a daytrip.

We've mentioned a few scenic driving trips near Denver. But they are virtually infinite, given the combination of roads and off-road experience. If you're looking for new ideas, you might check the "Minitour" feature that runs in *Weekend*, the Friday magazine of *The Denver Post*.

Do bear in mind, however, that snowstorms can render high mountain roads treacherous, if not impassable, from September through May. You might consider calling 639-1111 for Colorado State Highway Patrol's report on road conditions within two hours of Denver before taking off on a mountain jaunt during these months. Most mountain lovers who've lived in Greater Denver for any period of time can give you a horror story about sliding sideways on a snowy mountain pass, or worse. Particularly treacherous in heavy weather are high-altitude roads such as Berthoud Pass, Loveland Pass over the Continental Divide, the nearby Eisenhower Tunnel under the Continental Divide (on the way to Breckenridge, Arapahoe Basin, Keystone and Copper Mountain ski areas) or Vail Pass (on the way to Vail and Beaver Creek).

If conditions are bad, it's advisable to make sure your vehicle has good snow tires, if not studded tires. Or carry chains. If the chain law is in effect at a particular pass, that means those without chains will be turned back, no matter how good their tires are. And sometimes, the road will just be closed, period; so be aware of that possibility. It's really a pain to pull out of Vail heading east up I-70 and discover that they've swung the gates closed across the interstate.

Another worthwhile tip: I-70 and U.S. Highway 285 are Greater Denver's two main conduits into and out of the mountains. If there's any way to avoid it, do not return to Denver during the Sunday rush hour, which runs from late afternoon to early evening. These highways become absolutely jammed with traffic, and it kind of sours the mountain experience to spend an hour creeping along bumper-to-bumper. And that's if there isn't an accident that really clogs the road. This problem is worse in winter, when the ski areas all shut down their lifts at 3:30 to 4 PM. This unleashes a concentrated wave of traffic in often slick conditions when it's already dark. Sometimes you can barely figure out where the lines are that separate your car from the

cars hurtling and weaving around you, and there may be driving snow blinding everyone. Return in early afternoon. If you can't, then forget about rushing home for supper. Stop for dinner in the mountains, let the rush pass you by, then have a pleasant drive home.

We haven't mentioned the mountain resort areas in this section because you can already find them well covered in Ski Country, but they are certainly wonderful daytrip destinations year round. We've chosen a few of our favorite daytrips with outstanding special features that are sure to make you feel that a day's outing has been worth the drive.

One thing that's fun about daytrips in Colorado is that the roads you travel are usually quite spectacular for their geography. There's always some amazing or strange formation of land and rocks that makes you wonder at how it got there. Just a jolly good book to have along on any automobile trip is *Roadside Geology of Colorado*, by Halka Chronic. For most any route you travel in the state, the book has a section talking about why you're seeing what you're seeing along the road, and explaining how it got there. As of 1995, the price was $15, and any bookstore with an acceptable Colorado section should be proud to have it or ashamed not to.

Boulder

When you're driving up U.S. Highway 36 from Denver to Boulder, watch for the exit to the cities of Louisville and Superior. Don't take it. Just use it as a benchmark, because a stunning vista is about to punch you in the brain at the top of the next hill. In fact, if you haven't been to Boulder before, you should watch for a sign that says "Scenic Overlook," and take the exit to the right. During the warmer months, the

Many Insiders take their bikes along when daytripping in the mountains.

Boulder Convention and Visitors Bureau operates a visitor information center at the overlook. More importantly, you really need to absorb the view to get a full sense of what Boulder is all about, and Davidson Mesa, as this hill is known, is a primo vantage point.

Boulder nestles like a jewel in the scenic bowl of Boulder Valley. On the mountainsides rising from its western edges, you are struck immediately by the sight of the Flatirons, enormous sandstone monoliths that lean against the slopes like a row of fossilized aircraft carriers. Losing that vantage point as you drive down the hill and into town, you encounter a city of tremendous charm and diversity.

Detractors used to call it "the people's republic of Boulder" during the Vietnam era when students at the University of Colorado at Boulder, CU's main campus, added antiwar protests to the already offbeat lifestyles of this university town. Profiles of Boulder in national magazines continue to emphasize the offbeat, and there's plenty

of that. Boulder is a national mecca for alternative medicine, natural foods, spirituality and outdoor sports such as bicycle racing, mountain biking and technical climbing. The Naropa Institute, a national center for Buddhist studies, is here. It's the only fully accredited, Buddhist-inspired institution of higher education in North America, including bachelor's and master's degrees. And it's unconventional, colorful and photogenic. It's open all day for those who want to drop in, but it also has tours on weekdays at 2 PM. Call 444-0202 for more information. Celestial Seasonings, now an international power in the herbal tea business, was founded here and remains headquartered here. Want to take a tour of the company? Call 530-5300.

Celestial Seasonings is only one example of how Boulder's penchant for individualism and innovation also expresses itself in business entrepreneurism. This is a start-up town, where new companies pop up like spring flowers. Many are high-tech companies, and many have moved outward to other parts of Boulder County as they have grown. Storage Technology Corp., located in Louisville on the edge of Boulder Valley, for example, sprang from the Boulder high-tech community, and its employees have gone on to found numerous other high-tech companies. High-tech spin-offs are a fundamental part of the local culture, and technology here is high indeed, including major federal government laboratories such as the National Center for Atmospheric Research and the National Institute of Standards and Technologies. The University of Colorado, which did more than $143 million worth of research in the 1993-94 fiscal year, is nationally prominent in fields ranging from molecular biology to telecommunications. It's one of the main reasons why high-tech companies locate or start up here, and it works closely with that community. US West Advanced Technologies, the research and development arm of US West Inc., is located in the CU Research Park specifically to be close to its university research partners.

Despite the flaky image, often unfairly and shallowly reported by the outside press, Boulder has a wealth of cultural attractions and probably a greater concentration of good restaurants than you'll find in Denver with the possible exceptions of Denver's downtown and Cherry Creek area. You've got everything from the fine cuisine of the **Two Bitts & More** restaurant just off Boulder's downtown at 1155 Canyoun Boulevard to the hearty fare of restaurants like the **Red Robin Spirits Emporium** at 2580 Arapahoe Avenue.

Boulder also belies its offbeat image by the impressive strength of its business community. Boulder County has the state's highest percentage of employment in manufacturing, and it's way ahead in per-capita high-tech manufacturing. But don't expect to see Boulderites walking around in boardroom-elegant suits with grim, nose-to-the-grindstone expressions. Boulderites generally maintain an easygoing attitude. They're avid on the subjects of environmental responsibility and health consciousness.

All this is a rather long dissertation on one daytrip, but Boulder is by far the biggest nearby daytrip in breadth of offerings. The **Pearl Street Mall** is the center of the city. Formerly the main street of old Boulder, it's now a pedestrian mall lined with unique shops and restaurants and art galleries, flower gardens and street performers — a delightful stroll in any but the worst weather, except for the occasional panhandler or bourgeoisie-disdaining misanthrope. South on Broadway from Pearl Street and up the hill is **University Hill**, where you can enjoy a walk around the graceful campus of the University of Colorado at Boulder.

Go farther south on Broadway past the campus to Baseline Road, turn right on Baseline and go up a long hill. Just past Ninth Street you'll find on the left the entrance to **Chautauqua Park & Auditorium**. The Auditorium is a lovely setting for a summer evening concert. One of Boulder's biggest treats is a summer breakfast or lunch on the veranda of the 100-year-old Chautauqua dining hall, where you can gaze out at the mountains as you munch. Call the Chautauqua ticket service at 440-7666. To reach the Chautauqua Dining Hall, call 440-3776.

Chautauqua Park is also the city's prime entrée to **Boulder Mountain Parks**, some 8,000 acres of trails and rough climbing including Bear Peak, Green Mountain, Flagstaff Mountain, Mount Sanitas, and, of course, the Flatirons.

Another entrance to the park, and an attraction in its own right, is the **National Center for Atmospheric Research**, commonly referred to around Boulder simply as "EN-car." An architectural masterwork by master architect I.M. Pei, it perches like an Italian hill fortress on the redundantly named Table Mesa to the south of Chautauqua with views of the mountains and plains that make it a great spot just for weather gazing. You find it by going still farther south on Broadway from Baseline to Table Mesa Drive. Turn right, and keep going until you stop at NCAR. You can pick up a numbered tour guide in the lobby and take the self-guided tour, 8 AM to 5 PM Monday through Friday, and 9 AM to 3 PM on Saturday, Sunday and holidays. There's also a drop-in tour, which takes place at noon from Monday through Saturday from mid-June to Labor Day, and noon Wednesday only the rest of the year. The Exploratorium Museum in San Francisco has also given NCAR six interactive exhibits similar to those in San Francisco. And it's all free, except for the cafeteria, which is open to the public for breakfast and lunch from 7:30 to 9:30 AM and 11:30 AM to 1:30 PM. To find out about NCAR's guided tours and other information, call 497-1174. Outside NCAR, you can hike on 400 acres of the mesa top, including a handicapped accessible natural trail leading west behind the lab. And just west of the mesa, you get into the system of Boulder Mountain Park trails.

You can usually see climbers scaling the Flatirons, but the best place for close-up watching of technical climbers is Eldorado Canyon. Keep going south on Broadway from Table Mesa Drive until Broadway becomes Colo. Highway 93 as you pass into open country. Watch for the Eldorado Springs Drive turnoff on the right, just more than 5 miles out of Boulder. This is Colo. Highway 170, and about 8 miles of it takes you to **Eldorado Springs**. Back around the turn of the century this resort town used to be called "the Coney Island of Colorado" because of all the people who flocked here for the resort hotels and 76-degree springs. Pass on through it and into **Eldorado Canyon State Park** where you'll find a magnificent cut between high cliffs. You'll see little smudges of white all over the rocks, chalk from climbers' hands. In good weather, you'll see people dangling all over the canyon walls.

Colorado Springs

"The Springs," as locals call it, is an hour's drive south, 67 miles from Denver, the largest single cluster of tourist attractions in our daytrip-defining radius of 100 miles. It doesn't have as many natural wonders as Rocky Mountain National Park, but it has some great ones. And it has plenty of other attractions of human contrivance.

Pikes Peak is the biggest show in town, of course. You can drive to the top by taking U.S. Highway 24 west to Cascade and hanging a left on the same road that brings top auto racers from around the world every year for the Pikes Peak Hill Climb. Or you can do the dizzying trip on the Pikes Peak Cog Railway, officially known as the **Manitou and Pikes Peak Cog Railway**. Reach its terminal by driving west from Colorado Springs on U.S. Highway 24 to the Manitou Exit, west on Manitou Avenue and left onto Ruxton Avenue.

This is the highest cog railway in the world. Established in 1889, it's a historical as well as a sensory experience. During the 3½-hour round trip, you get more panoramas than you can stuff into your brain, including great views down on Manitou Springs and the Garden of the Gods. You get a great view of Denver on a clear day, just as Denverites can see Pikes Peak on a clear day. You can see a seemingly infinite expanse of mountains to the west, and you can even look into New Mexico.

Do take care not to exert yourself too hard and too long on the 14,110-foot summit: Oxygen is scarce up there, and altitude sickness is not a pleasant experience. Besides walking around and taking in the views, you can also unwind in the information center, the gee-gaw shop and the concession area.

The railway is only open from April to October and runs every day during that period. Reservations are required, since this is one of Colorado's big attractions. There's a $21 charge for adults and a $9.50 charge for children ages 5 through 11. Call (719) 685-5401 for information.

Garden of the Gods Park, 1805 N. 30th Street, (719) 634-6666, is another of Colorado Springs's most famous sights. A drive through the park reveals one of the most spectacular displays of dramatic red sandstone formations in Colorado. It's just northwest of downtown. **Cave of the Winds,** Colo. Highway 24 W. in Manitou Springs, is the biggest commercial cave in Colorado, and well worth taking the tour

through the underground passages and caverns. Call for tour information at (719) 685-5444. Cost is $8 for adults and $4 for children ages 6 through 15. They also have an outside laser light show each night at 9 PM, costing $5 for adults and $3 for children, with kids ages 6 and younger getting in free.

If you want to go a bit beyond the 100-mile limit of our daytrip definition, you will certainly enjoy the **Cripple Creek Narrow Gauge Railroad**. Cripple Creek itself is worth visiting, certainly, as one of Colorado's most famous old mining towns and a National Historic District in its own right, although the town has changed somewhat since gambling was legalized here in 1991. But the 4-mile round trip on this old-time steam railroad is rivaled on the Front Range only by the Georgetown/Silver Plume line for cool railroad Americana ($6.75 for adults, $3.50 children ages 3 through 12). Call (719) 689-2640 for information. A little farther out Colo. Highway 115 southeast from Colorado Springs is **Royal Gorge**, about an hour's drive from Colorado Springs, where you can drive across the world's highest suspension bridge 1,053 feet above the Arkansas River. Call Royal Gorge Bridge information at (719) 275-7507. By paying $10.50 for adults and $8 for children ages 4 through 11, you can drive or walk across the bridge, as well as ride an aerial tram across the canyon's history, a minitrain that takes you in the scenic mile circle ride and a carousel. They also have an incline railway, a cagelike ride that takes you all the way down to the bottom of the canyon to the river's edge.

There is so much more to see and do in the Colorado Springs area, including: the Victorian town of **Manitou Springs** and its natural hot springs; the **Cliff Dwellings Museum,** (719) 685-5242, 5 miles west of Colorado Springs on U.S. Highway 24; the historic **Broadmoor Hotel**, (719) 634-

Special Summer Events

Denverites don't mind the 45-minute trip to Central City or Boulder for the following summer performing arts events.

The **Central City Opera**, 292-6700, is a favorite summer tradition. Begun in 1932, the opera holds its performances in the historic Opera House in the old mining town of Central City, about 34 miles west of Denver. The incongruously grand opera house was built in 1878 and ceased operations from 1927 to 1932, at which time the Central City Opera Association took over the building and began restoration and performances. Such notables as Edwin Booth, Mae West, Helen Hayes and Beverly Sills have performed here. The coming of gambling to Central City in 1992 has drastically changed the formerly sleepy nature of the town, but the opera remains as charming as ever. Three

Photo: Daily Camera

MacDuff lays on to MacBeth at a recent performance of MacBeth at the Colorado Shakespeare Festival in Boulder.

operas are performed each summer, and all are sung in English. Ask in advance about specially priced youth performances, round-trip bus transportation from Lakewood and Cherry Creek and reserved parking — the last is highly recommended if you plan to drive yourself.

The summer concerts at Boulder's **Chautauqua Auditorium** are another reason to head west. Boulder's Chautauqua dates back to 1898, when a national movement brought the arts to numerous Chautauqua summer camps throughout the country. Before the evening concerts in the wonderful wooden auditorium, concertgoers can enjoy a picnic dinner under the big shady trees at the base of the Foothills or a sit-down dinner at the Chautauqua Dining Hall, 440-3776. Chautauqua concerts include both a popular music series, 440-7666 (box office) and the **Colorado Music Festival**, 449-1397, year round; 449-2413, summer ticketing; which emphasizes classical music.

The **Colorado Shakespeare Festival**, 492-0554, is another summer-only event in Boulder that draws audiences from Denver and beyond. Held at the outdoor Mary Rippon Theatre and indoor University Theatre on the

University of Colorado-Boulder campus, the annual event features both traditional and modern renditions of Shakespeare plays and non-Shakespearean classics. Tom Stoppard's *Rosencrantz and Guildenstern Are Dead*, for example, was a big hit of the 1995 season. Film actor Val Kilmer took part in a production one year, and other top performers and directors have likewise been attracted to this highly regarded event. "Falstaff's Fare," a box dinner, can be ordered and eaten on the lawn before the show begins. There are evening and matinee performances as well as special children's nights.

The **Colorado Dance Festival**, 442-7666, is now the third-largest dance festival in the nation. It has earned international recognition for its innovative programs of modern dance and performance art and has featured such acclaimed artists as Trisha Brown, Ralph Lemon and the late, great tap dancer Honi Coles. Some years the CDF organizes its one-month summer season around a theme, other years it's more free-form. Performances are held on the University of Colorado campus in Boulder.

7711, with its two great 18-hole golf courses; **Santa's Workshop at the North Pole**, (719) 684-9432, a little magic village/funland that kids can enjoy from mid-May through Christmas Eve; the **ProRodeo Hall of Fame**, and the **Museum of the American Cowboy**, both at (719) 528-4764.

Of all Colorado Spring's attractions, however, the very busiest is the **U.S. Air Force Academy**. You can spend a lot of time touring its 18,000 acres. The Academy doesn't have any one attraction that will blow your socks off, but it's intrinsically interesting simply because of its importance in the military world of aviation. You can take a self-guided driving tour around the grounds. You can walk the nature trail that winds along the ridge behind the school, with plenty of wind-through-the-pines atmosphere and Academy overlooks with benches. There's a very nice museum on the grounds. The most famous sight is the chapel, which is architecturally striking. Perhaps the best way to experience the Academy is by attending its spring graduation ceremony, where you can see the now-

ceremonial tossing of hats in the air by cadets and enjoy a performance by the Thunderbirds, the Air Force's famed jet-acrobatics team. You do need tickets in advance for this event, however. The tickets are free, but they generally come available about two weeks before the ceremony, which is always held on the first Wednesday after Memorial Day. Call the Academy's visitor center at (719) 472-2025 for tickets and other information.

Directly across I-25 from the north gate of the Air Force Academy is a particular favorite of ours, the **Western Museum of Mining and Industry**. It's a nice place for a picnic, with its 27 acres of rolling hills, trees, meadows, streams, beaver ponds and picnic tables. Most important, of course, is the museum itself: more than 15,000 square feet of exhibits in four buildings, along with outdoor displays. It's a big treat to watch them fire up the 1895 Corliss steam engine and watch the 17-ton flywheel go. You can see mining and milling demonstrations and even pan for gold. Admission is $5 for adults, $4 for seniors and students, and $2

Macky Auditorium is one of the historic buildings on the University of Colorado-Boulder campus.

Photo: Daily Camera/Vern Walker

for kids ages 5 to 12. Kids younger than 5 years of age get in free with a paying adult. The museum is open 9 AM to 4 PM Monday through Saturday, and noon to 4 PM on Sunday from March through November. From December through February, call ahead for winter hours, (719) 488-0880. To reach the museum, get off I-25 at Exit 156A, Gleneagle Drive.

Georgetown

Georgetown is a historic mining town that has been lovingly maintained and restored with a turn-of-the-century style that makes it look like one of those toy towns on an elaborate model railroad setup. John Denver used it as the site of one of his Christmas specials in the 1980s. It's a National Historic Landmark District that nestles deep in the head of a valley overshadowed by the steep slopes of several 12,000-foot mountains.

The biggest single attraction here is the **Georgetown Loop**, an old Western railroad train that hauls loads of tourists and train and history buffs from Georgetown uphill to Silver Plume, and back, which is about a 3-mile round trip. **Silver Plume**, by the way, is another great historic town to spend some time in. The train ride includes passage over a 100-foot trestle known as **Devils Gate Bridge**. We can't recommend this trip highly enough, and it's not just the scenery or the fun of riding. It's the historic element and the bits of cinder that fly from the stack of the horrendously puffing old engine and settle on the passengers behind. It's one of the few great antique train rides in Colorado and by far the closest one to Denver. Do it in the fall when the aspens are at high color, for a special treat. The railroad costs $10.95 for adults and $6.50 for children ages 4 through 15, with no charge for kids 3 and younger as long as they sit on a parent's lap. The train operates from May to October. Reservations are suggested. For reservations and information, call the Denver metro number, 670-1686, or the Georgetown number (303) 569-2403.

Georgetown itself went from a mining camp in 1859 to style itself as the "Silver Queen of the Rockies" by the 1870s. Now it's just a fun place to stroll around; it has shops, restaurants, museums, galleries and National Historic Register sites. Reach Georgetown by taking I-70 Exit 228, about 50 miles west of Denver.

You can also drive out of Georgetown south on the Guanella Pass Scenic Byway, which goes all the way to the City of Grant on U.S. Highway 285. The byway peaks out at Guanella Pass, elevation 11,669 feet, where you have wonderful views that include looking up at Mount Bierstadt. This pass is also a good place to get out of the car and look around, but don't stand up too fast in this altitude; the air is thin, and people have been known to faint from small exertions. Find a big rock and have a picnic. Or do some hiking. Heck, you can even hike to the top of Bierstadt. You're already so high that it doesn't take more than a couple of hours, even including the frequent stops to gasp and wheeze. We once encountered a 5-year-old boy on top of Bierstadt. With a parent, of course.

Georgetown has another neat little element. The State of Colorado chose a spot near the lake just east of Georgetown as the state's first **Watchable Wildlife Viewing Station**, although there are others now. Stop and see if you can spot the herd of bighorn sheep on the mountainsides. Often, you can even spot them from I-70 as you're whizzing by, although recently they've been harder to find because the herds went through a decimated-by-disease phase in 1994.

Georgetown visitor information is (303)

569-2555. From the Denver metro area call 623-6882. They also have a toll-free number, (800) 472-8230.

Grand Lake/Granby Loop

We call this the Grand Lake/Granby Loop drive because those are the two towns that anchor it on the western side of the Continental Divide. *National Geographic Traveler* mentioned this drive in its March/April 1994 edition, in an article called "50 Great Scenic Drives." Nobody around here was surprised.

You can experience Grand Lake/Granby Loop by driving from Denver to Estes Park and over Trail Ridge Road through Rocky Mountain National Park and down to Granby. Take U.S. Highway 40 from Granby south through Winter Park, over Berthoud Pass, connecting at Empire with I-70 back to Denver. It's almost 200 miles, a full day, especially if you stop along the way, which you should. Or, you may want to take the circle in the other direction. In fact, you may want to head the other direction only as far as Grand Lake, rather than making a full loop, and leave the Boulder, Estes Park and Rocky Mountain National Park stops for a trip of their own some other day.

Grand Lake is both the name of the city and the name of the big lake on the edge of which the city perches. And just south of Grand Lake is Lake Granby. You'll travel along their western edges and, looking east at the mountains rising from the lakes' other sides into Rocky Mountain National Park and Roosevelt National Forest, you could almost believe you're in Switzerland. The lakes are huge, deep blue and clear, usually decorated with sailboats and always lined with small resorts. Grand Lake is the state's largest lake created by glaciers. Grand Lake is a nice town in which to stop, walk around and maybe catch a bite to eat. Or, you might buy something and head out for a picnic at Lake Granby's Arapahoe Bay.

Arapahoe Bay is at the far southeastern end of Lake Granby. Its depths are a favorite fishing spot in June for the lake's big Mackinaw, or lake trout. You reach it by taking the first left turn off of U.S. Highway 34 at the southwestern tip of Lake Granby. A long gravel road passes over Granby Dam and skirts the southern edge of the lake. At the end of the bay you'll find campgrounds and some nice short hiking trails. You can follow the trail east past Monarch Lake and go as far as you want up toward or into the Indian Peaks Wilderness. It's a pretty area that makes a pleasant stopping point on your loop.

Head south to meet U.S. Highway 40 just west of Granby. You may want to take an added excursion west, or right, on Highway 40 along the scenic highway toward Steamboat Springs, at least as far as Hot Sulfur Springs, anyway. See our entry below on Hot Sulfur Springs. If not, take a left on Highway 40 to get back to Denver by way of Granby, Tabernash, Fraser, Winter Park, Berthoud Pass and down through Empire onto I-70 home. Most people just hustle through Empire, but there are some nice places to stop for refreshment there, and it's perhaps most famous as the home of **The Peck House**, Colorado's oldest operating hotel. Driving through Empire from Berthoud Pass, the Peck House, (303) 569-9870, is about ¾ of the way through town, a half block off U.S. Highway 40. You'll see it from the highway on your left, a big white building with red rim. It's a moderately priced hotel, ranging from $65 to $80 for a night. Check it out, and maybe dine in its restaurant.

Hot Sulfur Springs

This is our oddball recommendation. Hot Sulfur Springs doesn't have anything big that we can recommend, but that's why we're recommending it. If you want something more authentic and isolated than the developed recreation areas along Grand Lake, this tiny town of 347 is the place for you. It's just about 90 miles from the west side of Greater Denver, by way of I-70 to Empire, to Granby and west on U.S. Highway 40.

Actually, U.S. Highway 40 whistles past most of the town; so get off on any street to the right, and head down the hill where the Colorado River sparkles between the Riverside Hotel and the Hot Sulfur Springs Baths. The combination of the two make a great getaway.

The natural hot springs are heavy in sulfur and smell like it. The Utes, who used to roam this territory, bathed here for health and comfort. When outsiders built up a new Colorado, Hot Sulfur Springs became one of the great destinations for vacationers. It was one of the reasons why the Moffat Tunnel was built in 1928, letting trains come direct from Denver. No trains stop here now, and the springs have lost their prominence and seem kind of rundown compared to more patronized facilities in places like Idaho Springs and Steamboat Springs. But again, that's a good reason to come here — getting away.

The baths are both indoor and outdoor pools. The indoor baths are actually in caves, dimly lit, intimate old spaces with adjoining cots where you can wrap yourself and pass out. It's $8 for inside baths and $7 for outside pools. The baths are open 9 AM to 4 PM in May, 9 AM to 8 PM from Memorial Day to Labor Day. You can avail yourself of them during the winter months, a particular treat if you're cross-country skiing in the area, but they are only open by appointment. (The caretaker is more inclined to open them if you have a group.) Call the baths at (303) 725-3306.

The Riverside Hotel, across the bridge from the baths, is a blocky wooden structure that was built in 1908. Abe Renta, the energetically welcoming innkeeper, bought the hotel when it was rundown and had been closed for 1½ years. He spent 10 months sprucing it up and opened for business in 1983. The 19 rooms are old-fashioned in appearance, like the hotel rooms you might see in a cowboy movie or find a bit more fancied up in a modern bed and breakfast. Rates recently went up to $30 for a single room and $38 for a double. The hotel may be closed Monday through Wednesday in the winter months, when business slows down, and only dinner is served from September to May. The rest of the year, Abe opens for lunch and dinner seven days a week. The dining room has a potbellied stove and looks out on the Colorado River. You'll find mostly American cuisine, with some European accents. Call ahead for reservations, (970) 725-3589.

Idaho Springs

Idaho Springs, 32 miles west of Denver on I-70, is the first resort town and erstwhile mining town you hit on the way west.

It's also the mining town that is most visible as a mining town, thanks to the floes of yellow tailings spilling from holes that dot the mountainsides along I-70 here. If you want a closer look at this phenomenon, take the "Oh My God Road" from Idaho Springs to Central City, a narrow and scary road with even more holes and tailings dotting the hillsides.

Prospector George Jackson launched Idaho Springs in early 1859 when he pulled out nearly $2,000 worth of gold in one week. Miners flocked in, and the town was off. Two of your best choices for a look into the town's mining past are the **Argo Gold Mill** and the **Phoenix Mine**. You can't miss the Argo Gold Mill. It's the biggest structure on the north side of the valley, and "Argo Gold Mill" is printed in large letters on its front. Where much of the local ore was processed, this is now a museum and National Historic site that you can tour from May to October. The Phoenix Mine, sunk in 1872, is once again a working mine that you can tour guided by an experienced miner. Learn about the history, geology and the art of gold mining; dig your own ore; and pan your own gold. Call 567-0422 for more information.

Idaho Springs and the surrounding area have a lot of other attractions too, and one of them is simply the Clear Creek Ranger District office of Arapaho National Forest, 567-2901, where you can stop in to find out about other opportunities nearby. It's at 101 Chicago Creek Road. Coming from Denver on I-70, take the Mount Evans Exit,

The Broadmoor Hotel has attracted tourists to Colorado Springs for decades.

then turn left up Colo. Highway 103 and it's the first brown building on the right-hand side.

And of course, Idaho Springs has natural hot mineral springs. The **Indian Springs Resort**, listed on the National Register as a historic site, offers hot baths and a covered mineral water swimming pool. It's at 302 Soda Creek Road, just east of downtown. Call (303) 567-2191 for information.

For more information on these and other attractions, call the Chamber of Commerce's visitor information line at (800) 685-7785 or the Idaho Springs Visitors Center at 567-4382.

Mount Evans

If you love mountains, this is the best daytrip of them all. Not because there's a resort or town or some paying attraction at the end of it — just because this is the fastest route to the greatest vistas in the region. For out-of-town visitors here on business or some other short stay, with only a morning or afternoon to see the mountains, this is the best recommendation we can make. For anybody else, it's a must.

It's simple. Colo. Highway 5 to the top of Mount Evans is the highest paved road in the world and your chance to go to the top of one of Colorado's "fourteeners" without having to huff and puff up thousands of feet of forest and alpine meadow. You park at about 14,260 feet, wander around and look down and out 100 miles in every direction. The view is absolutely magnificent. It's more impressive than the view from Trail Ridge Road where it meets the Continental Divide in Rocky Mountain National Park, and it's just up the hill from Idaho Springs.

Take I-70 west out of Denver to Idaho Springs, about a 30-minute drive. Get off at Exit 240, which features a sign saying Mount Evans, and get on Colo. Highway 103. It winds uphill, to the intersection with Colo. Highway 5 at Echo Lake. The lake, by the way, is a nice place for a picnic and some fishing. Also, either on the way up or on the way down, stop at the Echo Lake Lodge, located at the intersection. Pause for a refreshment in their little restaurant, and browse among their gifts and souvenirs. Make sure to look out the window at their hummingbird feeder. In summer, you can expect to see the striking spectacle of ruby-throated hummingbirds swirling and hovering like bees just on the other side of the windowpane.

Head uphill on Colo. Highway 5 for another 14-mile trip to the top. Acrophobics should be warned that this stretch may produce whiter knuckles than any paved road in Colorado. The road is very narrow, especially on the ride down. Looking out from the passenger seat, your can easily imagine the car slipping off the side and cartwheeling into the abyss.

You will probably see mountain goats on the way up, and maybe even bighorn sheep. Several years ago, an ill-trained hunter wounded one near the highway, and tourists were treated to the sight of a bloody sheep running across the road pursued by the gun-toting hunter. Motorists stopped, and there was a hunter/driver exchange of angry words and fisticuffs.

Once at the parking lot, you can climb a short trail to the highest point and look down to the west on the Continental Divide, east over Denver and the Great Plains, north over the Roosevelt National Forest and south over the Pike National Forest. Bring along a state map; it's fun to try to identify some of the major peaks. If you like boulder fields, there are plenty to scramble around on. If you're a flatlander who hasn't been in Denver for at least three days, however, do bear in mind that there's only about half as much oxygen up here as there is at sea level. Don't exert yourself too hard or too long. Altitude sickness can hit you right away, or it can hammer you after you've been back in Denver for hours. We had one friend from outside Colorado who hiked 2,000 feet lower than this and had to be taken to the emergency room that evening when she got stomach cramps and began vomiting and frantically hyperventilating. Take it easy, drink lots of water and you should do fine. The road to Mount Evans is open only in the warmer months, and even then, weather can turn bad. To check on road conditions or ask other questions, call the Clear Creek Ranger District of Arapaho National Forest at 567-2901.

The Peak-to-Peak

The Peak-to-Peak Highway is so called because it follows the eastern slopes of more peaks than you can shake a stick at. It's basically the road that runs below the Continental Divide from the tourist mecca of Estes Park on the north to the historic towns and gambling meccas of Black Hawk and Central City on the south. Along the way there are plenty of turnoffs westward that will get you closer to Longs Peak, Mount Meeker, Chiefs Head Peak, Isolation Peak, Ouzel Peak, Mount Alice, Mount Orton, Mahana Peak and Copeland Mountain — and those are just some of the peaks along the first 10 miles. The highway is about 60 miles long and actually consists, north to south, of Colo. Highway 7, Colo. Highway 72 and Colo. Highway 119.

Take the Peak-to-Peak in either direction. The entire route is a winding road of beautiful vistas and lovely mountainsides. It's a worthwhile tour anytime but an especially great place to take in the views of autumn's golden aspens, generally in September. Ten miles south of Estes Park, you find the well-traveled turnoff for the **Longs Peak Trailhead**. This may be the most popular ascent of a Colorado "fourteener". It's a heck of a long slog. See the Hiking section of our Recreation Chapter.

Another 4 miles or so along, you'll find on the right the turnoff for the **Ouzel Falls Trail** at Wild Basin. If you want to get out of your car for a pleasant walk to a gemlike waterfall in the cool forest, this is the opportunity. The falls are only about 3 miles up the trail.

All along the Peak-to-Peak there are not only turnoffs to the west to reach scenic areas and other attractions, but also turn-

This may sound insane, but if your car overheats going up a mountain grade on a hot summer day, turn off the air conditioning and turn on the heater full blast (this sucks heat away from the engine). Make sure to open the windows, though.

Insiders' Tips

offs to the left that will take you back down to the flatlands in case you decide to bail out of the loop. You can come up these routes, and travel only part of the loop. At one of these points, the historic mining town of Ward, you can head east downhill via Lefthand Canyon or you can head west up to **Brainard Lake**. This crystalline, high mountain lake is a beautiful place where you can absorb spectacular views without walking more than a few steps from your car. Actually, you can just look out through the windshield, but the effect is better if you get out and inhale the mountain breezes.

Pass on south through Nederland (lots of nice drives west from here, too) and on down to Rollinsville. A drive west from here on a gravel road will bring you to the Moffat Tunnel, which connects Denver by railroad with points west. A trail up to the east of the tunnel makes a nice hike and is popular with cross-country skiers in winter.

From Rollinsville on down, the big tourist attractions are **Black Hawk** and **Central City**, which have become the places to go and gamble for Denverites since limited-stakes gambling was okayed by Colorado voters in 1991. Call (800) 542-2999 for information on Central City's lodgings and attractions. Also see our Nightlife chapter for more information.

Black Hawk is right next to Central City and was one of the first mining camps around Gregory Gulch, where gold was discovered in 1859. Central City, in the middle of Gregory Gulch, became the prominent population center because of its location, which claims the "richest square mile on Earth." Central City is a great old historic mining town, but a lot of people feel that its historic authenticity has been obliterated by all the new casinos. Well, Central City has become a favorite evening and weekend excursion for a lot of people looking for a little Las Vegas in their own back yard, but it's still a nice historic district as well. The **Central City Opera House** is still Colorado's reigning opera performance center during its summer season. It was built in 1861, burned in 1874, rebuilt in 1878 and during the latter part of the century was pulling in some of the biggest names in theater. Closed when the silver boom ended, it has been operating since it reopened in 1932. Call 292-6700 for opera information.

The **Teller House**, next to the opera, is Central City's historic hotel, perhaps most well known for the "Face on the Barroom Floor." The mystique of that woman's face is probably due more to the faded paint job and her mysterious expression than to its origin, because it doesn't hail from the boom days. It was painted in 1932. The **Gilpin County Historical Museum** is a better bet for a bit of history on this gold and silver town of yore, and it's located right in town. Call 582-5283 for more information about the museum.

Whether gambling has hurt or helped Central City and Black Hawk is a matter of opinion. Historic tourism wasn't paying the bills, many said, and gambling would bolster the economy so the historical aspects could get their just due. Gambling drove real estate sky high, drove out a lot of authentic residents and their businesses and required the gutting of historic buildings for new casinos, say detractors. At any rate, your Peak-to-Peak Highway tour is likely to run into heavy gambler traffic along here, bumper-to-bumper traffic on busy gambling nights. This area is well patrolled by police.

A short ride down the road will take you to I-70, if you're in a rush to get back home. But if you're here for the scenic route, you're well-advised to take a left on U.S.

Highway 6 down scenic Clear Creek Canyon to Golden.

Rocky Mountain National Park

With the possible exception of Yellowstone in Wyoming, Rocky Mountain National Park is the nation's most famous. And you can't say too much about it, since it's Colorado's hugest single immersion in nature that you can experience by auto and/ or short walks. It's a chance to see the full spectrum of Rocky Mountain nature in one gulp. You can roam from the darkest subalpine forests below to the sun-sprinkled meadows and granite grandeur of the continent's roof — 265,000 acres of it well-connected by roads and trails.

The best way to do the park by auto, of course, is **Trail Ridge Road**, 50 miles of U.S. Highway 34 that vaults over the park from Estes Park on the east to Grand Lake on the west. The drive over the top is one of the nation's great scenic routes, although its two lanes are well-jammed in the summer season. The opening of Trail Ridge Road by snowplow some time around Memorial Day is an annual Colorado event photographed for the Denver and Boulder papers, and it stays open until October. But you can access the park year round. The east side has plenty of lovely drives and hiking opportunities. To reach the west side in winter, take I-70 west from Denver to U.S. Highway 40 at Empire, then U.S. Highway 40 north to Granby, where you go right on U.S. Highway 34 to the park. Autumn and spring visits are particularly enjoyable. Do check it out on late summer or early autumn evenings when the elk are bugling, particularly in the Kewuneeche Valley on the western side.

The park headquarters can be reached for questions at (970)586-2371.

Photo: Daily Camera/Lourie Zipf

The Auraria Campus is close to downtown Denver and is home to three colleges.

Inside
Education

Education is a bright spot in any youthful and mobile population, and Colorado is no exception. When so many residents are recent and arrive by choice and quality of life is a primary reason for their arrival, they tend to put a high value on the educational facilities available to themselves and their children. So do the companies that make a community thrive. Corporate relocation consultants will tell you that one of the most important criteria that companies apply in choosing a new location is the educational system, not just because of what that says about the mentality of the region but also because it's an advantage in attracting good employees from other parts of the country.

The state stands at the educational forefront in many ways. In 1993, for example, Colorado became the third state after Minnesota and California to enact charter schools, which are publicly funded but run by groups of parents, teachers and other individuals who want to devise their own curriculum. Greater Denver now has charter schools in operation or pending in every one of its counties. The City of Denver, for example, by the 1995-96 year had a number of charter schools, including Clayton Charter School, P.S. 1 and Thurgood Marshall Charter School.

Colorado's public schools were made more accessible in 1994 by legislation creating "open enrollment" statewide, meaning you can enroll your kids in *any* public school at no extra cost. Got your eye on a school with some real nice programs but live outside the traditional enrollment area or the school is in another district? That problem has been eliminated by open enrollment. Of course, local children have priority, so it depends on whether space is available.

One of the best publications a parent can buy is *The Guide to Metro Denver Public Schools*, by Margerie Hicks. It lays out just about everything you could want to know about Greater Denver's 15 public school systems, its school districts and its individual schools and programs. It's available through Denver's Magnolia Street Press, 322-2822, and also through the Greater Denver Chamber of Commerce, 620-8029, and some local bookstores for $13.95. You can always look through a copy at a public library, but it's at least worth

Greater Denver's largest student populations are not in the City and County of Denver but in Arapahoe and Jefferson counties.

contacting Magnolia Press to make sure you are looking at the latest annual edition.

A valuable pre-college program for high school students is Project Upward Bound, operated by Metropolitan State College of Denver. Small, late-afternoon classes on Metro's Auraria Campus are geared for students from low-income families, students who need better preparation and students recommended by a high school teacher, counselor, principal, adult friend or community person. The program is designed to enhance development of basic skills, creative thinking, effective expression, independence in learning and positive attitudes toward learning.

For the younger set, Greater Denver has more than 60 Head Start centers. For information, contact Denver's Region VIII office of the U.S. Department of Health and Human Services, 292-3060.

The state of Colorado has a newcomer's packet to get you started on learning about the state's public schools; it's available through the Department of Education's Communications Center at 201 E. Colfax in Denver, 866-6646. You can also get a free copy of *A Parent's Guide to Colorado Public Schools* by calling the Governor's Office of Policy and Initiatives at 866-2155.

Colorado's colleges and universities in many ways stand among the nation's best. Colorado has a higher percentage of the population with bachelor's degrees than any state in the nation.

Higher education is available in a wide variety of forms in Greater Denver, the most obvious choices being the major institutions such as the University of Colorado and the University of Denver. Private colleges and universities are generally smaller but are numerous and diverse. In many ways the most important part of Greater Denver's higher-educa-

tion establishment is the community college system. At any one time, around 40,000 students are attending one of the area's five community colleges. These are public colleges so well distributed around Greater Denver that no resident is very far from one of them. They tend toward curricula that are career oriented and designed for accessibility by working students.

One handy reference to area colleges and universities is the *LEARN Directory*, produced by the Local Educational Adult Resource Network. You can get a copy by calling Melinda B. Anderson-Ghannam, Director of Admissions at National College, 758-6700. This book can be found at many local libraries.

Private elementary and secondary schools are another area of enormous choice, and parents shop carefully when looking into this option. How do you shop for a school? Ask other parents, of course, and research using guides such as this one. A more complete guide dedicated entirely to this subject is the $10.95 directory, *Colorado Private Elementary and Secondary Schools*, by Margerie Hicks, published by Magnolia Street Press, 322-2822. Our list of colleges and universities is by no means a full account of local adult educational opportunities. There are more specialized business, technical and other schools than you can shake your brain at. Colorado has nearly 200 private occupational schools, for example, ranging from the American Diesel & Automotive College to the Xenon International School of Hair Design. The bulk of these are in the Greater Denver area. They're fully listed and described in a handy reference known as the *Directory, Colorado Private Occupational Schools Approved to Do Business in Colorado*. To get a copy, contact the State of

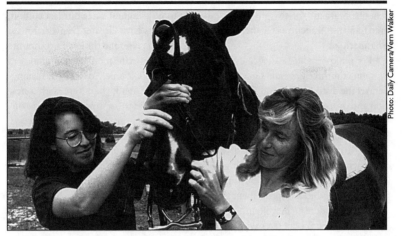

Photo: Daily Camera/Vern Walker

Students at Alexander Dawson School learn to ride and take care of horses.

Colorado's Department of Higher Education, Division of Private Occupational Schools, 894-2960.

Whatever educational needs and interests you may have, Greater Denver has an abundance of opportunities to offer, beginning with the public school systems.

Public Schools

ADAMS COUNTY SCHOOL DISTRICT No. 1 MAPLETON PUBLIC SCHOOLS
591 E. 80th Ave.
Denver   *288-6681*

Adams County School District No. 1, more familiar to most as Mapleton Public Schools, lies just north of Denver and includes part of the City of Thornton and some of unincorporated Adams County. With the third-smallest total enrollment in Greater Denver, the system has six elementary schools, two middle schools, one high school and one alternative school. Superintendent J. Tom Maes was named Colorado Superintendent of the Year in 1994. Although this system has Greater Denver's lowest percentage of teachers with advanced degrees, the highest pupil-teacher ratio and the second-lowest recent composite ACT (American College Test), it has one of the area's lower high-school dropout rates.

The district provides a lot of special opportunities for its diverse student body, including programs in back-to-basics, learning enrichment, accelerated classes, bilingual and multicultural education, Native American education and open enrollment for all schools based on availability.

ADAMS 12 FIVE STAR SCHOOLS
11285 Highline Dr.
Northglenn   *451-1561*

The Five Star Schools, Adams County's largest school district, the seventh-largest in the state, includes more than 22,600 students attending 36 schools in a 62-square-mile area serving Northglenn, Federal Heights and parts of Thornton, Broomfield, Westminster and unincorporated Adams County. In addition to 12 elementary schools, it includes six middle schools and three high schools, as well as the Bollman Occupational Center, Vantage Point Alternative School and two charter schools: Stargate, for the gifted and talented, and the Academy of Charter Schools, a basic school.

Per-pupil spending at Five Star Schools is among the three lowest in Greater Denver, yet the district still maintains graduation and dropout rates in the metro area's midrange. The mission of the district, "Success for all students through shared responsibility," is exemplified by the decentralized approach to shared decision making that exists in the district. Principals work in conjunction with school improvement teams to further student achievement at each school. The district operates with a well-established strategic plan, which is undergoing the five-year review process in school year 1995-96. Among the goals set by the district through its strategic plan is raising the graduation rate from the current 78.3 percent to the state goal of 90 percent. From 1994 to 1995, the rate increased by 2 percent. Another district goal is an increase in proficiencies for all students. The goal of increased enrollment by gender and ethnic diversity in higher level classes is being advanced by the district's Diversity Initiative. The district pushes "enhanced partnerships in learning" through increased home/school involvement.

ADAMS COUNTY SCHOOL DISTRICT 14
4720 E. 69th Ave.
Commerce City   289-3941

One of Greater Denver's smaller school systems, District 14 has seven elementary schools, two middle schools, one high school and one alternative high school. This district pulls students from Commerce City and areas in Thornton and unincorporated Adams County. It's solidly in the midrange of Greater Denver school districts as far as the education and salaries of its teachers and its spending per pupil. Its high school dropout rate has gone from second-highest to fifth-highest since our last edition, but it does have Greater Denver's lowest graduation rate, and the lowest composite ACT scores in the most recent rankings.

At the same time, Adams 14 has a gung-ho attitude about the future with a new commitment to improving its schools under the "Blueprint for Continued Success," a strategic planning document. The blueprint moves the community toward a common plan, with each school devising its own improvement plan. Among its special programs is Cities in Schools/Burger King Academy of the Rockies. Located at Adams City Middle School, 4451 E. 72nd Ave., Commerce City, it's a personalized alternative instructional program for students at risk of dropping out. With more than 43 percent of its students Hispanic, Adams 14 puts a lot of effort into bilingual education and accommodating cultural diversity.

ADAMS COUNTY SCHOOL DISTRICT 50
4476 W. 68th Ave.
Westminster   428-3511

School District 50 serves the City of Westminster, parts of Arvada and unincorporated Adams County with 16 elementary schools, four middle schools and two high schools. Although the average teacher salary is Greater Denver's second-lowest, and its spending per pupil is the third-lowest, it ties for Greater Denver's second-highest ratio of teachers to students. District 50 has a dynamic attitude about its school system. When the district had a graduation rate of 64.7 percent in 1992, it published a mission statement of achieving and maintaining a graduation rate of 95 percent by 1995. That's a pretty lofty goal, considering it would make the district by far the leader in that area. By 1993, the graduation rate had climbed to 76.8 percent, boosting it 40 percent of the way to the three-year goal.

In 1993 the district began an Odyssey of the Mind League to encourage students to develop creative thinking skills. The district also began the Graphics Communication Cluster, a prototype for a new method of integrating academic and technical education. Offered to 11th and 12th graders, it includes instruction in graphic arts, desktop publishing and video and electronic media.

The district puts out a special tabloid publication, *Focus on Excellence*, that highlights the service of individual teachers to encourage parents to get to know them. Adams County 50 pushes for technological innovation and offers such features as a computer-assisted instruction lab and a Writing-to-Read computer lab in every elementary school. It also offers an annual technology review conference.

AURORA PUBLIC SCHOOLS
1085 Peoria St.
Aurora 344-8060

Aurora Public Schools covers most of Aurora, which is Greater Denver's second-largest city. The district's mission is to develop its kids into "life-long learners who value themselves, contribute to their community and succeed in a changing world."

Strong emphasis is placed on student achievement in basic subjects. The district is committed to preparing students for life in the 21st century by helping them become self-directed learners, collaborative workers, complex thinkers, community contributors and quality producers. Special services and classes are offered for gifted and talented students, special education students and non-English speaking young parents, preschoolers and adults.

The district has seven elementary schools and two middle schools on year-round schedules. In total, the district has 28 elementary schools, seven middle schools and five high schools, one of which is an alternative high school.

Special classes in 50 skill areas are offered within the district at T.H. Pickens Technical Center, 500 Buckley Road, Aurora. Some programs offer credit toward an associate degree from the Community College of Aurora.

BRIGHTON PUBLIC SCHOOLS
630 S. Eighth Ave.
Brighton 659-4820

The closest thing to a small-town, country-school district in Greater Denver, Brighton Public Schools (District 27J), serves about 210 square miles of farmland around the 15,000 population of Brighton, the Adams County seat. As a school district, Brighton's enrollment is the second-smallest in Greater Denver. The district has five elementary schools, two middle schools, one high school and an alternative school. Brighton schools are staffed by about 250 professionally certified teachers, more than half of whom have master's degrees. The turnover rate of classroom teachers is 3 percent. In accordance with state law, district 27J is developing content standards for all academic areas. Included in this effort toward Standards Based Education are the improvement of instructional techniques as well as the assessment of skills and knowledge learned. The district has Greater Denver's second-highest spending per pupil and second-highest composite ACT scores in the most recent ranking, but the second-lowest graduation rate and second-lowest percentage of teachers with master's degrees or higher. The district's schools offer enrichment programs including bilingual education, programs in basic skills and accelerated education.

Photo: Daily Camera/Lourie Zipf

Community College of Denver is one of three colleges on the Auraria Campus.

CHERRY CREEK SCHOOL DISTRICT 5
4200 S. Yosemite
Englewood   *773-1184*

Covering Greater Denver's southeastern corner, District 5 encompasses Cherry Hills Village, Glendale, parts of Aurora, Englewood, Greenwood Village and some of unincorporated Arapahoe County. It includes the rapidly growing and well-to-do communities of new businesses and young families along the northern edge of Douglas County and wraps around the Denver Technological Center.

Cherry Creek School District 5 has some impressive statistics, including Greater Denver's highest average teacher salary and second-highest teacher-student ratio. It has 29 elementary schools, six middle schools, four high schools and one magnet school. Since 1990, The U.S. Department of Education has named one of the elementary schools, Indian Ridge Elementary, and two of the high schools, Smoky Hill High and Cherry Creek High, as Schools of Excellence. Smoky Hill High has one of Colorado's three International Baccalaureate programs in which advanced studies give students a jump on college. Every elementary and middle school in the district makes special accommodations for gifted and talented students.

DENVER PUBLIC SCHOOLS
900 Grant St.   *764-3200*

As the workhorse school system of Denver's central city population, Denver Public Schools has one of Greater Denver's greatest education challenges. It also provides some of Greater Denver's greatest educational opportunities.

The Denver school system provides parents with a lot of choices, including special programs for the 15,000 or so students in the district who have limited English proficiency. Other choices include the Challenge Highly Gifted program, three fundamental academies, two extended-day schools, a Montessori school, a laboratory school and an International Baccalaureate program, which was the first in the state. The system is still the only district to have the IBP program at all three levels — elementary, middle and secondary.

Denver's magnet schools are educational venues that parents prize for their kids. Seven elementary schools, four middle schools and three high schools offer the magnet concept, which means that they offer some special program not ordinarily part of the regular curriculum that draws chosen kids from other schools. The Denver School of the Arts at Cole Middle School, for example, where arts education is combined with academics, is one of the most sought-after educational venues among Denver parents. Unfortunately, many audition, and many must be turned away. The Computer Magnet program at George Washington High School is another popular program where students extend their knowledge about the use of computers beyond what is available at other schools. Knight Fundamental Academy and Traylor Fundamental Academy teach traditional basics with strict behavioral standards — Knight pulling kids from all schools east of University Boulevard and Traylor pulling from the west. Morey Fundamental, a magnet school newly created in 1994 at Morey Middle School, provides a place where Knight Academy kids can continue in the magnet concept.

Denver had two charter schools under way by fall of 1995: Clayton Charter School and P.S. 1. Another, Thurgood Marshall Charter School, is scheduled to start operating in fall 1996.

Denver Public Schools leads Greater Denver in teacher/pupil ratio and per-pupil spending, but it is still struggling with the lowest graduation rate.

Mitchell elementary school and Garden Place Academy were honored by *Redbook* magazine as two of America's best elementary schools for overall excellence.

Since 1991, Denver Public Schools has governed each of its schools using a collaborative decision-making (CDM) team. Each team is made up of parents, teachers, the principal, students and a business community representative. All told, Denver has 78 elementary schools, 18 middle schools, 10 high schools and two alternative schools. Special facilities include the Fred N. Thomas Career Education Center at 2650 Eliot Street, 964-3000, enrollment 1,000, where secondary students attend half-day career education training. The Emily Griffith Opportunity School at 1250 Welton Street, 572-8218, is the adult education arm of Denver Public Schools, offering more than 350 classes at more than 120 locations.

DOUGLAS COUNTY SCHOOL DISTRICT
620 Wilcox St.
Castle Rock   *688-3195*

This district's 19 elementary schools, one charter school, three middle schools and three high schools cover a far-flung area ranging from the southern edges of Jefferson and Arapahoe counties much of the way to Colorado Springs. Douglas is a fast-growing county, the second-fastest in the United States. In January 1995, the district welcomed its 20,000th student. Due to a successful $81.2 million bond election

---

Contrary to one popular perception, the recent increase in public school enrollment that has some communities pushing for new schools is not a result of the recent high inflow of immigrants from other states. Most of the student population growth is attributed to kids born in Colorado.

Insiders' Tips

in 1993, nine new schools have been funded, including a new high school in Highlands Ranch, another high school in Parker and a replacement middle school in Castle Rock.

The majority of the county's elementary and middle school students go to school on a four-track, year-round calendar, a rotation of nine weeks in school followed by three weeks of vacation, throughout the year.

Despite the lowest average teacher salaries in Greater Denver, Douglas County has the highest graduation rate and the lowest dropout rate. How do they do it? The system overall places a high value on educational excellence. Cherokee Trail Elementary School in Parker was named by *Child Magazine* as one of the 10 best schools in the nation. Greater Denver's first charter school, Academy Charter School, is located in Castle Rock. Beginning in the 1994-95 school year, the county approved a teacher-compensation plan linked to performance rather than longevity.

Douglas County is one of four school districts partnering in the Expeditionary Learning School, a K-9 school that has won national grants and acclaim for its challenging learning program.

ENGLEWOOD SCHOOLS
4101 S. Bannock St.
Englewood 761-7050

Also known as Arapahoe County School District No. 1, this district educates a little more than 4,500 students, Greater Denver's third-smallest enrollment, in the City of Englewood.

Englewood was not shy about its educational ambitions when it adopted a student-created name for its only alternative high school: Colorado's Finest Alternative High School. Either *Redbook* magazine was swayed by the name, or it found

the name accurate, because the magazine in 1994 named this school as the best in the state. The school was devised by the Englewood School District for kids at risk of dropping out. Englewood has recently shown Greater Denver's highest high school dropout rate. Aside from the regular curriculum at Colorado's Finest, the 530 students participate in teacher-run counseling groups of 25 students, complete 20 hours of community service in their senior year and can take college courses for credit. This school accepts students from anywhere in the state.

Englewood's other schools include Englewood Senior High School plus two middle schools and five elementary schools.

JEFFERSON COUNTY PUBLIC SCHOOLS
1829 Denver West Dr.
Golden 982-6808

Jefferson County makes up Colorado's largest school district with 83,000 students and a budget of $350 million. Just as Jefferson County has one of Greater Denver's fastest-growing populations, it also has one of the fastest-growing student loads, with Greater Denver's second-lowest ratio of teachers to students. But everybody seems to want to get their kids into Jefferson County. Hundreds of parents from surrounding school districts use open enrollment to have their children attend the Jefferson County schools.

What is it about Jeffco that makes it so desirable? Well, it's a nice place to live, right up against the mountains with a lot of upscale neighborhoods and light-industry, white-collar employment. Also, the school system has Greater Denver's highest percentage of teachers with master's degrees or higher and the second-highest average teacher salary.

Jeffco in 1991 established a task force of

parents, staff, students and community members to recommend how student learning could be improved. The task force's efforts have blended with the district's work in 1994-95 to determine what students should know and be able to do. Teams have drafted high, achievable-content standards for students in reading, writing, math, science, history and geography. In 1995-96, standards will be drafted for economics, civics, foreign languages, art, music and physical education.

Jeffco has a "least-restrictive environment" policy for special education students that gives primary responsibility for a special-needs student's education to the neighborhood school. The school district also has a Multicultural Learning Center that provides multicultural resources for teachers across the district.

As of 1995, Jeffco was pursuing these lofty goals in neighborhood schools — 88 elementary schools, 18 middle schools and 14 high schools — as well as a wide range of educational choice programs. These include open enrollment where space is available, schools within a school, alternative schools and self-governing charter schools. A brochure called *Choices* is available from the school district's Communications Services office, 982-6808.

Jeffco passed a $325 million bond issue in 1992, the largest general obligation bond issue in the state's history. By spring 1995, 186 projects had expanded or renovated old buildings, replaced four older buildings, and opened eight new schools. Construction will continue through 1997.

LITTLETON PUBLIC SCHOOLS
5776 S. Crocker St.
Littleton   347-3386
Pulling students from the City of Littleton and neighboring unincorporated zones, Littleton Public Schools is an-

other one of those districts that does a good job with its money. The district serves 15,700 students in Littleton and parts of unincorporated Arapahoe County, including 15 elementary schools, four middle schools, three senior high schools, one alternative middle school and one alternative high school program.

LPS students consistently rank above state and national averages on standardized tests. Littleton has Greater Denver's highest composite ACT score in recent rankings, the second-highest average teacher salaries and the second-lowest high school dropout rate. Of LPS' 1,000 teachers, 650 hold master's or doctorate degrees, and more than 600 exceed 10 years of teaching experience. LPS places a high value on small class sizes, which range from 20 to 27 for elementary and 26 to 32 for middle and high school classes. School choice is available to all district residents through an open enrollment/transfer policy.

LPS also enjoys a high level of community involvement and support. Parents, community members, businesses and senior citizens donated more than 179,000 hours to the schools during 1993-94, the equivalent of 86 full-time employees.

SHERIDAN SCHOOL DISTRICT NO. 2
4000 S. Lowell Blvd.
Denver   761-8640
Greater Denver's smallest school district, Sheridan has a total enrollment of just more than 1,900 in two elementary schools, one middle school and one high school. It serves the City of Sheridan, which surrounds the Englewood Municipal Golf Course and pieces of Englewood. Since our last edition, the district's graduation rate has gone from fifth-highest to second-highest in Greater Denver.

Besides the Sheridan Preschool Program and the Area Vocational School, District No. 2 has a Mentally Tough program that fuses principles of sports physiology and motivational psychology to improve student performance, concentration and overall health.

Private Schools

Not every private school in the area is included here, of course, but you will find the larger, as well as many smaller, schools that come to us by word-of-mouth recommendation. Some accept only one sex, and many of them are religion-based private schools. None of the religious schools profess to turn away students on the basis of their religion or lack of religious commitment. Actually, however, religious schools require students to take religious instruction, and lack of adequate preparation can in some cases disqualify a student. In Herzl Jewish Day School, for example, students need to have a sufficient grounding in the Hebrew language, and the Yeshiva Toras Chaim School is particularly heavy in Talmud and Torah.

ACCELERATED SCHOOLS
2160 S. Cook St.
Denver   758-2003
215 Students/K-12/Coed
$6,250-$12,250

Students, including the gifted and the learning disabled, study independently through individually prescribed instructional and motivational systems. Heavy use of computer instructional programs increases time spent on prescribed learning tasks and gives immediate feedback with an emphasis on practical business applications. Regular day students are in learning centers from 9 AM to 1:05 PM. The school offers accelerated reading and college classes for extra credit, as well as field trips and other activities. Transportation to and from home is included in tu-

ition. Housing is available for students who need it. Contact David Harris or Jane Queen.

ALEXANDER DAWSON SCHOOL
4801 N. 107th St.
Lafayette   665-6679
235 students/6-12/Coed
$7,800-$9,050

This college-prep school, located on a 135-acre campus 35 minutes north of Denver, also offers five-day boarding ($15,500) and seven-day boarding ($18,250). The school has a need-based financial aid program with over $300,000 in grants, which go to 25 percent of the students. Grades 6-8 are all day students. Typically, the school has 45 boarding students, about a third of the upper school. The rigorous academic program includes an emphasis on the arts. Alexander Dawson takes part in interscholastic athletic competitions, including canoeing, skiing and horsemanship. Stables with horses are on campus. The school has a new library; in 1992 the new middle school was completed; and dormitories, kitchens and dining rooms were renovated in 1992. A new gym and a renovation to the art center are expected to be completed by fall 1996.

BEACON COUNTRY DAY SCHOOL
6100 E. Belleview Ave.
Denver   771-3990
150 Students/PreK-8/Coed
$5,700

Beacon Country Day School is a private, nonprofit school on a large acreage in Greenwood Village. The programs use each child's interests to promote learning in classrooms designed for small learning groups. The grounds have a pond and a variety of natural ecology for children to explore. This school also has ponies that the children learn to care for and ride.

Photo: Daily Camera

The Dalton B. Trumbo Fountain area at the University of Colorado-Boulder is dedicated in the name of free speech.

BETHLEHEM LUTHERAN SCHOOL
7470 W. 22nd Ave.
Lakewood   233-0401
450 Students/PreK-8/Coed
$1,200-$2,300

Bethlehem Lutheran is part of the national network of Lutheran schools, the largest Protestant school group in the country. It offers a quality education in the Christian environment and has received National Lutheran School Accreditation. It has a good music program, computer lab instruction and interscholastic athletics, as well as an advanced reading program for students in third through sixth grades.

CHRISTIAN WAY SCHOOLS
14700 E. Mississippi Ave.
Aurora   751-2014
250 Students/K-6/Coed
$1,150 for K; $2,250 for 1-6

Christian Way Schools offers traditional secular academic studies combined with religious instruction. A nonsectarian Colorado corporation, the Christian Way Schools is sponsored by independent, autonomous Christian churches and Churches of Christ in Colorado. The school professes not to be in rebellion against public education but rather to be an extension of the home and church.

COLORADO ACADEMY
3800 S. Pierce St.
Denver   986-1501
650 Students/PreK-12/Coed
$4,000-$9,950

Among Colorado's most respected private schools, Colorado Academy is in southwest Denver on a lovely 75-acre campus. It's a college preparatory program emphasizing a well-rounded education in academics, fine arts and athletics with a 10-1 ratio of students to teachers. Bus transportation is available.

COLORADO CATHOLIC ACADEMY
11180 W. 44th Ave.
Wheat Ridge   422-9549
50 Students/1-12/Coed
$1,500 1-8; $2,000 9-12

Near the western edge of Wheat Ridge, this Academy offers a traditional curriculum and teaches the Catholic faith. Students attend daily Latin Mass and Rosary.

DENVER ACADEMY

1101 S. Race St.
Denver   777-5870
280 Students/3-12/Coed
$8,950

The Academy applies a structured, closely supervised and highly personalized approach to educating students who have intellectual aptitude but need help realizing their potential. This school has a 6-to-1 student-teacher ratio.

DENVER CHRISTIAN SCHOOLS

2135 S. Pearl St.
Denver   733-9085
970 Students/K-12/Coed
$1,900-$4,810

Denver Christian Schools was established by a small group that settled here before World War I, many of whom were from the Netherlands and ill with tuberculosis. Since the first classes in 1917, DCS has grown to four schools at three Denver locations: Denver Christian Middle School and Denver Christian High School, both at 2135 S. Pearl; Van Dellen Elementary School, 4200 E. Warren Ave.; and Highlands Ranch Elementary School, 1733 E. Dad Clark Drive.

FAITH CHRISTIAN ACADEMY

6210 Ward Rd.
Arvada   424-7310
1,110 Students/K-12/Coed
$2,395

A unique, charismatic Christian school, Faith is open to anyone interested in a Christian education. The curriculum includes the full range of traditional subjects.

FOOTHILLS ACADEMY

4725 Miller St.
Wheat Ridge   431-0920
185 Students/K-12/Coed
$5,500 K-8; $6,500 9-12

Valued by alumni and children of alumni, this is one of those schools where word of mouth is the best advertising. The small and interactive classes expose children to basic skills as well as art, music, foreign languages, physical education and an extensive outdoor education program. Foothills emphasizes "experiential learning and exploration," with field trips and visiting artist programs, outdoor experiences and community projects and services. Once a month, they conduct a "mini-society" in which students buy and sell homemade goods, act out the workings of government and simulate success in the real world.

GRALAND COUNTRY DAY SCHOOL

30 Birch St.
Denver   399-0390
595 Students/K-9/Coed
$7,535-$8,555
Extras, $100-$850

Among Denver's premier private schools, Graland has a history of fostering academic and personal growth. Its enrollment is limited to maintain small classes and close interaction between teachers and students. Graland is in a residential neighborhood five miles south of downtown Denver.

GOOD SHEPHERD CATHOLIC SCHOOL

940 Fillmore St.
Denver   377-8018
425 Students/PreK-8/Coed
$2,000 Parishioners
$2,650 Non-Parishioners

Actually two schools, an elementary and a middle school, Good Shepherd is between Sixth Avenue and East Colfax Avenue, York Street and Colorado Boulevard. It's a Christian education along with core educational curriculum. The Enrichment program is a before- and after-school program, between 6:45 AM and 6 PM, that includes guided study time, structured play time and extracurricular activities. A Montessori program is also available for age 3 through grade 4.

HERZL JEWISH DAY SCHOOL
2450 S. Wabash St.
Denver   755-1846
315 Students/K-6/Coed
$5,690

This school's basic approach is an education emphasizing the students' connections within the Jewish community, but also their connection in the world at large. Along with a primary focus on integrated secular and Judaic education, the school pursues a pluralistic approach to Jewish education, emphasizing respect for both the diversity of Jewish cultures and other religions. Hebrew background is a requirement, because Hebrew is taught through all grades.

HOLY FAMILY HIGH SCHOOL
4343 Utica St.
Denver   458-8822
300 Students/9-12/Coed
$3,600-$4,000

Founded in 1922 as a parish high school, Holy Family's mission statement proclaims a Catholic-Christian learning environment that "stresses academic excellence, fosters mutual respect, demands responsibility and encourages self-growth." Besides the standard high school core curriculum, there are also courses in subjects such as theology, journalism, advanced computer applications, law and drama.

HUMANEX ACADEMY
3222 S. Vance St., Ste. 100
Lakewood   985-0050
56 Students/9-12/Coed
$7,600

This alternative high school is for students ages 13 to 21 who may not have been successful in other schools. Humanex is dedicated to the idea that every student can succeed in the proper environment. The school has a student-teacher ratio of 7-to-1, a closed campus, progress reports to parents every two weeks and parent notification within 20 minutes after school starts if the student does not show up.

KENT DENVER SCHOOL
4000 E. Quincy Ave.
Englewood   770-7660
580 Students/6-12/Coed
$9,900

Kent Denver has roots going back to the founding of the Kent School for girls in 1922 and the founding of the Denver Country Day School for boys. The two schools merged to create the present institution in 1974. Its challenging, college-preparatory curriculum produced an average SAT score of 1,075 in the graduating class of 1994, 173 points above the national average. Kent Denver has a campus of 200 acres with five academic build-

The need for new school construction is often highest in fast-growth communities with the lowest tax bases, and these are often right next to school districts with plenty of tax base and little need. In the Greater Denver region, Douglas County and Bennett are among these high-growth communities that are hard-pressed for school capital construction funding.

Insiders' Tips

ings that include 43 classrooms and laboratories, six studios for music, dance and art, two gymnasiums, six tennis courts and 20 acres of playing fields.

THE LOGAN SCHOOL
1836 Logan St.
Denver   830-0326
185 Students/K-8/Coed
$6,400

A school for gifted and creative children ages 4 through 14, The Logan School for Creative Learning boasts a stimulating academic program with hands-on learning experiences. Admission requires a minimum IQ test score of 125.

LUTHERAN HIGH SCHOOL
3201 W. Arizona Ave.
Denver   934-2345
360 Students/9-12/Coed
$3,175 Association church members;
$4,775 others

Owned by the Colorado Lutheran High School Association, Lutheran High has been operating since 1955 on a 12-acre campus in southwest Denver. It was named in 1991 as one of 222 national recipients (four in the state) of the National Exemplary School award for exceptional educational services with outstanding staff in an atmosphere conducive to achieving excellence.

MACHEBEUF CATHOLIC HIGH SCHOOL
1958 Elm St.
Denver   322-1819
360 Students/9-12/Coed
$3,600 if church affiliated; $4,000 if not

Students' "responsibility as children of God in a democratic society" is the underlying theme of education at Machebeuf — that and preparation for college. The school boasts more than 95 percent of its graduates enrolled in college by graduation, and it employs a full-time college admissions counselor. By graduation, the 63 graduates in the class

of 1995 had earned more than $1.7 million in scholarships.

MARANATHA CHRISTIAN CENTER
7180 Oak St.
Arvada   431-5653
935 students/PreK-12/Coed
$2,100

A Bible-believing, non-denominational educational center, with Christ-centered academics taught by qualified, born-again staff, Maranatha was opened in 1982 on an agricultural piece of land that previously had been occupied by a house and barn.

Now its 15 acres include more than 70,000 square feet of classrooms, offices, a gymnasium, locker rooms, a learning center, a library and a computer lab.

MILE HIGH ADVENTIST ACADEMY
711 E. Yale Ave.
Denver   744-1069
330 Students/K-12/Coed
$1,910-$4,075

This school dates back to a one-room school established by Seventh-Day Adventists in Denver in 1913. The themes here are academic excellence, individual resourcefulness and responsibility, Christian philosophy and making the world a better place within the student's sphere of influence.

MOST PRECIOUS BLOOD PARISH SCHOOL
3959 E. Iliff Ave.
Denver   757-1279
490 Students/Pre-K - 8/Coed
$2,075-$2,600 grades 1-8
$1,300-$1,562 for out-of-parish K
$695-$980 pre-K

You've got your standard curriculum here, along with religious instruction including morning prayer, Mass once a month and religious education. The school also features geography and spelling bees, science and art fairs, speech meets, and a "super citizens program" in which grades 3-5 choose a supercitizen from their class each month to be honored by the Colorado Optimists Club.

J.K. MULLEN HIGH SCHOOL
3601 S. Lowell Blvd.
Denver   761-1764
800 Students/9-12/Coed
$4,475

One of Denver's more well-known Catholic private high schools, Mullen was founded in 1931 as a home for orphaned boys. In 1965 it became J.K. Mullen Prep, a college-prep school for boys. It has been coeducational since 1989. It's conducted by the Christian Brothers, a religious teaching order.

OUR LADY OF FATIMA
10350 W. 20th Ave.
Lakewood   233-2500
500 Students/PreK-8/Coed
$700-$2,750

Catholicism, of course, is the philosophical bent of this school, with religious instruction in addition to the academic courses one expects. The school has an extensive athletic program as well as special features including a science lab and a computer lab. In the 1995-96 school year, Fatima became the first school in Colorado to link up with the Learn Star program, a California-based, satellite-mediated interactive computer system that allows Fatima students to compete on-line with other schools nationwide on a weekly basis.

REGIS JESUIT HIGH SCHOOL
16300 E. Weaver Pl.
Aurora   699-1598
730 Students/9-12/Men
$4,400

Regis has the Jesuit-school mystique of quality education with a public-ser-

vice mentality. Special senior projects, volunteerism, student retreats, counseling and peer tutoring are among the additions to regular curriculum here, as well as college credit earned from Regis University.

ST. ANNE'S EPISCOPAL SCHOOL
2701 S. York St.
Denver   756-9481
420 Students/PreK-8/Coed
$5,200-$8,200

A state- and nationally accredited school founded in 1950, St. Anne's gives students a broad traditional education with emphasis on balancing academic excellence, artistic endeavor and athletic achievement while engaging students in community service and moral development. Located on 10 acres in southeast Denver, the school encourages parental involvement.

ST. FRANCIS DE SALES SCHOOL
235 S. Sherman St.
Denver   744-7231
225 Students/K-8/Coed
$1,800

Since 1904 this Catholic school has been serving the same neighborhood south of downtown Denver, combining religious instruction and experiences with a strong basic curriculum and small classes.

ST. JAMES CATHOLIC SCHOOL
1250 Newport St.
Denver   333-8275
230 Students/Preschool-8/Coed
$1,960-$2,600

On Denver's far eastern side, just northwest of Lowry Air Force Base, St. James tries to provide a value-based education that emphasizes academic excellence, self-direction, responsibility, a genuine love of learning and the wherewithal to become solid Catholic citizens.

St. John's Academy

Fourth Ave. and Renegade Way
Denver   893-3735
125 Students/K-8/Coed
$4,125-$4,925

St. John's moved in the summer of 1995 to the former Lowry Air Force Base, but it's the same individually guided education school in which teachers encourage children to learn at their ability in a small, structured-class framework. A nonprofit corporation founded in 1981 by a group of parents and educators, St. John's takes a holistic approach toward teaching the child as a total person to foster positive self-images, goal attainment, an appreciation of structure and responsibility and respect for others.

St. Louis School

3301 S. Sherman
Englewood   762-8307
200 Students/K-8/Coed
$1,590 Catholic; $2,279 non-Catholic

Mastery of the basics is the focus at St. Louis School, along with art, music, computer training and programs such as Junior Achievement, Great Books and Community Resource. It's a Catholic-sponsored school, but a large part of the student body is non-Catholic. There's religious instruction, student-prepared Masses and special sacramental instruction.

St. Mary's Academy

4545 S. University Blvd.
Englewood   762-8300
695 Students/Coed PreK-8, Girls only 9-12
$5,900

St. Mary's Academy is a Catholic, independent school founded in 1864 by the Sisters of Loretto. In 1875, it awarded the first high school diploma in the Colorado Territory. Among its special features are its Early Learning Center, at the Denver Tech Center, and the all-girls' high school where the program is based on current research on girls' learning. St. Mary's emphasizes values-based education, small classes, strong curriculum, personalized attention and community service. And its Lacrosse team seems to be taking the state title on a regular basis.

St. Therese School

12000 Kenton St.
Aurora   364-7494
390 Students/K-8/Coed
$2,400

St. Therese's includes Catholic teaching with its conventional curriculum. It's staffed by Sisters of Charity as well as lay teachers. It includes a reading specialist and full-time teachers in physical education, computer science and music education.

St. Vincent de Paul School

1164 S. Josephine St.
Denver   777-3812
570 Students/Pre-8/Coed
$1,865-$2,565

A Catholic parish school, St. Vincent's primary purpose for existence is to pass on the Catholic faith, and it accompanies that mission with all the standard core academic subjects. Special features include a technology program and full-time teachers for computer education, art, music and physical education. The student-teacher ratio is 25-to-1.

Sts. Peter and Paul Catholic Elementary School

3920 Pierce St.
Wheat Ridge   424-0402
350 Students/PreK-8/Coed
$1,950 Catholics; $2,200 non-Catholics

One of the west side's better-known Catholic schools, Sts. Peter and Paul provides sound academics and Catholic values and traditions. Features of its integrated curriculum include a literature program, computers, art, music, speech and drama, Family Math and physical education.

Photo: Daily Camera/Lourie Zipf

Colorado Academy students wait for their buses.

SHRINE OF ST. ANNE CATHOLIC SCHOOL

7320 Grant Place
Arvada   422-1800
510 Students/K-8/Coed
$2,110

A high-quality, well-rounded curriculum in basic academics is accompanied by daily classes in religion. The school describes itself as a "Christian community witnessing to the gospel message of Jesus Christ." Special features include an education fair, a science fair and a life education program, which tackles real-world issues that students face and will face in life. New, or just a couple of years old, are the school's computer lab, science lab and library.

SILVER STATE BAPTIST SCHOOL

875 S. Sheridan Blvd.
Lakewood   922-8850
380 Students/K-12/Coed
$1,500-$2,300

Strong in music and orchestra, with daily Bible classes, Silver State has its own mix of standard educational curricula along with educational direction from the Bob Jones Press. The school also partici-

pates in interscholastic sports governed by the Colorado High School Sports Athletic Association.

THE DENVER WALDORF SCHOOL

735 E. Florida Ave.
Denver   777-0531
275 Students/K-11/Coed
$4,300

The "Waldorf Movement" emphasizes working with the whole child, not just the mind, everything evolving through art. The school doesn't use textbooks. Rather teachers present the subjects, and students, through what they've learned, create their own narratives and illustrations, their own textbooks. By eighth grade, a lot of them have already had chemistry, biology, geometry, algebra. Beginning in first grade, German and Russian languages are mandatory, and by 8th grade they also have the option of taking Spanish.

WESTLAND CHRISTIAN ACADEMY

430 S. Kipling
Lakewood   986-5509
285 Students/K-12/Coed
$1,500-$2,000

"Academic excellence in Christian education" is the motto of this school maintained by Westland Baptist Church. The Christ-centered and Bible-based education has a traditional academic curriculum and daily chapel service. The school has three main classroom buildings on a 4.6-acre campus.

YESHIVA TORAS CHAIM SCHOOL

1400 Quitman St.
Denver   629-8200
85 Students/9-12, plus Talmudical seminary/ Men
$9,500 Tuition and Board

This private orthodox Jewish high school would be one of many in New York, but here in the Rocky Mountain area it has been unique since its founding in 1967. Half of each day is spent in studying Talmud and Torah, and the other half is spent in secular studies.

Colleges and Universities

CHAPMAN UNIVERSITY

1400 S. Colorado Blvd. Ste 430
Denver   753-6551

This is an academic center of Chapman University, based in Orange, California, that offers accelerated evening classes for adult learners. The Denver center has between 100 and 150 students at any given time who are working on bachelor of science degrees in business administration and computer information systems, or master of science degrees in human resources management and development and sports medicine.

COLORADO CHRISTIAN UNIVERSITY

9277 W. Alameda, Service Rd.
Lakewood   202-0100

As the only major evangelical Christian university in the Rocky Mountain region, Colorado Christian University offers NCAS fully accredited undergraduate and graduate courses with 25 undergraduate majors. CCU also offers programs designed to serve the social and spiritual needs of all students. The University has an enrollment of more than 2,600 students in all programs. In addition to its Lakewood campus, CCU administers a Foothills campus in Morrison specializing in graduate-level education in counseling. The School of Graduate and Professional studies offers accelerated evening, weekend and on-site corporate classes (on-site training to company personnel) for adult learners, with centers at Lakewood's main campus, at the Higher Education and Advanced Technology Center at Lowry and in Colorado Springs and Grand Junction. It offers undergraduate and graduate degrees and a teacher-recertification program. CCU is a division II member of NCAA, competing in men's and women's basketball, soccer, track and tennis, in addition to women's volleyball and men's golf. CCU also owns and operates a radio network consisting of KWBI-Denver, KJOL-Grand Junction and KDHR-Glenwood Springs.

COLORADO SCHOOL OF MINES

1500 Illinois
Golden   273-3000

"Mines," as it's called, is a school of engineering, energy, environment and economics nationally known for academic rigor. That reputation was recognized recently when Mines was placed in the first tier of national universities in the annual *U.S. News & World Report* rankings of "America's Best Colleges." That magazine also ranked Mines as the 16th "best buy" ("quality education at a relatively reasonable cost") nationally, just behind Harvard. Mines was founded in Golden in 1874 because that city was the gateway to Colorado's booming minerals mining industry. A public school, Mines now focuses on areas such as engineering, engineering systems, chemical engineering, petroleum engineering, mining engineering, economics, geology and geological engineering. Degrees are also available in chemistry, geochemistry and physics. Its metallurgical, materials science, environmental science and engineering programs are among the best in the nation, and not surprisingly, Mines is strong in math and computer science.

Mines also has the benefit of a beautiful location. Golden is nestled against the Foothills behind South Table Mountain from Denver and retains a small-town atmosphere. Mines is on its uphill side, a close walk from downtown. Golden is also connected by I-70 and U.S. Highway 6 directly into Denver, by I-70 into the mountains and by U.S. Highway 6 W. through scenic Clear Creek Canyon into the Gilpin County/Clear Creek County historic mining areas and mountain communities.

Golden claims a higher per-capita concentration of Ph.Ds than Boulder, home of the University of Colorado.

COLORADO STATE UNIVERSITY
Fort Collins, Denver 573-6318

Colorado State University in Fort Collins is the state's most highly esteemed school after the University of Colorado, and in some ways it stands way out in front. CSU is ranked among the top 115 universities nationwide. Forty percent of its majors are not available anywhere else in the state. It's nationally famous for its College of Natural Resources and its School of Veterinary Medicine. Faculty member Marty Fettman was a space shuttle astronaut and the first veterinarian in space. CSU is the state's only land-grant university, and CSU's Agricultural Experiment Station and Cooperative Extension form the edu-

cation/research backbone of Colorado's agriculture industry.

CSU's Denver-area educational and technical services are found in a single location, the Colorado State University Denver Center. Located downtown in the Petroleum Building at 16th Street and Broadway are the educational services aimed heavily toward downtown Denver's working population. Housed in the Denver Center are study programs extended from the Fort Collins campus, the Executive MBA program of the College of Business, Cooperative Extension's Denver County office, the Colorado State Forest Service and the Mid-America Manufacturing Technology Center. Offerings include courses in education, vocational education, business and professional and personal advancement.

COLUMBIA COLLEGE
2530 S. Parker Rd.
Aurora 755-7561

This is actually an extension center of the Columbia College campus in Columbia, Missouri, but it's a sizeable operation. Some 700 students attend evening classes here, working toward associate and baccalaureate degrees in the liberal arts, business administration, computer information systems, psychology, criminal justice, history, government and other subjects. It's primarily adult education, with an average student age of 32.

EMBRY-RIDDLE AERONAUTICAL UNIVERSITY
6786 S. Revere Pkwy.
Englewood 790-8486

Since its founding in Cincinnati, Ohio, in 1926, Embry-Riddle has been devoted exclusively to aviation-related education. In addition to residential campuses in Arizona and Florida, it has 100 off-campus centers in the United States and Europe (including the Englewood location) dedicated to working adults in a nontraditional setting. Embry-Riddle is a four-year, regionally accredited institution with bachelor's and master's degrees including bachelor of science in professional aeronautics, management of technical operations, master of aeronautical science and master of business administration in aviation. The Denver center was started in 1993.

METROPOLITAN STATE COLLEGE OF DENVER

1006 11th Ave.
Denver   *556-3058*

Metro State, Colorado's third-largest college, is a cosmopolitan city college on a 175-acre oasis on the edge of Denver's downtown business district. Half of its student body is students of traditional college age (18-25), and half consists of nontraditional students — those over the age of 25 who have already been in the work force. This, of course, can be a delight to professors who find they are dealing not just with students fresh out of high school but with professional adults as well. And it's great for students, because they can learn from their peers as well as their professors. Metro State has a reputation as the working student's college, with an emphasis on applied education, and takes pains to accommodate that student with a lot of weekend and evening classes.

The main campus, the Auraria Higher Education Center, is unique. Metropolitan State College of Denver shares the campus with two other institutions, the Community College of Denver and the University of Colorado at Denver. The three schools together offer a more potent education package than any one could alone because they allow students to cross-register for classes in all

three schools and enjoy a combined menu of lectures, concerts, plays and student programs.

Metro State offers a full lineup of NCAA intercollegiate athletic competitions in 10 men's and women's sports. The teams use one of the region's best athletic facilities, the Auraria Events Center, which seats more than 3,000 and is used for a variety of campus-wide events.

Metro State has all the elements of a traditional university, such as extensive physical education facilities, one of Greater Denver's best libraries and a quiet, tree-lined campus. The historic 19th-century Bavarian-style brewery, the Tivoli, which until recently was an independent shopping center, has been transformed into one of the country's most picturesque student unions. The Tivoli houses shops, the campus bookstore, restaurants, a 12-screen theater, recreation rooms and nightclubs as well as student offices and services.

Although there are not on-campus dormitories, many students get assistance from the campus housing office to live on their own in surrounding apartments. Plus, Metro State is just an easy walk from downtown Denver, the Denver Center for the Performing Arts, Elitch Gardens amusement park, Coors Field, the nightlife and restaurants of Lower Downtown, and Mile High Stadium.

Oh yes, and Metro State has classes too, 2,400 of them each fall and spring. The emphasis at Metro State is on individual attention, with an average class size of just 23 students. Each class is taught by a master teacher; no student teaching assistants here. Summer offerings are also available.

Metro State has 50 majors and 69 minors in addition to the "build-your-own" contract major degree option. Degree offerings cover business, performing and visual arts, liberal arts, natural and social sciences, and specialty areas such as criminology, aerospace and aviation, and engineering technology.

Metro State also operates two other campuses that offer degree programs and specialty classes. Metro South, in Englewood, offers evening and weekend classes to more than 2,500 students from southeast Denver. Metro North, in Northglenn, serves the northern suburbs.

NATIONAL COLLEGE

1325 S. Colorado Blvd.
Denver   *758-6700*

Aimed at the career interests of the nontraditional adult student, the average student age here is 30. National College offers bachelor's degrees in accounting, applied management, business administration and computer information systems; associate degrees in accounting, applied management, business administration, computer information systems and travel and tourism; and diplomas in the areas of accounting clerk, business, computer operator, travel and airline careers.

REGIS UNIVERSITY

3333 Regis Blvd.
Denver   *458-4100*

Regis University got a nice big PR boost in the summer of 1993, when it was chosen as the spot where President Bill Clinton met with Pope John Paul II on the Pope's historic visit to Denver. Secret Service helicopters buzzed like flies over the surrounding residential neighborhoods. Regis has been around for a long time, founded in 1877, and it has a pretty 90-acre main campus, about 9,000 students and a sterling reputation as an educational institution. It's a Colorado Jesuit university, centered around the Ignatius Loyola philosophy of leaders in service of others. Regis pursues that philosophy in three colleges: Regis

College, The School for Professional Studies and The School for Health Care Professions.

Regis College itself is a relatively small school, with about 1,100 undergraduate students studying liberal arts, sciences, business and education. The student-faculty ratio is 16-to-1.

The School for Professional Studies has undergraduate and graduate programs in business, education and computer sciences and offers classes in Denver, Colorado Springs, Loveland, Boulder, Sterling, three Colorado mountain locations and Wyoming.

The School for Health Care Professions is particularly well-known among the Greater Denver nursing community. Its graduate and undergraduate programs include nursing, physical therapy and health care administration and management.

UNIVERSITY OF COLORADO

Boulder   *492-1411*

Known in the vernacular as CU, this flagship institution of higher education in Colorado was founded in 1876, the year in which Colorado became a state. Today it is a university of international prominence. The university's campuses in Boulder, Denver and Colorado Springs, (719) 593-300, have a combined student body of about 45,000, and each campus has its own specific mission.

The University of Colorado at Boulder, or CU-Boulder, is where the university started, and it's still its largest and most important campus. Placed in the beautiful setting of Boulder's University Hill, its 786 acres of rural Italian-style buildings and complexes of Colorado sandstone make it one of the nation's most aesthetically pleasing campuses. A 1991 book, *The Campus as a Work of Art,* by Thomas Gaines, ranked CU-Boulder fourth among 50 of the "most artistically successful campuses in the country." Because of nearby skiing and the many outdoor activities available, and because it's often the campus of choice for wealthy students who want a most excellent place in which to spend their campus years, some people think of CU as a "party school." But CU-Boulder is far more than the place where film actor and director Robert Redford played on the baseball team and waited tables in a local bar.

CU-Boulder excels as both a teaching and a research university. *U.S. News & World Report* in 1994 ranked it among the nation's best buys for instate tuition. In 1995, the same magazine ranked CU-Boulder fourth in the nation for its environmental law program and among the top 25 in the nation (the only state institution so ranked) for its master's of music program, its biology doctoral program, its chemistry doctoral program, its graduate psychology program, its graduate education program, and its graduate engineering program. CU, which received $17 million in NASA funding in 1993-94, has 13 alumni who have flown in space.

CU-Boulder's leading programs include telecommunications, aerospace engineering and atmospheric and space physics. The department of molecular, cellular and developmental biology is ranked among the top 10 national doctoral programs by the National Research Council. The chemistry and biochemistry department boasts 1989 Nobel Laureate Thomas Cech among its teaching faculty. CU-Boulder funneled more than $143 million into research during the 1993-94 fiscal year, and it has a separate 147-acre research park nearby, which includes US West Advanced Technologies as a tenant.

These and other programs, including the schools of law, business and administration, education, journalism and mass communications, arts and science, music, architecture and planning, offer more than 2,500 courses in more than 150 fields of study to some 25,000 students.

UNIVERSITY OF COLORADO AT DENVER
1250 14th St.
Denver   556-3287

Established in 1912 to make the state university available in Denver, this is still Denver's only public university. CU-Denver, or "CU in the City," today has 83 undergraduate and graduate programs. CU-Denver shares the 175-acre Auraria Higher Education Center campus with Metropolitan State College of Denver and the Community College of Denver. Students can cross-register for classes in all three schools. The more than 6,100 undergraduate students at CU-Denver are therefore part of a much larger student body and enjoy academic and extracurricular opportunities greater than those provided by CU-Denver alone. Undergraduate class size averages 22 students.

Being 26 miles away from CU's main campus in Boulder has not detracted from CU-Denver's prominence. *U.S. News & World Report* in 1992 ranked it as one of the nation's top 15 academic regional universities and one of the three best education buys in the West. A five-minute walk from downtown Denver, CU-Denver makes the opportunities of a state university available to working students in an urban environment. Strong programs include its School of the Arts, business and administration, engineering and applied science, architecture and planning, and education.

UNIVERSITY OF COLORADO
HEALTH SCIENCES CENTER
4900 E. Ninth Ave.
Denver   399-1211

This is Colorado's only academic health center and the seat of medical research in the region. The 40-acre campus offers baccalaureate and graduate programs in medicine, nursing, dentistry, pharmacy and health-related fields. It includes two hospitals, University Hospital and the Colorado Psychiatric Hospital, as well as eight research institutes. The center is as prominent nationally in research as it is regionally in medical education, and renowned in numerous fields including transplants, cancer, neuroscience, molecular biology, perinatal care and cardiovascular services.

UNIVERSITY OF DENVER
2199 S. University Blvd.
Denver   *871-2000*

This is the oldest independent university in the Rocky Mountain region, founded in 1864, and the reason why one of Denver's main north/south thoroughfares is named University Boulevard. In a residential area eight miles southeast of downtown, the University of Denver, called "DU" by locals, is a good combination of big-university experience and small liberal-arts-college atmosphere. The campus includes 100 buildings on 125 acres. Its Lamont School of Music and its College of Law are located on the university's Park Hill campus, formerly Colorado Women's College. The student body counts about 8,600. About 3,000 of those are graduate students, and plenty of faculty members are at the forefront of research in their fields. Still, the university is a good place to spend one's undergraduate years. The student-faculty ratio is 13-to-1 for undergraduates. Class sizes average 20 students, and 29 percent of classes have nine or fewer students. Undergraduate degrees are available in arts, fine arts, music, music education, science, business administration, accounting, chemistry, electrical engineering and mechanical engineering. Campus Connection, a mentoring program, joins each new freshman with a faculty adviser in his or her major area of study and arranges special campus functions including an annual retreat in Estes Park for all new freshmen.

UNIVERSITY OF PHOENIX
3151 S. Vaughn Way
Aurora   *755-9090*

This is the Colorado Campus of the University of Phoenix, which is based, of course, in Phoenix, Arizona, but has 29 campuses in seven states, Puerto Rico and Hungary. To attend you have to be at least 23 years old and have at least two years of full-time work behind you. This university focuses on degree programs and services for working adults. Students from US West, for example, take classes at their company, and UP designs customized educational programs and seminars for many other companies as well. Degrees range from nursing and business administration to educational administration, computer information systems and technology management. UP has about 3,000 students in metropolitan Denver, Colorado Springs and Grand Junction.

WEBSTER UNIVERSITY
12500 E. Iliff Ave.
Aurora   *750-6665*

Webster University is based in St. Louis, Missouri, and has about 10,335 students worldwide; about two-thirds of them graduate. The Denver Campus in Aurora has about 250 students taking graduate courses in business administration, business, computer resources and information management, health services management, human resources development, human resources management, and procurement and acquisitions management. All programs are designed for working adults and offered in the evening format.

Community Colleges

ARAPAHOE COMMUNITY COLLEGE
2500 W. College Dr.
Littleton   794-1550

Arapahoe Community College's 7,500-plus students attend classes on a 51-acre campus adjacent to Littleton's downtown and just east of the South Platte River, which affords great mountain views to the west. It was established by ballot as Arapahoe Junior College in 1965 as the first two-year college in Greater Denver when west-side residents decided there was a need for a local junior college. It joined the Colorado State System of Community Colleges in 1970 as Arapahoe Community College.

Arapahoe leans toward two-year associate's degrees that help students enhance their careers with a degree or certificate, often while working. Some 60 percent of its students are working students. But courses can also transfer to a four-year college or university. The college has more than 70 degree and certificate programs in both academic and vocational areas, with more than 2,400 classes per year. The average class size is 17 students, and the average cost of education here is 10 to 60 percent less than most Colorado four-year schools.

The college also operates satellite classrooms at the Triad, at I-25 and Orchard Road, and at Deer Creek Middle School in South Jefferson County.

COMMUNITY COLLEGE OF AURORA
16000 E. Centretech Pkwy.
Aurora   360-4700

Community College of Aurora has been the community college of Greater Denver's east side since its founding in 1983. It moved to a new 35-acre campus just west of Buckley Air National Guard Base in 1991

and, with the closing of Lowry Air Force Base, Community College of Aurora opened a second campus there in the fall of 1994, the Lowry Higher Education Center. Like other community colleges, it accommodates adult learners. The 5,400 students average 31 years in age.

Community College of Aurora offers the full range of courses needed by students planning to transfer to four-year institutions with associate of arts and associate of science degrees. It has vocational programs that focus on an associate of applied science degree and training for employment certification. And it provides a menu of courses that serves a wide variety of interests by east-siders interested in learning. The college's faculty development program, which trains faculty in better methods of teaching students, has won several national awards and has been used as a model for schools across the country.

COMMUNITY COLLEGE OF DENVER
1111 W. Colfax Ave.
Denver   556-2600

With about 12,000 full-time and part-time students, this is Greater Denver's "inner-city" community college. It shares the Auraria Higher Education Center's 175-acre campus with Metropolitan State College of Denver (MSCD) and the University of Colorado at Denver. Around 37,000 students can cross-register in the courses of all three schools.

The college offers degree programs in the full range of college subjects, as well as transfer courses for the baccalaureate degree, occupational programs for job entry skills or upgrading, remedial instruction and GED prep, continuing education, community services and cooperative programs with the other schools.

FRONT RANGE COMMUNITY COLLEGE
3645 W. 112 Ave.
Westminster 466-8811

The community college of Greater Denver's north side, Front Range Community College is Colorado's largest community college. It has about 11,000 students at its 80-acre Westminster main campus, with another 6,000 on campuses in Fort Collins, Longmont and Boulder and from Loveland High School. Front Range has 64 degree and certificate programs, including associate's degrees in arts, science and general studies, as well as degrees and certificates in applied sciences.

Front Range offers classes for GED, English as a second language, literacy courses and classes for students with learning disabilities. Front Range is the leader among local community colleges in delivering courses at business and industry work sites, including companies such as AT&T in Westminster, Geneva Pharmaceuticals in Broomfield and Rocky Flats in Jefferson County, where Front Range has 600 employee-students. Front Range's hazardous materials technology program, by the way, is well known nationally and one of the first such programs in the country. Front Range is also the only place in the West teaching hearing people to interpret for the deaf. Its nursing program won acclaim as a 1994 program of excellence, and in addition to its vocational programs, it has 60 courses that transfer to four-year schools. Locals can also take a lot of fun, lifelong learning courses such as handwriting analysis and garden management.

RED ROCKS COMMUNITY COLLEGE
13300 W. Sixth Ave.
Lakewood 988-6160

Red Rocks claims to be the fastest-growing institution of higher learning in the state, and given its location, that's not hard to believe. Its 140-acre main campus perches on the western edge of Lakewood, in some of Jefferson County's fastest-growing territory. It's also near the site where a major developer recently announced plans for a prestige shopping center to rival the Cherry Creek shopping mall, not a bad idea considering all the wealth in the mountain communities to the immediate west. Red Rocks' enrollment of 7,200 students in the winter and 3,500 in the summer represents a 62-percent growth over the last six years.

Red Rocks was founded in 1969 as a two-year institution. It also serves northwest metro suburbanites with the Arvada Education and Training Center in Arvada and mountain communities with the Mountain Area Center in Conifer.

Its largest enrollments are in math, followed by sciences, computer information systems, English, psychology, fire science technology and criminal justice. More than half of the student reasons for attending Red Rocks are job-related. The college has special programs in construction technology, film/video technology, medical assisting and precision joining technology. The Red Rocks Institute does customized training for businesses; it served 4,000 employees in 41 companies and 446 small businesses in the 1994. The Red Rocks OSHA Training Institute is one of four sites in the nation designated by the U.S. Department of Labor for OSHA training. A Computer Access Center trains individuals with disabilities to use adaptive computer technologies.

Photo: National Academy of Nannies

Denver is home to the National Academy of Nannies.

Inside
Child Care

Greater Denver's child-care scene is much like that in any other youthful, growing area of the country: It's insufficient. Not that you should be discouraged— it seems like you always manage to find something, and there are some very nice somethings indeed. Friends of ours in Jefferson County, for example, suddenly losing their day-care provider, were worried. But they found a place in the day-care program at the Lakewood YMCA, and lo and behold, their child suddenly had swimming and gymnasium as part of his day-care activities.

Still, anyone who has tried to find quality day care will attest that it can be difficult. Waiting lists of more than a year are not uncommon. The day-care deficit is likely to be more of a problem in the higher-growth sub zones of Greater Denver. Highlands Ranch, on Denver's southern perimeter, is one such place, booming with young families. Yet Highlands Ranch parents, like parents everywhere in the area, make do. Sometimes it means the inconvenience of driving a good distance outside the route between work and home. But it's worth it if you can find a place you're happy with.

"Happy with" means a place where your children can be happy and spend their time doing something more constructive than sitting with six other children in the living room of a small apartment staring at a TV. That's a scene you'll find in some of the day-care situations to be found in Greater Denver homes. But you can also find day-care homes with plenty of room, facilities and activities, and wonderful, well-equipped yards to play in. Don't grab the first place you see, much as that may be the temptation to the hard-pressed parent.

Then there are the day-care centers, established not in homes but in facilities specifically designed for day care and employing multiple care-givers.

Colorado has just more than 1,000 licensed day-care centers and more than 3,000 day-care homes. Greater Denver has more than half of these, nearly 4,000 in all.

Douglas County has less than 300 day-care homes, yet Douglas County has the highest per capita number of day-care facilities. Jefferson County has the second-highest per capita and by far the largest number overall. Next in per capita concentration is Arapahoe County, and it's second-highest in total number. Next-to-last in per capita is Adams County.

The City and County of Denver has the lowest per capita, but in the single category of day-care centers, it leads.

School-age child-care programs that provide before- and after-school care is increasingly recognized by school districts as a way of putting their facilities to better use both in serving the community and in generating revenue. Greater Den-

Photo: Daily Camera

There are many resources to help parents find child care in the metro area.

ver has more than 300 such programs, and Arapahoe and Jefferson counties rank No. 1 and No. 2 respectively in the number available.

Preschools, part-day educational facilities that take care of kids anywhere from 2½ to 4 hours per day, are increasingly popular for early education, early socialization and helping parents get some extra time off to work or just to keep them from going insane. Greater Denver has about 200 of these.

Obviously, Greater Denver has plenty of child-care facilities with striking variations in the number and availability of facilities depending on where you are. A lot of them have waiting lists, so don't wait until the day of need has arrived to make your arrangements.

Surprise drop-in visits are a good way of finding out what a day-care facility looks like. Most day cares, of course, prefer that you call ahead and make an appointment, but even if you get turned away shortly after entry, what you see can be revealing. A reporter for Denver's *5280* magazine pulled a drop-in survey a couple of years ago and found wonderful places. That reporter also found places with stressed and yelling teachers, inadequate caretaker-to-child ratios, unpleasant odors, dirty facilities, poor security and loud rock music being played during nap time.

One thing you might want to do, once you've scanned the possibilities and settled on what look like some good ones, is check on day-care providers be-

fore you commit by calling the **Colorado Department of Human Services' Licensing Verification**, 866-5958. If you have the correct name and/or street address of the provider, the licensing verification department can look it up on the computer and let you know if the place is licensed and when the license was issued; the department can also provide other general information. Want to know if any complaints have been filed against your candidate daycare providers? Call licensing verification and ask to speak to Marlene Romero. She can set you up with an appointment to come in and view the file, providing you make a file review appointment at least 72 hours in advance.

It's probably a good idea. We know a couple who hired a day-care provider and found out later that a previous customer had lodged a complaint of child-battering. Most day-care providers are undoubtedly fine people, but a little paranoia is always a good thing when your kids are involved. Licensing verification only works for day-care providers licensed by the State of Colorado. Unlicensed day care is caveat emptor.

You can seek day care on your own, or you might want to save time by using one of the dozen or so referral agencies in the Greater Denver area. The **Work and Family Resource Center at Community College of Denver** is perhaps the most extensive of local referral agencies. It's a nonprofit agency with a data base of all licensed child-care providers in the Greater Denver area, including nannies, day-care centers and private child care. For free referrals and information about choosing quality child care, call them on their Community Line, 534-2625. Go through a voice-messaging question-and-answer session, and they'll call you back with perhaps three to five possibilities that match your criteria; you do the legwork from there. Community Line will continue to provide referrals free until you find what you're looking for. They also have a for-charge "Cadillac" service in which they do all the legwork, but this is a contract service available only to employees of customer companies. They also have "4 Parents Helpline" that provides information and referrals on a wide spectrum of parent support. The Work and Family Resource Center serves parents and child-care providers in nine counties, including those of Greater Denver.

Some referral agencies are more area-specific. **Family First Resource and Referral**, 969-9500, a nonprofit agency housed at Red Rocks Community College, helps families locate quality child care in Jefferson, Gilpin, Park and Clear Creek counties. It has a data base of about 1,200 family child-care providers and between 200 and 300 day-care centers. It also maintains a data base of family service agencies, in case you're looking for information on housing, counseling programs, parenting classes or other family services.

Among the other child-care information sources are the **Jefferson County Child Care Association**, 969-8772; the **Colorado Child Care Association**, 860-7174; **Mile High United Way's Child Care Resource and Referral** program, 433-8900, and **Child Care Aware**. The latter resource is what you will be referred to if you call the Denver YWCA, which used to have a referral program but no

longer does. Call Child Care Aware at its (800) 424-2246 number, and you will be talking to someone in Minnesota. Created by agencies including the **National Association of Child Care Resource and Referral Agencies**, Child Care Aware takes calls nationally and puts parents in touch with referral agencies in their area.

If you want a nanny, Denver is a good place to find one. **The National Academy of Nannies**, 333-6264, 1681 S. Dayton Street, in Denver, claims distinction as the oldest privately owned nanny training school in the nation. It started in 1983. A lot of parents may not be in the income bracket where they can afford the $1,200 to $1,400 per month, plus $1,500 placement fee and medical benefits that graduate nannies start at, but wait! Don't skip the rest of this paragraph! By virtue of having this West Point of nanny schools in the community, local parents can get a student nanny for just $825 per month and no additional benefits. Of course, student nannies are cheaper partly because they are available only on a live-in basis, while graduate nannies can live in or live out.

You can also go the less formal nanny route of simply advertising in the newspaper and interviewing prospects to find someone to take charge of the kids on a full-time, daily basis. The Academy prefers the term "baby-sitters" for those without formal NANI training and certification, but as long as you get a caring and competent person, you may not give a hoot for such fine distinctions.

Then there's the au pair route. A lot of people enjoy having a European au pair for the relatively low cost and the cosmopolitan experience of getting a live-in childcare helper while exposing the kids to a foreign culture. Two referral agencies for au pair services are **Au Pair in America**,

(800) 727-2437, and **AuPairCare**, (800) 288-7786.

If your needs go no further than simple baby-sitting services, one of your best options is to advertise through local high schools and churches. Put an advertisement up on their bulletin boards, and it can be the start of a long string of baby-sitters who, as they reach graduation and go on to full-time jobs or college, keep passing down recommendations to subsequent generations of younger sitters from the same institutions.

And, of course, there are your neighbors. People who never bothered to make much effort in neighbor-schmoozing before they had children suddenly find reasons why neighbors are good people to know. Part of it is the sense of security these contacts can provide, and part of it is because the kids often initiate neighborhood relationships and force their parents to get involved. But a real good incentive we've found is all those unidentified teenagers who suddenly become intensely interesting as possible neighborhood baby-sitters.

Photo: Daily Camera/Lourie Zipf

The Health Sciences Center is part of the University of Colorado.

Inside
Medical Care

There's no such thing as a great place to get sick, but if there were, Greater Denver would be it for the Rocky Mountains and Great Plains. As you'd expect, being the state's capital city and big population concentration, there are outstanding medical facilities in Greater Denver, a regional medical center.

It's not only the regional center as far as quantity of medical services, but it's a standout in quality as well. The *Places Rated Almanac* (1993) listed the Denver metro area as 43rd out of 343, or in the top 15 percent, of metropolitan areas nationwide in the quality of its health care.

Around the Denver area you'll find some 60,000 people working in health services, including more than 600 family practitioners, 1,500 medical specialists and 770 surgical specialists. At the beginning of 1995, there were 17 short-term general hospitals with some 5,580 beds, but to say how many there are right now is tough.

Our informational listing of Greater Denver hospitals is as current as possible, but the hospital picture is a rapidly moving target in these days of medical market upheaval. First of all, two of Greater Denver's

hospitals got the axe in early 1995. Included in our 1995 listings but left out this year, Mercy Medical Center was closed by vote of its board of directors, although its owner, Provenant Health Partners, plans to convert its campus into a center for out-of-hospital services. As part of the federal spending cut fervor, Fitzsimons Army Medical Center was nominated for closure by the Base Realignment and Closure Commission.

Beyond these more easily describable developments, however, rages a maelstrom of consolidations, acquisitions, partnerships and facilities changes as the hospital scene's ownership and services move around like a game of musical chairs.

Aurora Regional Medical Center, for example, was known as Humana Hospital-Aurora until Kentucky-based Humana Inc. split into two corporate entities in March 1993, and the Center became part of Galen Health Care Inc. In September 1993, another merger brought the Center under Texas-based Columbia Healthcare Corporation. In February 1994, Columbia merged with HCA-Hospital Corporation of America to become Columbia HCA Healthcare Corporation, now the biggest

One of the best ways to get a physician reference is to call a hospital. Most of the big ones have their own free physician referral service.

healthcare system in the United States. Other Greater Denver facilities owned by Columbia are North Suburban Medical Center, Columbine Psychiatric Center, Plum Creek Medical and Rocky Mountain Health Care Centers. Rose Medical Center was purchased by Columbia in 1995.

Columbia at the end of 1993 announced its intention of investing $200 to $300 million in Greater Denver by the year 2000, building a network of hospitals, psychiatric facilities and medical clinics and capturing 15 to 20 percent of all Greater Denver's hospital business. It's happened faster than that.

In 1993, P/SL Healthcare System, which had grown to include Presbyterian Denver Hospital, Aurora Presbyterian Hospital and Centennial Healthcare Plaza, merged with Swedish Medical Center to form HealthONE, which became Colorado's largest healthcare system. In 1994 HealthONE added Rocky Mountain Rehabilitation Hospital and Bethesda Psychiatric System.

In 1995, Columbia formed a partnership with HealthONE, raising its market share to more than 33 percent.

Meanwhile, Provenant Health Partners and Rocky Mountain Adventist Healthcare were holding talks in mid-1995 about forming a partnership that would have more than 20 percent of Greater Denver's hospital business. Provenant Health Partners is a comprehensive medical delivery system that forms an umbrella of ownership including Provenant St. Anthony Central Hospital, and Provenant St. Anthony Hospital North. It also included Mercy Hospital before that hospital closed in spring of 1995. Rocky Mountain Adventist includes affiliates PorterCare Hospital, Platte Valley Medical Center, PorterCare Hospital-Littleton and PorerCare Hospital-Avista, in Boulder County.

At the same time, Lutheran Medical Center and Saint Joseph Hospital joined together to form their own health plan, Primera, and were also considering a partnership with Mutual of Omaha. The National Jewish Center for Immunology and Respiratory Medicine formed an affiliation with University Hospital and Children's Hospital, in which 11 clinics would be transferred to National Jewish from the other hospitals and National Jewish would transfer in return most of its hospital beds.

It's enough to make one's head spin, but Greater Denver is still home to the state of the medical art, where hospitals and physicians work hand-in-hand with university researchers and high-technology companies. University Hospital, at the University of Colorado's Health Sciences Center University Hospital in Denver, was ranked as one of the 25 best hospitals in the country in the 1994-1995 edition of *The Best of Medicine* by Herbert J. Dietrich, M.D., and Virginia H. Biddle.

Pulmonary medicine is one example of a field in which Greater Denver enjoys worldwide renown. Some of the major hospitals in Greater Denver — including Craig and National Jewish hospitals and Swedish and Lutheran medical centers — originally began as tuberculosis treatment centers back in the days when tuberculosis patients came to Colorado for the healthy air. Not surprisingly, Greater Denver is a leader in pulmonary research and technology. If the University of Colorado's Health Sciences Center is not the world leader in pulmonary research, it's darned close. Research and expertise at institutions such as Presbyterian/St. Luke's Medical Center, National Jewish Center for Immunology and Respiratory Medicine, Rose Medical Center and the Web-Waring Lung Institute are one of the main reasons why some of the world's most advanced pulmonary technol-

*T*he shortest
distance between
you and quality
health information
isn't always
a straight line.

It can be the telephone cord
connecting your home
and ASK-A-NURSE®.

Twenty-four hours a day,
every day of the year,
ASK-A-NURSE is on call for you.
Think of us as your direct line for fast,
factual health answers
and informed physician referrals.
ASK-A-NURSE (303) 777-6877
TDD (303) 722-3833

© UNISON 1995

Porter Care
Adventist Health System

ASK-A-NURSE is a community service of Porter*Care* Adventist Health System.

ogy manufacturers make their homes in the Denver area.

Denver's other research and medical advancement highlights include the Belle Bonfils Blood Center, the Eleanor Roosevelt Institute for Cancer Research, the Barbara Davis Child Diabetes Center and the C. Henry Kempe National Center for the Prevention and Treatment of Child Abuse.

So, where do you go to look for information on doctors, hospitals and treatment centers? You can go to the extremes of research, for example, by getting a directory of Colorado hospitals from the Colorado Hospital Association, 758-1630, for $100. Or, you could just check the phone book under "Hospitals" or "Physicians." Mile High United Way is a great place to start when seeking all kinds of community service information, and medical service is no exception. You can call their United Way HelpLine at 433-8900. You can also find Greater Denver's medical and other community services in exhaustive detail by purchasing Mile High United Way's book, *Where to Turn*, a $30 value. Call Mile High United Way's HelpLine, or their administrative offices at 433-8383 to find out how to get the book.

Denver has physician referral services galore, of course, and you may want to start with the free physician referral services offered by many hospitals, including **Children's Hospital physician referral**, 861-0123; **University Physicians Inc.**, 270-6328, a service associated with University Hospital; **Ask-A-Nurse**, 777-6877, operated by the Adventist Healthcare System, including PorterCare Hospital, PorterCare Hospital-Littleton, PorterCare Hospital-Avista and the Platte Valley Medical Center; **Columbia Direct**, 450-4600, a physician and health services information bureau, offered by Aurora Regional Medical

Center; the **Healthy Directions line**, 450-4600, offered by North Suburban Medical Center; the **Rose Referral Source**, 320-7673, offered by Rose Medical Center; **CallONE**, a service of HealthONE, 788-6000; the **HealthONE Support Line**, 869-1999, for information and referral for emotional and addiction problems; **Med Search**, 866-8000, a service of Saint Joseph Hospital; **Provenant Health Partners**, 629-3814; or **Lutheran Medical Center**, 425-2255.

You can also get referrals from a lot of other organizations besides hospitals. Probably the best-known physician referral service is **Prologue**. It advertises extensively and has a catchy acronym phone number, 4-HEALTH.

You can call **Colorado Health Care Network**, 892-9085, for general physician information and referral, and the **Clear Creek Valley Medical Society**, 232-1428, can connect you with physicians in Jefferson County.

Greater Denver has more than 100 nursing homes and more than a dozen hospices, some operated in association with hospitals. A fine source of local nursing home referrals and information is **Community Housing Services**, 831-4046.

Emergency services in Greater Denver are sophisticated, including two medical helicopter groups and four certified Level I trauma centers. A good number to keep on the telephone if you have kids is that of the **Rocky Mountain Poison Center**, 629-1123, or 620-9565 for the deaf or hearing impaired.

There are plenty of 24-hour crisis counseling lines as well, including **Comitas Crisis Center Inc.**, 343-9890, and **Suicide and Crisis Control**, 756-8485. Adams County offers crisis counseling for residents of Adams County (except for Aurora) through the **Adams County Mental Health Cen-**

Photo: Daily Camera

The Greater Denver area offers basic and emergency medical care, but is a regional healthcare center as well.

ter, 287-8001. Adams and Arapahoe County offer counseling for residents of Aurora, Strasburg, Watkins and Bennett through the **Aurora Community Mental Health Center**, 693-9500. The **Arapahoe Mental Health Center**, 795-6187, has an emergency line serving Arapahoe and Douglas counties, but not Aurora. Denver residents can call the **Alcohol, Drug and Psychiatric Care emergency line**, 436-6266, at the Denver City & County Department of Health and Hospitals. Residents of Jefferson, Clear Creek and Gilpin counties can call the **Jefferson Center for Mental Health**, 425-0300. There are also two ethnic-specific counseling lines: The **Asian/ Pacific Center for Human Development**, 393-0304; and a **Hispanic line**, 458-5851, through Servicios de La Raza Inc.

Hospitals

Denver

BETHESDA HOSPITAL
4400 E. Iliff Ave.   *758-1514*
A division of HealthONE, this is a psy-

chiatric treatment center that offers the full spectrum of care for all ages. Founded in 1910 as a tuberculosis sanitorium, Bethesda is a not-for-profit center that manages about 90 inpatient beds and a variety of outpatient programs from a 20-acre campus in a residential area of Denver. Recent additions include the Center for Trauma and Dissociation, purchased in 1994 from Healthcare Concepts, and the Eating Disorders Program.

CHILDREN'S HOSPITAL
1056 E. 19th Ave.   *861-8888*
The name says it all. Kids. Children's Hospital is a healthcare system caring for kids with the full spectrum of needs from wellness and prevention through the most complex care. Children's was named by *U.S. News & World Report* as one of the top-10 hospitals nationwide in caring for kids, and it was the only hospital so recognized between Chicago and Los Angeles. Serving a 12-state region, Children's has been an innovator in medicine since it was founded in 1908, with firsts including the largest and most successful

pediatric heart transplant program, the nation's first pediatric transport system, and the discovery of Toxic Shock Syndrome. Children's mission focuses on clinical care, research, education and advocacy. Beyond the walls of the hospital, Children's offers pediatric services throughout the metropolitan area, the state and the region through partnerships with other healthcare institutions and clinics. Children's also operates four offsite specialty care centers in Aurora, Arvada, Wheat Ridge and Highlands Ranch. The hospital itself handles about 10,000 inpatient and 250,000 outpatient visits yearly. Children's is also affiliated with the University of Colorado Health Sciences Center to pool pediatrics expertise and enhance treatment and research.

COLORADO MENTAL HEALTH INSTITUTE

3520 W. Oxford Ave.   *761-0220*

This is the state psychiatric hospital, charged with providing treatment and services for the mentally ill. It was founded in 1960 and was rather revolutionary for its time as a completely open facility with no locked units. Areas of specialty fall in three treatment divisions: children/adolescents, adult psychiatry and geriatrics. An inpatient facility only, with 249 beds, this hospital is based on a treatment team approach — a patient's team consists of a psychiatrist, a psychologist, a social worker, psychiatric nurses and mental health clinicians. The team also has special education teachers for children and adolescents.

DENVER GENERAL HOSPITAL

777 Bannock St.   *893-6000*

This is Colorado's largest public hospital, operated by Denver Health and Hospitals, a City of Denver agency. That agency delivers acute-care, community health and public health services; Denver Gen-

eral is the acute-care portion. To a large extent Denver General is the safety net for Greater Denver folks regardless of their social or economic status. Nearly half of all charges for inpatient and outpatient services come from people without health insurance, and more than a third are from people covered by Medicaid and Medicare. Licensed for 349 beds, Denver General also emphasizes adolescent and adult inpatient psychiatry and handles some 3,000 childbirths a year. With expertise in managing difficult or problem deliveries, the hospital has maintained one of the lowest average Cesarean section rates (12.5 percent) in the country for more than a decade. Denver General's Rocky Mountain Regional Trauma Center serves the entire Rocky Mountain region. With more than 3,000 trauma patients annually, it is the busiest Level I trauma center in the area. During 1993-94, DGH bolstered its trauma capability with a new state-of-the-art emergency department, a surgical intensive care unit, operating suites and a laboratory. The hospital is also headquarters for the city's 911 medical emergency system, where dispatchers received more than 50,000 calls in 1994, more than 12,000 of which came to DGH. The hospital is an educational and training point for University of Colorado Medical School students, interns and residents. And all of DGH's 150 full-time physicians are also faculty at the Medical School. **Community Health Services**, 436-7430, operates 10 health centers throughout Denver and 10 student health clinics in Denver Public Schools. **Denver Public Health**, 436-7200, monitors communicable diseases such as AIDS, tuberculosis, measles and hepatitis. It operates several outpatient clinics for diagnosis and treatment of these and many other diseases. Through its Environmental Health Division, Public Health also provides a wide range of non-clinical services such as air and water pollution monitoring, restaurant inspections, licensing for day-care facilities and personal boarding-care homes, and operation of the Denver Municipal Animal Shelter.

NATIONAL JEWISH
CENTER FOR IMMUNOLOGY
AND RESPIRATORY MEDICINE
1400 Jackson St.   *388-4461*

People with asthma and other chronic respiratory diseases come here from all over the world because National Jewish has an international reputation as a leading — if not the leading — medical center for the study and treatment of chronic respiratory diseases, allergic diseases and immune system disorders.

One of those Denver medical centers that began at least in part to serve tuberculosis patients, it started in 1899 with the opening of the National Jewish Hospital for Consumptives. Today this nonsectarian medical center's staff of 570 serves patients with 248 beds and offers outpatient services at its Cohen Clinic, which doubled in size with the completion of a $5-million expansion in fall of 1994. National Jewish keeps at the forefront of its medical niches by devoting more than $10 million each year to research focusing on allergies, asthma and the immune system. One out of every five pediatric allergists in the United States was trained here.

National Jewish operates a free telephone information service known as **Lung Line** to answer questions and forward some literature on subjects such as acute bronchitis, asthma, emphysema and pneumonia. Call 355-LUNG if you're in Colorado, or (800) 222-LUNG if you're not, for the 8 AM to 5 PM service.

PORTERCARE HOSPITAL
2525 S. Downing St.   *778-1955*

Formerly Porter Memorial Hospital, PorterCare, on Denver's southern border, is a 368-bed, acute-care hospital that boasts more than 1,200 physicians. A not-for-profit organization, it's one of four — along with Platte Valley Medical Center in Brighton, PorterCare Hospital-Littleton and PorterCare Hospital-Avista in Boulder County — affiliated under Rocky Mountain Adventist Healthcare. It was founded in 1930 by Denver pioneer and businessman Henry M. Porter after he was impressed by his treatment at California hospitals that were owned by the Seventh-Day Adventist Church. He and his daughter gave the church $315,000 and 40 acres to start a hospital in Denver. The hospital's mission is "to serve as a continuation of the healing ministry of Christ." Its specialties include cancer care and cancer support, heart care and healthy heart programs, the Clyde G. Kissinger Center for Sight, the Porter Birthplace, Porter Breastcare, a center for treatment of substance abuse and eating disorders, transplant services and education programs in areas such as stress management, weight control and nutrition counseling, smoking cessation and alcohol education. A

Need specialized medical attention for your pet? Colorado State University is one of the leading veterinary schools in the nation, and Greater Denverites often take their pets there for chemotherapy or other advanced veterinary needs.

Insiders' Tips

new addition, Independence Square, helps patients return to normal activities by simulating situations patients will encounter when discharged from the hospital.

PRESBYTERIAN/
ST. LUKE'S MEDICAL CENTER
1719 E. 19th Ave.   839-6000

A division of HealthONE, this absolutely huge medical center has more than 1,000 physicians and more beds (674) and staff than any competitor in Greater Denver. You would be hard put to dispute its claim to being the most comprehensive health care provider in the Rocky Mountain West, given its amazing range of services including virtually everything you would traditionally expect of a general hospital to things such as The Mothers' Milk Bank, the Denver Broncos Sports Medicine Rehabilitation Center, the Sleep Disorders Center, the Colorado Gynecology and Continence Center, the Institute for Limb Preservation, the Senior Citizen's Health Center, the Hyperbaric Medicine Center, psychiatric services, organ and tissue transplants, Addictions Recovery Centers and a wide variety of women's and pediatric services. The list goes on and on until your head swims. The Family Birth Place was named as one of the top-10 maternity units in the United States by *Child* magazine in March 1995. Close to Pres/St. Luke, as the locals call it, The Inn at Presbyterian offers convenient lodgings to people undergoing pre-admission testing and to families of patients at very reasonable rates. Pres/St. Luke's was the anchor of the P/SL Healthcare System before that system merged with Swedish Medical Center in late 1993 to form HealthONE, and now it's the big guy in HealthONE.

PROVENANT
ST. ANTHONY HOSPITAL CENTRAL
4231 W. 16th Ave.   629-3511

St. Anthony Hospital Central was the founding hospital of Provenant Health Partners (PHP), which includes two acute-care hospitals, a continuum of senior care and a network of clinics and programs aimed at community needs in the Denver area. It runs a network of rural outreach clinics along the Front Range and the eastern Colorado plains. PHP has a "gospel-based" mission and is a member of the Sisters of Charity Health Care System of Cincinnati and contributes a sizeable portion of its services to unpaid community service, including charity care. St. Anthony Central was built by the Sisters of St. Francis in 1893. St. Anthony Central operates one of the area's four certified Level I trauma centers and is home base to Flight for Life, probably the best known of Greater Denver's helicopter emergency rescue services. The hospital is an innovator in cardiovascular surgery and services and was one of the first hospitals to provide a chest pain emergency center. It's also one of 11 sites in the nation to offer gamma knife surgery, which entails the use of gamma rays to eliminate deep-seated tumors and other malformations in the brain. St. Anthony Hospital Central is a 350-bed facility. Just down the street is the Provenant Senior Life Center, formerly Beth Israel Hospital, which now offers a 24-bed acute rehabilitation unit, a 12-bed geriatric psychiatric unit, a 42-bed extended-care facility and a long-term nursing home. Also just down the street is the Gardens at St. Elizabeth, a residential and specialized-care facility for seniors.

Photo: Daily Camera/Lourie Zipf

The Auraria Student Union is in the Tivoli, which was a brewery
and a shopping mall in its past lives.

ROSE MEDICAL CENTER
4567 E. Ninth Ave. 320-2121

Rose Medical Center is well known to an awful lot of Greater Denverites as the place where their children, grandchildren, nieces and nephews were born. It's second to Saint Joseph Hospital in the number of births that take place there, but in the ratio of childbirths to total hospital beds, it's the biggest in the area. That's not surprising considering its emphasis on women's health services, education, parent education classes, infertility and high-risk pregnancies. The Rose Women's Center has a satellite location in Littleton. The Rose Breast Center performs more mammograms than any other facility in the Denver area. And the Rose Children's Center is strong on in-patient, ambulatory and emergency services for infants, children and adolescents. All this is not to say that Rose is just for women and children, and neither is that why it's named Rose. Opened in 1949 and named after Denver World War II hero General Maurice Rose, the Medical Center claims its Rose Men's Health Resource is the region's "first comprehensive, primary-care-oriented health program designed especially for men." Among the general list of hospital services provided by Rose's 1,400 employees is advanced oncology research and Colorado's first coronary care unit. With 420 licensed beds, it was also the first adult, acute-care metro medical center to formally affiliate with the University of Colorado Health Sciences Center, which is right next door. Not surprisingly, Rose is a big-time teaching hospital. Other Rose special features include a Surgical Treatment of Emphysema program and Rose Sports Medicine, a comprehensive program of services for sports injuries and conditions, with its own 24-hour sports injury and referral and consultation service, 320-2100. Rose in 1994 created what it calls an ortho-pedic center of excellence, the Rose Institute for Joint Replacement.

SAINT JOSEPH HOSPITAL
1835 Franklin St. 837-7111

Denver's oldest private hospital, Saint Joseph was founded in 1873 by the Sisters of Charity of Leavenworth, Kansas, and they still own it. In 1994 and 1995, the hospital was designated as one of the top-100 hospitals in the United States by Mercer Management Consulting and Health Care Investment Analysts, and it has a national reputation for the quality of its heart care. It's the busiest childbirth center in Denver and Colorado. With more than 5,000 births per year, Saint Joseph is the birthplace of 10 percent of Colorado's babies. The hospital's Maternal/Fetal Medicine program and Level III Neonatal Intensive Care Nursery ensure that babies needing extra help get the best care available before and after birth. Saint Joseph excels in other services including oncology, orthopedics, gastroenterology and pulmonology. Saint Joseph also has average patient charges among the lowest of the metro area's hospitals.

SPALDING REHABILITATION HOSPITAL
900 Potomac St. 782-5700

Although Spalding is officially in Denver, it's actually located all over the place. The hospital's 146 licensed beds are in fact located at other hospitals. At each of these, Spalding operates as a wing or unit specializing in the treatment of stroke, brain injury, chronic pain, neck/back injuries, neurological disorders, multiple sclerosis and orthopedic problems. Spalding was founded in 1965 as a stand-alone hospital but sold that facility in 1992 and went the "hospital-within-a-hospital" route to save on costs and also to bring care to people in their own communities. Now people who

Photo: Daily Camera/Lourie Zipf

Saint Joseph Hospital is one of the major medical centers in the hospital area near downtown Denver.

move from acute-care to rehabilitation care can just move down the hall rather than having to move to another location in downtown Denver. Spalding Downtown is now at Presbyterian/St. Luke's Medical Center. Spalding South is at Swedish Medical Center. Spalding West is at Lutheran Medical Center. Spalding North is at Longmont United Hospital in Boulder County. Spalding also operates a unit at United Medical Center in Cheyenne, Wyoming.

UNIVERSITY HOSPITAL
4200 E. Ninth Ave.   *399-1211*

If the state of the medical art is what you're looking for, it's said, a research hospital is a good place to go. University Hospital is part of the University of Colorado Health Sciences Center. Besides having one of Greater Denver's three certified Level I trauma centers and full general hospital services, University Hospital is physically connected with Colorado's major health research base, which pulls in $133 million annually in research and training grants. The University of Colorado, known

around here as CU, has its School of Medicine here. The schools of nursing, pharmacy and dentistry are also on site, as is the Colorado Psychiatric Hospital. At any one time, University Hospital's 258 beds and outpatient services are attended by about 500 full-time doctors and 800 graduate doctors in training, as well as the rest of a total health professionals roster of more than 1,500. University pulled off the nation's first successful liver transplant, and it has plenty of other accomplishments to brag about since it was created in 1921. Pushing the medical frontiers, CU has given the hospital special expertise in areas ranging from heart surgery to cancer. The hospital's National Cancer Institute-designated Cancer Center, for example, does specialized experimental cancer treatments in conjunction with its research.

VETERANS AFFAIRS MEDICAL CENTER
1055 Clermont St.   *399-8020*

Through the VA Med Center, the federal government delivers health services to people who have previously served in the military. With 276 beds in use, it provides medical, surgical, neurological, rehabilitation and psychiatric care. The Center also has a 60-bed Nursing Home Care Unit and reaches out to other parts of Front Range Colorado through outlying clinics and a mobile MEDIVAN program. Among their special programs are care and treatment for aging veterans, female veterans, ex-POWs, Vietnam-era veterans and issues relating to Agent Orange and the Persian Gulf. The Center is also a major research site, the 14th largest in the Veterans Administration, with projects including a Schizophrenia Center, a VA Alcohol Research Center and an AIDS Clinical Trial Unit.

Adams County

FITZSIMONS ARMY MEDICAL CENTER
Between Potomac and Peoria sts.
Aurora 361-8313
Fitzsimons in 1995 was nominated for closure by the Base Realignment and Closure Commission. A variety of groups and federal, state and local officials have tried to change Uncle Sam's mind about that, but it doesn't look good. Fitz laid off some 40 doctors in the first few months after the announcement. If it isn't taken off the federal hit list, Fitzsimon's commander said in June 1995, it could be down to three or four doctors by mid-1996, although complete closure would not be expected until 1999.

Until closure is a certainty, however, Fitzsimons remains on its square-mile campus north of E. Colfax Avenue between Potomac and Peoria Streets. It has been the place to go for some 65,000 active-duty, retired, reserve and National Guard military personnel and their dependents in the Greater Denver area, serving 12 states for the entire Department of Defense and another 12 states just for the Army. It also provides public health service for four In-

dian reservations in South Dakota, North Dakota and Wyoming. The first hospital was built here in 1918, and the current hospital was built in 1941. As well as being a full-spectrum general hospital, it had until 1995 an extensive program of activities for disabled personnel. In fact, an amputee-ski program developed here during the Vietnam War was the forerunner of what is now the National Sports Center for the Disabled in the mountain ski-town of Winter Park.

MEDIPLEX REHAB-DENVER
8451 Pearl St.
Thornton 288-3000
This is a comprehensive medical rehabilitation facility for adult inpatients and outpatients with traumatic brain injury, stroke, amputation, orthopedic conditions, arthritis, neurological disorders, pulmonary conditions, psychiatric disorders or other disabling conditions. It's a 118-bed facility near I-25 just off the 84th Avenue Exit. Comprehensive brain injury rehab services include coma rehabilitation, acute brain injury rehabilitation and neurobehavioral rehabilitation. Comprehensive rehab includes multiple trauma, neurologic, stroke, orthopedic, amputee, arthritic and neuromuscular rehabilitation. Pulmonary rehab includes ventilator rehab, ventilator management and pulmonary restoration. There's a substance abuse program for people with disabilities and a restorative care program for patients who can't be discharged home or to an alternative level of care.

NORTH SUBURBAN MEDICAL CENTER
9191 Grant St.
Thornton 451-7800
This 200-bed hospital, near I-25 off the Thornton Parkway Exit, is one of four hospitals owned by Columbia/HCA

Healthcare Corporation. North Suburban provides comprehensive primary care and specialty healthcare services to the northern Greater Denver communities. Its services include: inpatient and outpatient medical surgical care, 24-hour emergency services, neonatal intensive care (level II), obstetrics, reproductive health, rehabilitation, orthopedic surgery, physician referral, oncology, women's health, diagnostic imaging (MRI, Breast Diagnostic Center, CT Scan), cryosurgery, urology, geropsychiatric mental health programs, senior transportation, home health, hernia repair, laboratory and pathology, cosmetic surgery, physical/occupational therapy, and a state-of-the-art cardiac catheterization lab.

PLATTE VALLEY MEDICAL CENTER
1850 Egbert St.
Brighton   *659-1531*

Platte Valley stays fairly busy because of its proximity to U.S. Highway 85 and I-76. It's also the closest hospital to the new Denver International Airport. Founded as Brighton Community Hospital in 1960, it came under the management of Rocky Mountain Adventist Health Care in 1980. A new hospital was built in 1982, and the name was changed in 1985. With 58 beds, it's one of Greater Denver's smallest acute-care hospitals, but it provides a solid spectrum of general hospital care ranging from coronary care and cardiac rehabilitation to perinatal and pediatric services. Among all hospitals in Greater Denver, Platte Valley is second only to Rose Medical Center in the ratio of childbirths to hospital beds. Generally it serves people from Adams and Weld counties.

PROVENANT
ST. ANTHONY HOSPITAL NORTH
2551 W. 84th Ave.
Westminster   *426-2151*

One of three major hospitals owned by Provenant Health Partners (see Provenant St. Anthony Central, in Denver), St. Anthony North was built in 1971 to serve the northern suburbs. This 196-bed hospital is oriented toward the needs of young families in a growing community. The emergency room is one of the state's busiest. Major medical specialties include family practice, pediatrics, cardiology and obstetrics, with advanced intermediate and intensive care nurseries. It also plays an educational role, offering parent education classes, wellness seminars, obstetrics classes, sick child day care and health promotion activities for businesses. It also trains physicians from across the nation in laser surgery.

Arapahoe County

AURORA PRESBYTERIAN HOSPITAL
700 Potomac St.
Aurora   *363-7200*

Aurora Presbyterian's women's services, oncology services, occupational medicine and surgical specialties are among the highlights of this 146-bed hospital less than a mile south of Fitzsimons Army Medical Center and just west of I-225. An emer-

Denver General Hospital had a big turnover not long ago when the city got serious about its rule that city employees have to live in Denver.

Insiders' Tips

gency medicine and full-service acute-care hospital, it has the busiest emergency department in Aurora, and it's home to AIR LIFE, one of Greater Denver's two helicopter emergency medical evacuation services. Since a merger with Swedish Medical Center in 1993, APH is part of HealthONE, Colorado's largest hospital system. It has pediatrics, psychology, a Women's Center with complete obstetrics and gynecology services and comprehensive cardiac and cancer care. It also has The Strawberry Place, a low- or no-cost residence where patients or their families can stay when, say, a cancer patient comes in from out of town for radiation therapy. Aurora Pres began in the 1950s when a local women's club was instrumental in getting a certificate of need filed for a hospital in Aurora and began raising seed money through bake sales and similar activities. The hospital was finally built and launched in 1976.

AURORA REGIONAL MEDICAL CENTER
1501 S. Potomac St.
Aurora   *695-2600*

Aurora Regional Medical Center opened in 1974 as Aurora's first full-service, acute-care civilian hospital. Located near I-225 and Mississippi Avenue, not far from the Aurora Mall, the hospital is licensed for 200 beds and has about 700 physicians on its medical staff. The hospital's campus includes the main hospital building and five medical office buildings. It was known as Aurora Community Hospital until 1983, when it changed its name to Humana Hospital-Aurora to reflect its ownership by Humana Inc. In 1993, the name changed again to reflect its ownership by Galen and then Columbia/HCA. The Center offers comprehensive cardiovascular services, including open-heart surgery, an open-heart unit, a cardiac care

unit, a telemetry unit and a cardiac rehabilitation unit. It also has comprehensive women's services, including a Breast Diagnostic Center, an obstetrical and gynecological unit, and childbirth, well-baby and newborn intensive care. Among its other specialized programs are the Colorado Spine Center, which provides advanced services and expertise to people with unusually difficult or complex spinal conditions, a Spine Imaging Center and a male impotency program.

CRAIG HOSPITAL
3425 S. Clarkson St.
Englewood   *789-8000*

Craig Hospital dates back to 1907 when it started as a tuberculosis colony by Frank Craig, who himself was a tuberculosis sufferer. Today, Craig Hospital is dedicated exclusively to patients with spinal cord and brain injuries. Some 10,000 of them have been treated and rehabilitated since Craig converted to a rehabilitation facility in 1956. Another of those Greater Denver hospitals with an international reputation in a specialized niche, Craig pulls the majority of its patients from outside Colorado. It supports that widespread patient base with an air transport team that flies an average of 200,000 miles a year in a specially equipped air-ambulance, a Lear jet and other aircraft. About a mile south of the Denver border in Englewood, Craig tries to maintain a casual, home-away-from-home atmosphere because it's a long-stay hospital that encourages family involvement in a patient's progress. In fact, Craig expects to complete in 1996 a $10 million addition to the hospital known as the Transitional Care Facility. In these apartment-like units, patients during the last phase of their inpatient stay can work on adjusting to independent life. The units are designed to hold the patient's family

Photo: Daily Camera/Lourie Zipf

Presbyterian and St. Luke's were once two separate hospitals.

members as well, so family can help with the adjustment. Acute-care patients can be managed almost immediately after injury by Craig physicians and therapists in neurotrauma units at adjacent Swedish Medical Center and at Provenant St. Anthony Hospital Central in Denver. The hospital has 80 beds, and other facilities include outpatient services, a neuroscience laboratory and a fertility clinic.

PORTERCARE HOSPITAL-LITTLETON
7700 S. Broadway
Littleton 730-8900

PorterCare Hospital-Littleton (formerly Littleton Hospital-Porter) was opened in 1989 in response to growing development in south Greater Denver, from Littleton and Englewood to Highlands Ranch and Castle Rock. It's just north of C-470, near the intersection of Broadway and Mineral Avenue. The next hospital to the south is in Colorado Springs. PorterCare Hospital-Littleton features services including obstetrics and gynecology, pediatrics, surgical services, radiology, cardiopulmonary, rehabilitation and 24-hour emergency care. All of its rooms are pri-

vate, billed at semi-private rates. The hospital's Family Life Center offers a wide selection of classes and programs. In addition, the hospital serves its community with Ask-A-Nurse, a 24-hour, free health information and physician referral service. This 105-bed hospital is owned by PorterCare Adventist Health System and represents an extension of the Adventist healing mission. Other hospitals in the system include PorterCare Hospital (formerly Porter Memorial Hospital) in south Denver, PorterCare Hospital-Avista (formerly Avista Hospital) in Louisville and Platte Valley Medical Center in Brighton.

ROCKY MOUNTAIN
REHABILITATION INSTITUTE
900 Potomac St.
Aurora 367-1166

Established in 1989, this 80-bed medical rehabilitation hospital offers rehab programs for people who've had serious illnesses or injuries, including stroke, spinal cord injury, traumatic brain injury, neurological disorders, arthritis, cancer and others. The hospital has special programs in neurological rehabilitation, cancer rehabilitation, occupational rehabilitation, spinal cord injury rehabilitation, lung health, speech and language pathologies, functional restoration and pain management and an orthopedic program for those recovering from hip fractures, joint replacement, amputation or other serious orthopedic procedures. In the Denver area, the Institute also operates two satellite facilities: The Headache and Neurological Rehabilitation Institute of Colorado in Northglenn and the Commerce City Physical Therapy Center.

SWEDISH MEDICAL CENTER
501 E. Hampden Ave.
Englewood   788-5000

A division of HealthONE, Swedish serves as a regional center for the most complex trauma, neurological and infertility cases. A not-for-profit, 328-bed acute-care hospital, it's one of four certified Level I trauma centers in Greater Denver. Because it shares its campus with two major regional rehab hospitals, Craig Hospital and Spalding Hospital, it is well positioned to provide continuum care for victims of spinal cord injury, stroke, neurological disorders and complex orthopedic problems. Critical health care includes cardiovascular and pulmonary services, oncology services and emergency and trauma services. Special facilities include the Women's Midlife Health Center, the Center for Reproductive Medicine and a Radiation Therapy Department. The Laser Center has state-of-the-art treatment for removing port-wine stains, spider veins, birthmarks, moles, tattoos, etc.

Douglas County

COLUMBINE PSYCHIATRIC CENTER
8565 S. Poplar Way
Littleton   470-9500

Mental health and chemical dependency services are provided by this 80-bed hospital owned by Columbia Healthcare Corporation. It's on the southwest corner of C-470 and Quebec Street on the northeastern fringe of Highlands Ranch, and it is the only hospital in Douglas County. Numerous day and evening outpatient programs as well as inpatient programs are available for adolescents, adults and seniors. The hospital offers free assessments both on site and at its Castle Rock satellite office.

Jefferson County

CLEO WALLACE CENTER HOSPITAL
8405 W. 100th Ave.
Westminster   466-7391

Cleo Wallace Center is Colorado's largest and most comprehensive psychiatric facility dedicated to the treatment of psychiatric, emotional and behavioral problems in children and adolescents. Cleo Spurlock Wallace was a local schoolteacher who saw a need for special services for troubled youth, which was why she started the center in 1943. Today, the center has a 74-acre campus with an inpatient hospital unit, residential facilities, day treatment and outpatient services for children and adolescents with psychiatric problems, and for their families. The center has six units, two hospital and four residential, with 112 beds total. It runs a school certified by the Colorado Department of Education, each classroom having both a teacher and a paraprofessional to integrate treatment into education. It also has a building with an indoor swimming pool, gym, weight room and game room. John Wayne used to come here for fund-raising events; he was a member of the Sigma Chi fraternity, which selected Cleo's hospital/school as its special charity. The center has a similar facility in Colorado Springs.

LUTHERAN MEDICAL CENTER

8300 W. 38th St.
Wheat Ridge   425-4500

Back in 1905, what would one day become the 100-acre site of the present Lutheran Medical Center was established as the Evangelical Lutheran Sanitorium tent colony, a place to care for people with tuberculosis. In 1962, Lutheran opened as a 220-bed not-for-profit hospital. Today Lutheran Medical Center consists of the 409-bed Lutheran Hospital as well as Lutheran Home Care Services, Business Health Services, Lutheran Rehabilitation Services, Lutheran Senior Services, Lutheran Medical Center Foundation, West Pines at Lutheran Hospital (mental health services) and Medical Centers of Colorado, a network of walk-in urgent care centers located throughout metropolitan Denver.

Lutheran offers comprehensive cardiac, oncology, obstetric/gynecological, orthopedic, urology, pulmonary and women's health services. In 1994, a new Level III emergency department opened featuring urgent and convenient care services and treatment. Lutheran also has a variety of community education programs.

Lutheran serves the community with such programs as EZ Care, which provides minor acute-care, preventive care and health education at community sites for those with no health insurance or inadequate health insurance coverage, and is involved in the development of local school science curriculums.

In 1994 and again in 1995, Lutheran Hospital was designated as one of the top-100 hospitals in the nation by Health Care Investment Analysts of Baltimore and Mercer Health Care Provider Consulting of New York, based on quality of care, delivery of care and financial capabilities.

Across from the Colorado State Capitol (yes, the dome does have real gold on it) in downtown Denver stands the Pioneer Monument, with one statue depicting famed mountain man and explorer Kit Carson.

Inside
Retirement

Greater Denver isn't exactly a retirement mecca like Arizona or Florida, yet its sunny and mild climate makes it a great place for seniors to live. Darned good thing because more seniors are coming up from the ranks of juniors. The Denver Regional Council of Governments in 1993 forecast that those 60 years of age or older would increase from 13 percent of the local population to 20 percent by the year 2013.

The City and County of Denver has by far the greatest number of independent and assisted-living facilities for seniors in the area, but when you seek word-of-mouth recommendations on finding the most desirable places for retirement living, Denver's outlying areas, and especially the suburban counties, tend to get the most praise.

That may not be fair to Denver's senior communities. It may simply say more about life being more difficult for the elderly in an urban setting. At any rate, the ultimate choice comes down not to what area you want to live in but more specifically to which retirement community you want to live in.

There are a variety of information sources that can help you make your decision. Referral agencies such as **Elderly Housing Choices**, 831-4046, are a good place to start. Elderly Housing Choices is part of a nonprofit organization known as Community Housing Services Inc. It provides free housing referrals that you can use as a start in comparing costs, availability and other factors.

Housing Connections is another one, 831-4788, offering lists of everything from subsidized senior housing to retirement communities. Then you have organizations such as **Senior Housing Options**, 595-4464, a nonprofit corporation that owns and/or manages 16 assisted-living properties and HUD-subsidized properties.

Before shopping for a retirement community, make a list of the amenities you want. Do you need transportation? Where to? Transportation to a particular kind of shopping area? Central City for gambling and nightlife? Don't want to cook? Want to keep a pet? What kinds of activities do you want? Dances, games, music? How close do you want to be to family or friends? Don't go in cold, just asking to be sold. Have a written roster of your requirements, so you can see how each retirement community scores on that roster.

Insiders' Tips

You can do your own word-of-mouth research by asking other seniors you meet in groups such as the **American Association of Retired Persons**, which has an office in Denver, 830-2277, and the **Association for Senior Citizens**, 455-9642. The **Aging Services Division of the Denver Regional Council of Governments**, 455-1000, offers information and referral services for seniors, as well as a Nursing Home Ombudsman Program. You can hobnob with seniors at any of Greater Denver's numerous senior centers. Call **Mile High United Way's Senior Information Source**, 433-0403, to find the senior center nearest you and get other senior-related information. For other senior tips as well as just a lot of good ideas about enjoying the area, you might take a look at *Uniquely Denver: A Discovery Guide to the Mile High City For Those Over 50*, written by Virginia Brey and published by American Source Books, Lakewood, Colorado. You might also get a copy of *The Denver Business Journal Top 255 Lists*, an annual publication of the *The Denver Business Journal*, 837-5500. We've mentioned it before, because it's a great resource for all kinds of area information. One of its lists is the top 25 retirement communities.

And don't forget *The Beacon Review*. This is Greater Denver's biweekly newspaper for "the better side of 40." It has an annual listing of retirement communities, but it's also a great resource for all kinds of senior news and issues in the area. You can pick it up for free at King Soopers stores, as well as at various banks, restaurants, senior centers and recreation centers in the five-county area. If you can't find it, call *The Beacon Review* at 692-8940.

Once you know what part of Greater Denver you'd like to live in and have some good options in mind, call these places and have them send you their brochures and information packages. If you're still interested, go and check them out in person to get a sense of what they're like. Arriving around meal time is a good idea, because that's a great time to get a feel for how the personnel work and relate to their residents. Of course, most communities have marketing folks who are willing and eager to give you a guided tour.

Worth paying attention to as well is the neighborhood of each candidate retirement community: whether it's clean, pleasant and quiet; whether there are parks and/or shopping within walking distance and whether the surroundings are congenial to the elderly. Greater Denver's four-lane traffic arteries such as Wadsworth Boulevard are not congenial, with the timing of their intersection signals apparently designed on the theory that pedestrians are little more than potential road kill. When the "WALK" symbol light finally comes on at an intersection, not even a speed-walking teenager can make it more than half way across before the red "DON'T WALK" symbol appears.

In mentioning a few of the more-talked-about examples of retirement communities in Greater Denver, we by no means intend to slight the many wonderful places not mentioned. We have tended to look specifically at places with independent and/or assisted living in which seniors have their own homes or apartments. These are the mid-range of a spectrum of senior living and care options, that range from nursing homes to prestige single-family developments. Assisted living simply means that assistance is available for such needs as medication reminders; help with dressing, grooming and bathing; close medical and health monitoring; laundry; in-apartment meal services and rehabilitation programs. Typically, both independent and assisted-living units have call buttons at stra-

Photo: Daily Camera/Crissy Pascual

Many Denver-area retirement communities are close to parks and recreation areas.

tegic locations, so residents can summon help if needed.

Overall, these senior living communities tend to look little different from any other nice, upscale apartment or condominium communities. Unlike most such communities, however, they are truly communities, with a great deal more attention paid to providing communal dining and gathering areas and community activities and services. Typically, meals are included as part of your rent, although this may vary. Housekeeping is a fairly standard service. There's not a one of these senior communities that doesn't have a calendar of social activities; many have their own newsletters, and all of them have their own transportation services to area shopping and other attractions. You are likely to have your own garage or carport space and storage lockers. Senior communities are a far cry from our traditional images of senior living as institutionaliza-

tion and a wonderful affirmation of the idea that the later years can indeed be golden.

CANTERBURY GARDENS

11265 E. Mississippi Ave.
Aurora   *341-1412*

Canterbury Gardens was the first independent and assisted-living community for seniors in Aurora when it opened in the late 1970s, and some of the pioneer residents are still there. The Gardens consists of two-story structures built around two ponds in a landscaped courtyard with a gazebo. This community actually consists of two sections: Canterbury Gardens, the independent living section, and The Inn at Canterbury Gardens, which is assisted living. Independent living units are one- and two-bedroom apartments with up to two bathrooms, and assisted-living units are studios. Some have private patios or balconies. Canterbury is owned and operated by Crossings Corporation of Tacoma, Washington, a company that specializes in developing and managing retirement communities. Canterbury includes a fireside lounge, library, TV and movie lounge, a beauty/barber shop, a full-service dining room with soup and salad bar, private dining, complimentary van service for scheduled trips, an ice cream shop, guest apartments and a hobby and crafts room. Monthly independent living rent for a single person ranges from $795 to $1,610, and $1,075 to $1,930 for assisted living.

CHERRY CREEK RETIREMENT VILLAGE
14555 E. Hampden Ave.
Aurora   693-0200

Cherry Creek has a nice location in a residential neighborhood and across the street from Aurora's public Meadow Hills Golf Course. It's one of the region's newer senior communities, a three-story buff-colored building with a large circle drive and two atriums for relaxing and entertaining.

Some apartments have patios or balconies. Every unit has a window over the kitchen sink that looks out into one of the halls. Monthly rent ranging from $750 for a studio to $1,645 to a two-bedroom deluxe apartment covers amenities ranging from continental breakfast and weekly housekeeping to excursions. Meals and other amenities are available at a nominal charge. The Village has card and game rooms, an exercise room, a library, a country store, billiards, an arts and crafts area, restaurant-style dining and a private dining room. Independent and assisted living are provided. It's owned by Lifecare Centers of America, Cleveland, Tennessee.

THE COURTYARD AT LAKEWOOD
7100 W. 13th Ave.
Lakewood   239-0740

Three blocks east of Wadsworth Boulevard and a couple blocks south of Colfax Avenue in Lakewood, the Courtyard is in a quiet residential neighborhood. Every apartment in the three-story building has a view of the center courtyard, where there are flowers, rock gardens and a pond. The Courtyard is managed by two husband-and-wife teams who live on the premises.

Beyond the living quarters, the Courtyard's amenities include a giant-screen TV room, a large kitchen for group activities, a beauty shop, library, billiards areas and a spa. Single-occupancy units range from $1,250 to $1,750 per month. The Courtyard is owned by Holiday Retirement Corporation.

DAYTON PLACE
1950 S. Dayton St.
Aurora   751-5150

Dayton Place is right on the western edge of the City of Aurora's south side, just off Parker Road, a major thoroughfare that runs northwest to Denver and southeast past the Cherry Creek Reservoir State Recreation Area. Dayton is a three-story complex that has an open feeling, in part due to its suburban location and perhaps in part due to its setback on large grounds with a lot of meandering walkways, gardens and outdoor patios. Dayton Place has a general store, chapel, beauty and barber shop, TV lounges, a billiards room and a card and

---

Insiders' Tips

A retirement community is as good as you make it. Once there, get to know your neighbors, get to know the other residents and join in. Don't isolate yourself. Isolation, say senior Insiders, is probably the worst thing seniors can do to themselves.

Retirement communities offer classes and hobby areas.

activities room. Apartments range from $1,390 to $1,690 per month for assisted living. Independent living ranges from $1,145 to $1,570. Dayton Place is owned by CMD Corporation.

HERITAGE CLUB

2020 S. Monroe St.
Denver   756-0025

The Heritage Club has a good reputation for elegant living at affordable prices. The apartments are luxurious. The dining room really looks like something in an upscale downtown restaurant with a menu to match, and there's a private dining room for special occasions. Heritage Club has a private library, exercise room with whirlpool and spa, an on-premises bank, country store and ice cream parlor, a billiards room, a cards and games room, an arts and crafts studio and a beauty and barber shop, as well as shuffleboard, a putting green and horseshoes. The bay windows and balconies are a nice feature, since the Heritage Club is located in the University Park neighborhood, a very pleasant part of the city southeast of Colorado Boulevard's intersection with I-25. It's managed by American Retirement Corporation of Brentwood, Tennessee. It has both assisted and independent living, and rental costs range from $1,220 to $3,985.

MERIDIAN

10695 W. 17th Ave.
Westland   232-7100
1805 S. Balsam St.
Lakewood   980-5500
9555 W. 59th Ave.
Arvada   425-1900
3455 S. Corona St.
Englewood   761-0300

Denver's western suburbs in Jefferson County have the largest number of retirement communities. One of the most extensive retirement residence organizations that gets mentioned in a positive light is Meridian, which actually has four retirement communities in Greater Denver. All of them are owned by Legan Corporation, a Denver company that also owns a Meridian in Boulder. Each is managed independently, but all are essentially the same: nicely appointed buildings on campus-like settings, with elegant interiors and formal furniture. The only major difference is that the Balsam Avenue Lakewood Meridian and the Englewood Meridian have nursing home sections, while the other two have independent and assisted living only. Monthly rents range from $1,570 to $3,400 for the high-end, two-bedroom apartment at the Englewood Meridian; $1,445 to $1,840 at the Arvada Meridian; $1,570 to $2,395 at the S. Balsam Lakewood Meridian; and $1,445 to $1,810 at the W. 17th Avenue Lakewood Meridian.

PARK PLACE
111 Emerson St.
Denver   *744-1950*

Right in the heart of Denver, this 18-story independent and assisted-living community resembles one of those quiet-elegance hotels that get known by word-of-mouth. Its elegance is immediately apparent in the dark wood and rich upholstery of the lobby, lounge and formal dining room, but the atmosphere is maintained throughout. It's next to Hungarian Freedom Park on the south side of Speer Boulevard, south of Denver's downtown and not far from the Cherry Creek shopping area. The Cherry Creek greenbelt and its pedestrian/bicycle path runs along Speer Boulevard out front. Park Place has an indoor swimming pool with a hot tub and exercise room, as well as a convenience store, beauty and barber shop, library, card lounge, patio dining area and auditorium. They don't have a rate sheet, because the units are quite individualized, but rent ranges from $1,575 to $2,400 per month. Park Place is owned and managed by American Retirement Corporation, Brentwood, Tenn.

PORTER PLACE
1001 E. Yale Ave.
Denver   871-9200

Porter Place is on the campus of PorterCare Hospital in Denver's University neighborhood on the northernmost edge of Englewood. In addition to independent and assisted living (with studio, one-bedroom and two-bedroom apartments), it also offers small studio apartments at $39 per day for visiting family and friends of residents. Porter Place is affiliated with PorterCare Hospital and PorterCare Hospital-Littleton, but that doesn't mean it looks like a medical facility. The interiors are as lovely as can be, from the grand piano and high ceilings of the lobby to the pleasant tranquility of the library. There are flower gardens and outdoor patios, a chapel, activity rooms, a gift shop, a beauty and barber shop, a big-screen TV room, a parlor, a card room and a craft room. And you have access to the hospital's Porter Health Club. Single-occupancy prices range from $1,095 to $1,895 monthly.

SPRINGWOOD
6550 Yank Way
Arvada   424-6550

The Springwood Retirement Community is a "beautiful facility," and that's from an administrator of a competing retirement community. It's just off the Yankee Doodle Park in a nice residential section of Arvada. It has a full-time social director, as well as facilities such as dining room, maid service, laundry and dry cleaning, a general store, a library, a chapel, a hair salon, a game room and an exercise facility. Lutheran Medical Center provides input to Springwood's healthcare and health-promoting activities. Springwood offers a variety of one-and two-bedroom apartments, with two-way intercom and emergency buzzers, ranging from $1,225 to $1,785 per month for single occupancy, with $250 extra for double occupancy. Springwood also offers assisted living at its Nightingale Suites, which range from $1,345 to $1,945 per month for single occupancy. The cottages at Springwood are 1,100-square-foot residences built on their own private cul-de-sac at Springwood's campus, with foyer, living room, dining room, covered patio, master bedroom with its own bath and oversized walk-in closet, a guest bedroom, a second bathroom, a laundry/utility room and attached garage. The cottages cost $1,145 per month for one person; $1,295 for two.

TREEMONT OF DENVER
10200 E. Harvard Ave.
Denver   696-0622
Treemont's interiors are bright and open, yet reminiscent of the club spaces in an Ivy League university, with a lot of dark wood and formal, Old World style. The exterior and grounds also have something of a country club atmosphere, overlooked by a second-story exterior deck. Treemont is in the northwest corner of Denver's Hampden neighborhood, just west of Au-

rora near the pleasant green spaces of Babi Yar Park and the private Los Verdes Golf Club. Although it's basically an independent-living community, it has a formal Assisted Living Program managed by a professional social worker with nursing support. Under the same roof, Treemont also includes a dining room, beauty and barber shop, game room, library and multipurpose room. Apartments range from $995 to $1,785 per month, with assisted-living plans running an additional $350 to $450 per month.

VILLAS AT SUNNY ACRES
2501 W. 104th Ave.
Thornton   452-4181
Just about the most-often mentioned word-of-mouth recommendation for retirement communities, the Villas at Sunny Acres is a large facility on a campus-like setting just south of Stonehocker Park in Thornton. The northern suburbs are quiet areas with good mountain views and a lot of remaining open space, and the Villas' landscaped grounds include two fishing lakes as well as gardening areas for residents. To that Sunny Acres adds amenities including home healthcare, 10 libraries, a new 3,000-square-foot fitness center, a whirlpool, pool tables, a woodworking and carpentry shop, lounges, dining rooms including a new restaurant, a convenience store and beauty and barber shops. You can live at the Villas by paying monthly rent, which ranges from $820 for one person, or you can choose their unique Life Care package. That means you pay an entry fee that starts at $33,100 for one person in addition to a monthly service fee ranging from $614. The Life Care entry fee prepays for all future long-term and short-term nursing care.

Photo: Daily Camera/Lourie Zipf

The neighborhood near the Colorado State Capitol is called Capitol Hill.

Inside
Neighborhoods and Real Estate

An overwhelmingly seller's market in the last few years, Greater Denver's housing market of late is beginning to hold more promise for the buyer. Homes aren't being snapped up as rapidly as they were in 1994, the peak year for residential construction. Net in-migration to the state has slipped from 70,000 in 1993 and 60,000 in 1994 to 40,000 in 1995. With consumer demand cooling, new building permits in the first half of 1995 were 20 percent lower in number than the level of early 1994, according to the Home Builders Association of Metro Denver. But if the market isn't hot, it's still pretty warm. The median price of a new home in Greater Denver plus Boulder County increased nearly 12 percent from 1994 to 1995, reaching $174,000 in mid-1995, according to Home Builders Research data reported in *The Denver Post*. Of course, Boulder County skewed that a bit, having the highest median price of a new home at nearly $198,000, and most of the home buying opportunities are existing homes anyway.

A full picture of Denver's residential scene, from home prices to intangible atmospherics, would require a book much larger than our entire guide. There are more than 70 officially designated neighborhoods in the City and County of Denver alone, not to mention the tremendous diversity in surrounding counties and their numerous cities and communities. Nevertheless, we've scanned variations in Greater Denver's residential fabric and costs.

Neighborhoods

Denver

As Greater Denver's urban center, the City and County of Denver covers the widest range of neighborhood types and home prices, from the humble to the posh. Aside from touching on some of the more well-known neighborhoods, with a few others tossed in for geographic variety, the most general statement we can make is that you can find any level of living you want in the City and County of Denver, from the serene suburban scene to the intense downtown experience.

Want to know more about a Denver neighborhood? One of your best sources may be the local neighborhood association. Stop by the Denver Planning Office, 200 W. 14th Avenue, and pick up an extensive list of neighborhood and homeowners groups for $4.

Insiders' Tips

Downtown Denver includes the Union Station area on the north, the Auraria neighborhood and the Civic Center area on the southwest and reaches east to Broadway, where it borders the North Capitol Hill and Capitol Hill neighborhoods. This is where you live if you like the downtown lifestyle; and here you almost certainly live in a condo. **Lower Downtown**, the red-brick historic area between the central business district and Union Station and the Central Platte Valley, is particularly popular of late. In fact, LoDo, as true Denver hipsters call it, is hot, owing largely to the revivification of the Central Platte Valley in general and the rise of the new Coors Field in particular. It's so hot that proposed developments include a plan by Arnold Schwarzenegger for a multiuse development taking up most of a block along Blake Street including the Arnold's Planet Hollywood nightclub as well as an eight-screen movie complex, retailers, loft space and parking. Condo prices here are going to be some of the highest in the region, if not the highest. Downtown Denver condo asking prices ranged as high as $875,000 in the first half of 1995, but they also ranged as low as $45,000 and averaged $230,000.

Downtown Denver is cool, but an anomaly as far as residential opportunities. Condo prices are high, and single-family homes are virtually nonexistent. In the rest of Denver, homes outnumber condos by a considerable margin and homes were selling in 1995 for an average just under $89,000. Of course, you can't expect that kind of price average everywhere. In **southeast Denver**, that part of the city east of Broadway and south of Colfax Avenue, single-family homes sold at an average of $170,774. Condos also vary, with the highest average asking price at $230,000 and selling price at $215,000-plus in downtown

Denver. Southeast Denver is where the condos have been selling most rapidly, 1,142 of them from January 1 to mid-August 1995, versus 150 sales in southwest Denver, 12 in northeast Denver and 6 in northwest Denver. Denver's second-highest quadrant as far as single-family home prices is **northeast Denver**, that part of the city east of Broadway and north of Colfax Avenue, with average home-sale prices around $93,000, and condos running around $61,000. In **southwest Denver**, west of Broadway and south of Colfax Avenue, single-family home-sale prices have been lower than in northeast Denver, averaging $89,000, but more of them have been selling. And southwest Denver has been selling a lot more condos than the northeast, and at higher average prices of about $82,000. **Northwest Denver**, north of Colfax Avenue and west of Broadway, has been selling fewer homes and fewer condos than the other parts of the city, with the lowest average sale price for single-family homes of $85,000.

Just east of downtown Denver, you can find historic neighborhoods that are much less molested by the revivification boom shaking Lower Downtown. **North Capitol Hill** and **Capitol Hill**, bounded roughly by 20th Avenue and Sixth Avenue, Clarkson Street and Broadway, were among the first of Denver's housing developments in the 1800s. While those in the working class were making their homes down by the river and in other outlying sections, the aristocrats were populating this area east and upslope from the business district. Here you find most of the historic mansion tours, and this stretch of Grant Street was once known as "Millionaires Row." In recent years, people have come to appreciate the historic charm of the area and its accessibility by foot to downtown. Now a lot of those mansions have been converted to condominiums, offices and bed and breakfasts, and there are a lot of cultural and fine-dining opportunities close by. Sales of Capitol Hill residences in 1995 were averaging around $133,000, and condos around $76,000.

Still, the Capitol Hill area lies along East Colfax, which has a bad reputation for sleaze and crime. Many prefer to live farther east in the **Cheesman Park** or **City Park West** neighborhoods. The Cheesman Park neighborhood, bounded by University Boulevard and Clarkson Street, Colfax and Sixth avenues, surrounds one of Denver's finer parks. Its name is Cheesman Park, and it borders one of Denver's finest amenities, the Denver Botanic Gardens. Cheesman Park neighborhood contains two historic districts and has a feel of urban gentility.

Things start to get more expensive as you move toward the **Country Club** neighborhood on the south, which borders on Speer Boulevard just across from the Denver Country Club. Less "discovered" as of yet, City Park West is an urban treasure trove of historic homes going back to Denver's silver boom of 1880 to 1893. Bounded by Clarkson Street, University Boulevard and Colfax and 23rd avenues, it's located between North Capitol Hill and City Park, Denver's largest central park, containing the Denver Zoo and the Denver Museum of Natural History. It's a moderate walk from the Botanic Gardens, a reasonable walk from downtown, and it has a hospital complex on its northern edge. The 17th Avenue strip of fine restaurants and entertainment runs right through it.

Washington Park is Denver's other big, well-known public green space, and the Washington Park neighborhood is one of Denver's most popular living areas. It has a lot of homes built in the early-to-mid-1900s, with 1995 sale prices averaging

about $165,000 and condos averaging $129,000. It's convenient to transportation as well, bordering on I-25 to the south and Colorado Boulevard to the east. The Denver Country Club is just north of it.

Just east of the Denver Country Club is fashionable **Cherry Creek**. Bounded by University Avenue and Colorado Boulevard, Sixth and Alameda avenues, it's an area of large-to-moderate size homes, expensive condos and a heck of a lot of shopping. It's Greater Denver's premier retail and arts area, as detailed in our Shopping chapter. It has a gracious ambiance, it's a fun place to visit and shop, and it's highly sought as a habitation. In fact, it's another one of those hot areas like Lower Downtown. Residential sales in 1995 averaged $244,000 and ranged as high as $925,000.

Directly west of Cherry Creek is **Hilltop**, another prestige living area of nicely cared-for streets adjacent to the major north/south corridor of Colorado Boulevard. Home sales in Hilltop in 1995 averaged $263,000, while condos went for prices between $280,000 and $336,000. **Park Hill**, to the north, just west of City Park, is an area of handsome old homes and large mature trees. In the last couple of years, however, Park Hill residents have hired their own patrolling security force due to concerns about crime. Residential sales in 1995 averaged $156,000.

One area that has become particularly interesting of late is the area known as **Far Northeast Denver**. The map of Denver is essentially a square with two little pods extending like stubby legs from the southeast and southwest corners; or at least that's what it would look like were it not for the Far Northeast Denver neighborhoods of **Montbello**, **Gateway** and **Green Valley Ranch**. Protruding east/northeast from the bulk of Denver, these neighborhoods stand out not just geographically but also as a focus of growth expected as a result of the new airport.

Montbello and Green Valley Ranch are established neighborhoods with a combined total of about 22,000 residents, but that number has been projected to grow to 35,000 by the turn of the century. These are quiet neighborhoods, although there's been some complaining about noise since the new Denver International Airport opened. They're new areas; the oldest home in Montbello is about 30 years old, and the oldest home in Green Valley Ranch is about 10 years old. They're low-crime areas with panoramic views of the mountains, room for another 9,400 dwellings and a lot of open space, including the Green Valley Ranch 18-hole golf course slated for 1996 completion. Yet, they're still the extreme edge of Denver's urban fabric, places where residents can take a walk and see a deer or an eagle in flight, and maybe even hear coyotes howling late at night.

Gateway, between Montbello and Green Valley Ranch and directly bordering the new airport on the north, is where Denver planners envision big-time development. Already launched are the beginning stages of a planned $1 billion Denver International Business Center just a few miles from the terminal. Denver publications have referred to the Gateway as "our first 21st Century neighborhood," and represented it as a future community of 65,000 people with strong economic links to the airport. Although it was annexed by Denver to link the city with the airport, it's not yet officially a neighborhood. It's still mostly 4,500 acres of empty land, except for some wheat farming, but Denver planners envision it as a new employment area on the level of downtown Denver and the Denver Tech Center, which is only one-sixth the size of Gateway.

We've given a lot of mention here to the central and eastern parts of Denver, perhaps more than is fair. But this is where the oldest neighborhoods, the big-name neighborhoods and the well-known neighborhoods are.

A lot of people, however, prefer the west side of the city. It's the smaller part of the city, it's closer to the mountains and it generally has a feeling of being near to its country roots. It doesn't seem like a part of the central city; it's not sandwiched between downtown and the airport, between downtown and the Denver Tech Center, between downtown and the industrial areas of northern Denver, between downtown and Lowry Air Force Base. It's not surrounded by I-25, I-70 and I-225.

Northwestern Denver is the city's smallest quadrant, bounded by West Colfax Avenue on the south and 52nd Avenue on the north, Sheridan Boulevard on the west and the South Platte River on the east. The **Highland** and **Jefferson Park** neighborhoods, stretching west from the high ground above the South Platte, were where Denver put its first residential neighborhoods west of the South Platte. Around the turn of the century, there was a large ethnic Italian neighborhood here. Descendants of truck farmers in what is now the western suburbs still tell of taking their produce downtown for delivery to Italian produce salesmen who would cry their wares in the streets. These neighborhoods now have a rich ethnic mix and some fine ethnic restaurants, including Latin American and Vietnamese. **Sloan Lake**, **West Highland**, **Berkeley** and **Regis** are some of the neighborhoods to the west that are pleasantly equipped with quiet streets and the greenery of lawns and parks around small lakes. These northwestern neighborhoods are as old as a lot of east Denver neighborhoods between downtown and Colorado Boulevard, but they're across the river, up

Cherry Creek is one of Denver's most popular neighborhoods.

the hill and over the ridge from the central city. One has more of a feeling here of being removed from the urban bustle.

Southwest Denver is larger and more extensive, more dynamic and growing than the west side of the city. Certainly, it has its older neighborhoods close in, such as **Val Verde** and **Sun Valley**. Val Verde, meaning "green valley," was a separate town established in 1873 and annexed into Denver in 1902. Bordered by Sixth and Alameda avenues, the South Platte River and Federal Boulevard, it is today an ethnically diverse neighborhood with a large industrial and warehousing base. As you move southwest toward southern Lakewood, however, you get a sensation of increasingly newer urban landscape. Not that there haven't been homes in this area since the 1800s, of course; just that it wasn't developed as early and extensively as the northwest. One of Denver's few areas where truly major new development is taking place is the **Marston** neighborhood that juts down into unincorporated Jefferson County on southwest Denver's farthest southwestern point. Near Marston Reservoir you'll find particularly high-quality residential living. The Marston area produced a real estate sensation in 1995 when a California developer announced that the 445-acre, historic Grant Ranch, spanning the boundaries of Denver, Lakewood and unincorporated Jefferson County, was to become a $500-million development. Supposedly it will include up to 2,200 new homes priced from $140,000 to $600,000. Generally, however, southwest Denver vies with northwest Denver for the city's lowest overall housing prices, and a much larger percentage of its population consists of married couples and families.

Adams County

Adams County is often viewed as the area's most blue-collar, working-class county, and that has a lot to do with the heavy industry and warehousing around Commerce City, northeastern Denver and the I-76 corridor leading northeast. **Commerce City**, Adams County's industrial/warehousing heartland, where twice as many people work as live, certainly has some of the county's lowest housing prices.

In the **North Suburban East** area, of which Commerce City comprises the primary residential component, home sales in the first half of 1995 averaged $69,500, ranging from $33,000 to $203,000, with condo sales averaging $62,350.

One of the first things you may notice in driving north on I-25 to **Thornton**, **Westminster** and **Northglenn** is a sensation of climbing to higher ground. **Federal Heights**, a community between Westminster and Thornton, is well-named. You're actually looking down at the tops of downtown Denver's highest buildings. Much of this northern area seems to be on high ground, and since there is little in the way of high-rise buildings, Denver's northern suburbs have some of the grandest views of the Rockies.

Westminster is Greater Denver's closest northside city to the mountains. Westminster spreads all over the place, so it isn't easily categorized. It's roughly centered around the Westminster Mall just off U.S. Highway 36, the "Boulder Turnpike," at 88th Avenue. To the west, 88th Avenue contains the most extensive complexes of shopping and shopping centers on Greater Denver's north side. To the north, there are attractive housing developments clustered and scattered through a lot of open country with big-sky views.

The eastern half of Westminster, in Adams County, and the western portion of Northglenn, some unincorporated Adams County land and a tiny eastern point of Arvada, are the area known to Realtors as the **North Suburban West**. This is the area contained in the vertical rectangle between Sheridan Boulevard on the west and I-25 on the east, 120th Avenue on the north and Denver on the south. Homes in the NSW are close to Denver and are Adams County's highest priced, averaging $122,424. This area has a lot of new homes

to offer. For a take on western Westminster, see Jefferson County below.

Just north of Westminster, mostly in Boulder County but with a good quarter of its population in Adams County, and a smaller portion in Jefferson County, is the City of **Broomfield**. Originally a residential community, it's fast becoming a business development area thanks to its strategic position between Boulder and Greater Denver and to the rampant development of business and industrial parks along U.S. Highway 36. While Broomfield is also seeing a lot of residential development, it is in some part a nice, older community where more affordable living can be found for those working in Greater Denver, Boulder or Louisville. Single-family homes in Broomfield were selling between $75,000 and $410,000 in 1995, and averaging $141,000. Condo sales were averaging $84,500 and ranging from $35,000 to $166,000.

The **North Suburban Central** area, between I-25 on the west and the South Platte River on the east, Denver on the south and 144th Avenue on the north, contains the bulk of the City of Thornton, eastern Northglenn and patches of unincorporated Adams County. Here home sales averaged $107,000 and ranged from $38,000 to $356,900. Condos averaged $64,000. A good deal of Thornton, in fact, has a moderate-to lower-income population, and that in a community with a suburban feel. It spreads thinly in many places on what was open country not too long ago.

Another arm of Westminster protrudes west to wrap around two sides of Standley Lake, one of Greater Denver's greatest water recreation resources, right on the edge of unincorporated Jefferson County.

Westminster's eastern half, near Northglenn and Thornton, is where you'll find the most condo activity, although availability is limited compared with Denver, Arapahoe and Jefferson counties.

Brighton, the Adams County seat to the northeast, is seeing a lot of growth but still has the benefit of a small-town atmosphere within an easy, 15-mile commuting distance of Denver. Home prices are moderate, with 1995 sales having averaged about $102,000.

Southeast of Commerce City, the City of **Aurora** has its industrial centers in its northern Adams County side, along the I-70 corridor near the new Denver International Airport. Here in north Aurora homes are among Adams County's less expensive with average sale prices in the first half of 1995 at $74,800, though sales ranged as high as $255,000.

Arapahoe County

Most of the City of Aurora lies in Arapahoe County. This is where the bulk of the city's office and R&D (research and development) centers are found. It's also where the homes are higher priced, averaging $121,000 in early 1995. Condos were going for an average $68,000. The area is close to the Denver Tech Center business area on the south and is well connected north/south by I-225 to both I-70 and I-25. Aurora's more than 180,000 households represent a young population with a median age of 31 years. The average salary of residents is about $2,000 higher than the average for the Denver metro area and about $5,000 higher than Colorado and the nation. The unemployment rate was lower than Greater Denver as a whole in 1992, but that rate took a hit from the 1994 closing of Lowry Air Force Base, where about 9,500 were employed. The city is pursuing a number of strategies to alleviate that hit, including the redevelopment of the base and of nearby Stapleton International Airport.

South and southeast of Aurora is perhaps Greater Denver's area of the highest-priced homes. The region is known among Realtors as the **Suburban Southeast**, roughly defined by the Arapahoe County Line, County Line Road on the south and Aurora on the north. The northwestern segment contains about half of **Greenwood Village** and most of **Cherry Hills Village**.

The bulk of this area lies in unincorporated Arapahoe County east, west and north of Centennial Airport. It includes the Denver Tech Center. Home prices here tend to be skewed rather dramatically upward by prestige pockets such as Cherry Hills Village, one of Greater Denver's most upscale communities with residences selling in 1995 for an average of about $509,000. Cherry Hills Village, for example, has absolutely no commercial base — not even a gas station — and the only nonresidential features are two private schools and the Cherry Hills and the Glenmore country clubs. Greenwood Village, just south of Cherry Hills, wrapping under the Denver Tech Center and up its eastern side, is another highly desired living area with residences sold there in 1995 averaging about $488,000.

Move a little to the west, and you'll find the area directly below the City of Denver known as the **South Suburban Central** region, which includes the Cities of **Littleton**, **Englewood**, about half of **Greenwood Village** and a substantial patch of unincorporated Jefferson County between Greenwood Village and County Line Road, Littleton and I-25. Overall, the South Suburban Central area has been selling houses at an average of $170,000 and condos at around $98,000.

The unincorporated part of South Suburban Central is generally an area of clean, new neighborhoods with the kind of convoluted street patterns that make life confusing for pizza delivery but peaceful for residents. It has a country feel, being the last neighborhood south of Denver before you arrive at Douglas County. There are some good shopping complexes along County Line Road; the Denver Tech Center is just up I-25; and C-470 (part of this is a toll road) provides fast access west and up to I-70 near Golden.

The City of **Littleton** grew out from an old downtown established in 1890 on what is now its northwestern edge along the South Platte River. It still has that old, traditional community atmosphere, but it also has its newer areas reaching south to Douglas County and C-470. The South Platte River runs north/south through nearly the entire length of the city, and the extra green spaces that make the city a particularly pleasant place to live.

Englewood, like Littleton, is one of the southern suburbs with an old downtown established in the 1800s along Broadway; and also like Littleton, it has a small-town appeal. But it's closer to Denver, and its business corridor along South Santa Fe Drive on the city's west side is home to hundreds of manufacturing, industrial and service companies. On the city's east side, it borders Cherry Hills Village.

Douglas County

Anyone who has lived in Greater Denver for 10 years or more, and doesn't make the drive south through Douglas County very often, is likely to be struck by the number of new residences, set well apart like estates and speckling the landscape seen from I-25 south. It's an area of rolling hills and open spaces with views of the mountains and the feel of the Great Plains.

In a 1994 *Wall Street Journal* story reporting on 20 of the nation's "fastest-growing, wealthiest and most educated areas," Douglas County was No. 1. It added 6,200 residents in 1994 and 5,400 residents in 1995. Douglas County is a huge area, with just a few small cities in the Denver area that have old and well-established downtowns, places like **Larkspur**, **Franktown** and the county seat of **Castle Rock**. Otherwise, you'll find very little in the way of residential buildings that aren't either ranches, farm structures or the large and expensive homes that are popping up like crazy in planned communities with names like Castle Pines Village, Deer Creek Farm and The Meadows. These are among the 20 to 30 planned communities along the Denver/Colorado Springs corridor that are expected to bring Douglas County's population as high as a half million by the year 2030. Extending more than halfway to Colorado Springs, the majority of Douglas County homes sold in 1995 averaged a selling price of around $210,000, with condos averaging around $141,000.

Highlands Ranch is the Douglas County community best-known by Denverites, partly because it now represents a continuum of the Greater Denver urban fabric. It lies on the northern edge of Douglas County directly south from the City and County of Denver. With 23,000 residents and growing like crazy, it's supposed

Photo: Daily Camera/Lourie Zipf

City Park West is home to some of Denver's most historic homes.

to top out at a population of 90,000 by the year 2020, and it won't be too surprising if at some point it is incorporated as a city. It's already starting to look like one, with its well-established schools and community centers; its huge central green space, the Northwest Community Park, that branches through the main, western cluster of the community; and the large Highland Heritage Regional Park on the growing eastern cluster. The average single-family home here has been selling for $199,000, with a range of $110,000 to $710,000. Condos have been going for $60,000 to $265,000, averaging $122,000.

Jefferson County

Here is where home buyers can choose from the widest variety of landscapes, simply because Jefferson County has both the bulk of Greater Denver's mountain communities and a large percentage of the area's flatland communities. The mountain communities are a big attraction. After a hot summer day at work in Denver, their residents can retreat to cool mountain evenings among the pines. Of course, it can be less

of a treat in the winter when you have to commute through the more severe snow conditions of the mountains. Sport-utility vehicles tend to be popular among mountain community commuters.

Jefferson County's flatland communities, however, still offer the attraction of being near the mountains, and Jefferson County in general has a good reputation for quality-of-life factors such as good schools, relatively low crime and nice neighborhoods. Actually, flatland is a bit of a misnomer here, because Jefferson County's eastern half, being close to the mountains, tends to go up and down across a lot of ridges and valleys.

Realtors over in Aurora and far eastern Denver tend to think you can find there the same quality of house and yard you can find in Jefferson County for maybe $15,000 less. It may be true that you pay such a premium for being in Jefferson County, but of course it's a big place and cost/benefit depends on where you are. On average, Jefferson County is moderately well-to-do, with a median household effective buying income of more than $42,000, versus $27,000 for the City and County of

Denver. In the 1994 *Wall Street Journal* story reporting on 20 of the nation's "fastest-growing, wealthiest and most educated areas," Jefferson County ranked No. 18.

Jefferson County South is the county's most expensive housing region bordering directly on Denver, but homes only average around $178,000. The vast majority of residences here are in the area bounded roughly by U.S. Highway 285 on the north, Sheridan Avenue on the east and C-470 on the south and west. Bulging into that area on the northeast corner is the City and County of Denver's **Marston** neighborhood, which surrounds Marston Lake. Denver tried to annex most of the rest of this area back in the 1970s but was rebuffed by Jefferson County and the courts. It's an unincorporated area, but one with a lot of consciousness of itself as a unique community right on the edge of the mountains. It has rejected efforts at incorporation as a city, but it holds its own community festivals, and it has its own organization of homeowners associations known as the Council of Homeowners Organizations for Planned Environment. South Jeffco also has some nice housing south and west of C-470, in Ken Caryl Valley on the other side of the Dakota Hogback, for example, where there's a mix of everything from townhomes to million-dollar mansions.

Immediately to the north is the City of **Lakewood**, the giant of Denver's southwest side and third-most populous city in Greater Denver after Denver and Aurora. Unlike many suburbs, Lakewood is a major employment center, with the Denver Federal Center, strong retail communities and substantial light industry. At the same time, it has a lot of semi-rural areas right inside the city limits. Lakewood's older neighborhoods lie to the east, where the city meets with about half the entire western border of Denver. On the west, it

reaches into the Foothills, where its 6,000 acres of parks include Green Mountain and the surrounding William Frederick Hayden Park. It touches the City of **Morrison**, a Greater Denver small town hidden in one of the red rock-rimmed valleys in the Rocky Mountains' first folds. Lakewood-area residences have been selling at an average of around $146,000, but sales have ranged as high as $545,000. Condos have averaged sale prices of $80,000 but have ranged as high as $172,000.

North of Lakewood is the City of **Wheat Ridge**, also bordering Denver. It has developed largely since World War II. Before that it was largely a farming area known more for fruits and vegetables and carnations than wheat. Wheat Ridge also has that uniquely rural flavor characteristic of many suburbs here. Foxes come up into the neighborhoods at night from the Clear Creek greenbelt. Deer sometimes blunder into busy Wadsworth Boulevard at morning rush hour. Walkers in serene suburban neighborhoods are sometimes surprised to see people passing on horses. Home sales here have averaged $126,000 and ranged up to $365,000, with condos averaging $71,000 and ranging up to $215,000.

Driving west on 32nd Avenue and passing out of Wheat Ridge as you go under I-70, you are on the way to the City of Golden, on the other side of South Table Mountain. Between I-70 and South Table Mountain, however, you begin noticing nicely groomed new neighborhoods primarily on the left. You are on the north side of a loosely defined area known as **Applewood**, which includes bits of Lakewood, Golden and Wheat Ridge but is mostly in unincorporated Jefferson County. Applewood is a name often heard on the lips of westsiders considering a move to a new home.

Keep going west on 32nd Avenue, around South Table Mountain and past a row of Adolph Coors Co. subsidiary companies and finally past the brewery itself, and you'll be coming in a sort of back door to **Golden**. Largely hidden from Denver on the west side of South Table Mountain, its eastern sides scrunching up against the Foothills, Golden has kept an identity apart from the rest of the metro area. It has an Old-West downtown and it's a charming small town. But it's also a big town. Once a Coors-company town, it's now mainly a high-technology and university town, largely influenced by the culture of the Colorado School of Mines just up the hill from Washington Avenue, its main street. New neighborhoods have been climbing up the side of South Table Mountain, growing south toward Heritage Square and Morrison and spreading east toward Lakewood. The level of education among Golden's population is one of the highest in the Greater Denver area, and its homes have been selling for an average of $185,000 and ranging up to $490,000.

Northeast of Golden and north of Wheat Ridge is one of the big boys of Denver's west side, the City of **Arvada**. Looking north from the top of the literal ridge that is the center of Wheat Ridge, you can see on the next ridge top 3 miles away the historic center of Arvada, now known as Olde Town Arvada. But Arvada has spread considerably from that historic beginning, out to the "horse country" of the far west side. Arvada's central area consists largely of homes typically built in the 1950s and 1960s. Home sales here have averaged $135,000 and ranged to $465,000.

Arvada, north of 80th Avenue, and Westminster, west of Sheridan Boulevard, pretty much define the residential majority of the area known as **Jefferson County North**. The parts of the two cities in this area — north, east and south of Standley Lake — are more like each other than they are like their respective city centers. A lot of new homes have gone in here in the last five or 10 years, primarily tract homes with some high-end custom homes and some of the patio homes preferred by empty-nesters. Jefferson County North homes were selling in 1995 in the average range of $93,000. There are lots of younger families here and a lot of shopping close by, along N. Wadsworth Boulevard. The area has an out-in-the country feel to it because you're looking west across the last prairie before the mountains, over the big empty spaces that contain Rocky Flats, the erstwhile bomb factory now beginning a long cleanup phase. It's a short shot north on Wadsworth to Broomfield and U.S. Highway 36 to Boulder.

West beyond Rocky Flats and Golden, off Colo. Highway 93, there are growing mountain developments up side roads such as Coal Creek Canyon, Golden Gate Canyon and Crawford Gulch. This is known as **Mountain Jefferson County North**, where residences have been selling around $157,000 on average.

Greater Denver's big mountain communities, though, tend to be off I-70 and U.S. Highway 285. Here communities such as **Genesee**, **Evergreen**, **Conifer**, **Aspen Park**, **Indian Hills**, **Kittredge** and **Hidden Valley** offer a lot of new, high-end living across ridge tops with fantastic vistas and hidden, pine-covered valleys and hillsides. The only drawback is the 30-minute commuting time from Evergreen to Denver, assuming no traffic jams, and 45 minutes to an hour from areas farther out (and those times are in good weather).

Homes up in this neck of the woods tend to average around $275,000, and condos around $162,000, based on 1995 sales, although they're likely to run higher, of course, in the prestige subdivisions. Riva Chase homes, for example, were going for

Photo: Daily Camera/Lourie Zipf

This house is in the Capitol Hill neighborhood.

an average of more than $500,000 in 1995. There are some older, less-expensive properties, though they're harder to find. But the bulk of opportunities are in burgeoning, although tasteful, developments.

Friends of ours who live in an older Genesee ramshackle in a side canyon, just off I-70 near Exits 253 and 254, have expressed the opinion that people up there look down on them because they're not millionaires. They're probably just paranoid. Genesee residential sales in 1995 only averaged around $357,000, with condos averaging around $157,000.

Evergreen is probably the largest, most-established community near I-70, about 8 miles south of it, actually, on Colo. Highway 74. There are more than 7,000 people in the City of Evergreen — 20,000 including the nearby communities of **Kittredge** and **Bergen Park** — and there's even a downtown, just below the dam that holds back Evergreen Lake. Evergreen also has shops, restaurants and the Little Bear bar, which pulls people up from Denver for its great musical evenings and singles scene. Housing here is more mixed than in the prestige suburb of Genesee. You're more likely to find inexpensive homes, but of course you can also find homes at $600,000 and up.

Mountain communities down U.S. Highway 285, in the Conifer/Aspen Park area, have Denver commuting times closer to an hour, but here you find properties in all price ranges, with some horse properties and more available space. You're looking at homes in this area averaging $188,000 sale prices in 1995.

Real Estate Resources

You can get more information on the local real estate market, Realtor licensing and ethics and other information involving the sale or purchase of homes, by contacting the following agencies:

Colorado Association of Realtors Inc., 790-7099

Denver Board of Realtors, 756-0553

Douglas/Elbert Board of Realtors, 688-0941

Evergreen-Conifer Association of Realtors, 674-7020

Jefferson County Association of Realtors, 233-7831

North Metro Denver Realtor Association, 451-5757

South Metro Denver Realtor Association, 797-3700

Real Estate Firms

The following are among Greater Denver's more well-known real estate brokerages:

THE KENTWOOD MOORE CO.
5690 DTC Blvd.
Englewood 773-3399

A one-office operation based in the Denver Tech Center, The Kentwood Moore Co. specializes in upper-price homes and does most of its brokerage in the south metro area, as well as some of the more expensive properties in the inner city. It offers the complete range of real estate services, including corporate relocations, condo conversions and new home sales. The company's 34 sales associates average around 15 years of experience. Average annual sales volume has been around $240 million.

MOORE AND CO.
390 Grant St.
Denver 778-6600

The largest independently owned real estate company in Colorado, Moore and Co. sold local properties worth more than $1 billion in 1994, and was looking at $1.1-1.2 billion in 1995. Moore and Co. has 430 agents and 19 Denver area offices. It is active all over the Denver area, north to Loveland and in Breckenridge, Frisco and Winter Park — with 10 metro and nine outlying offices throughout the state. The company sells a lot of new construction, as well as resale, and did $117 million in relocation business in 1994.

PERRY & BUTLER REALTY INC.
101 University Blvd., Ste. 100
Denver   394-2221

This Colorado company, founded in 1963, has 315 sales agents and 10 branch offices serving metropolitan Denver, Boulder and Longmont. It has a relocation division and sells residential real estate in the whole spectrum of incomes and price ranges. Local sales volume in fiscal year 1994 was $475 million.

RE/MAX MOUNTAIN STATES INC.
5445 DTC Pkwy.
Englewood   770-5531

Re/Max is really the real estate giant of the area. Re/Max has some 40 offices in Greater Denver, and each of them is independently owned and operated. When the *Denver Business Journal*'s April 28-May 4, 1995 issue rated the top Denver-area residential real estate brokers in terms of sales volume, 16 out of the top 23 were Re/Max offices. They're all joined together by the Re/Max International Referral Roster System.

COLDWELL BANKER
VAN SCHAACK & CO.
6041 S. Syracuse Way, Suite 300
Englewood   773-1820

Coldwell Banker Van Schaack & Co. focuses on the metropolitan Denver area. It has 428 full-time licensed agents and it had a 1994 sales volume of $677 million, according to the *Denver Business Journal*.

Residential Builders

The following are among Greater Denver's larger home builders:

MELODY HOMES
11031 Sheridan Blvd.
Westminster   466-1831

Melody Homes focuses on homes in the $100,000 to $180,000 range, building ranch style, tri-levels, multi-levels, two-stories —

it varies from place to place. Melody has recently concentrated its construction on subdivisions in Westminster, Thornton, unincorporated Arapahoe County southeast of Denver, Brighton and Erie.

PULTE HOME CORP.
15150 E. Iliff Ave.
Aurora   751-3700

Pulte Home Corp. has been building in 12 communities from Boulder to Douglas County, Aurora to Lakewood, including Highlands Ranch and masterplanned communities such as Signal Creek in Thornton and Green Mountain in Lakewood. Pulte Homes generally range from the low $120,000s to the $250,000s, averaging about $165,000. Pulte did about $81 million in sales in 1994, building almost 500 homes. Pulte's single-family homes, ranch and two-story homes, range in size from 1,300 to 3,000 square feet.

RYLAND HOMES
8787 Turnpike Dr., Ste. 220
Westminster   426-0111

A local division of a national home builder, Ryland builds from Thornton to Lakewood, Boulder to Parker. It builds homes ranging in price from $127,000 to $337,000; the average price is around $160,000. Ryland's been building in the metro area since 1986, and nationally for nearly 30 years. Among Ryland's awards has been the MAME Award for best house in the metro area, an award given by the Homebuilders Association of Metropolitan Denver.

RICHMOND HOMES
4600 S. Ulster St., Ste. 400
Denver   773-2727

Richmond Homes is Colorado's No. 1 builder, started here in 1977 and now a national company with Denver headquarters.

In the Denver area, Richmond sold more than 1,800 homes in 1994. It has homes in every price range, from townhomes to custom homes.

US HOME CORP.
5970 Greenwood Plaza Blvd., Ste. 310
Englewood   779-6100

Most of US Home's Greater-Denver building goes on in Douglas County or the far northwest quadrant, with the exception of the Wyndemere development in Thornton, Pride's Crossing in Aurora and The Meadows at Westwoods Ranch in Arvada. US Home also builds from Fort Collins to Colorado Springs, and in 1995 built a total of around 1,200 homes along the Front Range, 600-800 of those in the metro Denver area.

The company's homes range typically from the low $100,000s to the low $200,000s, with an average price of homes sold in 1995 at about $155,000. In January 1995 US Home Corp. was named the 1994 National Builder of the Year by *Professional Builder* magazine, its third time for this honor.

VILLAGE HOMES OF COLORADO
6 W. Dry Creek Cr., Ste. 200
Littleton   795-1976

Builder of about $93 million worth of homes in 1994, Village Homes works in more than a dozen different areas of Greater Denver including Arvada, Thornton, Arapahoe County, Douglas County, Littleton and Lakewood. Homes average around $185,000 but range from the mid $130,000s to the $250,000s.

Photo: Daily Camera/Lourie Zipf

A businessman takes a cellular-phone break on the 16th Street Mall.

Inside
Business and Industry

Colorado's economy, according to a local truism, always moves in the opposite direction from the national economy. So the writers at *Time* magazine may perhaps be forgiven their enthusiasm when they focused on Colorado in their 1993 cover story, "Boom Time in the Rockies."

Compared to the rest of the nation in the first few years of the 1990s, Greater Denver's economy may have seemed to be booming. But in actuality, especially compared to local conditions in the 1970s and early 1980s, the economic conditions might more accurately be described as a "boomlet." And slow growth is just fine, because Denverites know all too well just how bad the crash that follows a boom can be.

The "Dynasty" television series set in Denver a decade ago was well-suited to the mood of the times. As the oil boom heated up, skyscrapers popped up like gushers and transformed the city's skyline.

The fact is that the oil boom was mostly a real-estate boom. The oil business never accounted for more than a small fraction of local employment, but commercial building speculators and investors went wild. By the time the skyscrapers were completed, many of them were largely empty and hunting desperately for potential tenants. The fact that the computer industry, in which Colorado was a growing minipower, slumped in the mid-1980s as well, was also a drag.

By the late 1980s, however, with office vacancy rates at record levels and new housing starts and real-estate value increases at the lowest levels in decades, Greater Denver had become very price-competitive for new businesses and citizens. At the same time, the area's economic base was becoming more diverse and resilient. By the early 1990s, the combination of cost attractions plus reawakening local industry had set the area on course for its recent miniboom. In 1995, a local miniboom milestone was set with the first major "speculative" office building projects since the 1980s. Speculative means buildings are constructed without committed tenants, an indicator of faith in the market. They included a $110-million, eight-building office development in the Denver Technological Center and another $60-million office development in Southeast Denver. Speculative industrial construction has also gone bonkers, with 500,000 square feet of it predicted to break ground in 1995 and another 1 million square feet in 1996.

A decade ago, some Coloradans used to bemoan the fact that the state didn't have more Fortune 500 companies. Now, with the big boys downsizing nationwide, Colorado is counting its relative lack of megacompanies as a blessing. From 1992 to 1994, Colorado has seen a net in-migration of some 160,000. A good portion of the 110,000 more jobs created than lost in the state during that same period can be credited to small companies, many of them relocating to Colorado from California and other areas where the economic bloom of the '80s has wilted.

Colorado is expected to continue outpacing the nation in economic growth during the next decade, particularly in Greater Denver, which *Fortune* magazine in 1993 named as one of the nation's top-10 business cities. The arrival of tens of thousands of immigrants from recessionary economies elsewhere in the nation bolstered local businesses ranging from real estate and retail to furniture manufacturing and appliance sales. Coming out of a series of record ski seasons, with summer resort facilities rapidly developing, out-of-staters are accounting for most of the $6 billion-plus now being earned by Colorado's tourism industry. In-migration in 1995-1996 is slowing, however, and job growth is expected to fall more in line with the rest of the nation. Still, the Business Research Division of the University of Colorado's Graduate School of Business projected the state's net in-migration at 40,000 in 1995, with an employment growth of 55,300 in the same year. Colorado's unemployment rate in 1995 went the lowest it had in 17 years. Colorado's thriving economy left the state

government with a surplus of $427 million at the end of June 1995.

High-technology companies are prominent in Greater Denver's manufacturing sector, thanks in part to the national research centers that were established here during and after World War II, and to the dense cluster of academic and medical research communities. Colorado has been promoting high technology in every way it can through such agencies as the Colorado Advanced Technology Institute, which focuses on four different designated research centers for biotechnology, information technology, advanced materials processing technologies and advanced manufacturing technologies.

Besides promoting economic diversity, high tech is also helping the area ride out cutbacks in defense, government and other major industries, which have eaten into the workforces of local private-sector companies as well as federal installations such as Lowry Air Force Base's Technical Training Center, which began closing in 1994 and by 1995 had eliminated some 4,500 jobs and 3,000 students from the economy.

A *Denver Business Journal* survey found that nondefense federal jobs decreased by 2,000 in Greater Denver just between March 1994 and March 1995. Greater Denver's private-sector defense industry tends to be oriented more toward research and development than making weapons, so it is perhaps suffering less than might otherwise be from federal cutbacks. Martin Marietta Corp., one of the area's largest employers, has gone from about 14,000 employees in the 1980s to some 7,000 today. Yet Martin Marietta locally has been strengthened lately with its retooling as a technology company. Following the purchase of General Dynamics in 1994, the company's largest local segment, its Astronautics Group, actually showed a slight in-

Jila Maler has opened a branch of her successful custom Boulder clothing business in Cherry Creek.

crease in employment for the year. Now following the corporation's merger with Lockheed Corporation in 1995, resulting in the new company, Lockheed Martin, the corporation as a whole is expected to show an overall increase of perhaps 1,000 in Colorado employment for 1995.

Even more so than the big contractors, the support industries and skills bases that have grown up in the area as a result of the defense industry are making the transition to commercial markets.

Generally, Front Range Colorado feels justified in styling itself as "Silicon Mountain," after California's Silicon Valley, and Greater Denver is the base of that mountain. Greater Denver certainly is not among the nation's big population centers, yet look at maps showing state by state where industries are located and where they're most rapidly growing. Colorado jumps out in many knowledge-based enterprises, including computer hardware, software and peripherals, scientific instruments and medical equipment. Greater Denver, again, is the focus of Colorado's map. It's among the national leaders and fastest-growing

areas in two industries in which the United States is still the undisputed world leader: biotechnology and telecommunications. The Denver/Boulder area has recently been labeled "Telecom Valley." Greater Denver is the only major population center one satellite bounce away from both coasts, and Greater Denver is the headquarters of the world's largest cable company, Tele-Communications Inc. Hughes Communications in 1994 finished its $120 million Direct TV facility in the Douglas County seat of Castle Rock to begin national satellite TV service in competition with the cable industry.

High-technology products are what the manufacturing crowd likes to call value-added, which means they pack more value into the weight of product than, say, soybeans or carpeting. This means export demand. Since well before the downtown opening of the Denver World Trade Center in 1988, the state has been doing handsprings to get foreign investors and trading partners to pay attention. Colorado exports of $4.6 billion in 1994 represented a 30 percent increase over 1993. Agriculture accounted for 19 percent of exports. The rest was manufactured products led by industrial machinery and computer equipment, electronics, primary metals and rubber and plastic products. Located midway between Canada and Mexico, its two biggest trading partners, Greater Denver expects the new Denver International Airport to be a big export advantage.

New business growth is largely small business growth, and a study by the *Denver Business Journal* in May 1995 revealed that Greater Denver ranks fourth nationwide in the number of small businesses per capita.

Greater Denver's two main employment centers are downtown Denver and the south I-25 corridor around the City of Greenwood Village's Denver Technological Center, a complex of office buildings and light industry on Denver's southeast corner. Denver planners envision a new business cluster employing tens of thousands in tourism and international business in the Gateway, some 4,500 acres of land around Denver International Airport's entrance.

Where the Businesses Are: A Regional Profile

The City of Denver is the first place to look for jobs and businesses. It's got nearly half of Greater Denver's jobs, after all, and those jobs focus most strongly in the downtown area around Denver's 17th Street, "the Wall Street of the Rockies." Statewide industries tend to put their administrative offices in Denver, so Denver is a national business center for mining and agricultural businesses, thanks to the state's leadership in natural-resource industries. Various Colorado counties can claim first or top-rank place in national cattle production, oil-well drilling and production of oil, natural gas and helium. Denver has more head-

quarters of major gold-mining companies than any city in the nation.

Denver leads Greater Denver as an employer in finance, insurance, real estate, banking, services, government, air transportation, construction, communications businesses, wholesale and retail trade, the manufacturing of food products and nonelectrical machinery. Construction began in 1995 in Denver on a new Merrill Lynch regional headquarters that is expected to employ up to 5,000 people within a decade.

Jefferson County actually leads Greater Denver in overall manufacturing, thanks to the county's high level of education and high-tech industries as well as to such gargantuan manufacturing companies as Martin Marietta Astronautics Group, the Adolph Coors Brewing Company and the Rocky Flats Plant, a government nuclear weapons plant. Although employment at all of these companies has downsized recently — capsized might be a better word for Rocky Flats, where cleanup has replaced production as the point of its employees' existence —Jeffco has plenty of manufacturing to spare. It leads Greater Denver's employment picture in production of fabricated metals, nonelectrical machinery (which includes computers) and scientific and medical instruments. Jefferson County, particularly in Westminster and Broomfield, has also been part of a major land rush in business-park development projects along the U. S. Highway 36 corridor between Boulder and Denver.

High-technology or information-based industries aren't the exclusive purview of any one area. Adams County has its share of companies such as Lockheed Information Technology. Arapahoe County has plenty of high-tech companies, with a particular strength in aerospace employers such as Hughes Aircraft and McDonnell Douglas. Ultimate Electronics in 1995 be-

The National Renewable Energy Laboratory

The Denver area is distinguished by its large number of national research centers such as the National Institute of Standards and Technology, the National Oceanic and Atmospheric Administration, the National Center for Atmospheric Research . . . the national this and the national that.

Arguably the most distinctive and important of the national-somethings is the National Renewable Energy Laboratory, the Department of Energy laboratory commonly referred to as NREL ("En-Rel"). Located in the Jefferson County community of Golden, this is America's center of research and development on renewable energy and energy-efficient technologies.

NREL was founded as the Solar Energy Research Laboratory in 1977, but its fields of interest grew quickly beyond the pursuit of solar energy to wind energy, biofuels, waste management, superconductivity, energy-efficient buildings and industrial processes and other ways of providing alternatives to — and enhancing the yield of — the world's declining fossil-fuel reserves.

More than a research institution, however, NREL plays midwife to the birth of new American industries and promotes the fortunes of the nation's nascent commercial renewable-energy sector. Look at the gigantic wind turbines spinning on the windswept flats of NREL's National Wind Technology Center at the base of the Foothills north of Golden, and you can see the new generation of commercial products that NREL funding and technical expertise has helped to produce. These products can now generate power

Photo: National Renewable Energy Laboratory

The National Renewable Energy Laboratory's Solar Energy Research Facility, located in Jefferson County near Golden, is the nation's research and development center for solar energy technologies, superconductivity and related materials science.

that is price-competitive with fossil-fuel sources. Worldwide wind power capacity is expected to grow from some 4,000 megaWatts today to 50,000 megaWatts by the year 2010, and NREL is dedicated to making sure United States companies get a piece of the pie. United States wind power technologies supported by NREL are going into utility power grids around the world. $11 million in DOE funds funneled through NREL turbine development efforts just in 1995-96, for example, had by mid-1995 resulted in current and projected sales of those turbines by United States companies amounting to $300 million.

The Solar Energy Research Facility, snuggled against South Table Mountain west of NREL's office headquarters, is a futuristic complex that was completed in 1993 and houses 42 laboratories. Here research and development concentrate on photovoltaics, superconductivity and related materials sciences. As in wind power, NREL works in solar energy technology development with United States companies and has done much to promote the spread of their products in developing countries.

NREL's technical and financial assistance has helped United States companies in everything from converting corn and cellulose to ethanol and producing electricity from garbage, to improving batteries and recycling carpets. You go nuts if you try to figure out everything that goes on at this amazing place, but a good way to get some appreciation for it is to visit the NREL Visitors' Center just off I-70 in Golden. You can call them at 384-6565 for information.

gan building a $15 million headquarters in Thornton, with anticipated employment of 270.

As a white-collar employer, Arapahoe County isn't very far behind Denver itself. In fact, the County's Denver Technological Center in Greenwood Village and other business parks such as Greenwood Plaza and the Inverness Business Park, make the I-25 corridor from Hampden Avenue almost a twin city to Denver. Arapahoe County, by the most recent estimates, had 60,000 fewer residents than Jefferson County but about 15,000 more jobs. The Denver Tech Center and the I-25 corridor are probably the cause of that odd imbalance.

Arapahoe County is a close second to Denver and leaves the rest of Greater Denver far behind as far as employment in com-

munications. It contains MCI's regional offices, US West headquarters and cable giants Tele-Communications Inc. and Jones Intercable. US West in 1994 opened two service centers in Arapahoe County that add another 3,600 employees. Arapahoe County is also second only to Denver in printing and publishing businesses, engineering services, business services and insurance.

In some ways, the economies of Jefferson County and Arapahoe County are very similar. Their populations and average wages, for example, both lie between the highs of Denver and the lows of Adams and Douglas counties. They're also close cousins in their leading or near-leading portions of employment in nonelectrical machinery production and scientific and medical instruments industries. Outside Denver, Jefferson and Arapahoe are the two giants of engineering services employment, with Arapahoe exceeding Jefferson by 50 percent. Both are big in construction, health services and retail trades.

Employment by the federal government concentrates in Denver and Jefferson County. Geography has made Denver the regional center for just about every federal agency, from courts to the EPA. Outside Denver, federal government employment in Jefferson County is more than twice that of the other three counties combined, thanks to such facilities as the National Renewable Energy Laboratory and the Denver Federal Center. The Federal Center, just off U.S. Highway 6 in Lakewood, is a kind of mini-Washington, D.C., although jobs have been getting the axe there recently in record numbers.

As a regional transportation hub, Greater Denver is a big air transportation, trucking and warehousing employer. Denver, which owns the big airport, has 95 percent of employment in air transportation. But Adams County has 57 percent more employment in trucking and warehousing than the rest of Greater Denver combined, and it contains 37 percent of all trucking and warehousing in the state of Colorado. Adams County enfolds both Stapleton International Airport and its successor, Denver International Airport, and provides added incentive for shippers to locate there.

Sandwiched between I-70 and I-25 and crosscut by I-76, Adams County has a strong surface transportation advantage as well. And warehousers enjoy an abundance of good land west and north of Commerce City. But the center of this industrial area is Commerce City, aptly named because it's the only city in Colorado with a larger working population than resident population. Its working population outnumbers its residential population by almost a two-to-one ratio. Commerce City has a lot of heavy industries, including the Conoco and Total Petroleum refineries as well as the area's heaviest concentration of electrical machinery manufacturing.

The Workforce

Economic growth is expected to slow somewhat in the near future, with construction employment having passed its peak in 1994, but that doesn't mean that employment opportunities won't keep growing overall. In fact, a Coopers & Lybrand survey of 61 local CEOs in 1995 showed that worker shortages — particularly for skilled workers — are a serious local concern. The result is significant increases in wages, perks and benefits, employment advertising and the use of temporary workers.

Greater Denver now employs close to 900,000 and from 1993 to 1998 was projected to add more than 100,000 new jobs. Professionals are in particular demand, some 32,000 more professional positions being created from 1993 to 1998. Services are looking for another 22,000 jobs over that same period. Clerical workers will be able to choose from about 13,000 new jobs. So will those working in sales. Blue-collar workers can anticipate 12,000 new jobs and administrators and managers about 10,000.

Greater Denver may be in the national boondocks in the minds of some coastal urbanites, but that doesn't mean its workforce isn't full of ethnic diversity. The first European language spoken in Colorado was Spanish. When Japanese businessmen come calling, they are often met by descendants of Japanese-American Coloradans who have been here for generations, their ancestors being most famous for their contributions to the truck farming industries of the Arkansas River valley and other regions.

Hispanics today make up nearly one-fourth of Greater Denver's population. Hispanics own about 5,000 businesses in the metropolitan area. Ninety percent of them were born in the state, and about the same percentage remains bilingual.

Denver's black population has been a part of Denver's history long before the city's first black newspaper started publishing in 1881. As many as one-third of all cowboys in the Old West, it has been estimated, were black. Before the turn of the century, Denver's black population was reputed as among the most progressive in the nation, and entrepreneurism and business ownership have been a part of that tradition from its start.

On average, Greater Denver might well claim to have one of the nation's most sophisticated workforces. The most recent national census showed that Colorado leads the nation in the percentage (18 percent) of its population that has bachelor's degrees. The only competitors that even come close to that figure are Washington, D.C.,

and Connecticut, both with 16 percent. Only Washington, D.C., and four other states exceed Colorado in the percentage of citizens with advanced degrees. And Colorado leads the nation in the number of businesses per capita connected to the Internet, according to *The Denver Post*.

Greater Denver has no problem pulling the best and the brightest away from other parts of the country. Colorado's natural beauty and quality of life are nearly always cited by employment recruiters as prime advantages in attracting an educated workforce.

Suggested Reading

More information on the economy, business community, labor market and relocation options is available from a wide variety of agencies.

The Denver Job Bank. Subtitle: *The Job Hunter's Guide to Denver*. Published by Bob Adams Inc., 260 Center Street, Holbrook, Massachusetts 02343. An extensive compendium of employment opportunities arranged by categories of business.

The Top 25 Lists, a supplement to *The Denver Business Journal*, 1700 Broadway, Suite 515, Denver, Colorado 80290, 837-3500. A magazine-format guide to the top 25 (or more) businesses/organizations in more employment categories than one can imagine. Includes address, phone number and extensive additional information on each business/organization.

Directory of Colorado Manufacturers, a directory of more than 4,500 companies. Published by the Business Research Divi-

Insiders' Tips

The Denver Public Library has a respectable collection of government documents and the very useful data therein, but our designated government repository library is Norlin Library at the University of Colorado at Boulder.

Photo: Daily Camera/Lourie Zipf

The Denver Tech Center is one of the hubs of business in Greater Denver.

sion, Graduate School of Business Admin-istration, Campus Box 420, University of Colorado, Boulder, Colorado 80309-0420, 492-8227.

Job-hunters can get a good idea of the skills in demand from *Occupational Supply/Demand Report* for State Planning Region 3 (Denver/Boulder Labor Market Area); and from the *Occupational Employment Outlook*, 1993-1998, Denver-Boulder Region. Both are produced by the Colorado Department of Labor and Employment, Labor Market Information, 1515 Arapahoe St., Denver, Colorado 80202, 620-4856. The department also provides wage data.

Economic Reports and Forecasts

Several leading economic forecasts are available to help new or potential residents and businesses see how the economy and its various niches are doing and what they are expected to do. The State of Colorado's pre-eminent forecast is *Focus Colorado, Economic and Revenue Forecast*, which comes out quarterly from the office of Nancy McCallin, chief economist for the Colorado Legislative Council, 866-4782. The September issue is typically the one that spends the most time analyzing the economies of specific counties and regions.

Academia's biggest analysis and forecast of the local business climate is the *Colorado Business Economic Outlook Forum*, produced annually in December by the University of Colorado's College of Business and Administration. Cost is $25.

The most popular private-sector fore-cast is the one produced each year by Tucker Hart Adams, chief economist for Colorado National Bank, 585-5060.

Contacts

Regional

Colorado Department of Labor and Employment, Job Service Center
393 S. Harlan St.
Lakewood   937-0760

Colorado Office of Business Development
1625 Broadway, Ste. 1710
Denver   892-3840

Colorado Association of Commerce & Industry
1776 Lincoln St., Ste. 1200
Denver   831-7411

Public Service Company of Colorado, Economic Development
1445 Market St.
Denver   294-2280

Denver Regional Council of Governments, Development Services
2480 W. 26th Ave., #200B
Denver   455-1000

By County

DENVER
Business Support Services
The Downtown Denver Partnership Inc.,
511 16th St., Ste. 200, Denver   534-6161

Greater Denver Chamber of Commerce, Business Development
1445 Market St., Denver   620-8029

Denver Mayor's Office of Economic Development
216 16th St., Ste. 1000
Denver   640-7100

ADAMS COUNTY

Adams County Economic Development
11990 Grant St., Ste. 220
Denver   450-5106

ARAPAHOE COUNTY

South Metro Denver Chamber of Commerce
7901 Southpark Plaza
Littleton   795-0142
(Serves Arapahoe County and parts of Denver and Douglas counties.)

DOUGLAS COUNTY

Southeast Denver/Douglas County Economic Development Council
9605 Maroon Cr., Ste. 210
Englewood   792-9447

JEFFERSON COUNTY

Jefferson Economic Council
1726 Cole Blvd., Bldg. 22, Ste. 210
Golden   202-2965

Pope John Paul II and President Clinton addressed the crowds at
World Youth Day in Denver in summer 1993.

Inside
Places of Worship

Greater Denver has an active and involved religious community, with all major denominations represented. There are both Japanese and Vietnamese Buddhist congregations, a sizeable Greek Orthodox community, a Korean Christian Church and many Catholics, Methodists, Baptists, Mormons and Jews. This diversity dates back even to before Colorado was a state; by the time of statehood in 1876, 20 religious denominations had been organized in Colorado. St. Joseph Hospital, the first of Denver's many church-affiliated hospitals, was founded in 1873, and Jews and Catholics, as well as many Protestants, were conducting services in and around Denver at that time. Present-day Congregation Emanuel can trace its beginnings back to its incorporation in 1874 and, even before that, to the establishment of the Hebrew Burial Society in 1859. Similarly, enough Catholics were in Colorado during the territorial period that the Rocky Mountains were removed from the authority of Santa Fe and recognized as a separate vicariate in 1868. The first Bishop of Denver, Joseph Machebeuf, was consecrated in 1887.

Denver is truly an ecumenical city. The Mormon faith is strong here but does not have the kind of influence it enjoys elsewhere in the Rocky Mountains. Similarly, Catholicism, which swept into Denver from the San Luis Valley, is not as dominant a force as it is in some other Southwestern cities.

Certainly Catholics got plenty of attention when Pope John Paul II visited Denver in August 1993 for World Youth Day. The Pope's mass at Cherry Creek State Park was a most historic occasion and attracted nearly 500,000 people. Year round, pilgrims travel to the **Mother Cabrini Shrine**, 20189 Cabrini Boulevard in Golden, 526-0758, for prayer and contemplation. The shrine is open to the public daily, and mass is celebrated each morning. Take I-70 west to the Morrison Exit 259, then take U.S. Highway 40 (the frontage road) west about a mile.

Also in Morrison, scenic **Red Rocks Park** is the site of an annual nondenominational Easter sunrise service that fills the 9,000-seat natural amphitheater to capacity in good weather. Take I-70 west to the Morrison Exit 259, and turn south

---

Get up early for the Easter Sunrise Service at Red Rocks Park in Morrison — when the weather's good, the ampitheater fills to capacity.

Insiders' Tips

toward Morrison; watch for signs marking the entrance to Red Rocks on the right.

In this brief chapter, we want to introduce you to just a few of the more historic or unusual houses of worship in the metropolitan area. It would not be practical to list every place of worship in Denver, nor would it be appropriate for us to suggest one rather than another. To find a specific place of worship for yourself and your family, consult the listing of religious organizations at the end of this chapter or the Yellow Pages under churches, mosques, religious organizations and synagogues. The *Church Guide* lists some (but not all) of the Christian churches in the area and is available free of charge in local supermarkets and chambers of commerce.

Also, we have in most cases avoided mentioning hours of services, as these are subject to change. Where we have given specific times, it's advisable to call ahead to confirm.

Historic Houses of Worship

Denver's oldest existing churches are located downtown. Many of them are described in a booklet of six walking tours in downtown Denver known collectively as *The Mile High Trail*, which is available for $1.50 at the Greater Denver Chamber of Commerce, 1445 Market Street, or the Denver Visitors Information Center, 225 W. Colfax Avenue.

The oldest extant church building in the city is found on the Auraria Campus, where it functions as the college art gallery. The small Romanesque/Gothic building now known as the **Emmanuel Gallery** was built to serve an Episcopalian congregation in 1876 and was converted into a Jewish synagogue in 1903. Services ceased in 1958 and the building was purchased by Wolfgang Pogzeba, who used it as an art studio until 1973.

Nearby is **St. Cajetan's**, one of three Catholic churches clustered in this area. Each church served a different ethnic group. Built in 1925, St. Cajetan's services attracted Spanish-speaking Catholics until the construction of the Auraria campus in the 1970s prompted the congregation to relocate. Today this lovely blue-and-white structure is a performing-arts and meeting space for the campus.

Built in a Romanesque style, **St. Elizabeth's Church**, also on the Auraria campus (off Speer Boulevard) has a cornerstone date of 1896 and is still an active Catholic parish. It traditionally served a German congregation. Services are held midday during the week and on Saturday evenings and Sunday mornings. The church is open from 9 AM to 3 PM for those who would just like to take a peek inside. Call 534-4014.

The **Denver Buddhist Temple**, at 1947 Lawrence Street, was established in 1916 by Japanese immigrants, but today about a third of its congregation is not Japanese-American. Sunday morning services are held in both Japanese and English. The temple is associated with the Jodo Shin Shu sect of Buddhism and is also the headquarters for eight other Buddhist temples in Colorado, Wyoming and Nebraska. Group tours are given on Wednesdays; the priests appreciate advance notice at 295-1844.

Trinity United Methodist Church, 1820 Broadway, is one of Denver's most distinctive churches as its Gothic style contrasts with the modern banks and office buildings that tower over it. Built in 1887, the church has an active and growing congregation and has been made wheelchair accessible. Call 839-1493.

Nearby at 1900 California Street, the **Holy Ghost Church** provides an even more dramatic contrast between old and

Historic St. Elizabeth's Church, completed in 1896, still is an active Catholic parish.

new. Built in 1943 by May Bonfils in memory of her parents, who were prominent early Denverites, the Catholic church is now tucked under a gleaming green glass skyscraper, the 1999 Broadway Building, which was constructed around and over it in the mid-1980s. The church is the only one in the archdiocese built exclusively for daily exposition of the blessed sacrament and offers a Latin High Mass on Sundays, as well as daily masses. Call 292-1556.

Episcopal services in the high church tradition are held at **St. Andrew's Church**, 2015 Glenarm Place, a Gothic-revival structure designed by Ralph Adams Cram and completed in 1909. The church is noted for its art-deco stained-glass windows. There is a Wednesday service and a Tuesday evening prayer and Eucharist. There are weekend services as well. Call 296-1712.

The twin bell towers of the **Cathedral of the Immaculate Conception**, 1530 Logan Street, pierce the Denver skyline not far from the secular golden dome of the state capitol. Completed in 1912, the cathedral became the first Minor Basilica

west of the Mississippi in 1979. Visitors can go inside to see its beautiful stained-glass windows from 6 AM to 6 PM daily. For information about services, call 831-7010.

Temple Emanuel, at 1595 Pearl Street, was designed in an unusual Moorish style. Built in 1898 to serve Denver's oldest and largest Jewish congregation, the building now functions as a music and performing-arts center (Congregation Emanuel itself has moved to 51 Grape Street.) Temple Emanuel's 950-seat auditorium and ballroom are the site for a variety of musical and dance events. Call the Temple Events Center at 860-9400 for a schedule.

Architecturally significant churches can be found outside the downtown area too. **Park Hill United Methodist Church**, 5209 Montview Boulevard, is a Southwestern-style church built in the 1920s. The church became integrated in 1961 in the heyday of the Civil Rights movement, when its first black members joined. Today the church serves a racially mixed congregation. Call 322-1867.

St. Thomas Episcopal Church, a few blocks away at 2201 Dexter Street, is an

St. Cajetan's served Spanish-speaking Catholics until the Auraria Campus was built.

excellent example of the Spanish Baroque style. The church has an elaborately carved entryway, a central courtyard and a red tile roof. With a reputation for being inclusive, the church draws from a wide geographic and demographic base. The church is wheelchair-accessible and offers a Sunday service signed for the deaf. Call 388-4395.

Old St. Patrick's Mission Church, 3325 Pecos Street, was designed in 1907 in the manner of old Spanish missions. Granted landmark status, the church is adjacent to **Our Lady of Light Monastery,** which houses an order of Capuchin Poor Clare sisters from Mexico. The neighborhood today is still largely Spanish-speaking. Mass is held on Sundays. Call 433-6328.

Not far from St. Patrick's is **Our Lady of Mt. Carmel Church,** 3549 Navajo Street, which celebrated its 100th anniversary in 1994. The church traditionally served an Italian congregation, and although Italians still make up a substantial part of the congregation, the neighborhood has become more of a melting pot (a Brazilian restaurant is across the street from

the church). Masses are held weekdays and Sundays; call 455-0447 for times and more information.

One of the prettiest churches in Denver is the **Evans Memorial Chapel** on the University of Denver campus. Started in 1873 but not operational until 1878, this sandstone treasure originally stood at 13th and Bannock streets. The chapel was given to the Methodist Church by John Evans, Colorado's second territorial governor, in memory of his daughter Josephine. It was moved to its current site stone by stone in 1959 and listed on the National Register of Historic Places in 1974. Although the non-denominational chapel is still used by some student religious groups, its principal use is for weddings. Catholic mass is observed every Sunday. Call 871-4442.

Religious Television Programming

The sermon from the **Riverside Baptist Church,** 2401 E. Alcott Street, 433-8665, is broadcast on Channel 2 at 7:30 AM each Sunday. Check local listings for other religious programming.

Resources

COLORADO COUNCIL OF CHURCHES
1234 Bannock St.   825-4910

AFRICAN METHODIST EPISCOPAL CHURCHES OF COLORADO
3100 Richard Allen Ct.   320-1712

CHRISTIAN CHURCH (DISCIPLES OF CHRIST)
2080 Kline St.
Lakewood   274-8567

EVANGELICAL LUTHERAN CHURCH IN AMERICA
7000 N. Broadway No. 401   427-7553

THE GREEK ORTHODOX CATHEDRAL OF THE ASSUMPTION
4610 E. Alameda Ave.   388-9314

ROCKY MOUNTAIN CONFERENCE UNITED CHURCH OF CHRIST
7000 N. Broadway No. 420   428-0045

UNITARIAN UNIVERSALISTS
1510 Glen Ayr Dr., Ste. No. 4
Lakewood   238-4051

AMERICAN BAPTIST CHURCH
1344 Pennsylvania St.   831-7231

EPISCOPAL DIOCESE OF COLORADO
1300 Washington St.   837-1173

NATIONAL BAPTIST CONVENTION
195 S. Monaco Pkwy.   355-0297

CATHOLIC ARCHDIOCESE OF DENVER
200 Josephine St.   388-4411

PRESBYTERY OF DENVER (PRESBYTERIAN CHURCH U.S.A.)
1710 S. Grant St.   777-2453

ROCKY MOUNTAIN UNITED METHODIST CONFERENCE
2200 S. University Blvd.   733-3736

DENVER BUDDHIST TEMPLE
Tri-State Buddhist Headquarters
1947 Lawrence St.   295-1844

CHURCH OF JESUS CHRIST OF LATTER-DAY SAINTS
Denver North Mission
11172 N. Huron St., Ste. No. 21
Northglenn   252-7192

Denver South Mission
2001 E. Easter Ave.
Littleton   794-6457

REORGANIZED CHURCH OF JESUS CHRIST AND LATTER-DAY SAINTS
Denver Stake & Regional Office
9501 Lou Dr.
Denver   426-5900

COLORADO MUSLIM SOCIETY
P.O. Box 24564
Denver   696-9800

SYNAGOGUE COUNCIL OF GREATER DENVER
P.O. Box 102732
Denver 80250   759-8485

Faith on the Frontier, a book compiled by the Colorado Council of Churches in 1976, was used as the source for much of the historical data in this chapter. *Denver: The City Beautiful* by Thomas J. Noel and Barbara S. Norgren (Historic Denver, Inc.) contains a brief section on Greater Denver church architecture, and is a wonderful resource for anyone interested in Denver's architectural history.

Inside
Media

Greater Denver is not exactly a media center, at least not in the sense of New York or Los Angeles. It doesn't produce a lot of television programs or magazines, although it does occasionally show up in movies. Still, at least in part because Greater Denver is home to telecommunications industry giants Jones Intercable and Tele-Communications, Inc., it may very well become a major stop on the information highway. And Denver does have something that most comparably sized cities don't: two daily newspapers.

Newspapers

Denver is one of the very few U.S. cities remaining with two independent daily newspapers. Over the years, rumor has had it that either *The Denver Post* or the *Rocky Mountain News* was on the verge of folding — and although such rumors continue, as of this writing both papers are holding on. They fight each other for readership and advertising, and each has its fans and detractors. The *News* leads in daily circulation, a fact that it touts loudly whenever new circulation figures are released. The *Post* prefers to emphasize trends over raw numbers: it's gaining readers while the *News* has been losing them. Both are morning papers, but while *The Denver Post* is a broadsheet, the *Rocky Mountain News* has a tabloid format.

For readers, the newspaper war has

KCNC-TV 4 newsman Bob Palmer is one of the most-recognized faces and voices in Denver television.

meant improved color in both papers and fiercely competitive subscription rates. As in most cities, the dailies have special sections depending on the day of the week. Looking for recipes and food stories? Pick up the Wednesday edition of either paper. Looking for something to do on the weekends? Pullout weekend entertainment guides are published each Friday.

Hate it or love it, many Denverites pick up *Westword*, the city's weekly arts and entertainment paper. Why not — it's free and has comprehensive lists of what's going on around town.

There are also many community papers, too many to list here. Specialized publications are always coming into and out of existence to serve a particular region (downtown) or interest (art).

Dailies

ROCKY MOUNTAIN NEWS
400 W. Colfax Ave.
Denver   892-5000

The first issue of the *Rocky Mountain News* — four pages, 500 copies — came out in 1859, published by William N. Byers. In 1901, the first year that accurate measurements could be made, the upstart *Denver Evening Post* surpassed the *Rocky Mountain News* in circulation for the first time; the two papers have battled for readership and advertising ever since. The *News* was purchased in 1926 by Scripps-Howard during a decade of particularly acrimonious competition, and in 1928, having disposed of or incorporated their other competitors, the *Post* and the *News* called a truce. But in 1993 when the *News* temporarily dropped the price of its Sunday issue from 75¢ to 25¢, Greater Denver saw the return of the kind of drastic price-cutting that characterized the 1920s. The *News* is generally more conser-

vative in its editorial viewpoints than the *Post*, but this varies depending on the topic.

THE DENVER POST
1560 Broadway
Denver   820-1010

The *Post* has a long and colorful history. It was founded in 1895 by Harry Heye Tammen and Frederick Gilmer Bonfils. The early *Post* was a prime exemplar of sensational journalism, relying on stunts and gossip to attract readership. In the '20s, Tammen and Bonfils got themselves entangled in one fine mess, the Teapot Dome scandal. Originally vehemently opposed to questionable oil leases in Wyoming, the *Post* dropped the issue when paid to do so. Tammen died of cancer in 1924, and Bonfils resigned in 1926.

After Bonfils died in 1933, ownership passed largely to his daughters. In the 1960s, May Bonfils sold her stock to S.I. Newhouse, head of a chain of newspapers and magazines. Helen Bonfils contested the sale, and after years of litigation, Newhouse finally dropped his bid to gain control of the *Post* in 1973.

The *Post* was sold to the Times Mirror Company, owners of the *Los Angeles Times*, in 1980, and sold again to William Dean Singleton of the Dallas-based MediaNews Group in 1987.

The *Post* switched from evening to morning distribution in 1982.

Weeklies

WESTWORD
1621 18th St.
Denver   296-7744

Owned by New Times, a national publisher of "alternative" papers, *Westword* is known for its muckraking investigative stories and is depended upon for its arts and entertainment coverage. Not

KMGH-Channel 7 is one of Denver's major TV stations.

everyone admires the weekly paper's zeal in pursuing stories, as is evidenced by heated letters to the editor. But a few of its articles, such as a recent investigation of the Rocky Flats grand jury proceedings that examined who should be held responsible for environmental crimes, have won awards and national media attention. *Westword* is distributed free throughout Greater Denver and hits the streets late Tuesday afternoon. You can find *Westword* in boxes on street corners all over town. Its art/dining/ entertainment listings are superb.

SENTINEL NEWSPAPERS
1224 Wadsworth Blvd.
Lakewood   *239-9890*
This company publishes weekly newspapers for residents of Arvada, Lakewood and Wheat Ridge, and an on-line edition of the *Daily Times*.

THE DENVER BUSINESS JOURNAL
1700 Broadway
Denver   *837-3500*
The weekly *Denver Business Journal* covers local business news in depth, with specialized sections including one on small businesses. The paper comes out on Friday and is available by subscription or throughout downtown Denver for a single copy price of $1.

BROOMFIELD ENTERPRISE
26 Garden Cr.
Broomfield   *466-3636*
This community paper is owned by Boulder Publishing, which publishes the *Daily Camera*, Boulder's daily newspaper. The *Enterprise* is delivered free to Broomfield residences and carries news of Broomfield, Greater Denver's most northwestern community. Regular offerings include news and

Greater Denver has more industries related to cable television than any place outside New York City.

Insiders' Tips

feature stories, editorials and classified ads. Coverage is strong on government, business, schools and sports. The paper also publishes special sections ranging from homes and gardens to election issues.

Weekly newspapers are published for residents of Englewood, Highlands Ranch, Littleton, Evergreen, Golden, Greenwood Village and Westminster. If you live there or are interested in news about these communities, check for these papers at local newsstands.

Magazines and Special Interest Publications

5280
5280 Publishing, Inc.
P.O. Box 4194
Denver 80204   832-5280

Denver has seen its share of city magazines come and go. The new kid on the block, *5280*, "Denver's Mile-High Magazine," debuted in 1993. (For those who don't know, 5,280 feet equals 1 mile.) It's fresh, independent and has a lively design. *5280* is published bimonthly. Single issues are $2.95 at newsstands throughout the city.

COLORADO HOMES & LIFESTYLES
COLORADO BUSINESS MAGAZINE
Wiesner Inc.
7009 S. Potomac, Englewood   397-7600

Two magazines with long track records are *Colorado Homes & Lifestyles* and *Colorado Business Magazine*, both Wiesner Publications. *Colorado Homes &*

Lifestyles, published bimonthly, is a wealth of information about home and garden design, while the monthly *Colorado Business* surveys the movers and shakers in the state, with an emphasis on Denver.

COLORADO EXPRESSION
New West Publishing
10200 E. Girard Ave., Ste. 222B
Denver   751-0696

Poised somewhere in terms of longevity — and focus — between *Colorado Homes & Lifestyles* and *5280* is *Colorado Expression*. The summer issue of this glossy quarterly is worth picking up for its annual statewide listing of art galleries. The fall issue features a dining and entertainment guide. Single copies are $3.

THE BLOOMSBURY REVIEW
1028 Bannock St.
Denver   892-0620

A bimonthly book "magazine" of reviews and interviews, *The Bloomsbury Review* is printed on newsprint and available free of charge at local bookstores. TBR has a national audience but emphasizes regional writers. You'll find an occasional bestselling writer profiled in here, but TBR's mission is to call attention to good, but lesser known, writers.

COLORADO PARENT MAGAZINE
2430 S. University Ave., Ste. 205
Denver   320-1000

Formerly *Denver Parent*, this monthly magazine includes a comprehensive calendar of events and classes of interest to parents in the Greater Denver area. The free paper comes out the first of each month

and can be picked up in about 800 different locations around town, including libraries and bookstores. They also publish an annual A-Z comprehensive directory of local resources for parents each December ($4.95). In July they distribute a free birthday guide, with listings of restaurants, party planners, suppliers and the like.

HIGH COUNTRY NEWS

119 Grand Ave.
Paonia   (970) 527-4898

An environmentally oriented newspaper, *High Country News* is published by the intrepid husband-and-wife team of Ed and Betsy Marston in Paonia, Colorado. The much-praised paper focuses on issues intrinsic to the West, such as use of public lands and water and grazing rights. This sharp biweekly is highly recommended to Greater Denver newcomers who would like to know more about the region they now call home. It's available at Tattered Cover Bookstore and other locations throughout the city.

OUT FRONT

244 Washington St.
Denver   778-7900

A gay and lesbian newspaper, *Out Front* is published every two weeks (with a break at Christmas). The paper is free and is available at local bars, restaurants, gay businesses and bookstores. It's noted for its entertainment and nightlife listings. Mail subscription is available for a small charge.

Radio

Nothing but the Rocky Mountain weather changes as much as Denver radio stations. One day you're listening to jazz, the next day the station has gone country-Western. Consider that caveat when tuning in to the stations listed below, and for an up-to-date list, check the entertainment pages in *The Denver Post* and the *Rocky Mountain News* and the "Friday Magazine" in the *Daily Camera*.

ADULT CONTEMPORARY

KOSI 101.1 FM
KQKS 104.3 FM (Top 40)
KWMX 107.5 FM
KGOL 107.9 FM

CLASSICAL

KCFR 90.1 FM (National Public Radio)
KVOD 99.5 FM

COUNTRY

KYGO 1600 AM and 98.5 FM
KLMO 1060 AM
KZDG 92.5 FM
KGLL 96.1 FM
KUAD 99.1 FM

CHRISTIAN

KLZ 560 AM (Contemporary)
KLT 800 AM (Country)
KPOF 910 AM (Classical)
KRKS 990 AM & 94.7 FM
KQXI 1550 AM (Music/talk/sports)
KWBI 91.1 FM

KIDS

KKYD 1340 AM

JAZZ

KHIH 95.7 FM
KUVO 89.3 FM

MEXICAN/SPANISH

KCUV 1150 AM
KBNO 1220 AM
KJME 1390 AM

NATIONAL PUBLIC RADIO

KGNU 88.5 FM (Alternative music, folk)
KCFR 90.1 FM (Classical)
KUVO 89.3 FM (Jazz)

NEWS/TALK/SPORTS

KHOW 630 AM
KNUS 710 AM
KTLK 760 AM
KOA 850 AM

Denver's newspapers include dailies, The Denver Post *and* Rocky Mountain
News *and the alternative weekly* Westword.

OLDIES
KXKL 1280 AM and 105.1 FM('60s-'70s)
KEZW 1430 AM ('40s-'70s)
KIMN 100.3 FM ('70s-'80s)
KTRR 102.5 FM ('70s-'80s)
KRFX 103.5 FM (classic rock)

ROCK AND PROGRESSIVE ROCK
KNRX 92.1 FM
KXPK 96.5 FM
KBCO 97.3 FM and 1190 AM
KTCL 93.3 FM
KBPI 106.7 FM
KALC 105.9 FM

SPORTS ONLY
KKFN 950 AM
KYBG 1090 AM

URBAN CONTEMPORARY
KDKO 1510 AM

Television

Greater Denver is the nation's cable
television capital, with industry giants Tele-
Communications, Inc. and Jones Intercable
both headquartered here. The Denver area
is also home to Direct TV, a Hughes Communication subsidiary that competes with
the cable industry. Direct TV operates its
national direct satellite service out of Castle
Rock. As a practical matter, however, cable
TV here is like cable TV everywhere: you
pay your money; you watch your programs.
For service in your area, call the cable companies' customer service numbers: Jones
Intercable (Kittredge, Idledale, Evergreen,
Brighton, Broomfield and portions of
Littleton), 978-9770; TCI, Mile Hi
Cablevision, (Denver), 744-9696; TCI
(suburbs), 930-2000.

MAJOR LOCAL TV STATIONS
AND THEIR NETWORK AFFILIATES
KWGN Channel 2 (Independent/WB)
KCNC Channel 4 (CBS)
KRMA Channel 6 (PBS)
KMGH Channel 7 (ABC)
KUSA Channel 9 (NBC)
KBDI Channel 12 (PBS)
KTVD Channel 20 (Independent/UPN)
KDVR Channel 31 (Fox)
KUBD Channel 59 (Telemundo)

Photo: Meals on Wheels

Volunteers pack Meals on Wheels for delivery.

Inside
Community
Services Directory

As always, the phone book is the first source for community service numbers. Phone books are delivered when phone service is hooked up. Call 375-0707 or (800) 422-8793 to have one sent to you (there's a charge for out-of-area deliveries). Our Government Services and Utilities chapter also contains many useful numbers; look there for information on whom to call to register to vote, get a driver's license or hook up electric service.

AIDS

COLORADO AIDS PROJECT
837-0166

Air pollution

COLORADO HEALTH DEPARTMENT
Air Pollution Control Division
(complaints, advisories, permits)   692-3100

CLEAN AIR COLORADO
Air Quality Advisory Line   758-4848

Animals

COLORADO DEPT. OF AGRICULTURE
Animal Cruelty Section   239-4158

DENVER DUMB FRIENDS LEAGUE
(HUMANE SOCIETY OF DENVER)
2080 S. Quebec St.
Denver
Adoptions and general information 751-5772
Cruelty investigations   750-0310, 696-4941
Lost and Found   751-9688

DENVER DUMB FRIENDS LEAGUE
(WEST SHELTER)
305 Sheridan Blvd.
Lakewood   233-7387

Cable Television Companies

JONES INTERCABLE
Kittredge, Idledale, Evergreen and parts of Littleton   978-9770

TCI (MILE HI CABLEVISION)
Denver   744-9696
Other suburbs   930-2000

Child Abuse

ADAMS COUNTY
DEPT. OF SOCIAL SERVICES
287-8831

ARAPAHOE COUNTY
DEPT. OF SOCIAL SERVICES
795-4825

DENVER CHILD ABUSE ASSISTANCE
727-3000

**DOUGLAS COUNTY DEPT.
OF HEALTH AND HUMAN SERVICES**
688-4825

**JEFFERSON COUNTY
CHILD ABUSE HOTLINE**
271-4357

**FAMILY AND COMMUNITY
EDUCATION & SUPPORT (FACES)**
782-9337

Community Service Organizations

AMERICAN RED CROSS
722-7474

CATHOLIC CHARITIES
388-4435

**CATHOLIC YOUTH/FAMILY AND
CHILDREN/SENIOR SERVICES**
Lakewood   238-0521

HISPANIC SENIOR OUTREACH SERVICE
Commerce City   287-1587

Services for the Disabled

**DENVER COMMISSION FOR
PEOPLE WITH DISABILITIES**
640-3056, TDD: 640-3840

**LEGAL CENTER SERVING
PEOPLE WITH DISABILITIES**
722-0300

Ethnic Services

**THE ASIAN/PACIFIC CENTER
FOR HUMAN DEVELOPMENT**
Counseling   393-0304

SERVICIOS DE LA RAZA
Hispanic Counseling Line   458-5851

DENVER INDIAN CENTER
General   936-2688
Social services & adult ed   937-1005

HISPANIC SENIOR OUTREACH SERVICE
Commerce City   287-1587

Gay and Lesbian Services

GAY & LESBIAN YELLOW PAGES
863-9232

**GAY, LESBIAN AND BISEXUAL
COMMUNITY SERVICES CENTER**
831-6268

Healthcare

For more information, see our Medical Care chapter.

IMMUNIZATIONS
Denver General Immunization Clinic
436-7230

**HOSPICE AND NURSING
HOME REFERRALS**
Community Housing Services   831-4046

**PHYSICIAN REFERRAL SERVICES
(HOSPITAL AFFILIATED):**
Children's Hospital physician referral
861-0123

University Physicians Inc.   270-6328

Ask-A-Nurse   777-6877

Columbia Direct/Aurora Regional Medical Center
450-4600

Rose Medical Center Referral Source
320-7673

CallONE   788-6000

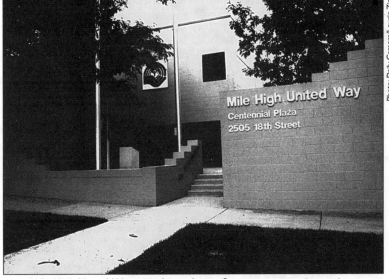

Photo: Daily Camera/Lourie Zipf

Mile High United Way is a clearinghouse for many community services.

Med Search (St. Joseph Hospital)	866-8000
Provenant Health Partners	629-3814
Lutheran Medical Center	425-2255
Clear Creek Valley Medical Society	232-1428

PHYSICIAN REFERRAL SERVICES
(OTHER THAN HOSPITALS)

Prologue ("Dial 4-HEALTH")	443-2584
Colorado Health Care Network	892-9085

Infertility

RESOLVE OF COLORADO

support group	469-5261

Legal Assistance

LEGAL AID SOCIETY OF METRO DENVER
837-1313

LEGAL CENTER SERVING
PEOPLE WITH DISABILITIES
722-0300

Libraries

DENVER

Denver Public Library	
10 W. 14th Ave. Pkwy.	640-6200

Denver has numerous branch libraries. Call for information about locations and specializations. In Denver and the other metro counties, hours at branch libraries vary, so it's best to call ahead.

ADAMS COUNTY

Main library	
10530 Huron St., Northglenn	452-7534
Branch libraries:	
Brighton Branch	
575 S. Eighth Ave.	659-2572
Commerce City Branch,	
7185 Monaco St.	287-0063
Perl Mack Branch	
7611 Hilltop Cr., Denver	428-3576
Thornton Branch	
8992 Washington St.	287-2514

● ARAPAHOE COUNTY

Main library (Koelbel Library)
5955 S. Holly St., Littleton — 220-7704

Castlewood Library
6739 S. Uinta St., Englewood — 771-3197

Glendale branch, Glendale Community Center
Corner of Cherry St. and Tennessee Ave.
691-0331

Sheridan branch
3201 W. Oxford Ave. — 789-5422

Smoky Hill Library
15430 E. Orchard Rd., Aurora — 693-7449

Southglenn Library
2052-A E. Arapahoe Rd., Littleton — 797-9597

DOUGLAS COUNTY

Highlands Ranch
48 W. Springer Dr. — 791-7703

Louviers Branch
7885 Louviers Blvd., Louviers — 791-7323

Oakes Mill Branch
8827 Lone Tree Pkwy., Littleton — 799-4446

Parker Branch
19801 E. Main St. — 841-3503

Philip S. Miller Branch
961 Plum Creek Blvd., Castle Rock — 688-5157

JEFFERSON COUNTY

Main libraries:

Columbine Library, 7706 W. Bowles Ave.
Littleton — 932-2690

Standley Lake Library, 8485 Kipling St.
Arvada — 456-0806

Evergreen Library
Colo. Hwy. 73 at Buffalo Park Rd. — 674-0780

Lakewood, 10200 W. 20th Ave. — 232-9507

Major branch libraries:

Golden, 923 10th St. — 279-4585

Villa Library
455 S. Pierce, Lakewood — 936-7407

Arvada, 8555 W. 57th Ave. — 424-5527

Westminster Public Library
3031 W. 76th Ave. — 430-2400 Ext.. 2300

Mental Health

COMITAS CRISIS CENTER INC.
343-9890

SUICIDE AND CRISIS CONTROL
756-8485

ADAMS COUNTY
MENTAL HEALTH CENTER
(all of Adams County except Aurora)
287-8001

AURORA COMMUNITY
MENTAL HEALTH CENTER
(Aurora, Strasburg, Watkins and Bennett)
693-9500

ARAPAHOE MENTAL HEALTH CENTER
(Arapahoe and Douglas counties, but not Aurora)
795-6187

DENVER ALCOHOL, DRUG &
PSYCHIATRIC CARE EMERGENCY LINE
436-6266

JEFFERSON CENTER FOR MENTALHEALTH
(Jefferson, Clear Creek and Gilpin counties)
425-0300

Planned Parenthood

Arvada	425-6624
Aurora	671-7526
Denver (Capitol Hill)	832-5069
Denver (20th and Vine sts.)	321-2458
Glendale	320-1630
Lakewood	988-3821
Littleton	798-0963

Poison Control

ROCKY MOUNTAIN POISON AND DRUG CENTER
629-1123

Rape

RAPE CRISIS HOTLINE
322-7273

ENDING VIOLENCE EFFECTIVELY
322-7010

Recycling

DENVER RECYCLES
640-1675

Road Conditions

Within two hours of Denver	639-1111
Major highways in the state	639-1234
Colorado State Patrol	239-4501

Senior Services

For more information see our Retirement chapter.

SENIOR ANSWERS AND SERVICES
333-3482

HISPANIC SENIOR OUTREACH SERVICE
Commerce City   287-1587

Ski Conditions

COLORADO SKI COUNTRY USA
825-7669

Substance Abuse

AL-ANON
321-8788

ALCOHOLICS ANONYMOUS
322-4440

COCAINE ANONYMOUS
421-5120

MILE HIGH COUNCIL ON ALCOHOLISM AND DRUG ABUSE
825-8113

Suicide

SUPPORT LINE
869-1999

Transportation

TRAIN
Amtrak   (800) 872-7245

BUSES
Greyhound/Trailways bus lines
293-6555 or (800) 231-2222

RTD   299-6000

Denver International Airport   342-2000

MAJOR AIRLINES

America West	(800) 235-9292
American	(800) 433-7300
Continental Airlines	398-3000
Delta	(800) 221-1212
Frontier	(800) 432-1359
MartinAir Holland	(800) 366-4655
Mesa Airlines	(800) 637-2247
Mexicana	(800) 531-7921
Northwest	(800) 225-2525
TWA	(800) 221-2000
United Airlines/United Express	(800) 241-6522
USAir	(800) 428-4322

No-frills carriers include:
Vanguard   (800) 826-4827

TAXIS

Yellow Cab	777-7777
Zone Cab	444-8888
Metro Taxi	333-3333

United Way

Mile High United Way Helpline   433-8900

Victim Assistance

DENVER VICTIMS SERVICE CENTER
Hotline   894-8000, TDD: 860-9555

VICTIM OUTREACH INFORMATION
980-1112

Volunteer Opportunities

BIG BROTHERS OF METRO DENVER
377-8827

BIG SISTERS OF METRO DENVER
744-3323

HABITAT FOR HUMANITY
292-4114

METRO VOLUNTEERS
832-6060

PROJECT ANGEL HEART
(Meals for homebound people with AIDS)
388-1315

RSVP
Volunteers of America, Retired and Senior Volunteer Program
Denver, Douglas and western Arapahoe counties
477-2340

VOLUNTEERS FOR OUTDOOR COLORADO
(trail building and maintenance)   830-7792

Weather

DENVER AREA WEATHER,
TIME AND TEMPERATURE LINE
337-2500

NATIONAL WEATHER SERVICE FORECAST
398-3964

Women's Services

BATTERED WOMEN'S
SUPPORT GROUP/SAFEHOUSE
830-6800

ALTERNATIVES TO FAMILY
VIOLENCE CRISIS LINE
Adams County   289-4441

ARAPAHOE COUNTY SHELTER
343-1851

DOUGLAS COUNTY CRISIS CENTER
Shelter and Hotline   688-8484

WOMEN IN CRISIS
Jefferson County   420-6752

Youth

COMMISSION ON YOUTH
640-2621

Inside
Government Services and Utilities

Denver has been Colorado's capital since before Colorado was a state, but it wasn't the first territorial capital. Colorado City, near present-day Colorado Springs, holds that honor. Golden followed in 1862 and Denver five years later. In 1876, 100 years after the United States declared its independence, Colorado became the Union's 38th state. The Centennial State celebrates its statehood on August 1 every year, and state offices are closed.

Virtually all state offices are in Denver; the Colorado Legislature and Supreme Court convene here, and the governor's mansion is located at 400 E. Eighth Avenue, not far from the gold-domed capitol building at Broadway and Colfax. The Colorado Legislature is typi-

cally in session from mid-January through mid-May. Tours of the capitol are offered on weekdays, but visitors might want to keep in mind Otto von Bismarck's famous dictum that people who like laws and sausages should never watch either one being made. See the entry in Tours and Attractions for more information.

Greater Denver has the second-largest number of federal workers in the country — only Washington, D.C., has more. Most of these employees have offices downtown, but many work at the Denver Federal Center, a vast complex in Lakewood bordered by Sixth Avenue to the north, Alameda Avenue to the south, Kipling Street to the east and Union Boulevard to the west. The U.S. Mint in downtown Denver is a top tourist attraction and another indication of the sig-

The Denver City and County Building is the hub of local government.

nificant federal presence in the city. In addition, Denver is the site of the 10th Circuit Court of Appeals, which has jurisdiction over federal cases from Colorado, New Mexico, Utah, Wyoming, Oklahoma, Kansas and some tax and agency appeals.

The Denver City and County Building is due west of the state capitol on the other side of Civic Center Park. The city clerk's office and the various branches of the Denver courts — juvenile, probate and district — are found in this building.

Denver is unique in the state in that it is both a city and a county and combines the functions of the two. But residents of the city of Aurora, in Adams and Arapahoe counties, or of Golden, in Jefferson County, will deal with different levels of government depending on whether they wish to register their cars, register to vote or get tags for their dogs. To make things even more complicated, special districts exist with the sole function to provide, say, fire protection or water service; and on top of that, school district boundaries don't necessarily stop and start at the various city limits.

To determine which entities apply to any particular address, call the county assessor's office, give the residence address, and ask which city, school and special district taxes are assessed on that property.

Voting and the Legislative Process

Generally, bills are written and approved by the Colorado Legislature and signed into law by the governor. Colorado's current governor, Roy Romer, is a Democrat who was re-elected to a third term in 1994.

A recent significant trend in Colorado has been the increased use of ballot initiatives, citizen-sponsored proposals that are put on the ballot for a statewide vote in November. Such a proposal, if it wins voter approval, essentially becomes law without going through the usual deliberative process. This was the case with the controversial Amendment 2 ballot initiative, commonly known as the "Anti-gay Rights Amendment," which was later declared unconstitutional by the Colorado Supreme Court.

Denver is governed by an elected city council and elected mayor, who serves a four-year term. Wellington Webb, the city's first black mayor, was re-elected to a second four-year term in 1995.

Voter Registration

Register to vote when obtaining or renewing a driver's license or at the county clerk's office; check the individual county listings that follow for phone numbers and addresses. A person must have resided in Colorado for 25 days before he or she is eligible to register, and registration must be done at least 25 days before an election. General elections are held in Colorado in even-numbered years.

To vote in the state primary election, held in August in even-numbered years, it's necessary to declare a party affiliation. This can be done at the polls on primary day.

Driver's Licenses and Automobile Registration

New residents are required to obtain a Colorado driver's license within 30 days of moving to the area. Licenses are valid for five years from your last birthday. Colorado has a mandatory front-seat seat belt law.

Automobile registration is handled at

the county level. The following items are required to obtain Colorado license plates and registration: an emissions certificate; verification of vehicle identification number; out-of-state title (if applicable); current registration; and evidence of lien if the vehicle is financed. In some cases additional information may be required.

Telephone Service

Local telephone service is provided by US West Communications. For new residential telephone service anywhere in the Denver metropolitan area or to change or disconnect service or for billing questions, call (800) 244-1111.

It's necessary to dial "1" before making long-distance calls to another area code. In April 1995, Colorado got its third area code, 970, which applies to the region north and west of Denver. This includes Fort Collins, Greeley, and the mountains including the Summit County and Vail ski areas. South Colorado and southeast of Greater Denver, including Colorado Springs and vicinity fall within the 719 area code. The 303 area code covers Greater Denver and Boulder. Central City and Black Hawk, in the 303 area code, recently joined the metro calling area and are no longer a long distance call from Denver.

Utilities

Public Service Company of Colorado provides gas and electric service throughout the Greater Denver area. The customer service number is 623-1234.

Post Offices

The blue pages of the phone book contain a list of Greater Denver post offices. The Terminal Annex, on Wynkoop Street one block west of Union Station, is open from 4:30 AM to 10:30 PM daily. The General Mail Facility, 7500 E. 53rd Place, is open 24 hours a day. For recorded postal information, call 297-6100. During regular business hours, call 297-6000 to speak to a post office employee; be prepared for a busy signal.

County Government

The following useful phone numbers and addresses are listed by county first, then by city. In Denver, as noted, the functions are combined. Remember that police serve cities; the comparable law enforcement agency at the county level is the sheriff's office.

Denver City and County

1437 Bannock St.
Denver 80204

General Information	*640-5555*
Animal Control	*698-0076*
Assessor	*640-3021*
Fire and Rescue Services	*Emergency 911*
Non-emergency	*640-3435*
Police	*Emergency 911*
Non-emergency	*640-2011*

Don't know what fire protection or school district an address is in? Call the county assessor with the residence address for complete information on taxing entities.

Insiders' Tips

Motor Vehicle Division	576-2882
Public Works (trash and sewer)	640-1000
Voter Registration	640-2351
Water Department	893-2444

For complaints regarding city services and agencies, call the Mayor's Office of Citizen Response, 640-5151.

Adams County

450 S. Fourth Ave.
Brighton 80601

General Information	659-2120
Animal Control	288-3294
Assessor	654-6038
Fire and Rescue Services	Emergency 911
Sheriff	Emergency 911
Non-emergency	654-1850
Motor Vehicle Division	659-2120
Voter registration	654-6030

Arapahoe County

5334 S. Prince St.
Littleton 80120

General Information	795-4400
Animal Control	795-4685
Assessor	795-4600
Fire and Rescue Services	Emergency 911
TDD	795-4785
Sheriff	Emergency 911
Non-emergency	795-4711

Motor Vehicle Division	
Aurora	343-1840
Littleton	795-4500
Voter Registration	795-4511

Douglas County

101 Third St.
Castle Rock 80104
(Clerk and recorder are at 301 Wilcox St.)

General Information	660-7400
Animal Control	660-7529
Assessor	660-7450
Fire and Rescue Services	Emergency 911
Sheriff	Emergency 911
Non-emergency	660-7505
TDD emergency	660-7500
Motor Vehicle Division	660-7440
Voter Registration	660-7444

Jefferson County

100 Jefferson County Pkwy.
Golden 80419

General Information	279-6511
Animal Control	271-6616
Assessor	271-8666
Fire and Rescue Services	Emergency 911
Sheriff	Emergency 911
Non-emergency	277-0211
Motor Vehicle Division	271-8100
Voter Registration	271-8111

The Colorado State Judicial Building is in downtown Denver.

Cities and Towns

Arvada (Jefferson County)*

8101 Ralston Rd.
Arvada 80002

General Information	421-2550
Fire and Rescue Services	Emergency 911
Police	Emergency 911
Non-emergency	431-3060
Public Works (Utilities)	431-3030
Elections	431-3010
Water and Sewer	431-3035
Water and Sewer billing	431-3070

*A very small portion of Arvada is in Adams County

Aurora (Adams and Arapahoe counties)*

1470 S. Havana St.
Aurora 80012

General Information	695-7460
Fire and Rescue Services	Emergency 911
TDD	366-1558
Non-emergency	341-7552
Police	Emergency 911
TDD	366-1558
Non-emergency	341-8630
Public Works	695-7300
Elections	695-7122
Water and Sewer	695-7388

*A very small portion of Aurora is in Douglas County

Bow Mar (Arapahoe and Jefferson counties)

5395 Lakeshore Dr.
Littleton 80123

General Information	797-3174

Brighton (Adams and Weld counties)

22 S. Fourth Ave.
Brighton 80601

General Information	659-4050
Animal Control	659-3322
Fire and Rescue Services	Emergency 911
Non-emergency	659-2629
Police	Emergency 911
Non-emergency	659-3322

Public Works (including water and sewer)
659-4050

Broomfield (Adams, Boulder and Jefferson counties)*

1 DesCombes Dr.
Broomfield 80020

General Information	469-3301
Fire and Rescue Services	
Emergency	452-6262
Non-emergency	452-9910
Police	
Emergency	466-2345
Non-emergency	438-6400
Water and Sewer	438-6319
City Clerk/Elections	438-6332

* A portion of Broomfield is in Weld County

Castle Rock (Douglas County)

680 N. Wilcox St.
Castle Rock 80104

General Information	660-1015
Fire and Rescue Services	Emergency 911

Non-emergency	660-1066
Police	Emergency 911
Non-emergency	660-1000
City Clerk/Elections	660-1015
Utility billing	660-1015

Cherry Hills Village (Arapahoe County)

2450 E. Quincy Ave.
Cherry Hills Village 80110

General Information	789-2541
Fire and Rescue Services	Emergency 911
Non-emergency	773-8282
Police	Emergency 911
Non-emergency	795-4711

Columbine Valley (Arapahoe County)

5931 S. Middlefield Rd. Ste. 101
Columbine Valley 80123

General Information	795-1434
Fire and Rescue Services	Emergency 911
Police	Emergency 911
Non-emergency	795-4711

Commerce City (Adams County)

5291 E. 60th Ave.
Commerce City 80037

General Information	289-3600

Animal Control	288-3294
Fire and Rescue Services	Emergency 911
Non-emergency	288-0835
Police	Emergency 911
Public Works (trash, street maintenance, snow and ice removal)	289-3700
City Clerk/Elections	289-3611
Water and Sewer	288-2646

Edgewater (Jefferson County)

2401 Sheridan Blvd.
Edgewater 80214

General Information	238-7803
Fire and Rescue Services	Emergency 911
Non-emergency	237-2860
Police	Emergency 911
Non-emergency	278-2000
City Clerk/Elections	238-7803

Englewood (Arapahoe County)

3400 S. Elati St.
Englewood 80110

General Information	762-2300
Animal control	762-2343
Parking, snow removal	762-2340
Fire and Rescue Services	Emergency 911
Non-emergency	761-7490

Police	Emergency 911
Non-emergency	761-7410
Water and Sewer	762-2635
City Clerk/Elections	762-2405

Federal Heights (Adams County)

2380 W. 90th Ave.
Federal Heights 80221

General Information	428-3526
Fire and Rescue Services	Emergency 911
Non-emergency	428-3526
Police	Emergency 911
Non-emergency	428-3526
TDD	428-5225

Glendale (Arapahoe County)

950 S. Birch St.
Glendale 80222

General Information	759-1513
Fire and Rescue Services	Emergency 911
Non-emergency	759-1513
Police	Emergency 911
Non-emergency	759-1511
Public Works (Utilities and sewer)	759-1513

Golden (Jefferson County)

911 10th St.
Golden 80401

Take advantage of early voting or voting by mail to avoid election-day lines.

Insiders' Tips

General Information	384-8000

Fire and Rescue Services	Emergency 911
Non-emergency	278-2932

Police	Emergency 911
Non-emergency	279-2557

Public Works (Water and Sewer)	384-8151
Water and Sewer Emergencies (after hours)	279-2557

City Clerk/Elections	384-8000

Greenwood Village (Arapahoe County)

6060 S. Quebec St.
Greenwood Village 80111

General Information	773-0252

Fire and Rescue Services	Emergency 911
Non-emergency	773-8282

Police	Emergency 911
Non-emergency	773-2525

Lakewood (Jefferson County)

445 S. Allison Pkwy.
Lakewood 80226

General Information	987-7000

Animal Control	987-7111

Fire and Rescue Services	Emergency 911

Police	Emergency 911
Non-emergency	987-7111

City Clerk/Elections	987-7080

Water and Sewer Information	987-7615

Littleton (Arapahoe County)

2255 W. Berry Ave.
Littleton 80165

General Information	795-3700

Animal control	794-1551

Fire and Rescue Services	Emergency 911
TDD	794-1555 or 911
Non-emergency	795-3800

Police	Emergency 911
TDD	794-1551 or 911
Non-emergency	794-1551

Snow Removal and Trash	795-3751

City Clerk/Elections	795-3780

Water and Sewer — see Denver listings

Morrison (Jefferson County)

321 Colo. Hwy. 8
P.O. Box 95
Morrison 80465

General Information	697-8749

Fire and Rescue Services	Emergency 911
Police	Emergency 911
Non-emergency	697-4810

Mountain View (Jefferson County)

4176 Benton St.
Mountain View 80212

General Information	421-7282
Fire and Rescue Services	Emergency 911
Police	Emergency 911
Non-emergency	425-1748

Northglenn (Adams County)

11701 Community Center Dr.
Northglenn 80233

General Information	451-8326
Animal Control	911
Fire and Rescue Services	Emergency 911
Non-emergency	452-9910
Police	Emergency 911
Non-emergency	288-1535
Water and Sewer (Turn on/shut off)	450-8770
City Clerk/Elections	450-8755

Parker (Douglas County)

20120 E. Main St.
Parker 80134

General Information	841-0353
Fire and Rescue Services	Emergency 911
Police	Emergency 911
Non-emergency	841-9800
Public Works	840-9546

Sheridan (Arapahoe County)

4101 S. Federal Blvd.
Sheridan 80110

General Information	762-2200
Fire and Rescue Services Emergency	911
Police	Emergency 911

Thornton (Adams County)

9500 Civic Center Dr.
Thornton

City Clerk/Elections	538-7230
Fire and Rescue Services	Emergency 911
Non-emergency	452-9910
Police	Emergency 911
Non-emergency and TDD	288-1535
Public Works (streets and sanitation)	538-7348
Water and Sewer Maintenance	538-7411
Water and Sewer Billing	538-7370

Westminster (Jefferson and Adams counties)

4800 W. 92nd Ave.
Westminster 80030

General Information	430-2400
Fire and Rescue Services	Emergency 911
TDD	426-0007
Police	Emergency 911
TDD	426-0007
Non-emergency	430-2400
Water and Sewer	430-2400
City Clerk/Elections	430-2400

Wheat Ridge
(Jefferson County)

7500 W. 29th Ave.
Wheat Ridge 80215

General Information	234-5900
Animal Control	235-2926

Fire and Rescue Services	*Emergency 911*
Police	*Emergency 911*
TDD	235-2900
Non-emergency	237-2220
City Clerk/Elections	234-5900

Index of Advertisers

Index

ORDER FORM
Fast and Simple!

Mail to:	Or:
Insiders Guides®, Inc.	**for VISA or**
P.O. Drawer 2057	**MasterCard orders call**
Manteo, NC 27954	**(800) 765-BOOK**

Name _____

Address _____

City/State/Zip _____

Qty.	Title/Price	Shipping	Amount
	Insiders' Guide to Richmond/$14.95	$3.00	
	Insiders' Guide to Williamsburg/$14.95	$3.00	
	Insiders' Guide to Virginia's Blue Ridge/$14.95	$3.00	
	Insiders' Guide to Virginia's Chesapeake Bay/$14.95	$3.00	
	Insiders' Guide to Washington, DC/$14.95	$3.00	
	Insiders' Guide to North Carolina's Outer Banks/$14.95	$3.00	
	Insiders' Guide to Wilmington, NC/$14.95	$3.00	
	Insiders' Guide to North Carolina's Crystal Coast/$12.95	$3.00	
	Insiders' Guide to North Carolina's Mountains/$14.95	$3.00	
	Insiders' Guide to Myrtle Beach/$14.95	$3.00	
	Insiders' Guide to Atlanta/$14.95	$3.00	
	Insiders' Guide to Boca Raton & the Palm Beaches/$14.95	$3.00	
	Insiders' Guide to Sarasota/Bradenton/$14.95	$3.00	
	Insiders' Guide to Northwest Florida/$14.95	$3.00	
	Insiders' Guide to Tampa Bay/$14.95	$3.00	
	Insiders' Guide to Mississippi/$14.95	$3.00	
	Insiders' Guide to Lexington, KY/$14.95	$3.00	
	Insiders' Guide to Louisville/$14.95	$3.00	
	Insiders' Guide to Cincinnati/$14.95	$3.00	
	Insiders' Guide to the Twin Cities/$14.95	$3.00	
	Insiders' Guide to Boulder/$14.95	$3.00	
	Insiders' Guide to Denver/$14.95	$3.00	
	Insiders' Guide to Branson/$14.95	$3.00	
	Insiders' Guide to Civil War in the Eastern Theater/$14.95	$3.00	

Payment in full (check or money order) must
accompany this order form.
Please allow 2 weeks for delivery.

N.C. residents add 6% sales tax _____

Total _____

Who you are and what you think is important to us.

**Fill out the coupon and we'll give you
an Insiders' Guide® for half price ($7.48 off)**

Which book(s) did you buy? _____

Where do you live? _____

In what city did you buy your book? _____

Where did you buy your book? ❏ catalog ❏ bookstore ❏ newspaper ad

  ❏ retail shop ❏ other _____

How often do you travel? ❏ yearly ❏ bi-annually ❏ quarterly

  ❏ more than quarterly

Did you buy your book because you were ❏ moving ❏ vacationing

  ❏ wanted to know more about your home town ❏ other _____

_____

Will the book be used by ❏ family ❏ couple ❏ individual ❏ group

What is your annual household income? ❏ under $25,000 ❏ $25,000 to $35,000

  ❏ $35,000 to $50,000 ❏ $50,000 to $75,000 ❏ over $75,000

How old are you? ❏ under 25 ❏ 25-35 ❏ 36-50 ❏ 51-65 ❏ over 65

Did you use the book before you left for your destination? ❏ yes ❏ no

Did you use the book while at your destination? ❏ yes ❏ no

On average per month, how many times do you refer to your book? ❏ 1-3 ❏ 4-7

  ❏ 8-11 ❏ 12-15 ❏ 16 and up

On average, how many other people use your book? ❏ no others ❏ 1 ❏ 2

  ❏ 3 ❏ 4 or more

Is there anything you would like to tell us about Insiders' Guides? _____

_____

_____

Name _____ Address _____

City _____ State _____ Zip _____

**We'll send you a voucher for $7.48 off any Insiders' Guide® and a list of available
titles as soon as we get this card from you. Thanks for being an Insider!**

BUSINESS REPLY MAIL
FIRST-CLASS MAIL PERMIT NO. 20 MANTEO, NC

POSTAGE WILL BE PAID BY ADDRESSEE

THE INSIDERS GUIDE
PO BOX 2057
MANTEO NC 27954-9906